The John Doe Associates
Backdoor Diplomacy for Peace, 1941

R. J. C. Butow. "A fascinating account of how the private efforts of three men ... fostered confusion and further complicated the course of Japanese-American relations in the crucial 12 months preceding Pearl Harbor. ... An exciting tale which reads more like fiction than fact. Highly recommended."—*Library Journal.* This book tells for the first time the story of the secret, and in the end damaging, efforts of the John Doe Associates to avert war in the Pacific by influencing the Hull-Nomura diplomatic conversations. Illustrated. $16.95

The Chinese City Between Two Worlds

Mark Elvin & G. William Skinner, Editors. Twelve scholars trace the role of cities in Chinese history from 1842-1949, emphasizing the urban roots of the Chinese Revolution. Topics include the treaty ports, the growth of financial institutions, revolutionary mobilization, warlord control, educational development, social reform, religious change, administrative transformation, and patterns of migration. *Studies in Chinese Society.* $18.75

The Revolutionary Left in Spain, 1914-1923

Gerald H. Meaker. "One of the few really major books on modern Spanish history."—*Stanley G. Payne.* This first comprehensive history of the burgeoning of the revolutionary Left begins with the profound impact of the First World War and the Russian Revolution on the labor movement. It traces the ideological evolution, internal divisions, and interaction of the two main movements, ending with the collapse of the Restoration regime and the advent of a military dictatorship. $18.95

 Stanford University Press

New from Columbia

THE WITNESS AND I

O. EDMUND CLUBB

This is the shocking story of how O. Edmund Clubb, when Director of the State Department's China Office, was forced to leave his job because of allegations of Communist sympathies by Whittaker Chambers. A quarter century later, our governmental system still has the scars from that period.
$9.95

COMPUTERS AND THE SOCIAL SCIENCES

ALAN BRIER and IAN ROBINSON

The aim of this concise, critical introduction is to assist readers in gaining a knowledge of practical computing in their area of interest. Useful to professionals or students, this work offers further insight into the growing uses and potential of computers in modern society
cloth, $12.50; paper, $6.00

THE UKRAINE IN THE UNITED NATIONS
A Study in Soviet Foreign Policy, 1944–1950

KONSTANTYN SAWCZUK

Professor Sawczuk tells the little-known but significant story of how one of the states in the U.S.S.R. became a founding member of the United Nations at the San Francisco Conference which set up the U.N.
East European Monographs $10.00

DETERRENCE IN AMERICAN FOREIGN POLICY: THEORY AND PRACTICE

ALEXANDER L. GEORGE and RICHARD SMOKE

Based on case studies of deterrence strategy since World War II, the authors show the limitations of deterrence in the modern world and suggest such alternatives as positive incentive and negotiation to settle international disputes.
cloth, $17.50; paper, $6.95

 COLUMBIA UNIVERSITY PRESS

Address for orders: 136 South Broadway, Irvington, New York 10533

VOLUME 416   NOVEMBER 1974

THE ANNALS

of The American Academy *of* Political
and Social Science

RICHARD D. LAMBERT, *Editor*

ALAN W. HESTON, *Assistant Editor*

INTERGOVERNMENTAL RELATIONS
IN AMERICA TODAY

Special Editor of This Volume

RICHARD H. LEACH
Professor of Political Science
Duke University
Durham, North Carolina

PHILADELPHIA

International Standard Book Numbers (ISBN)

ISBN 0-87761-183-1, vol. 416, 1974; paper—$3.00

ISBN 0-87761-182-3, vol. 416, 1974; cloth—$4.00

Issued bimonthly by The American Academy of Political and Social Science at Prince and Lemon Sts., Lancaster, Pennsylvania 17604. Cost per year: $15.00 paperbound; $20.00 clothbound. Add $1.00 to above rates for membership outside U.S.A. Second-class postage paid at Lancaster and at additional mailing offices.

Editorial and Business Offices, 3937 Chestnut Street, Philadelphia, Pennsylvania 19104.

CONTENTS

INTERLOCAL RELATIONS

A COMPARATIVE PERSPECTIVE

BOOK DEPARTMENT

INTERNATIONAL RELATIONS AND POLITICAL THOUGHT

EUROPE

UNITED STATES POLITICS
AND HISTORY

SOCIOLOGY

ECONOMICS

Contents

PREFACE

This is the third volume of THE ANNALS to be devoted to the topic of intergovernmental relations: the first, a pioneering effort edited by the late, eminent W. Brooke Graves in 1940, and the second, a worthy follow-up edited by Harry Reynolds in 1965. With a twenty-five year lapse between the first two volumes, one might legitimately ask why a third volume was deemed necessary in only nine years. The answer emerges clearly on a perusal of the articles that follow: intergovernmental relations have become central to the operations of American government—they are at its very core and are likely to remain so. Moreover, they have come to be institutionalized in government operations and to be recognized by scholars and lay citizens alike as being of central importance to the functioning of American government. Also, of course, the Johnson and Nixon administrations focused attention on intergovernmental relations as did none of their predecessors. Thus, nine years is none too soon for a reappraisal of so vital a force in American government. Indeed, periodic appraisals would now seem to be in order.

Authors of the articles that make up this issue were all first choices: each is an acknowledged expert on his subject. Together, their final products constitute as perceptive an analysis of American intergovernmental relations as is currently possible. Appreciation is a mild word for my feeling about their efforts.

RICHARD H. LEACH

Intergovernmental Relations:
an Analytical Overview

By DEIL S. WRIGHT

ABSTRACT: The distinctive features of American intergovernmental relations (IGR) are specified, and the last half-century of policy trends in the United States are viewed through the conceptual lens provided by the IGR perspective. Several distinctive features of IGR set it apart from the more commonplace term, federalism. These features include a multiplicity of units, the primacy of public officials' attitudes and actions, informal working patterns, the prominence of administrators, and a policy emphasis. Five phases of IGR form a matrix for classifying recent United States political developments. The phases are: (1) conflict, (2) cooperative, (3) concentrated, (4) creative, and (5) competitive. The challenges presented by the complexity and interdependencies of IGR point toward a management emphasis. Intergovernmental accomplishments appear to hinge on the successful management of complexity.

Deil S. Wright holds A.B., M.P.A., and Ph.D. degrees from the University of Michigan. His teaching career includes membership on the faculties of Wayne State University, the University of Iowa, the University of California at Berkeley (as visiting professor) and the University of North Carolina at Chapel Hill. He joined the University of North Carolina faculty in 1967 as Professor of Political Science and as Research Professor, Institute for Research in Social Science. He has authored or coauthored books, monographs, research reports and articles in the fields of state and local government, public administration, intergovernmental relations and public finance.

WILLIAM Anderson, one of the intellectual parents of the intergovernmental relations field, once claimed that "intergovernmental relations is, I believe, a term indigenous to the United States, of a relatively recent origin, and still not widely used or understood."[1] Since Anderson's assertion in 1960, the phrase intergovernmental relations (IGR) has experienced wider usage, but whether the term is clearly or adequately understood remains questionable. Brief attention to the definition and features of IGR is therefore appropriate if not mandatory.

GAINING FORCE BY UNUSUALNESS: THE DISTINCTIVE FEATURES OF IGR

We need look no further than the author quoted above for a starting point in clarifying IGR. Professor Anderson says that IGR is a term intended "to designate an important body of activities or interactions occurring between governmental units of all types and levels within the [United States] federal system."[2] It is possible to use his general definition as a starting point to elaborate the concept of IGR.

First and foremost, IGR occurs within the federal system. American federalism is the context, not the totality, of IGR. IGR encompasses more than is usually conveyed by the concept of federalism, where the emphasis is chiefly on national-state relationships with occasional attention to interstate relationships. IGR recognizes not only national-state and interstate relations, but also national-local, state-local, national-state-local, and interlocal relations. In short, IGR includes as proper objects of study all the permutations and combinations of relations among the units of government in the American system.

Anderson also assists us in making a second important point about IGR. "It is human beings clothed with office who are the real determiners of what the relations between units of government will be. Consequently the concept of intergovernmental relations necessarily has to be formulated largely in terms of human relations and human behavior . . ."[3] Strictly speaking, then, there are no intergovernmental relations, there are only relations among officials in different governing units. Individual interactions among public officials is at the core of IGR. In this sense it could be argued that federalism deals with the anatomy of the system, whereas IGR treats its physiology.

A third notion implicit in IGR is that relations are not one-time, occasional occurrences, formally ratified in agreements or rigidly fixed by statutes or court decisions. Rather, IGR is the continuous, day-to-day pattern of contacts, knowledge, and evaluations of government officials. A major concern is with the informal as well as with the formal, the practices as well as the principles, pursued in both competitive and cooperative interjurisdictional patterns. This third facet of IGR reads into the concept those activities—as well as research studies—that have previously gone under the title of cooperative federalism, which the late E. S. Corwin defined as one in which governmental units "are regarded as mutually complementary

1. William Anderson, *Intergovernmental Relations in Review* (Minneapolis: University of Minnesota Press, 1960), p. 3.

2. Ibid., p. 3.

3. Ibid., p. 4.

parts of a single governmental mechanism all of whose powers are intended to realize the current purposes of government according to their applicability to the problem at hand."[4] These words from a constitutional law scholar provide the desirable emphasis on the working, problem-oriented informalities of IGR and at the same time are a reminder of the formal, legal, institutional context within which those relationships originate and flourish.

It has been shown that IGR recognizes multiple unit relationships, that it respects the primacy of public officials acting in an interjurisdictional context, and that it is concerned with informal working relationships in institutional contexts. A fourth distinguishing characteristic of IGR is its awareness of the role played by all public officials. Automatically assumed as integral and important to IGR are mayors, councilmen, governors, state legislators, members of Congress and others. But in recent years more attention has been paid to the actions, attitudes and roles of appointed administrators. The increased focus on administrators as relevant IGR participants is a natural outgrowth of the increasingly important role played by public bureaucracies in government. The concern for the administrative aspects of IGR also arises, however, from attention to informal working relationships and from the academic leanings of most of the writers who have staked out claims to the IGR field. A majority of these persons have been oriented toward public administration and have also held a strong interest in state and local government.

4. E. S. Corwin, *The Passing of Dual Federalism*, Virginia Law Review 36 (February 1950), p. 19.

A fifth and final distinctive feature of IGR is its policy component. Federalism has, to a large extent, translated questions of policy into questions of law and relied upon the courts for their resolution. Economic and political complexities, combined with rapid rates of social and technological change, have greatly reduced the capacity of courts—and legislatures—to deal with continuous pressures for policy change. The secular shift from regulatory politics to distributive and redistributive politics signaled new power relationships and configurations to which the term federalism could be applied only with awkward and ambiguous modifiers, such as direct, private, functional, economic. From its origins in the 1930s, IGR was recognized as anchored in politics and suffused with policy. It retains those features in the 1970s.

IGR cut its teeth on the massive political and policy issues that remained following the Supreme Court decisions on the social welfare legislation of the New Deal. It reached early adolescence in grappling with federal aid to education, urban development and civil rights. It is now attempting to claim maturity on issues related to citizen participation and effective services delivery systems. Near the policy core of IGR have been fiscal issues. These have been dominated by allocational issues: Who shall raise what amounts by what method from which citizens, and who shall spend how much for whose benefit with what results? This "fiscal fixation" has sometimes skewed diagnoses of and prescriptions for IGR problems, but the main point stands: IGR is centrally concerned with policy. As the Kestnbaum Commission noted in 1955, "The crucial questions now are questions of policy: What level ought to move? Or should both?"[5] These questions, the commission added, are ones on which the criteria for judgment "are chiefly political, economic, and administrative rather than legal."[6]

The five distinctive features of IGR are summarized in table 1. These characteristics combine and interact to produce new directions, vectors, and results in the conduct of public affairs in the United States. A new term or phrase to describe these special features therefore seems amply justified. The term IGR alerts one to the multiple, behavioral, continuous and dynamic exchanges occurring between various officials in the political system. It may be compared to a different, novel and visual filter or concept that can be laid on the American political landscape. It permits one to observe, classify and cumulate knowledge without obscuring other relevant data which prior political concepts have provided.

5. Commission on Intergovernmental Relations, *A Report to the President for Transmittal to the Congress* (Washington, D.C., June 1955), p. 33.
6. Ibid., p. 33.

PHASES OF IGR

"To follow still the changes of the moon," Shakespeare

To say that the American political system has evolved and changed is trite. The significant questions in dealing with change are ones centering on the frequency, mechanisms, direction, and effects of change. It is possible, for example, to understand aspects of the solar system by studying carefully the phases of the moon. Similarly, a better grasp of the American political system may hopefully be gained by identifying and analyzing five phases of IGR.

In each of the five IGR phases, three main components are considered. First, what were the main problems dominating the public agenda during each phase? Second, what were the perceptions held by the main participants that seemed to guide or direct their behavior in each phase? Third, what mechanisms and techniques were used to implement intergovernmental actions and objectives during each period? Additional elements will help describe each phase, orient the reader, and reveal the effects of changing in-

TABLE 1
DISTINCTIVE FEATURES OF INTERGOVERNMENTAL RELATIONS

1. ALL UNITS (MULTIPLE ENTITIES)
National   Municipalities
States   Special districts
Counties   School districts
	4. ALL PUBLIC OFFICIALS
	(ADMINISTRATORS)
	Elected officials
	  a. legislators
	  b. executives
	  c. judges
	Appointed administrators
	  a. generalists
	  b. functional specialists or
	     program professionals

2. INTERACTIONS OF OFFICIALS (INFORMAL) Behavior Perceptions Beliefs Preferences	
3. CONTINUOUS AND CUMULATIVE (REGULARITIES) Day-to-day contacts Working relationships Cumulative patterns	5. POLICY EMPHASIS (FISCAL FOCUS) Financial issues Anchored in politics Suffused with policy

tergovernmental behavior patterns. These elements are a one-word descriptor, a metaphoric or graphic characterization, and an indication of the approximate dates in which each IGR phase peaked or climaxed.

The five phase descriptors employed here, together with rough date designations are: (1) conflict (pre–1937); (2) cooperative (1933–1953); (3) concentrated (1945–1960); (4) creative (1958–1968); and (5) competitive (1965–?). A condensed and summary chart of the successive phases is offered in table 2. Added to that overview are verbal and graphic expositions of the phases with important caveats. The phases are clearly indicated as successive ones with some overlapping of dates among the periods. While the dates have been selected with deliberateness, they are not sharp and arbitrary cutting points. Forces and tendencies bringing one or another phase

to its climax were present or had antecedents in prior periods. Also, caution is necessary on terminal dates. None of the phases ends in any exact or literal sense. Each phase produces carryover effects beyond the years designated in table 2. Indeed, it is probably most accurate to think of the current state of intergovernmental affairs as resulting from overlaps of the cumulative and successive effects of each IGR phase.

Conflict (pre-1937)

The chief concern of the conflict phase of IGR was the effort to identify and implement "proper" spheres of governmental jurisdiction and neatly defined boundaries for officials' actions. This emphasis operated at the state-local level as well as between national and state governments. Dillon's rule, as a principle for interpreting narrowly the

TABLE 2
PHASES OF INTERGOVERNMENTAL RELATIONS (IGR)

PHASE DESCRIPTOR	MAIN PROBLEMS	PARTICIPANTS PERCEPTIONS	IGR MECHANISMS	FEDERALISM METAPHOR	APPROXIMATE CLIMAX PERIOD
Conflict	Defining boundaries Proper spheres	Antagonistic Adversary Controversy Exclusivity	Statutes Courts Regulations	Layer cake federalism	pre–1937

Cooperative	Economic stress
	International threat
		Collaboration
		Complementary
		Mutuality
		Supportive
			Policy planning
			Broad formula
			  grants
			Open-ended
			  grants
			Tax credit
				Marble cake
				federalism
					1933–1953

Concentrated	Program needs Capital works	Professionalism Objectivity Neutrality Functionalism	Categorical grants Service standards	Focused or channelled federalism (water taps)	1945–1960
Creative	Urban-metropolitan Disadvantaged clients	National goals Great society Grantsmanship	Program planning Project grants Participation	Fused-foliated federalism (proliferated)	1958–1968
Competitive	Coordination Program effectiveness Delivery systems Citizen access	Disagreement Tension Rivalry	Revenue sharing Reorganization Regionalization Grant consolidation	Picket fence federalism (fragmented)	1965– ?

powers of local governments, was not only an assertion of state supremacy but also a consequence of the search for the exact limits of local power. Guiding this search was an expectation of exclusive powers. Public officials' perceptions reflected these adversary and antagonistic patterns of interaction.

These conceptions and attitudinal postures by participants were anchored in deeper societal values of competition, corporate organizational forms, profit and efficiency. Residual elements of this phase remain today on the urban-metropolitan scene in the so-called market models of metropolitanism and in the search for the political jurisdiction to perform most efficiently a particular function—for example, should an activity be assigned to a city or to an areawide body?

The manner in which problems of jurisdiction were resolved in the conflict model of IGR was through statutes and the courts. Growing social and economic complexity subsequently brought regulatory agencies and commissions into being to referee jurisdictional boundary disputes. The Interstate Commerce Act of 1887 created the first of the great regulatory commissions and was a major breach in the century-old "administrative settlement" between the national government and the states.[7] It broke the long-standing presumption against the creation and growth of a national administrative establishment. Attempts to locate the scope of federal regulatory power under the commerce clause and other authority have persisted to the point that under a recent court ruling *all* electric generating and

transmission companies fall under the rate-making authority of the Federal Power Commission.

Other illustrations of the continued adversary, conflict-oriented pattern of national-state relations abound. Environmental and health concerns recently precipitated a jurisdictional dispute over the spheres of national and state power to regulate the safety levels of a nuclear generating plant in Minnesota. National standards set by the Atomic Energy Commission (AEC) specified one level of allowable millirems of radiation escaping from the reactor into the atmosphere. The Minnesota Pollution Control Agency set the permissible level of millirems at only two percent of that sanctioned by the AEC. The Northern States Power Company brought suit in the federal court challenging the state standards and requesting permission to construct the nuclear power plant without regard for the Minnesota regulations. At issue in the case was the application and intent of federal statutes dealing with atomic energy. The court ruled in favor of the exclusive jurisdiction of the national government and invalidated the more restrictive state regulations.[8]

These recent court decisions probably come as close to reflecting current economic realities, social interdependencies, and technological necessity as pre-1937 courts and legislatures thought they were reflecting economic, social and technological separatism. That supposed separatism—however limited, qualified or restricted in practice—gave

7. Leonard D. White, *The States and The Nation* (Baton Rouge: Louisiana State University Press, 1953), pp. 9–10.

8. *Northern States Power Co.* v. *State of Minnesota*, 447 F. 2nd 1143 (1971); *see also, Science* 171 (8 January 1971), p. 45, and Harry Foreman, ed., *Nuclear Power and the Public* (Minneapolis: University of Minnesota Press, 1970).

credence to the metaphor of "layer cake federalism" as a crude means of describing national, state and local disconnectedness.

Cooperation (1933–1953)

Several authors have ably argued and amply demonstrated that intergovernmental collaboration in the United States existed throughout the 19th and 20th centuries.[9] That such collaboration was of major significance or the dominant fact of our political history is less clear. It does seem possible, however, to point to one period in which complementary and supportive relationships were most prominent and had high political significance. That period is the cooperative phase from 1933–1953. The prime elements of national concern during those two decades were the alleviation of widespread economic distress and response to international threats. It seems logical and natural that internal and external challenges to national survival would bring us closer together.

The means by which increased collaboration occurred were several and varied. Most pertinent for our concerns were such approaches as national policy planning, tax credits, and categorical grants-in-aid. Most of the dozen or so grant programs enacted during the depression period were broad formula grants, with a few being open-ended. Special emergency funding arrangements were instituted during the depression years and repeated in selected federally-impacted areas in wartime. As one observer noted in 1943:

9. Morton Grodzins, *The American System: A New View of Government in the United States* (Chicago: Rand McNally, 1966); Daniel J. Elazar, *The American Partnership: Intergovernmental Cooperation in the Nineteenth Century United States* (Chicago: University of Chicago Press, 1962).

Cooperative government by federal-state-local authorities has become a byword in the prodigious effort to administer civilian defense, rationing, and other war-time programs. . . . Intergovernmental administration, while it is a part of all levels of government, is turning into something quite distinct from them all.[10]

The IGR collaboration that persisted during these years was present on such unusual occasions as the 1952 steel seizure confrontation; prior to his seizure effort, President Truman polled state governors for their views.

The prime IGR mechanism, as well as the major legacy of this cooperative period, was fiscal. Substantial and significant fiscal links were firmly established. These established conduits were harbingers of more to come. They also served as important illustrations of a new and differently textured model of intergovernmental patterns, the well-publicized "marble cake" metaphor. The marble cake characterization appears to have been coined by Professor Joseph McLean of Princeton University in the early 1940s for the visual or contrast effect with the layer cake conception. Professor Morton Grodzins probably had the greatest impact in popularizing and elaborating the marble cake concept.

Concentrated (1945–1960)

The descriptor employed for this IGR phase stands for the specific, functional, highly focused nature of intergovernmental interaction that evolved and dominated the Truman-Eisenhower years. From 1946 to 1960, twenty-nine major new grant-in-aid programs were established, a

10. Arthur W. Bromage, "Federal-State-Local Relations," *American Political Science Review* 37, no. 1 (February 1943), p. 35.

number that doubled the total number of programs enacted before and during the depression and wartime eras. The expanded use of categorical grant programs was accompanied by increased attention to service standards and program measurement.

Guiding this growing functional emphasis were corps of program professionals in each of the specialized grant fields, such as airport construction, hospital construction, slum clearance and urban renewal, urban planning, waste treatment facilities, library construction, and so on. The pervasiveness of professionalism enhanced the service standards emphasis by covering the domain with a cloak of objectivity and neutrality. These fit comfortably into Professor Herbert Kaufman's conception of the autonomy accompanying "neutral competence" in public administration contrasted with the control over policy by a strong executive leader.[11] The professionalism, specialized grants and growing insulation also coincided neatly in time, as well as thematically, with Professor Frederick Mosher's view that the 1950s confirmed the triumph of the "professional state" in the public service.[12]

What aims or ends guided and provided the rationale for this surge of activity? Two appear to be most prominent. One was a capital works, public construction push. Between 1946 and 1960, state and local capital outlays increased twelvefold while current operating expenses rose by a multiple of four. Federal grants for highways, hospitals, sewage plants, and airports underwrote much of the state-local effort to meet deferred wartime needs and respond to changing technology and population configurations, especially its suburbanization.

A second motive force propelling intergovernmental action in this period was the political realization that government generally, and IGR especially, was capable of responding to particularistic middle class needs. The New Deal may have had its most telling political effect in making the American middle class acutely aware of the positive and program-specific capabilities of governmental action. Effective political action based on this awareness came after World War II and was reinforced by several conditions.

One condition already mentioned was suburbanization. It constituted the urban frontier and reinforced the myth of Jeffersonian ward republics. Another was the predisposition for using intergovernmental mechanisms because they also meshed with the historical political tradition of localism. In addition, IGR techniques fitted middle class values of professionalism, objectivity and neutrality. It appeared that objective program needs rather than politics were being served. Like reform at the turn of the century, IGR appeared to take a program out of politics.

Those political values coincided with an important structural change at the national level: the legislative reorganization of Congress in 1946. The most significant result of this event for IGR was the creation and stabilization of standing committees with an explicit program emphasis. These congressional committee patterns soon became the

11. Herbert Kaufman, "Emerging Conflicts in the Doctrines of Public Administration," *American Political Science Review* 50, no. 4 (December 1956), pp. 1057–1073.

12. Frederick Mosher, *Democracy and the Public Service* (New York: Oxford University Press, 1968), esp. ch. 4, "The Professional State."

leverage points and channels through which influence on program-specific grants flowed. Furthermore, the committees developed their own cadre of professional staff members with functional and programmatic inclinations.

The flow of influence combined with the concentrated or focused flow of funds in the 1946–1960 period prompts one to employ a hydraulic metaphor in depicting this phase of IGR. The national government had become an established reservoir of fiscal resources to which a rapidly increasing number of water taps were being connected. The functional flows of funds could be facilitated by those knowledgeable at turning on the numerous spigots, that is, the program professionals. Cooperation was prominent during this period, but it occurred in more concentrated and selectively channeled ways.

A crude effort to express the water tap phase of IGR is made in figure 1. The intergovernmental flow of funds for 1950 is shown by the lines connecting the national-state and state-

FIGURE 1

PUBLIC EXPENDITURES BY TYPE AND BY LEVEL OF GOVERNMENT AND THE INTERGOVERNMENTAL FLOW OF FUNDS, FISCAL YEAR 1950
(in billions of dollars)

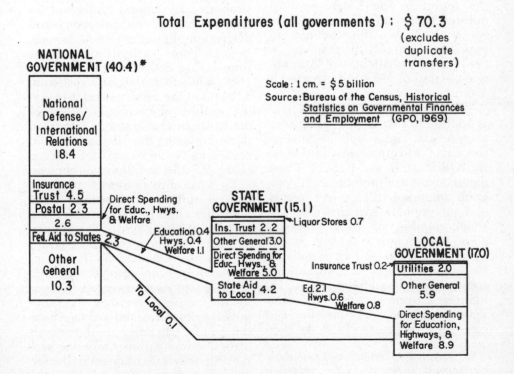

Total Expenditures (all governments): $70.3 (excludes duplicate transfers)

NATIONAL GOVERNMENT (40.4)*

Scale: 1 cm. = $5 billion
Source: Bureau of the Census, Historical Statistics on Governmental Finances and Employment (GPO, 1969)

National Defense/ International Relations 18.4

Insurance Trust 4.5
Postal 2.3
2.6
Fed. Aid to States 2.3
Other General 10.3

Direct Spending for Educ., Hwys. & Welfare

Education 0.4
Hwys. 0.4
Welfare 1.1

To Local 0.1

STATE GOVERNMENT (15.1)
Liquor Stores 0.7
Ins. Trust 2.2
Other General 3.0
Direct Spending for Educ., Hwys. & Welfare 5.0
State Aid to Local 4.2

Insurance Trust 0.2
Ed. 2.1
Hwys. 0.6
Welfare 0.8

LOCAL GOVERNMENT (17.0)
Utilities 2.0
Other General 5.9
Direct Spending for Education, Highways, & Welfare 8.9

* Excludes interest on the national debt ($4.4 billion)

DSW 7/ 1 /72

local spending sectors. This phase of IGR confirmed the interconnected and interdependent nature of national-state-local relations.

Creative (1958–1968)

The foundations for the creative phase of IGR were formed and filled in the cooperative and concentrated periods. The dates delimiting this phase are again somewhat arbitrary, but they mark a decade of moves toward decisiveness rather than drift in American politics and public policy. The election of a heavily Democratic Congress in 1958 and the 1964 presidential results were the political pegs to which this phase of IGR was attached. An added input that contributed to direction and cohesiveness, if not decisiveness, was the report of the Eisenhower-appointed President's Commission on National Goals. The commission, appointed partially in response to the Russian challenge of Sputnik, was created in 1959 and reported in 1961.[13]

The term Creative Federalism is applied to this decade because of presidential usage and because of the novel and numerous initiatives in IGR during the period. Three mechanisms are prominent: (1) program planning, (2) project grants, and (3) popular participation. The sheer number of grant programs alone is sufficient to set this decade apart from the preceding periods. In 1961 the Advisory Commission on Intergovernmental Relations (ACIR) identified approximately 40 major grant programs in existence that had been enacted prior to 1958. By 1969

13. Report of the President's Commission on National Goals, *Goals for Americans* (Englewood Cliffs, N.J.: Prentice-Hall, Spectrum Series and the American Assembly of Columbia University, 1960).

there were an estimated 160 major programs, 500 specific legislative authorizations, and 1,315 different federal assistance activities, for which money figures, application deadlines, agency contacts, and use restrictions could be identified. Federal grants jumped in dollar magnitude from $4.9 billion in 1958 to $23.9 billion in 1970. At the state-local level, state aid to local governments rose from $8.0 billion to $28.9 billion over the 1958–1970 span.

Numbers and dollars alone are insufficient to distinguish the creative phase. Planning requirements, for example, were attached to 61 of the new grant programs enacted between 1961 and 1966. The tremendous growth in project grants as contrasted with formula grants increased the diversity of activities supported by federal funds and increased further the autonomy and discretion of program professionals. Project grant authorizations grew from 107 to 280 between 1962 and 1967, while formula grants rose from 53 to 99 in the same period. Finally, the public participation requirements tied to some grants increased the complexity, the calculations, and occasionally the chagrin of officials charged with grant allocation choices.

To what ends or aims were these federal initiatives directed? What were the chief problems addressed by this activism? At the risk of great oversimplification, two major policy themes are identified: (1) an urban-metropolitan emphasis and (2) attention to disadvantaged persons in the society through the antipoverty programs and aid to education funds. The latter problem needs little documentation. Only one supporting item is mentioned for the former. Between 1961 and 1969 the percentage of all federal aid that went to urban areas increased from

55 percent to 70 percent, as total dollar amount so allocated went from $3.9 billion to $14.0 billion.[14]

Supporting the urban and disadvantaged emphases of this phase were selective but significant views held by important actors. President Johnson's speech first mentioning Creative Federalism also contained a phrase of larger and more popular political importance, that is, "The Great Society." As one observer has noted: "The Great Society was, by definition, one society; the phrase was singular, not plural."[15] How much this consensus politics push owed to the popularity of national goals efforts in the late 1950s and early 1960s is unknown. The unitary emphasis was evident, however. The president's preference on the need for centralized objective-setting made his 1965 moves toward planning-programming-budgeting a natural offshoot of views which held that our governmental system was a single system. Indeed, the basis for such revisionary thinking had been spelled out in a 1961 speech by Senator Joseph Clark entitled "Toward National Federalism."[16]

Accompanying these national and unitary sets of participants' perspectives was a subsidiary theme. It grew out of the expansion and proliferation of federal grants. This was the grantsmanship perspective that formed around the poverty and project grant programs. Playing the federal grant game became a well-known but time-consuming activity for mayors, managers, governors, universities, and, of course, for the program professionals.

This creative phase of IGR contains a paradox. Federal grants expanded massively in number, scope, and dollar magnitudes. The diversity that accentuated grantsmanship tendencies, however, moved from political and policy assumptions that were common—if not unitary—in their conception about the aims of society. The paradox is one of proliferation, participation, and pluralism amid convergence, consent, and concord. The prominence of the latter set suggests that "fused" is an appropriate metaphor by which this IGR phase can be characterized. An effort to show visually the coalesced character of IGR at the end of the creative period is provided in figure 2. The ties between national-state and state-local sectors are broad and weld the segments into a closely linked system. The visual contrast between figures 1 and 2 helps confirm the shift from a focused to a fused model of the IGR system.

The contrasting component present in this creative phase has not yet been noted. Figure 2 conveys the impression of intense interconnectedness and interdependence. What it does not convey is the diversity, proliferation, and fragmentation of the national-state fiscal links. There may be a superficial appearance of fusion, but the scores of specific and discrete categorical grants require additional adjectives to describe this period, such as the fused-foliated or proliferated phase.

Other, more crude metaphors that could be used are flowering federalism and spaghetti federalism. Both terms attempt to capture the elaborate, complex, and intricate features of IGR that developed in this phase.

14. *Special Analyses, Budget of the United States, Fiscal Year 1971* (Washington, D.C., 1970), pp. 228–229.

15. James L. Sundquist, *Making Federalism Work: A Study of Program Coordination at the Community Level* (Washington, D.C.: The Brookings Institution, 1969), p. 12.

16. George Washington University, *The Federal Government and the Cities: A Symposium* (Washington, D.C.: George Washington University, 1961), pp. 39–49.

FIGURE 2

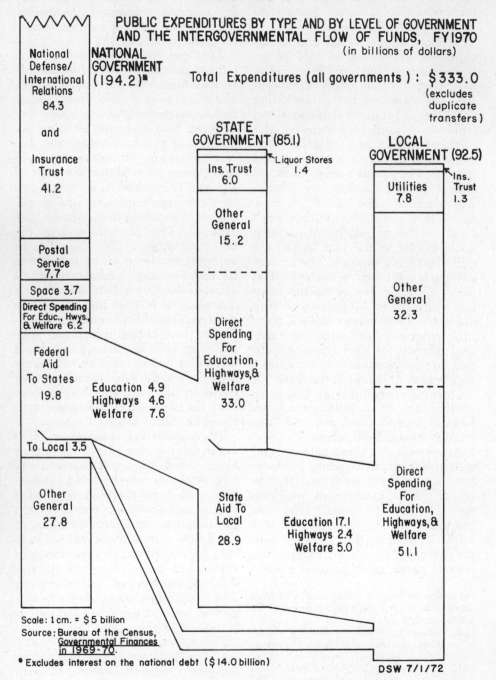

PUBLIC EXPENDITURES BY TYPE AND BY LEVEL OF GOVERNMENT
AND THE INTERGOVERNMENTAL FLOW OF FUNDS, FY1970
(in billions of dollars)

NATIONAL GOVERNMENT (194.2)*

National Defense/International Relations 84.3

and

Insurance Trust 41.2

Postal Service 7.7

Space 3.7

Direct Spending For Educ., Hwys., & Welfare 6.2

Federal Aid To States 19.8

Education 4.9
Highways 4.6
Welfare 7.6

To Local 3.5

Other General 27.8

Total Expenditures (all governments) : $333.0
(excludes duplicate transfers)

STATE GOVERNMENT (85.1)

Ins. Trust 6.0

Liquor Stores 1.4

Other General 15.2

Direct Spending For Education, Highways,& Welfare 33.0

State Aid To Local 28.9

Education 17.1
Highways 2.4
Welfare 5.0

LOCAL GOVERNMENT (92.5)

Utilities 7.8

Ins. Trust 1.3

Other General 32.3

Direct Spending For Education, Highways,& Welfare 51.1

Scale: 1 cm. = $5 billion
Source: Bureau of the Census, Governmental Finances in 1969-70.

* Excludes interest on the national debt ($14.0 billion)

DSW 7/1/72

Competitive (1965–?)

The proliferation of grants, the clash between professionals and participation-minded clients, the gap between program promises and proven performance, plus the intractability of domestic urban and international problems, formed a malaise in which IGR entered a new phase.

A different statement of central problems emerged when the administrative consequences of prior legislative whirlwinds became the center of attention. Issues associated with bureaucratic behavior and competence came to the forefront. One talisman earnestly sought was coordination. Others in close association were program accomplishment, effective service delivery systems and citizen access. Attention shifted to administrative performance and to organizational structures and relationships that either hindered or helped the effective delivery of public goods and services.

A sharply different tack was taken regarding appropriate IGR mechanisms. Pressure grew to alter and even reverse previous grant trends. Grant consolidation and revenue sharing were mentioned, popularized, and ultimately proposed by a Republican president on the basis of both program effectiveness and strengthening state and local governments. Some progress was made in the grant consolidation sphere, but as of 1973 the ACIR reported 69 formula grants and 312 project grants in existence. On the federal administrative scene, moves were made toward regionalization and reorganization. With the strong support of mayors, governors and county officials, general revenue sharing slipped through a divided Congress.

A flood of other developments in the late 1960s and early 1970s underscored the competition present in the system and also signaled efforts to reduce it. Perhaps the more visible actions and initiatives came at the national level, but in numerical terms and potential significance, important policy shifts occurred at the state and local levels. It is impossible to compress the numerous trends that were competition-inducing and to acknowledge some that eased competitive tendencies. Only three policy patterns will be mentioned as illustrations of tension-promoting developments: (1) economic opportunity programs and their chief implementation mechanisms—community action agencies; (2) "white flight" and the polarization of central city-suburban relationships, especially along racial lines; and (3) elimination or funding reductions in several grant programs by the Nixon administration in 1973 —some of which were achieved by the impounding of funds.

Countervailing tendencies in the direction of reduced tensions and increased cooperation appeared during this competition-dominated phase. At the local level, prompted and supported by national action, councils of governments sprang into existence in large numbers. One major aim was to foster metropolitan and regional coordination, especially through the A-95 grant review process. At the state level, herculean tax efforts were made to: (1) expand state services, (2) greatly increase state aid to local governments, and (3) meet the enlarged state-level funding requirements to match the vastly expanded federal grant monies.[17] Tension-reducing aims can

17. For example, state funds to match federal aid increased from $5.1 billion in 1964 to an estimated $18.4 billion in 1972;

also be attributed to such national-level actions as new departures with interstate compacts, the Partnership for Health Act (P.L.89–749), the Intergovernmental Cooperation Act of 1968 (P.L.90–577) and the Intergovernmental Personnel Act of 1970 (P.L.91–648).

The developments noted above reflected contrasting sets of perspectives that old as well as new participants brought to IGR. A statement by Senator Edmund Muskie—Democrat, Maine—in 1966 will serve as one example: "The picture, then, is one of too much tension and conflict rather than coordination and co-operation all along the line of administration—from top Federal policymakers and administrators to the state and local professional administrators and elected officials."[18] Similar views about the unwarranted degree of disagreement, tension, and rivalry among and between officials prompt the use of "competitive" for this phase of IGR.

The competition, however, is different in degree, emphasis, and configuration from the interlevel conflict of the older, layer cake phase. It is more modulated, and it acknowledges the lessons learned from the intervening periods of cooperation, concentration and creativity. For example, the current competitive phase appears reasonably realistic about the interdependencies within the system and the inability to turn the clock back in IGR. The three statutory enactments cited above bear witness to reasoned and reality-oriented approaches to IGR.

The nature of the competition in the present IGR phase is indicated in part by Senator Muskie's remarks. He mentions professional program administrators and state-local elected officials. It is the tension between the policy generalist, whether elected or appointed, and the program-professional-specialists that currently produces great static and friction in IGR. This cleavage is another reason for describing this phase of IGR as competitive. A visual representation of the fractures and rivalry characterizing this phase is offered in figure 3. The metaphor of the picket fence, referred to in former Governor Sanford's book, *Storm Over the States*,[19] was the original stimulus for this formulation. The seven public interest groups, often called the Big Seven, have parted ways from the functional specialists. Their common interest in revenue sharing, grant consolidation and similar proposals represents a reassertion of the executive leadership doctrine and a challenge to the program professionals' doctrine of neutral competence.

A second type of competition can also be discerned from figure 3: the competition between the several functional program areas. Each vertical picket represents an alliance among like-minded program specialists or professionals, regardless of the level of government in which they serve. As early as the mid-1950s these interlevel linkages of loyalties were identified and criticized as "vertical functional autocracies."[20]

see, Deil S. Wright and David E. Stephenson, "The States as Middlemen: Five Fiscal Dilemmas," *State Government* 47, no. 2 (Spring 1974), pp. 101–107.

18. U.S., Congress, Senate, *Congressional Record*, 89th Cong., 2nd sess., 1966, 112, p. 6834.

19. Terry Sanford, *Storm Over the States* (New York: McGraw-Hill, 1967), p. 80.

20. Advisory Committee on Local Government, *An Advisory Committee Report on Local Government* (submitted to the Commission on Intergovernmental Relations, Washington, D.C., June 1955), p. 7.

FIGURE 3

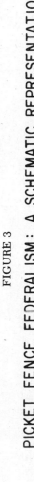

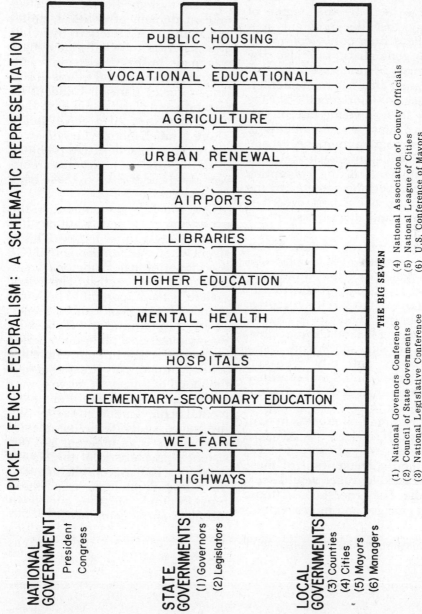

PICKET FENCE FEDERALISM: A SCHEMATIC REPRESENTATION

PUBLIC HOUSING

VOCATIONAL EDUCATIONAL

AGRICULTURE

URBAN RENEWAL

AIRPORTS

LIBRARIES

HIGHER EDUCATION

MENTAL HEALTH

HOSPITALS

ELEMENTARY-SECONDARY EDUCATION

WELFARE

HIGHWAYS

NATIONAL GOVERNMENT
President
Congress

STATE GOVERNMENTS
(1) Governors
(2) Legislators

LOCAL GOVERNMENTS
(3) Counties
(4) Cities
(5) Mayors
(6) Managers

THE BIG SEVEN

(1) National Governors Conference
(2) Council of State Governments
(3) National Legislative Conference

(4) National Association of County Officials
(5) National League of Cities
(6) U.S. Conference of Mayors
(7) International City Management Association

DSW 6/15/74

© Copyright 1974
Deil S. Wright

Other epithets used against these patterns are: balkanized bureaucracies, feudal federalisms and autonomous autocracies. These terms emphasize not only the degree of autonomy that the program specialists have from policy control by political generalists, but also the separateness and independence that one program area has from another. This lack of horizontal linkage prompts interprogram, interprofessional and interagency competition. The cross-program competition combined with the generalist-specialist split helps confirm the contention that the competition depicted by the picket fence model best describes the current and most recent phase of IGR.

Both competitive patterns were captured in the words of local officials as quoted by James Sundquist. Speaking in the late 1960s, the director of a local model cities program contended that "Our city is a battleground among federal Cabinet agencies."[21] Similar sentiments came from mayors and city managers whose limited control and coordination powers over federal programs caused them to feel like spectators of the governmental process in their own cities. If, in fact, this competitive model is applicable to IGR today, then a recognition of these tensions and cleavages would seem to be the first-order task of those seeking changes and improvements in IGR.

21. Sundquist, *Making Federalism Work*, p. 27.

CONCLUDING COMMENT

IGR has become a distinctive dimension of activities in the American political system. It refers to a significant domain of political, policy and administrative actions by public officials. An acknowledged emphasis was made in this discussion on the meaning, features and trends in IGR (as a term or phrase). Concept explication and clarification have their uses; but they also have limits. There is much more to be said about the realities, practices and problems of IGR. Subsequent articles are appropriately addressed to these types of concerns.

One concluding comment on this exposition is offered in anticipation of the analyses that follow. This is an era when the *management* of IGR is a matter of major moment. James Sundquist observes that "The federal system is too important to be left to chance."[22] His book can be seen as an effort to critique and reconstruct the organizational philosophy undergirding effective intergovernmental action. Sundquist's treatment and the mood of this essay move toward a similar conclusion: intergovernmental achievements hinge on coping successfully with complexity. Complexity is an inherent and persistent characteristic of the several features of IGR. Accomplishments in the intergovernmental arena therefore depend on the successful management of complexity.

22. Ibid., p. 31.

How Fares Federalism in the Mid-Seventies?

By David B. Walker

ABSTRACT: American federalism and the intergovernmental relations that sustain it are in a major transitional period. The recent emergence of several different theories—especially Creative Federalism and New Federalism—are symptomatic; yet neither of these schools of thought were applied consistently, nor were they in conflict with each other in all instances. Moreover, neither provides helpful answers to some of the emerging problems confronting the system. The many changes in fiscal federalism are another dimension of this transition. The federal government still plays a dominant role in economic affairs, but a reduced one in intergovernmental financial assistance. Most states have strengthened their revenue systems, are enjoying surpluses or balanced budgets, and are beginning to act like major fiscal middlemen. All levels now have large intergovernmental components in their budgets, making fiscal relations more interdependent than ever before. Administratively and jurisdictionally, a number of myths have emerged that impede the management of the system's current business. These include such notions as: all categorical grants have similar operational traits, block grants are easy to administer, decentralization is devolution, devolution of authority to elected officials is a simple undertaking, local governmental fragmentation preserves local autonomy, and all general units of local government are general governments. A clearer understanding of the sources of conceptual confusion, a greater awareness of the new features of fiscal federalism, and a better appreciation of current administrative and jurisdictional conditions are vital for policy makers at all levels.

David B. Walker is Assistant Director, Governmental Structure and Functions, Advisory Commission on Intergovernmental Relations. Previously, he was Staff Director, U.S. Senate Subcommittee on Intergovernmental Relations. He received his B.A. and M.A. degrees from Boston University and his Ph.D. from Brown University. Dr. Walker has taught at American University, Howard University, Northwestern University's Medill School (Washington program), the University of Maryland, and Bowdoin College. He has written several articles on different facets of contemporary American intergovernmental relations.

AS THE nation approaches the Bicentennial, the condition of American federalism, and of the countless intergovernmental relations sustaining it, roughly resembles that of the British Constitution and of mother country/colonial relationships of two hundred years ago. Conceptually, the so-called system is in ferment. Fiscally, it is in a state of flux and of some fear. Managerially, it is in considerable confusion. In terms of the public, its major institutional components enjoy remarkably low esteem in the electorate's eyes. In short, the nonsystematic system is in a time of major transition. Though a Third American Revolution is not the likely result of these domestic tensions, post-Bicentennial intergovernmental relations will be markedly different from what we had in the sixties and early seventies.

CONFLICTING CONCEPTS

The academic, public administration and policy making arenas, to cite only the more obvious, recently have been caught up in a fairly major effort to define, redefine and debate federalism's record, real meaning and needed reforms. No other period in this century can match this one in its capacity to produce divergent interpretations of how the system should and does function. So we are confronted with theories of dual, cooperative, permissive, creative, and new federalism, with a nation-centered or state-centered emphasis in most of them. Moreover, each of these interpretations is capable of commanding intellectual, political and popular support.

In the contemporary world of politics, programs and administra-

tion, the debate is largely dominated by Creative and New Federalists, and the basic divisions are chiefly between adherents of these two schools of thought and action. This is not to say that spokesmen of either group are political theorists or are even aware of all the principles comprising their respective creeds.

Creative Federalism, after all, never received a rounded presidential exposition. One of its best interpreters was not even a member of the Johnson administration, but a journalist, and one of its best analyses lies buried in a doctoral dissertation gathering dust in the library at the American University. With the New Federalists, there has been far more rhetoric and ready phrases and more newspaper and journalistic coverage. Yet the most thoughtful explanation of the new view came from a man who was never among the top Nixon advisers and who is now busy monitoring the operations of general revenue sharing at Brookings.

Most of the exponents of Creative and New Federalism, then, have been and are men of practical affairs—concerned with political, program and/or administrative matters. Most have not attempted to formulate a comprehensive view of the system, but have hammered out their precepts in the context of specific issues and problems—largely from the vantagepoint of their positions in the executive or legislative branches of the national government.

Both of these operational theories have been classed as variations of cooperative federalism and properly so. Both, after all, stress partnership, the sharing of responsibilities and revenues, and activism at all levels. The apparent differences arise chiefly from their contrasting methods, differing views of the federal role, and varying interpretations of the partnership ideal.

The Creative Federalists ostensibly placed heavy emphasis on national goals while relying on categorical grants as a means of implementation. They had an expansive view of the system which included private sector participants and focused on programs and their goals, rather than on jurisdictions as such. They emphasized urban and city problems as much as state and rural concerns and worried little about the degree to which they further "marbleized" the cake of federalism.

The New Federalism, reacting in large measure to what was considered to be the thrust of Creative Federalism, supported the following: decentralization of federal program authority to field offices, devolution of power and greater discretion to state and local governments, enactment of general and special revenue sharing programs, a curbing of categorical grants-in-aid, strengthening general governments and politically accountable state and local officials, streamlining the service delivery system generally, and some sorting out of responsibilities for certain functions by governmental levels.

In practice, of course, these contrasting approaches sometimes were followed, sometimes not. The Johnson administration obviously had a lofty and near-panoramic view of the national purpose, and it relied heavily on the political leadership of the federal government to give definition and program content to this purpose. The traditional categorical grant-in-aid mechanism was relied on heavily to achieve its program goals. During the Johnson years, over 240 new grant programs were enacted, and the assistance dollars were more than doubled. Only one major Creative Federalism enactment—Medicare—departed from this fundamental reliance on intergovernmental ways of implementing program objectives. The Johnsonian effort to expand traditional aid programs, as well as to launch new ones, produced a remarkable array of governmental, quasi-governmental and even private sector recipients of grant funds, and a drastic redefinition of the partnership concept. Especially with its proliferation of project grants (about four-fifths of the 1968 total number), specific program purposes were heavily stressed, eligibility requirements were expanded to give administrators maximum discretion in selecting recipients, and middle managers acquired more delegated authority. Accompanying all this was a near tripling of the direct or indirect flow of assistance funds to urban areas, and an increase in the grant dollars that by-passed states to local governments—as of early 1969, some 70 programs permitted direct disbursement to local governments. Moreover, as the Creative Federalism years drew to a close, nine out of every 10 central cities in the largest metropolitan areas were receiving more federal aid on a per capita basis than their suburban counterparts. These operational thrusts, then, tend to conform to the precepts generally subsumed under Creative Federalism.

With New Federalism, there also has been some matching of theory and practice. The federal field structure was reorganized in 1969, with 10 standardized regions and common headquarters cities established, and, as of mid-1974 nine domestic federal departments and agencies were bound by this structure and served as members of the Federal

Regional Councils. Significant administrative discretion has been delegated to field offices in at least 190 grant programs. General revenue sharing now is law, and with it the discretion of states and general units of local government has been strengthened. The new manpower legislation of 1973 represents a major breakthrough on the block grant front by merging 23 categoricals into two, assigning to the field major administrative responsibilities, and giving significant discretion to the states and local "prime sponsors."

The Federal Assistance Review (FAR) program under the New Federalism explored various ways to streamline the administration of categorical grants, and Office of Management and Budget (OMB) Circular A-102, with its uniform requirements for many phases of the grant process, constitutes one of FAR's major accomplishments. Under its Integrated Grant Administration (IGA), OMB has launched 27 pilot programs in the joint funding of state, areawide, and local projects.

During the past five years, the New Federalism has curbed the growth in categoricals (thanks to some consolidations), OMB constraints on new departmental special purpose initiatives, and executive impoundments. General governments have been favored under the New Federalism's general and special revenue sharing proposals, with the states usually assured some sort of role. Finally, the broadly discretionary special revenue sharing bills, the nationalization of the adult public assistance categories—old-age assistance, aid to the blind, and aid to the permanently and totally disabled—in the 1972 Social Security amendments, and the ear-lier Nixon administration drive for the Family Assistance Program (FAP) reflect basic components of the New Federalism's not-too-successful effort to reassign key functions according to which level could best cope with them. In short, some of the key New Federalism precepts have found their way into practice.

With both of these versions of contemporary federalism, however, other developments were or are present—developments that suggest continuity and even a collaboration between them. The Creative Federalists, after all, launched the A-85 process in 1967 to give state and local elected executives a chance to react to proposed grant regulations. They also sponsored the first block grant in modern times, the Partnership for Health Act of 1966, and collaborated in producing the second, the Safe Streets legislation of 1968. They ultimately sanctioned the Intergovernmental Cooperation Act of 1968, with its many provisions geared to eliminating interlevel friction in grant programs and other operations. They began the staff work on reorganizing the federal regional boundaries and field structure, and their model cities program was one of the first attempts to achieve a common focus on the multiple needs of a specific area through a form of joint funding. Their Appalachian Regional Commission legislation and Public Works and Economic Development Act of 1966 provided major examples of multifunctional grant programs. Moreover, despite the proliferation of grant programs and participants, over three-quarters of all aid funds were channeled to state governments during the Johnson years. General governments and elected officials, block grants, and improvements in grant administration clearly were not forgotten items on Creative Federalism's agenda, and this was particularly the case during its last two years.

In like fashion, the New Federalism has not always adhered to its publicized principles. Decentralization of program authority to the field is only now beginning to affect the big money grants. Effective organization of the Federal Regional Councils for major liaison efforts with the states and localities still faces many hurdles, including the continuing basic weakness of their chairmen's positions, the variations in delegated discretion among the field units, and the politicization of many of the key positions in some of the departments' regional offices. The administration of the Partnership for Health and Safe Streets programs, the first two block grants, has been so uneven that the latter now has a major categorical string attached to it, and the former is subjected to several strings, plus a current HEW effort to revamp it wholly. Moreover, while general governments are supposed to be favored under the New Federalism, federally encouraged single purpose substate regional bodies have grown during the past six years to more than 1,800.

Meanwhile, only modest efforts have been made to strengthen generalist-oriented regional units representing local general governments. In the case of general revenue sharing, the failure to develop a sensible operational definition of general governments produced a situation where a whole cluster of essentially limited governments, notably townships and some counties, enjoyed a fiscal windfall. Not unexpectedly, practical considerations have forced the New Federalists to assume a strongly centraliz-ing stance when they have confronted various issues in the fiscal, environmental, economic and energy fields.

Finally, the New Federalists realized that in order to decentralize, they first would have to centralize; this led to an erosion of departmental and cabinet discretion and a strengthening of the White House staff, the Domestic Council and OMB. In short, practice clearly has not always matched New Federalism precepts.

Continuing currents and new cross-currents form the confusing flow of impressions suggested by this brief analysis of the principles and practices of Creative and New Federalism—and no wonder. Both were a product of practical political considerations, not systematic analysis. Both produced their respective rationales after their component programs had been launched. Both had to confront the realities of American intergovernmental relations—with the Creative Federalists it was the states and to a lesser degree the cities, while with the New Federalists it was and is the Congress, and to a lesser extent the federal bureaucracy. Yet both in a sense have added to the conceptual confusion regarding the system.

To help curb this confusion and to narrow the ideological gap between the New Federalists in the federal executive branch and elsewhere and the less articulate but still redoubtable Creative Federalists in Congress and elsewhere, we need a clearer understanding of, and probably more solid research on, such propositions as these:

—Creative and New Federalism had as much in common as they had in conflict, yet neither at this point addresses the range of fundamental challenges confronting American federalism of the late seventies.

—Categoricals, block grants, and general revenue sharing now exist at both the federal and state levels as means of achieving intergovernmental fiscal transfers; each is needed, but each has different program and administrative—not merely money—implications; failure to appreciate fully these contrasting implications, especially in the case of block grants, will impede efforts to develop a more flexible, balanced and adaptive system.

—At the multistate and substate regional levels, the mismatch of new areas of functional concern and the jurisdictional boundaries of traditional general governments —states, counties, and cities— have produced 17 federal-multistate commissions in the water resources and economic development areas, approximately 1,800 single purpose substate regional districts under 19 different federal area-wide programs (law enforcement, comprehensive health planning, economic development, etc.), plus a roughly equal number of multijurisdictional special authorities and districts with direct operational and fiscal authority. Do these districting developments portend another triumph of the technocrats, or are they controlled or controllable by elected decision makers and/or the electorate? Do they facilitate or impede appropriate devolution and the development of more dependable service delivery systems?

—On the basic question of strength, the sixties saw a strong federal government, while the early seventies saw the emergence of strong states with an enfeebled federal government. In the earlier period, cities and counties focused on Washington, and in the latter they divided their attention equally with their state capitals. In light of the growing need for better public services, is the strong federal-state-local partnership formula merely an ideal or a practical necessity? Assuming the latter, what institutional, fiscal, functional and political party changes are required at each level to put this formula on an operating basis?

—Finally, and on a more broadly philosophic level, which levels of government—federal, state, or local—best reconcile majority rule with minority rights? Are the political processes of local governments basically majoritarian; those of most states, limited majoritarian; and those of the national government concurrent majoritarian—given the relative homogeneity of the local electorates, the greater heterogeneity of the state publics, and the massively heterogeneous national electorate? Phrased in terms of the American political tradition, does Jefferson dominate city halls and county courthouses; Madison, the State houses; and Calhoun, the U.S. Capitol? Also, if these propositions prove accurate, what significance do they have for the assignment of functions, and where are equity considerations given greater attention?

As America moves toward and beyond its Bicentennial, basic propositions and questions such as these need probing and testing if federalism's real conceptual agenda is to be confronted.

FINANCES IN FLUX

Fiscal federalism's recent record highlights certain major changes, the impact of which has yet to be analyzed and understood.

—Overall growth in expenditures and revenues since World War II exceeded the rate of population growth and even the pace of urbanization. Total federal-state-local outlays multiplied more than seven times between 1946 and 1972, reaching $368.3 billion by 1972; total governmental receipts more than sextupled, to $361.4 billion; and total taxes more than quintupled, reaching $274.7 billion.

—Intergovernmentally, federal expenditures grew by a multiple of 5.9, to $246.5 billion, in this period, and state-local spending by 13.5; federal revenues rose by 475 percent, while state-local receipts soared by 1,254 percent, reaching $174.6 billion. As proportions of the gross national product, federal taxes—exclusive of Social Security—represented 17.2 percent of the GNP in 1945, but only 14.1 percent in 1972. State-local taxes—again, exclusive of social insurance contributions—constituted only 4.4 percent of GNP in the earlier year, as opposed to 10 percent a generation later.

—The total general revenue pie (from own sources) in 1952 was divided 75 percent federal, 12 percent state and 13 percent local, but its 1972 counterpart had a 56 percent federal share, a 23 percent state portion and a 21 percent local sector.

—On the tax front, the federal income tax has been cut four times since 1952, while the number of states using both a broad-based personal income tax and general sales tax jumped from 17 in 1950 to 36 in 1974. Between 1959 and 1973, 525 rate hikes and 40 new tax enactments occurred at the state level, leaving only 10 without a broad-based personal income tax, five without a general sales tax and one without either.

—Among the 50 states, however, only a little over one-fifth are making heavy use of the income tax; 15 are exerting moderate; 14, meager; and 10, no effort at all. When gauging the relative state-local tax effort, 14 states captured a modest portion of their tax potential, 26 garnered a moderate share and 10 were tapping close to their full potential.

—Property taxes still are a major source of local revenues—about 82 percent of total local taxes from own sources. Because of their continuing importance, over one-third of the states reorganized or strengthened their property tax supervisory units in the last decade, with four states joining Hawaii in centralizing assessment, 15 establishing or beefing up assessor-training programs, 14 launching or revamping their assessment ratio studies, and a dozen adopting a full disclosure policy regarding the average level of assessment in a community.

—On the property tax relief front, all states now have instituted some form of help, with 29 taking action in 1973 alone; between 1970 and 1973, the number of states adopting state-financed "circuit breaker" types of relief programs jumped from 4 to 21.

—Within metropolitan areas, most

central cities have a disproportionate share of the disadvantaged and have experienced a dangerous eroding of their fiscal base. Meanwhile, the average local tax burden of the core city dweller in the 72 largest Standard Metropolitan Statistical Areas amounted to 6.8 percent of income in 1970, while the comparable figure for the suburbanite came to only 5.2 percent.

—In terms of intergovernmental fiscal transfers, federal grant outlays multiplied more than 33 times between 1946 and 1972, while state aid to localities rose from 34.8 percent of local general revenues (from their own sources) in 1946 to over 57 percent in 1972.

—Until the mid-sixties, all of the direct federal assistance took the form of project or formula-based categorical grants. But with the enactment of the Partnership for Health and Safe Streets block grants, plus general revenue sharing in 1972, the total federal aid packet became more diversified—15 percent going for general revenue sharing in 1973, 1 percent for block grants, and 84 percent for categoricals. The states have had some version of this tripartite aid approach for some time, with general support payments accounting for 10.2 percent of the total state aid in 1972. The state-by-state mix of aid as between categorical, block and general purpose has yet to be analyzed adequately.

—Functional transfers have been another recent development, with the federal government assuming full fiscal responsibility for the three adult public assistance categories in 1974, and the states moving gradually on a number of program fronts. As of 1971, 21 states provided more than half the combined state-local outlays for public schools; 21 met 95 percent or more of the nonfederal matching in public welfare; and 20 provided 40 percent or more of the total state-local expenditures for their criminal justice systems.

—Though relieved of the threat of a federal judicial mandate to reform their school support programs, several states have begun to move on this front, with nine adopting major equalization measures in 1973.

—Finally, in terms of overall outlays for domestic programs, the federal proportion, for both direct and intergovernmental purposes, rose from 34 percent of the total in 1953 to 47 percent in 1973. Put another way, the hikes in Social Security taxes and benefits and related medical outlays, the federal deficit of $133 billion (1953–1973), and the shift in federal budgetary priorities to the domestic sector from 24 percent of federal outlays in 1954 to 60 percent in 1973, more than offset the effect of the various federal tax cuts and the bootstrap fiscal efforts of state and local governments.

Steady growth in governmental activity at all levels, but especially at the federal and state levels; greater overall revenue efforts generally at the local and especially the state levels, with most of the latter now having systems that are highly responsive to economic growth; continuing uneven tax effort among the states and unequal tax burdens between most core cities and their suburbs; rapid expansion in the amounts and some basic changes in the form of intergovernmental fiscal transfers; some state efforts to reform the property tax and many more state efforts to provide property tax relief; the beginnings of some significant transfers of functions and portions of functions between the major levels; and a growing proportionate federal role in civil governmental program areas, despite expanding state-local spending from their own sources—these are some of the basic fiscal trends that have put federalism's finances in a current state of considerable flux. These developments portend a new set of fiscal conditions and concerns for policy makers at all levels.

The recent record reveals a greater "marbleizing" of the intergovernmental fiscal system than ever before. The budgets of all levels now involve a greater intergovernmental fiscal component, and the types of revenue are no longer fairly well separated by governmental levels. Increasingly, each level will be more conscious of the fiscal actions of the others. To date, only the transfer of functions represents a contrary trend, and thus far this has not reached major proportions, nor has it usually involved a transfer upward of administrative as well as fiscal responsibilities for services. Uneasiness and some anxiety are bound to arise when independent political jurisdictions have to operate in an increasingly interdependent era.

Despite the tight supply of federal assistance dollars, the economy, inflation and the energy crisis have forced state and local officials to continue to focus on Washington. After all, Phase II wage and price controls covered their jurisdictions as well as the private sector; inflation, some state and local officials say, has outpaced the flow of general revenue sharing dollars; and, according to some estimates, state gasoline tax collections could experience an anticipated short-fall of as much as $734 million during calendar year 1974. The federal government's role in maintaining economic stability clearly is as vital as ever.

At the same time, its intergovernmental fiscal efforts are less crucial. The federal government experienced a combined $47.7 billion deficit in FY's 1972 and 1973, while state and local governments enjoyed surpluses of $13.6 billion and $8.5 billion for those years. Not unexpectedly, this federal fiscal position generated a mood of retrenchment and executive branch-Congressional battles over program priorities. The latter, in turn, centered heavily on the relative size and scope of revenue sharing, proposed special revenue sharing and categorical assistance sectors. Yet in the many ensuing battles over authorizations, appropriations, vetoes, impoundments, and the 66 related court cases, state and local governments were not passive bystanders. Of more than passing interest was their success in several of the court cases and in having an intergovernmental fiscal impact provision inserted in the Senate version of the pending Congressional budgeting reforms.

Fiscal federalism, then, has entered an era in which the traditional levels are concerned with both the revenue and expenditure policies of each other. Despite the federal government's key role vis-à-vis the national economy, its relatively weaker fiscal position has prompted major concern in Washington over state and local fiscal actions. The states, on the other hand, are beginning to play a new and significant role as fiscal middlemen in the system—thanks to their stronger revenue situation, their position as the primary recipients of most federal assistance dollars, their status as the transfer agent for the bulk of federal assistance going to local governments, and their moves toward converting the local fiscal sector into an integral component of a unified state-local system. Yet the states still are very much affected by unilateral federal, local, and private sector economic and/or fiscal decisions. Meanwhile, with the heavy dependence of local governments on intergovernmental fiscal transfers and on the property tax, the exposed condition of their finances needs no further emphasis. In short, state and local governments still must watch Washington, despite the meager prospect of any freeing-up of discretionary federal dollars. Yet federal and local attention is now being drawn to state capitals, where some strong monetary middlemen are emerging. And neither the federal nor state governments can ignore politically or administratively the primary servicing units in the system: the local governments.

Such are some of the dimensions of this new interdependence. More times than not, however, adversary attitudes and debates over fiscal centralization versus decentralization have been the main response to this development. More appropriate would have been a full-fledged probe of what cooperative federalism in the fiscal area now entails, and whether the traditional means by which the federal government, the states and the localities have sought to influence each other's taxing and spending policies are still adequate.

Throughout the better part of the last three decades, the strong international position of the dollar, the informal but fairly clear allocation of different taxes to different governmental levels, and the relatively modest role of intergovernmental fiscal transfers provided the basis for a fairly open, loosely interacting system. All this is history now. Every level's expenditures and revenues are conditioned significantly by the actions or inactions of other levels. Officials at all levels and in different ways evidence concern over some facet of this new fiscal federalism. However, the partial, piecemeal, and informal procedural responses that have been produced to date may not suffice to quiet the anxieties and the very real uneasiness which this basic development has generated.

THE MANAGEMENT MORASS

Despite the attention recently given it, the management of federalism's business is still in a state of considerable confusion. Some of the muddle stems from the continuing controversy over systemic concepts and the administrative assumptions subsumed under them. Some of it clearly relates to the many changes in fiscal federalism, especially the differing program and management implications of each of the sectors comprising the new tripartite system for disbursing intergovernmental assistance. Yet much of the difficulty is rooted in the ponderous pace of our thinking about intergovernmental administrative matters as contrasted with the rush of policy and program developments at all levels.

In effect, a cluster of management myths has emerged which clouds our perception of the current condition of intergovernmental administration. Ten such myths merit attention.

—One fairly popular misconception is that all categorical grants are basically alike: narrowly defined, loaded with regulations, centralizing, proliferating and strengthening of middle management. Categoricals, of course, come in all sorts of shapes and and packages. The traits cited above, however, generally are more applicable to the project type, due to the absence of a precise, statutorily-established allocation formula, the greater discretion assigned to administrators, and the rapid rise in the number of, and the permissive eligibility provisions in, such grants. The far fewer formula-based grants, on the other hand, usually narrow the range of eligible recipients; they focus on governments, are governed by a fairly precise allocation scheme set forth in the legislation, and involve the bulk of categorical funds. These traits tend to curb the discretion of middle management and their capacity to glut a program with innumerable administrative regulations. The major exceptions are those formula-based grants that are open-ended, and here legislative bodies have tended to provide the stimulus for administrative constraints. In short, much of the on-going criticism should be directed toward some, but not all, of the categoricals.

—Another misconception is that a block grant is merely a big categorical program. In some respects this is true, especially when large formula-based categoricals are used as the sole basis of comparison; but a block grant is different. It arises when categoricals are merged, as in the case of the Partnership for Health and manpower programs, or when a broad program area that could be categorized is treated as a whole from the outset, as was the Safe Streets legislation. Rigorously defined eligibility provisions usually are stipulated. Both matching and apportionment formulas generally are applied. While significant discretion in terms of specific program emphasis usually is left to eligible recipients, the higher level government retains the power of substantive review prior to expenditures, and audits comprise a basic means of providing long term accountability. In contrast to categoricals, all of this suggests an unusual and arduous attempt to balance the broad functional concerns of higher level governments with the specific program needs of lower level governments. The record of the Safe Streets and Partnership for Health programs—the only two federal block grants with any real history—suggests that all the skills needed for striking such a balance have yet to be developed.

—Clearly related to this garbled view of block grants is the fairly commonplace misconception that "few strings" or "no strings" assistance monies are easy to spend. When phrased in terms of "freedom of choice is easy to cope with," the difficulties of this assumption become more apparent. Moreover, the block grant case studies confirm this. Both the Partnership for Health and Safe Streets programs began with few strings, and both have had more added to them. Both sought to expand state and especially gubernatorial discretion, and both provide many examples of program specialists', in effect, taking over. Both also sought a melding within states of narrow program concerns into a broad functional context, but both, not unexpectedly perhaps, have produced many examples of program winners, program losers, and politically accountable generalists unable to act as intergroup brokers. With general revenue sharing, its brief record bars any final conclusions regarding the ease or difficulty of spending decisions. However, as the program becomes a firm feature of state and local financial decision making, and as more sectors of the electorate become conscious of this fact, priority politics can be expected to emerge, and the challenge of choice will have to be confronted. This, after all, is one of the major objectives of the program.

—Still another source of current management difficulties is the fairly common tendency to equate decentralization with devolution. Decentralization involves the breaking up of concentrated authority at the center of a government and distributing it more widely among its subcomponents. Devolution, on the other hand, is the delegating of power or authority by a central government to lower-level governing units. The former, then, is a geographic and administrative concept applied to a single administrative system; the latter is a political concept involving power relationships between different levels of governments. With attempts to assign more program authority from Washington to the field offices, or state efforts to foster substate regional areas and units for delivering their services, case studies of decentralization are provided. Both occur within single administrative systems; both relate to better service delivery; and both entail potentially better liaison with other governments in the areas involved. However, neither of these decentralizing efforts involves any grant of power to other governmental units, and from the vantagepoint of these other units, the entire effort may be viewed as a subtle move to enhance the administrative strength of the higher level jurisdiction—as a variety of centralization, if you will. Devolution, on the other hand, is more accurately reflected in the federal general revenue sharing and block grant programs, as well as in state general support and local home rule undertakings. In short, devolution and decentralization serve very different goals, which may be compatible or sometimes in conflict. Both, however, are essential approaches to coping with differing facets of the assignment of functions question.

—Linked with the decentralization-devolution confusion is the frequently held assumption that decentralization can occur without some measure of significant prior centralization. Yet how does one mandate decentralization in an administrative system that lacks the effective power to mandate? Administrative centralization within a single department or administrative system is not just a proposition, but is actual practice in many federal, state, and local agencies. On the other hand, intradepartmental fragmentation and fractious disputes are also commonplace, and these are hurdles that decentralization must surmount. What the recent federal efforts to decentralize to the field offices reveals is that departments traditionally classed as collections of federal fiefdoms in Washington have experienced great difficulty in transferring major program authority to the 10 regions, and that only with the buttressing of a Secretary's role has some progress been made. Governors and mayors have faced comparable administrative resistance in some of their attempts to decentralize their service delivery systems. So there is the irony and perhaps the danger of having first to centralize and then to decentralize.

—With devolution, another dilemma (usually misunderstood) is faced. How does one devolve power in a system that is, in Elazar's phrase, already "noncentralized?" From one vantage-point, an easy answer can be produced. Discretion obviously can be assigned to other separate governmental units simply by cutting the number of administrative and other strings associated with intergovernmental fiscal transfers and by broadening the scope of an assisted program area. In this way, a range of choices can be conferred, recipient discretion can be expanded, and the decision making of lower level governments can be revitalized. But the more subtle dimensions of the dilemma arise with the question: can power be devolved so that elected officials and their generalist allies are the primary beneficiaries? The record of block grants and of the model cities program suggests that an affirmative answer here is only possible when the political and governmental systems of the recipient jurisdictions already have undergone significant reform efforts and have put these decision makers in an authoritative position. Where these officials are not on a par—practically and politically—with the program specialists and their interest group allies, the efforts of higher level generalists turn out to be more of a sham than a success. Another irony arises then. Effective devolution of power to key elected office holders can only take place when these officials already have been rendered powerful by indigenous reform efforts.

—Still another myth cluttering up the current management landscape is the assumption that administration is simply a matter of planning, organizing and delivering services within a single administrative system. For some, the system is the entire federal partnership, while for others it is limited to one of the governmental partners. Both groups overlook the vital jurisdictional issue. It is this jurisdictional factor, with its separate political, personnel and bureaucratic systems, that gives contemporary intergovernmental administration its distinctive, nonhierarchic, nonsystemic, non-superior-subordinate character. To view this maze of relationships as a unified system is to be misleading; but to treat the process as a series of disciplined servicing endeavors within a number of separate governmental jurisdictions is to ignore the ever-increasing interjurisdictional character of contemporary management.

—Linked with this jurisdictional issue is the political belief that local governmental fragmentation is a vital preserver of a noncentralized system and is somehow unrelated to current servicing difficulties. In days past, this may have been so; but with increases in intergovernmental fiscal transfers, and with the many servicing spillovers in urban areas, higher level intervention in one form or another has been demonstrated to be the prime result. Sometimes this has taken the form of court cases, sometimes of higher level assumption of a functional responsibility or its regulation, and sometimes of establishing new, usually single-purpose regional governmental entities. All of this has major administrative implications, especially at the new tier of ever-increasing governmental activity: the substate regional level. Here, some 1,800 federally encouraged planning and development districts, a comparable number of multijurisdictional special authorities and districts with operating responsibilities, and some 470 A-95 clearinghouses have been set up; and here, some 16 metropolitan areas are involved in reorganization efforts of the one-, two-, or three-tier variety of their own. The fragmentation generally at the substate regional level, growing out of the fragmentation at the local level, already represents a kind of cen-

tralization. Moreover, the very nature of the functional and jurisdictional conflict at this level guarantees additional state and federal involvement.

—A major myth involving local units is the assumption that all general governments are, in fact, general governments. The strength of this myth is reflected in a number of recent developments: the general revenue sharing legislation adopted it; the 1973 manpower program did not escape its attraction; and the pending better communities bills are grappling with its powerful pretensions. Moreover, state and local efforts to make the myth a reality have encountered their greatest hurdle in attempts to demolish the myth first. The myth, of course, arises out of unreal legal classifications and Bureau of the Census reliance on them. Yet many supposedly general purpose jurisdictions are really limited purpose units—halfway between single purpose districts and full-fledged multipurpose governments. Definitions are needed that make fiscal, functional and operational sense, especially in a period when the focus is on narrowing eligibility requirements, on emphasizing general purpose jurisdictions, and on reassigning servicing responsibilities or portions thereof. A jurisdiction's ability to raise revenue from its own sources, its pattern of expenditures, its degree of reliance on interlocal contracts, the presence of a large number of overlying independent special districts, and the range of its functions all provide clues as to whether, in actuality, it is a general or essentially limited purpose unit.

Without a better understanding of this middle category of local governments, federal and state assistance programs, especially of the general support and block grant type, and state policies on local governmental viability run the risk of failure.

—A final myth that is facing gradually the harsh glare of real world sunlight is the notion that the contemporary jurisdictional map of local government in America is sensible and satisfactory. Officials at all levels, for political and other purposes, pretend or actually believe this to be the case. Again the federal general revenue sharing and manpower legislation, along with state difficulties in developing and/or implementing local governmental viability policies, attest to the political strength of this belief. The combination of federal, state and local actions that have produced today's patchwork pattern of assorted single purpose units at the substate regional and subregional levels suggests, however, a rejection of this myth when having to cope with actual servicing problems. The failure to face frontally the gap between the jurisdictional area of most local general governments and the geographic reach of a growing number of governmental functions has major management implications. In the typical substate region, there is a generalist-dominated coordination unit, usually a council of governments that can not coordinate authoritatively; there are functional planning districts that can not link projects with plans; and there are single purpose authorities that can act, but outside of any process that would interrelate effectively these units' various regional operations. An umbrella multijurisdictional organization (called for in volume 1 of the Advisory Commission on Intergovernmental Relations' recent study, *Substate Regionalism and the Federal System*), regional and local reorganization (following the format of ACIR recommendations set forth in volume 3 of that series), and strong state intervention provide three alternate approaches to coping with this dilemma.

CONCLUSION

Conflict over concepts, finances in flux, and muddled intergovernmental management—these are three themes that have dominated much of the thought and action involving contemporary American federalism. Their ascendancy makes ours a time of transition. A safe prediction is that the system of the late seventies will be markedly different from the one we have known; but the nature of its basic intergovernmental relations will depend, in no small measure, on how the issues raised herein are resolved. Hopefully, the Bicentennial will engender a more concerted effort among thinkers, administrators, politicians and the public to rethink and respond to some of the more fundamental of these questions. With such an effort, the shallow ceremonialism of many commemorative efforts will be avoided, and potentially constructive actions will emerge that will help adapt this federal system and its intergovernmental sinews to the real needs of the nation as it enters its third century. What better way to keep the faith of the Fathers?

Intergovernmental Relations: a Fiscal Perspective

By Elmer B. Staats

ABSTRACT: The domestic functions of the federal-state-local partnership account for the most rapid increases in total government expenditures. Federal assistance now amounts to nearly one-fourth of state and local revenues. The General Accounting Office is engaged in evaluating the success of the many federal programs designed to assist state and local governments and in pursuing the task of stimulating improved auditing at all levels in an effort to provide a higher level of accountability. General revenue sharing demonstrates the clear need for federal-state-local cooperation if adequate audit coverage and accountability are to be achieved. The General Accounting Office is concerned that present methods of reporting revenue sharing expenditures do not provide the information needed to enable the citizenry to make informed judgments.

Elmer B. Staats is Comptroller General of the United States and, as such, heads the U.S. General Accounting Office. Before appointment as Comptroller General in 1966, he served as Deputy Director of the Bureau of the Budget under Presidents Truman, Eisenhower, Kennedy and Johnson. The author earned his Ph.D. degree from the University of Minnesota and is a member of the Board of Trustees of McPherson College and the American University. He is a member of the board of directors of the American Academy of Political and Social Science and past national president of the American Society for Public Administration.

IN JANUARY 1974, the president sent to Congress a budget calling for outlays of $304 billion, an increase of nearly $30 billion from the previous year, and more than two and one-half times the federal spending rate of only 10 years ago. Nearly three-quarters of the president's budget is beyond his control, as it is fixed by previous legislation or earlier decisions which cause money to be spent for such programs as veterans' pensions, Medicare, farm subsidies, student loans, or to pay for completion of defense contracts.

Although appropriation action for fiscal year 1975 has not been completed as of this writing, it is estimated that the government will incur a deficit of about $9 billion. Only once since fiscal year 1961 has there been a budget surplus. Furthermore, the total federal debt is expected to rise to over $500 billion by June 30, 1975.

However, when the trend of rising federal costs is viewed as a percentage of the gross national product (GNP), the perspective changes. In 1960 federal expenditures accounted for 19 percent of GNP. In 1970, federal expenditures, more than doubling since 1960, accounted for 20 percent of GNP and have continued at that level.

State and local government expenditures have increased far more rapidly than have those of the federal government—to over $200 billion from $13 billion in 1946. At the same time, our GNP, our personal spending, and even spending by the federal government have not climbed at even one-third that rate. The rapid growth of state and local government expenditures is explained essentially by the fact that demands for governmental services in this country have been much greater in those

areas of state and local governmental responsibility than in the area of federal responsibility. The great majority of government domestic functions has always been carried out by states and localities and, despite the cost of wars and related problems, it is in the domestic arena that the most rapid increases in public expenditures have occurred.

Public demands for services that local governments provide—education, police and fire protection, public welfare, water and sewage services, parks and recreation, and trash removal—have been increasing each year, and the end is not in sight. There is little doubt that the essential problems facing cities are the rising costs of local public services and inadequate sources of revenue, compounded by the heavy movement of population into large cities. Not to be overlooked are the pressing fiscal problems of the suburbs and rural America.

The federal government has responded to the needs of state and local governments chiefly through funds provided by grant-in-aid programs. In 1950 the federal government had 71 grant programs costing $2 billion. In 20 years the number increased to 530 programs or more, depending upon definition, costing $24 billion annually. Even this figure is badly out of date. The current budget (fiscal 1974), in approximate terms, estimates that federal assistance to state and local governments will total $52 billion. Federal assistance represents approximately 22 percent of total state and local revenues.

Each individual grant program has its own unique features and requirements which are burdensome, time-consuming and, in many cases, inflexible. This has resulted, in the past 10 years, in demands for consolidation of grants, simplification of procedures, and greater federal reliance upon state and local administration, including auditing. Yet little interest has been generated in achieving grant consolidation as would have been authorized in the proposed amendments to the Intergovernmental Cooperation Act of 1968. The amendments have failed to pass in the last three sessions of Congress. Similarly, special revenue sharing proposals of the current administration, which are essentially forms of grant consolidation, have met with only limited interest.

Grant programs have developed in response to national as well as local needs. Medical research, interstate highways, aviation facilities, pollution control, and a host of other programs must involve all three levels of government. Accordingly, three central questions need serious attention:

1. How should each level be involved?
2. What portion of costs should each level pay?
3. How can reliance upon state and local governments be increased?

We have long since learned that when the federal government reduces its income tax—still the most equitable tax devised—it does not follow that state and local governments will levy commensurate income taxes to offset the need for federal grants or increases in the property tax. We have long recognized that program objectives cannot be satisfactorily achieved without policies and priorities. State and local governments have themselves been in the forefront in seeking federal leadership in crime control, communicable disease control, safety for airways, and many other areas.

The federal government has not been alone in providing financial assistance to local governments. In terms of state fiscal involvement in local or federal-local program areas, many states, despite their own fiscal problems, expanded their commitment to help alleviate local and urban problems. Overall state aid to local governments increased from $20.2 billion in 1969 to an estimated $48.2 billion in 1974, almost a 140 percent increase. While these figures include undeterminable amounts of federal aid passing through the states to local governments, the financial commitment of states themselves is nonetheless substantial.

More than two-thirds of the $52 billion proposed in the 1974 federal budget for assistance to state and local governments will be spent in, or will affect directly, metropolitan areas—an increase of more than $22 billion in four years, mainly for law enforcement and public assistance.

The work of the General Accounting Office (GAO) encompasses the spectrum of federal activities. Starting in 1921, it was primarily concerned with assuring Congress as to the legality and fiscal integrity of federal expenditures. Later, it became increasingly involved in ways in which federal programs could be carried out more economically and efficiently. Still more recently, it has been deeply concerned with such basic questions as whether federal programs are working as they should, whether they need modification to make them work better, and whether they should be expanded, cut back or discontinued. The purpose of GAO, then, is not solely to reduce the cost of managing programs; GAO is equally concerned with developing recommendations to make them work better.

Much of the work of the General Accounting Office, especially in the area of federal domestic assistance programs, has intergovernmental aspects. Two years ago it established a group with specific responsibility for carrying out our work in the intergovernmental relations area. This group is responsible for conducting broad-based studies of federal activities impacting on state and local governments. These studies deal not with assessing individual federal programs, but rather with the system for delivering federal assistance, with emphasis on the state and local perspective of how federal programs are administered.

For example, in January 1974, the office issued a report to Congress on its assessment of Federal Regional Councils. I also testified on this subject before the Subcommittee on Intergovernmental Relations, House Committee on Governmental Operations.

The report noted that Federal Regional Councils were established to develop closer working relationships between large federal grantmaking agencies and state and local governments and to improve coordination of the categorical grant-in-aid system.

Although their experiences varied widely, most officials of states and larger units of local governments knew about the Councils. On the other hand, representatives of smaller units of local government generally were unfamiliar with them. State and local governments need information on federal grant-in-aid programs and on the opportunities for securing assistance from Councils. Unless governmental units had developed aggressive programs for seeking out and securing federal assistance, they usually had little knowledge of, or information on, federal grant-in-aid programs. Important factors contributing to the Councils' limited outreach, particularly with smaller units of local governments, were the limited staff resources available and the Councils' relatively brief experience in operating intergovernmental programs. Certain programs conducted by Councils helped state and local governments to coordinate the administration of federal assistance programs; however, these programs were experimental and reached only a limited number of potential recipients.

Councils were impeded from being more effective by factors such as:

—member agencies' lack of, or variations in, decentralized decision making authority;
—limits on the authority of Council chairmen;
—division of time and effort by Council members, staffs, and task force members between Council and agency affairs;
—insufficient participation by nonmember federal agencies in Councils' activities; and
—absence of formalized standards for planning work and reporting progress.

The conclusion is that, although these factors impeded the Councils' effectiveness, Councils can, within their existing framework, accomplish their purposes more effectively with stronger management direction by the Under Secretaries Group for Regional Operations. The Office of Management and Budget, the Under Secretaries Group, and Council chairmen generally agreed and concurred in the recommendations for making Councils more effective.

ACCOUNTABILITY AND THE AUDIT

The increased commitment of federal, state and local resources to fund the myriad of programs intended to improve the quality of life has been accompanied by an increased demand for information about governmental programs. Public officials and legislators at all levels and the general public want to know whether governmental programs are being conducted efficiently, effectively and economically. This demand for information has necessitated broadening the scope of governmental auditing so that the auditor must be concerned with three types of accountability:

1. fiscal accountability, which includes financial integrity, disclosure, and compliance with applicable laws and regulations;
2. managerial accountability, which is concerned with efficient and economical use of resources; and
3. program accountability, which is concerned with accomplishments and objectives, that is to say, whether the statutory objectives of the program have indeed been accomplished.

The complex relationship among the levels of government in the administration of programs similarly extends to the area of auditing. In recognition of the need for broad audits at all levels of government, the General Accounting Office two years ago published its *Standards for Audit of Governmental Organi-*

zations, Programs, Activities and Functions. These standards were developed over a period of nearly three years with the assistance of federal agencies, professional associations, and public interest groups that had an interest in governmental auditing.

The audit standards in their final form are a set of criteria that call for an audit of a much broader scope than the traditional financially-oriented governmental audit. The criteria are also quite demanding as to staff competence, independence and professional proficiency.

The standards have a significant impact on the auditing of governments either by independent public accountants or by organic audit groups. Under the standards, an audit will respond not only to the need to determine fiscal accountability, including compliance with applicable laws and regulations, but also will deal with the question of how well the entity is managed and to what degree individual programs are accomplishing their intended objectives.

Another aspect of auditing that is affected by the standards is the expansion of auditing on an intergovernmental basis. As more audit groups accept and implement the standards in the conduct of their work, it is anticipated that the quality of governmental auditing at all levels will improve.

A major effort is underway to encourage adoption and use of the standards at the state and local level. Some of the projects in process include:

—development of a model state statute and model local ordinance to provide a legal framework for effective audit of organizations;

—a study of alternative means by which state and local audit organizations can be reimbursed for auditing federal programs;

—development of a data bank on state audit organizations to eliminate the need for these organizations to respond to multiple inquiries for similar data;

—development of regional intergovernmental audit forums as a basis for federal, state and local audit organizations to exchange ideas and in general to strive for improved auditing (a national forum and two regional forums are in operation—six forums are in various stages of development); and

—participation with several units of local government in pilot audits to demonstrate the benefits of efficiency, economy, and program results audits, and to develop model audit programs for use in local units of government. (This project is being conducted in cooperation with the International City Management Association.)

REVENUE SHARING

Revenue sharing, perhaps more than any other program, makes clear the need for an intergovernmental effort to achieve adequate accountability and audit coverage. It also highlights the difficulties which must be overcome to satisfy the information needs of all levels of government.

Unlike traditional federal assistance programs, the Revenue Sharing Act (State and Local Fiscal Assistance Act of 1972) allows state and local governments considerable flexibility in the use of the funds with minimal federal supervision of the recipient governments.

In testimony on the administration's proposal for revenue sharing before the House Ways and Means Committee on June 24, 1971, I expressed reservations regarding the lack of accountability provisions in the proposed legislation.

The sheer number of recipient governments—over 38,000—would, as a practical matter, necessitate heavy reliance on audits by or for state and local governments. A study GAO had begun in 1970, which was still in progress when I testified, indicated that the auditing capabilities of most state and local governments did not meet standards the office considers adequate.

I recommended to the committee that the accountability provisions of the proposal be strengthened and that GAO be given the right of access to pertinent information for purposes of audit and examination. I felt that our presence would likely contribute to the advancement of the quality of state and local auditing, and reviews by GAO, as an agency of the legislative branch, would assist and be consistent with the traditional oversight role and responsibility of Congress.

The act, as passed, contains several accountability provisions. It requires state and local governments to provide for the expenditure of revenue sharing funds under the same laws and budgetary procedures they employ spending their own revenues. The intent of this provision is to ensure that the usual budgetary and expenditure approval mechanisms are applied to revenue sharing funds.

State and local governments are required to establish a separate trust fund account in which all revenue sharing receipts, including interest earned on the funds, are to be deposited. This provision was intended to facilitate review and evaluation of the program.

The act requires state and local governments to account to the Department of the Treasury and the public through periodic reports on their planned and actual expenditures of revenue sharing funds. The reports, in addition to being submitted to the Treasury Department, must be published in a newspaper having general circulation, and other news media must be given notice of publication. The intent of this provision is to facilitate scrutiny of the program by local citizens to help ensure wise expenditure of funds and to make government officials accountable to their constituents.

The act also contains requirements for audits and reviews of the program. The Treasury Department is responsible for conducting audits necessary to insure that recipient governments comply with the requirements of the act. In discharging this responsibility, Treasury is relying heavily on audits conducted by independent public accountants and state and local auditors.

GAO is directed by the act to assist congressional evaluation of the program by reviewing the work done by the Treasury Department and state and local governments. In carrying out this responsibility, GAO has already issued two reports to Congress[1] on its reviews of the program operation among

1. Comptroller General of the United States, *Revenue Sharing: Its Use by and Impact on State Governments* (Washington, D.C.: U.S. General Accounting Office, August 1973), and *Revenue Sharing: Its Use by and Impact on Local Governments* (Washington, D.C.: U.S. General Accounting Office, April 1974).

state and local governments, and several other studies are currently underway.

In both reports, GAO has commented on the difficulties involved in identifying what has actually happened as a result of the program. Because of the wide discretion recipients have in using the funds, revenue sharing represents merely an addition to the total resources available for government expenditure. Revenue sharing, aid from other governments, and a government's own resources can often be used to provide the same services. This creates an environment where funds can be easily displaced or substituted. Therefore, when a recipient uses revenue sharing for any purpose, there are a variety of effects which are not necessarily reflected by the direct use of the funds: (1) its own funds may be used to finance other programs; (2) it may be relieved of the need to increase taxes; (3) it may reduce taxes; or (4) it may experience a combination of these or other consequences.

Because budgetary choices among competing programs and decisions regarding the methods for financing a government's budget are typically based on total resources available to the government, it is extremely difficult, and probably impossible in many cases, to identify objectively the effects of revenue sharing. An objective identification of effects is further complicated by such factors as changing priorities and needs, changing amounts of resources available to a recipient from its own sources, and the relatively small contribution that revenue sharing makes to total state-local resources.

Because revenue sharing represents only a part of total resources, it is probably unrealistic to expect that the citizenry can make informed judgments from reports which describe expenditures contemplated or made with revenue sharing funds. For public disclosure purposes, it would probably be more meaningful for a government to report all of its expenditures along with an explanation of the part that revenue sharing played in the total fiscal program.

In a similar vein, GAO studies to date have convinced us that the information needs of federal policy makers (both Congress and the executive branch) are not met adequately by the present reporting system, which merely portrays activities being directly funded with revenue sharing. Such data, in order to be meaningful, should be integrated and related to total expenditures for state-local activities. The development of a comprehensive information system on the overall activities of state-local government would be of great value at the national level, not only in evaluating revenue sharing but in establishing priorities for federal domestic assistance programs. GAO has recently initiated an inquiry to consider the data base presently available and possible ways to make it a more meaningful policy instrument in the domestic field.

From GAO's perspective, revenue sharing has also given added emphasis to the importance of improving state-local audit capabilities. The traditional financial audit and audits of compliance with applicable laws and regulations fall short of informing the public and appointed officials as to how well funds and other resources are utilized.

Revenue sharing makes very clear the fact that today state-local programs are financed by a mixture of federal, state and local dollars, and that it is extremely difficult to determine whether a federal, state or local dollar was actually used in a particular program. There are simply not enough federal auditors, nor should there be, to evaluate economy, efficiency and effectiveness of state-local programs. Such a task properly rests with state and local governments.

The revenue sharing regulations encourage recipient governments to have their audits performed in accordance with GAO's standards. Hopefully this, along with GAO's other efforts, will prompt state and local governments to undertake the audit contemplated by the standards.

IGR and the Executive Branch: the New Federalism

By Thomas J. Graves

ABSTRACT: IGR and the New Federalism are synonymous. Former President Nixon summarized the New Federalism as "A cooperative venture among governments at all levels . . . in which power, funds, and authority are channeled increasingly to those governments which are closest to the people." IGR is essentially an art and primarily an exercise in the behavioral field. The thread which binds government officials intergovernmentally is the financing and administration of federal grants-in-aid and other forms of federal financial assistance. Concern in the executive branch for IGR developed in the last 20 years; thus its roots in American governance are not yet very deep. The views and support of public interest groups as well as the sympathetic attention of Congress are essential to the pursuit of IGR goals and objectives in the executive branch. In relations between levels of government, partnership rather than paternalism must prevail. The rise of stronger chief executives and decentralization of power from Washington are noted. Confidence of Americans in their own government is essential to achieving a federal system working in all parts, well-managed and equitably financed.

Thomas J. Graves since 1956 has been a specialist on intergovernmental relations for the Office of Management and Budget, Executive Office of the President. He is Federal Coordinator of Suggested State Legislation and liaison with the public interest groups as well as the National Association of State Budget Officers and other functional groups. Educated at Rutgers, N.Y.U., and Princeton University, he served as staff to the Commission on Intergovernmental Relations (1954), the Joint Federal State Action Committee (1957–59) and was interim Executive Director, Advisory Commission on Intergovernmental Relations (1959–60). He has served on Capitol Hill in a number of Senators' offices and was Director, Professional Staff, U.S. Senate Committee on Appropriations.

THE concept of American federalism has its roots in colonial development and the events which shaped the nation nearly 200 years ago. In a new continent a new system of government with its basic principles of freedom and the importance of the individual was the lasting result of the successful American Revolution whose Bicentennial we are soon to celebrate.

No system, however perfectly formulated in the beginning, will under the stress and strain of changing circumstances continue to work at a maximum level. After two centuries under a unique federal system, the time is none too soon for reexamining America's position and determining its future direction in order to cope successfully with the complicated problems of a free government in the third century of the nation's existence.

When former President Nixon was campaigning in 1968, he recognized the need for, and the desirability of, delving deeply into the ramifications of our federal system. Soon after taking office in 1969, he established an Office of Intergovernmental Relations in the Executive Office of the President, proposed to Congress a system of general and special revenue sharing, established the Ash Council to survey the executive branch of the federal government, and ordered a continuing study of ways and means to streamline federal grant-in-aid administration. Buttressing all of these actions was his underlying premise that the United States needs and must have a New Federalism.

THE NEW FEDERALISM

Since the end of World War II, the nation has been grappling for a solution to its most basic problem: the governance of a country of continental proportions with a burgeoning population and a new social consciousness. President Nixon came to office at a time when a broad consensus was emerging that the domestic programs of the federal government were in need of basic overhaul. The best indicator of this was the frustration of Americans throughout the nation—much of which was justified—about the inability of governmental institutions at every level to perform their assigned tasks. A large part of the problem of establishing a public opinion favorable to the Nixon administration's aims was the generally low esteem in which government at all levels—federal, state, county, city, school district and special district—is held.

President Nixon, consequently, was firmly committed to the concept of the New Federalism, the basic philosophy of which is summed up in the president's often repeated words:

A cooperative venture among government at all levels . . . in which power, funds, and authority are channeled increasingly to those governments which are closest to the people.[1]

Fundamentally, therefore, the New Federalism is a deep-seated commitment to bringing government closer to its citizens, to restoring faith and credibility to government at all levels, and to strengthening state and local governments in ways that will foster the wise and responsible local level leadership which gave this nation so much strength and vitality in the earlier days of the re-

1. Richard M. Nixon, *The New Federalism: An Address and Statements by the President,* Address to the Nation, 8 August 1969.

public. This concept guided many of the policies of the Nixon administration and was reflected in the budget, executive orders, legislative proposals, rules and regulations, and other executive branch actions.

INTERGOVERNMENTAL RELATIONS DEFINED

Intergovernmental relations is essentially an art, not a science, and is therefore not particularly susceptible to the measuring scales of general management and productivity. It is primarily an exercise in the behavioral field and could well be classified as relying very heavily on interpersonal relationships between and among government officials and centering upon a common concern.

In my view, IGR is synonymous with federalism—new or old—and all discussions of the subject necessarily and inevitably center on the administrative and financial complex of federal grants-in-aid (and other forms of such assistance) and the programs underlying these grants. This statement is in no sense a derogation of philosophical or fundamental questions regarding the true relationships that should exist between and among levels of government in the American system of federalism.

This is merely to say that the executive branch is confronted with the reality that the grant-in-aid is in the forefront and is the "warp and woof" of day-to-day intergovernmental relationships which must be performed if the system is to work at all. The grant structure is where IGR becomes an operating reality and where the battle is joined. It is an arena which rather perfectly fits Grover Cleveland's dictum that "We are confronted by a condition, not a theory."

EXECUTIVE BRANCH CONCERN FOR IGR

Executive branch concern for IGR, so defined, is a development of the last 20 years or so. While it has flourished and gained wide acceptance since 1955, IGR can hardly be said to be rooted very deeply in American governance in any sense —organizationally, systematically, traditionally or philosophically.

During the 1952 campaign and in the very early days of his first administration, President Eisenhower repeatedly expressed the view that the national government must leave to the states and local governments those things which they could best do for themselves, and that the role of the national government should be one of assisting in this objective. Among his first official acts was a call for legislation resulting in the appointment of the Commission on Intergovernmental Relations, which was created early in 1953 and which reported June 30, 1955. This commission, under the chairmanship of the late Meyer Kestnbaum of Chicago, addressed itself to the first fundamental review of federalism since the Constitutional Convention. The most significant quotation from the report of the commission is that:

The national government and the states should be regarded not as competitors for authority but as two levels of government cooperating with or complementing each other in meeting the growing demands on both.[2]

As a follow-up to the report, the

2. Commission on Intergovernmental Relations, *Report to the President for Transmittal to the Congress* (June 1955), p. 2.

president adopted a major commission recommendation and established a focal point for the continued consideration of intergovernmental relations. Governor Howard Pyle of the White House staff was designated as the Deputy Assistant to the President for Intergovernmental Relations, and the Bureau of the Budget was assigned the task of "backstopping" this new operation.

Specifically, Governor Pyle was directed, among other things, to maintain liaison with national organizations interested in this field, to grapple with problems concerning state and local governments, to follow through on the findings and recommendations of the Commission on Intergovernmental Relations with the assistance of Mr. Kestnbaum, and to make such special studies as might be required.

The Eisenhower administration's guiding philosophy on intergovernmental relations was summarized in the following statement of policy:

It is the goal of the administration, in the interest of public legislative, and State-local relations, to demonstrate its active concern with improving the relations of the National Government with State and local authorities.

Late in 1957, President Eisenhower, in a major address before the Governors' Conference at Williamsburg, proposed the establishment of a Joint Federal-State Action Committee, to be composed of representatives of the Governor's Conference and high-ranking federal officials. The committee would have three specific duties:

—to designate functions which the States are ready and willing to assume and finance that are now performed or financed wholly or in part by the Federal Government;

—to recommend the Federal and State revenue adjustments required to enable the States to assume such functions; and

—to identify functions and responsibilities likely to require State or Federal attention in the future and to recommend the level of State effort, or Federal effort, or both, that will be needed to assure effective action.[3]

The committee was subsequently appointed and included from the federal government three cabinet members, the secretaries of the treasury, labor, and health, education and welfare, Governor Pyle, the budget director, Mr. Kestnbaum, then serving as Special Assistant to the President, and the Special Assistant to the President for Public Works, General J. S. Bragdon. Representing the other half of this joint committee were the governors of New Hampshire, Maryland, Nebraska, Idaho, Texas, Mississippi, Rhode Island, Pennsylvania, Kansas and Illinois. Secretary of the the Treasury Robert Anderson and Governor Dwinell of New Hampshire were appointed co-chairmen.

On August 9 and 10 the committee held its initial meeting in Hershey, Pennsylvania, and it was decided that the following functions and taxes would be suitable for consideration and action at a subsequent meeting for transfer to the states: (1) the school lunch program, (2) vocational education, (3) natural disaster relief, (4) waste treatment facilities construction, (5) local telephone facilities construction, (6) local telephone service taxes, (7) admissions and a number

3. Dwight D. Eisenhower, *Address of the President before the National Governors' Conference* (Seattle, 1953).

of other excise and licensing taxes which are part of the normal policing powers of the states.

The Joint Committee was endeavoring to do something that had never been attempted before. This was the first time the president of the United States had invited the states to indicate which functions and which tax sources should be returned to them. It was the first time that a group of the highest federal and state officials had met for this purpose.

That the basic question of federalism would be a constant factor in the deliberations and negotiations in which the committee was engaged was evident from the very first meeting. From the executive point of view, it was obvious that the national government would give up some supervisory and fiscal powers, but this would not be a net loss since the executive branch of the state and perhaps even the local governments would be strengthened. This in itself is an example of the genius of the United States system, in that items are not lost but find their expression in the totality of government.

The Joint Federal-State Action Committee did not achieve its objective for reasons other than a lack of desire on the part of either the federal or state representatives. Out of this experience, nevertheless, came two highly worthwhile results: (1) the recognition of the fact that federal grants are and will remain an integral and essential part of our federal system, and (2) the creation of a permanent Advisory Commission on Intergovernmental Relations (ACIR) with broad representation of all the elements in our federal system.[4]

4. Dwight D. Eisenhower, *Address of the*

Since its very beginning the ACIR has proven to be a harmonious blend of solidly academic research effort and high level action designed to implement its recommendations for the improvement of government at all levels. With these beginnings, therefore, it is necessary to illustrate the IGR elements currently in the picture. A diagram of the federal government's present structure for dealing with interlevel problems is shown in figure 1.

In addition to the formal governmental bodies shown in figure 1, the IGR structure includes the following:

Public Interest Groups— the Big Seven

Council of State Governments
National Governors Conference
National Legislative Conference
National Association of Counties
National League of Cities
U.S. Conference of Mayors
International City Management Association

These groups represent elected public officials at the state, county and local levels, both executive and legislative, except for the International City Management Association, whose members are appointive officials responsible for administering city and county governments. All are located in Washington, D.C. except the Council of State Governments, which is headquartered in Lexington, Kentucky.

State-County-City Service Center

This is an organization of the Big Seven, the executive directors of which associations serve as the board of directors. It is designed to

President before the National Governors' Conference (Williamsburg, Va., 1957).

Executive Branch

OMB

Assistant Director for Management and Operations

Intergovernmental Relations and Regional Operations Division

White House

Domestic Council

Associate Director for Intergovernmental Relations

Federal Agencies

Various arrangements for the handling of intergovernmental relations, including the Treasury Department's Office of Revenue Sharing

Congress

Senate

Committee on Government Operations

—Subcommittee on Intergovernmental Relations

House

Committee on Government Operations

—Subcommittee on Intergovernmental Relations

General Accounting Office

The Comptroller General

ACIR

Composite group of executive and legislative branch members from federal, state and local levels, plus private citizens, national (not federal) in scope and reporting to both the president and Congress.

FIGURE 1

serve the common needs of these associations and is a means of bringing them together periodically.

Coalition of Governors, Mayors and County Officials

Governor Dan Evans of the state of Washington recently announced the formation of this coalition, which consists of the presidents of the Big Seven plus other prominent state and local officials. One of its first jobs will be to review administration proposals and try to agree on specific points which members want added to or deleted from proposed legislation. In addition, Governor

Evans is quoted as saying when the coalition was announced: "We hope by coalescing our views to convince Congress and the Administration that we deserve to be in on the formulation of programs and policies. . . . We want to initiate proposals rather than just respond."[5]

All of the above mechanisms operate at the national level and are concerned primarily with the action or inaction of the federal government—both executive and con-

5. Daniel J. Evans, *Speech before the National Governors' Conference* (Lake Tahoe, Nev., 1973).

gressional—in Washington. There is no counterpart organization for states, counties and cities to relate to the federal government in the field. Only the Council of State Governments has a field structure with well-established field offices. The other associations do have state (and occasionally regional) leagues of county and city officials. These vary considerably in effectiveness and staff resources and in their ability and willingness to relate to federal government operations. On the other hand, the official Federal Regional Councils and the Federal Executive Boards, as well as individual federal agency regional offices, are demonstrating an increasing competence and desire to relate to state, county and local officials, either individually or collectively.

All of this raises a significant problem for the federal government in the field—the dichotomy of serving the needs of individual states and localities as against the obvious advantages of dealing with them in groups.

RELATIONS BETWEEN GOVERNMENTS IN A FEDERAL SYSTEM

The relations between and among levels of government in the United States, like those between nations, require constant attention and careful consideration of the roles to be played by federal, state and local governments as they serve the people. That the interrelationships of government be at their best at all times is particularly important because the federal system recognizes that state and local governments must be free of domination or subordination by an all-powerful centralized government. If American democracy is to survive and flourish, the levels of government must be maintained in proper balance so that they will be responsive to the will and needs of the people. The Founding Fathers and all succeeding generations of Americans have recognized and acknowledged this basic truth. In one way or another, they have also recognized that the principle of partnership rather than paternalism must characterize the role of the federal government in its internal governmental relations.

In the maturation of the federal system, the remarkable aspect is that the basic principle remains the same: national power must not overshadow the development of state and local government, and the liberty of the people must be secure in all possible circumstances.

An understanding of federalism is the key to the understanding of the American method of governing. Professor Joseph E. McLean, now of the University of Pittsburgh Graduate School, first summed up the situation in an early pamphlet on "Politics is What You Make It," when he said:

Most of us think of our federal system as having three layers of government—Federal, State, and local—with each level assigned definite functions and responsibilities, and many of us believe that a specific service or function generally belongs exclusively to *one* layer of government. . . . Most of us fail to realize that this layer-cake is much more like a marble cake. There are many combined activities—administrative, financial, and political—which blend throughout the cake and ignore the layers. . . . Almost any public problem you can mention today involves all of the so called "layers" of government.[6]

6. Public Affairs Committee, *Public Affairs Pamphlet* (New York, April 1952).

One of the significant factors in the growth of government in this nation in recent years, however, has been the increasing recognition that state and local governments have again become strong and better able to administer those services and programs for which they are responsible. This development has occurred coordinately with the rise in power of the national government, which demonstrates a healthy and simultaneous growth factor. If continued, nurtured and expanded properly, government should be better able to cope with the manifold problems confronting it—some of which are now full-scale and some of which are on the horizon.

Concomitantly with the growth of state and local government capabilities, two other trends have developed. There has been a marked tendency in the direction of stronger executives, both elective and appointive. The many added responsibilities and duties of governors as full-time state chief executives are indicative of this trend. Even more exemplary is the widespread adoption of city manager plans for local governments and, in many instances, the adoption of strong mayor plans to replace outmoded commissions and other hydra-headed local executive branches.

The second trend is increasing concentration of power in Washington. Concentration of power at the Washington level, for any reason no matter how compelling, tends to weaken and vitiate the initiative of state and local governments. It likewise tends to strike at the roots of a truly federal system. On the other hand, not everything that the national government does is antithetical to the best interests of either the federal system or the citizens of other levels of government.

THE EXECUTIVE BRANCH, CONGRESS, AND IGR

A further problem the executive branch has had in its pursuit of IGR objectives has been the varying success and receptivity in addressing Congress as to its needs. Enactment of the Intergovernmental Cooperation Act of 1968, and the OMB Circulars which have emanated from that legislation, have increased executive-congressional relationships in a professional and nonpolitical manner to the general benefit of improved IGR as they affect federal domestic programs.

The enactment of general revenue sharing, the continued push for forms of special revenue sharing, and the development of other aspects of the New Federalism—administrative and fiscal—will increase the necessity for a good executive-congressional atmosphere in the continued development and success of IGR goals and objectives.

STRENGTHENING THE FEDERAL SYSTEM

Today the citizen is often too well aware that federalism as envisioned by the Founding Fathers is not working well in behalf of the people it is supposed to serve. Money alone is neither the expedient nor long-range solution; the management of money shares equal importance with the amount of money invested.

Strengthening of the federal system in all its working parts is essential to providing people with government services which, in the final analysis, are the only rationale for taxation. What these services are or should be and, more particularly, how they should be delivered, is a matter of public policy which is decided through the political process. The question of who is right or wrong in the advocacy of a particular program is a decision reached after much wrangling and soul-searching on the part of the proponents and opponents. The fact that such decisions are never so firm that they cannot be changed is one of the great strengths—not weaknesses—of American federalism.

The essential question is: What does the federal government intend to do about future intergovernmental administrative and fiscal relations; what are the new directions in federal aid policy?

The Nixon administration came into office with a particular desire to strengthen intergovernmental relations. President Nixon, in regard to the basic philosophy of government management, said:

I plan a streamlined Federal system, with a return to the States, cities, and communities of decision-making powers rightfully theirs. The President is a place where priorities are set, and goals determined. We need a new attention to priorities, and a new realism about goals. We are living in a time of great promise —but also of too many promises. We have had too much wishful imagining that all the ills of man could be set right overnight, merely by making a national commitment.[7]

The Nixon administration regarded reform of the federal aid system as a basic objective. A reformed system should:

—strengthen state-local political institutions, recognizing the primacy of their responsibility to their citizens;

7. Richard M. Nixon (various Presidential documents, messages and statements, 1969–73).

—enhance the capacity of state and local chief executives to coordinate and direct the resources available for state and local problem solving;
—promote the strengthening of state and local revenue systems; and
—encourage innovation and the demonstration of new ideas and techniques.

While categorical grants have proven to be effective in many instances, their rapid growth has caused serious problems in terms of:

—a bypassing of elected chief executives;
—overlapping programs and duplication at the state-local level;
—inflexibility and distortion of state and local budgets;
—additional administrative costs and program delays and uncertainties;
—an information gap about available grant programs which is difficult to close, and the placement of a premium on "grantsmanship"; and
—severe competition at all levels for capable administrative and technical personnel.

Those who have looked at the present revenue structure and expenditure pattern of the national, state and local governments would agree that there exists a strong need for basic reforms in present methods of financing the total pattern of government. The harsh and realistic facts of fiscal life are that:

—state and local program services are at a high level and are continuing to rise not only because of population growth but also because of necessitous and recognized higher standards of services to be performed;

—state and local revenue structures as presently devised are undergoing severe strain and the principal tax sources contain evident inequities;

—the continued use and improvement of the federal tax system to help state and local governments is a prime requisite in fiscal federalism;

—the present system of federal financial assistance to state and local governments is deficient; and

—the administrative machinery for providing domestic public services needs strengthening throughout the federal system.

In summary, the United States government needs the kind of appraisal that will have as its stated goal a compelling desire to make the machinery of government work in a manner that will sustain citizen confidence in the ability of government to provide necessary services under a system of taxation that puts the money where the action is at the right time and in the proper amount.

Recent discussions have sought to achieve relatively quick and broad solutions through such devices as block grants, shared revenues and tax credit mechanisms, with all of their possible modifications and permutations. These proposals have recognized that it is almost impossible for even the most intrepid state or local expert in grantsmanship to swing effectively a machete through the somewhat impenetrable jungle of categorical grant programs.

The federal government has progressed from a rigid adherence to categorical grants, to a softening of these by the use of project grants, to a grouping of related grants such as is found in the Partnership for Health statute. As Dr. Richard Nathan, former Assistant Director of OMB, has stated, ". . . it is highly desirable that we move away from narrow and highly specific federal aids and focus instead on new and broader federal aid instruments . . . The 'how-to-do-it' questions of policy implementation are increasingly becoming as important as the basic question of what needs to be done."[8]

While easing state and local financial problems, the rapid growth of aid programs has heightened the need for improved coordination to insure effective and efficient public services at the local level. This realization has stimulated the following generic approaches by the federal government to improving the administration of aid programs:

—broader, multifunctional approaches—to meld programs together at the local level as in model cities, community action agencies, neighborhood centers, and concentrated employment programs;

—consolidation of existing grant categories;

—improvements in funding arrangements—as in advance funding for education—to allow more time for planning—and the proposed Joint-Funding Simplification Act;

—utilization of regional councils of federal agencies in the field to coordinate federal programs at the point of impact;

—rationalization of regional boundaries and decentralization;

—greater consultation with state and local officials;

8. Richard Nathan, "Revenue Sharing and the New Federalism," *15th Annual Whearret Lecture* (Pittsburgh, Pa.: University of Pittsburgh, 1969).

—a concentrated review of present grant-in-aid regulations;

—passage of new legislation such as the Intergovernmental Cooperation Act—which improves the flow of information between elected officials at the federal and state levels, simplifies accounting requirements for federal grants, relaxes impediments of grant legislation to reorganization at the state level, and provides a number of other improvements, including a new educational program to increase the supply of trained public servants at all levels of government.

CONCLUDING COMMENTS

No one will contend that administrative improvements and new legislation taken together will achieve a system of revenue allocation and program responsibility that will enable each of the federal partners to handle his end of the game effortlessly and efficiently. The magic word, of course, is still *money*.

But if these vitally important questions of management are not tackled, money will continue to be wasted and, more importantly, a situation will be perpetuated in which, as Dwight Ink describes it, "help does not reach those who need it until months—sometimes years—after it should."[9] Or, as an able and knowledgeable economist has said: "It is precisely the management problem, and the political implications of the tremendous growth in federal assistance, that provide much of the fuel for the purely political aspects of the debate now in progress."[10]

9. Dwight Ink, *Address to Midwestern Regional Conference, United States Chamber of Commerce* (March 1973).
10. Nathan, "Revenue Sharing."

The American system, as a whole, is in need of:

—critical review and fundamental change;
—high level and outspoken thoughts about necessary changes; and
—a strengthening of state and local government capabilities to participate as full partners in a truly federal system.

Critical to this major task of the president and the executive branch is reforming the system, so that government is closer to the people whom it serves. This is a time of change-over and very necessary change and, as might be expected, it has its attendant agonies. The confidence of the American people in their own government at all levels and in all of its institutions—executive, legislative and judicial—must be restored. In a very real sense, this is the New Federalism—a federal system working in all of its parts, well managed and equitably financed, with full participation by all of the partners in both the decision making and operational phases of a government for which they share a common responsibility.

As the executive branch of the federal government meets its responsibilities for maintaining the federal system, it must constantly give recognition to the fact that government is dynamic and that it must make progress. It must be constantly alert to the changing needs of the times and the varying needs of the citizens it serves. It is no mean feat to govern a country which contains over 210 million persons living thousands of miles apart in regions which have marked differences in social, political and economic outlooks. Only a federal system could achieve the national unity which has existed in the United States since its founding.

The letter to President Eisenhower which transmitted the report of the original Commission on Intergovernmental Relations summarizes the whole subject in a few, exceedingly well-chosen words:

Many of the problems to which we have addressed ourselves have been with us since the founding of the Republic. They are likely to concern us for many years to come. No inquiry of this kind could possibly provide universally satisfactory answers to all of the difficult questions that are under discussion at any particular moment. We are hopeful that this Report will be regarded as the beginning rather than the end of a contemporary study of the subject of intergovernmental relations, and that it will stimulate all levels of government to examine their respective responsibilities in a properly balanced Federal system.[11]

11. Commission on Intergovernmental Relations, *Report to the President*.

The trend in governmental relations prompted Woodrow Wilson to observe nearly a half century ago that the "question of relationship of the States to the Federal Government is the cardinal question of our constitutional system. It cannot be settled by the opinion of any one generation because it is a question of growth, and every successive stage of our political and economic development gives it a new aspect, makes it a new question."

The coordinated attention which this problem will receive at the national level is a recognition on the part of this generation that the "new question" requires a new answer. To conclude, the United States needs a New Federalism, and the executive branch must play a very strong but not commanding role in its development. It is fully anticipated and wise to expect that President Ford will assume that necessary kind of leadership in the continuing maintenance, fostering and enhancement of American intergovernmental relations. This process is already well underway.

Intergovernmental Relations: from the Legislative Perspective

By Delphis C. Goldberg

Abstract: Federal assistance to state and local governments has expanded dramatically during the past decade, with most of this growth represented by special-purpose ("categorical") programs intended to promote social objectives of national importance. Even before the accelerated growth of these cooperative programs, periodic efforts were made to develop a more orderly grant-in-aid system. The proliferation of grants, particularly in the 1960s, made it more difficult for many state and local governments to compete for and administer federal aid programs and stimulated an intensified demand for grant simplification. General and special revenue sharing were the principal instruments of former President Nixon's New Federalism for promoting more orderly and simplified relations and for decentralizing decision making in fields of intergovernmental interest. These forms of assistance, however, conflict with a traditional congressional concern for targeting grants to more specific social objectives and maximizing accountability.

Delphis C. Goldberg has been the Professional Staff Member of the Intergovernmental Relations Subcommittee, U.S. House of Representatives, for the past 18 years. He previously served on the professional staffs of the Commission on Intergovernmental Relations and the President's Commission on Veterans' Pensions, and in administrative and research positions with the state of New York. He received his undergraduate education at Union College and the M.A. and Ph.D in Political Economy and Government from Harvard University.

The views expressed in this paper are those of the author and are not intended to represent the views of the subcommittee or its individual members.

AS THE nation nears its Bicentennial, one is struck by the extent to which legislative actions concerning intergovernmental matters are based on pragmatic rather than constitutional or philosophic considerations. Although students of government may argue about whether and for how long the United States federal system has been "dual," "cooperative," "creative," or "new," there is little doubt that the character of the public sector has been shaped in the past 40 years principally by political reactions to socio-economic forces and interest group pressures.

Continued expansion of the national government's involvement in domestic activities probably ranks as the most important development affecting our federal system in recent years. This trend, however, should not obscure the fact that the activities of state and local governments have also been substantially expanded.

Until the 1930s, the federal government was involved relatively little in programs providing social and economic services to the public. Its role was radically changed by the Great Depression. The federal government's superior fiscal position and the broad interpretation of national powers adopted by the Supreme Court combined in the face of severe economic distress to spawn new programs in areas previously considered the province of the states. This development continued and accelerated in the years following World War II.

Armed with ample capacity to raise revenue through taxation and the creation of debt, and with virtually no constitutional inhibitions, the only practical limitation on the national government's ability to engage in activities for the general welfare was its own self-restraint. Congress, in effect, became the forum for determining the division of powers in our federal system.

Another factor impacting on intergovernmental relations that has undergone considerable change in recent years is the demarcation between the public and private sectors. Although organized business groups once fought vigorously to restrain government expenditures at all levels, their efforts today appear to be directed more toward assuring that private industry receives an appropriate share of government contracts and other program benefits.

GROWTH OF THE PUBLIC SECTOR

Government expenditures have increased substantially in the past 20 years, both in absolute terms and in relation to the private sector of the economy. During the years 1954 to 1973, the combined expenditures of all levels of government rose from 27 to 32 percent of the gross national product (GNP), while expenditures for domestic programs alone nearly doubled—from 13 to 24 percent of GNP.[1]

This growth has been accompanied by significant changes in the division of responsibilities for raising and spending revenues. From 1954 to 1973, federal expenditures for domestic purposes increased nearly 2½ times in relation to GNP —from 5.4 to 12.9 percent. During the same period, expenditures of the

1. Unpublished data compiled by Advisory Commission on Intergovernmental Relations. Domestic expenditures exclude defense, international, space programs, and the estimated portion of net interest attributable to these functions. Percentages are based on expenditures by governments of their own funds.

states from their own funds increased from 3.4 to 5.7 percent of GNP, or about two-thirds, while local expenditures from local revenue sources rose slightly more than one-third—from 4.0 to 5.4 percent of GNP.[2]

It should be noted that the large expansion of the federal domestic budget relative to state and local expenditures has not been matched by a commensurate increase in the federal civilian workforce. In the two decades from 1954 to 1973, the number of federal employees concerned with domestic programs increased by approximately 46 percent. During the same period, state and local employment increased by 143 percent. Stated another way, federal employment decreased from 20 to 13 percent of the total. The comparatively large growth in employment at the state and local levels reflects both the impact of federal assistance programs and the expansion of such labor-intensive service activities as education, health, welfare, law enforcement and sanitation.

IGR ASSISTANCE

Federal assistance to state and local governments has increased dramatically during the past decade, from $10.9 billion in 1965 to $48.3 billion in 1974. In these 10 years, federal assistance doubled as a proportion of total federal outlays— from 9 to 18 percent—and the federal share of state and local expenditures increased from 15 to 23 percent. As recently as 1955, total federal assistance was $3.3 billion and amounted to only 5 percent of federal outlays and 10 percent of state-local expenditures.[3] Federal

assistance has clearly become an important factor in the revenue structure of state and local governments.

Similarly, the states have provided an increasing share of local revenues. In fact, the states assist local governments to a greater extent than the federal government assists state and local governments. Thirty-six percent of all local general revenue came from state payments in 1972, as compared with 33 percent in 1967 and 28 percent in 1962. In dollar amounts, state assistance has nearly doubled in each five-year period, from $11 billion in 1962 to $19 billion in 1967 and $37 billion in 1972.[4] However, some federal funds, estimated at 21 percent of the total in 1967, are included in the state payments.[5] The latter, it should be noted, includes both grants-in-aid and the local share of certain taxes collected at the state level.

While the amount of federal assistance has multiplied in recent years, grants-in-aid (which constitute approximately 99 percent of the total classified in the budget as assistance to state and local governments) have increased enormously in number and variety. The height of grant expansion occurred during the Ken-

---

2. Ibid.

3. *Budget of the United States Govern-*

ment, *Fiscal Year 1975*, Special Analysis N. Unpublished data for 1950 and 1955 from Office of Management and Budget. State and local expenditures include federal assistance. Federal assistance includes grants-in-aid and a small amount of shared revenues (as distinguished from general revenue sharing) but excludes net loans and repayable advances made to state and local governments.

4. U.S., Bureau of the Census, *State Payments to Local Governments 1972*, 1972 Census of Governments, vol. 6 (Washington, D.C.: Government Printing Office), table 1.

5. Advisory Commission on Intergovernmental Relations, *State Aid to Local Governments* (April 1969), p. 3.

nedy and Johnson administrations, when the number of separate authorizations more than doubled—from 160 to 379—in the four-year period 1963 to 1966.[6]

The velocity of this growth has complicated the federal aid landscape, has made it more difficult for many eligible communities and states to learn what grant programs are available and to qualify for them, and has given rise to a renewed and more intensive interest in restructuring the instruments used for carrying out intergovernmental programs.

SEARCH FOR MORE ORDERLY IGR

First Hoover Commission

In 1949, the first Hoover Commission recommended the establishment of a system of grants "based upon broad categories—such as highways, education, public assistance, and public health—as contrasted with the present system of extensive fragmentation."[7]

The commission did not attempt to identify the levels of government responsible for particular public functions, or which functions "require joint policy making, financing, and administration." Instead, it recommended that such an appraisal be made, and it further recommended a revision of our tax systems with a view to reducing tax overlapping and leaving the states

and localities adequate resources to meet their responsibilities.[8]

The Hoover Commission's Committee on Federal-State Relations was more explicit:

We believe that the Congress should make funds available to the states for general purposes rather than specific projects, so that the states will have more freedom in the planning and administration of their entire program of social, education, and health services. The many specific grants that now exist, with their attendant pressure groups, tend to distort the expenditures of the states in undesirable ways, to the neglect of other services that are not nationally aided. Each state legislature should be allowed more freedom for the working out of its own pattern of services, and we believe that the states are fully competent to assume this responsibility.[9]

Kestnbaum Commission

In sharp contrast to the Hoover Commission, the Commission on Intergovernmental Relations (Kestnbaum Commission) expressed a distinct preference for limited-purpose grants after a comprehensive two-year study of the federal system completed in 1955. The Kestnbaum Commission gave this explanation for its support of conditional grants:

It is the only technique that is in any sense self-limiting, both as to objectives and amounts of expenditure and as to the extent and nature of National control. When Federal aid is directed toward specific activities, it is possible to observe the effects of each grant, to evaluate the progress of aided activities, and to relate the amount of financial assistance to needs. There is more assurance

---

6. Advisory Commission on Intergovernmental Relations, *Fiscal Balance in the American Federal System* I (October 1967), p. 151.

7. Commission on Organization of the Executive Branch of the Government, *Federal-State Relations: A Report to the Congress*, March 1949, p. 36.

8. Ibid., p. 35.

9. Committee on Federal-State Relations: *Report to the Commission on Organization of the Executive Branch of the Government*, 28 September 1948, p. 13.

that Federal funds will be used to promote the Nation's primary interests. Finally, the direct control exercised by the National Government is confined to limited and well-defined governmental activities, leaving other areas of State and local responsibility relatively unaffected.[10]

The Kestnbaum Commission also cautioned against federal grants in the form of broad subsidies—for example, general revenue sharing—in preference to conditional grants:

It has been argued that a subsidy policy would provide maximum help to the States that most need funds, give all States an opportunity to use money where they feel their need is greatest, preserve for them a larger and more independent governing role, and relieve the National Government of administrative burdens and of the difficult task of selecting specific objects of aid. The National responsibility would be limited to the minimum supervision needed to prevent fraud.

Experience with different types of grants, however, suggests that subsidies would not materially relieve pressures for National action for specific objectives. Other factors that are responsible for the establishment of existing grant programs would still remain. . . .

In short, if a system of subsidies were adopted, there is no assurance that the funds would be used to provide all the services thought necessary by the National Government. There would still be pressure for National programs for specific objectives. The end result would be a piling of conditional grants on top of subsidies, as in Canada and Australia, or enlargement of the field of direct National provision of services, or both.[11]

10. Commission on Intergovernmental Relations, *A Report to the President for Transmittal to the Congress* (June 1955), pp. 122–23.

11. Ibid., pp. 121–22.

Joint Federal-State Action Committee

Exactly two years after the Kestnbaum Commission reported to the president in June 1955 without recommending the termination or transfer of any federal grant programs, President Eisenhower invited the National Governors' Conference to join with him in creating a task force charged with three responsibilities:

1. to designate functions which the states were ready and willing to assume and finance that were then performed or financed wholly or in part by the federal government;
2. to recommend the federal and state revenue adjustments required to enable the states to assume such functions; and
3. to identify functions and responsibilities likely to require state or federal attention in the future and to recommend the level of state or federal effort, or both, that would be needed to assure effective action.

The resulting Joint Federal-State Action Committee recommended, in December 1957, that the states assume full responsibility for the federally-aided programs of a vocational education and waste-treatment plant construction in exchange for relinquishment by the federal government of a portion of its tax on local telephone service.

It was disclosed in congressional hearings that none of the 10 lowest-income states could obtain sufficient revenue from the federal tax source proposed for relinquishment to replace the grants recommended for discontinuance. On the other hand, the telephone tax would have produced more than four times as much revenue as California and New York needed to carry on those activities. In all, 20 states would have been financially disadvantaged by the transfer plan, even though it would result in a net loss of more than $50 million a year to the federal government.

Because of this defect in the committee's transfer proposal, the Governors' Conference concluded that it could not support it until the tax relinquishment recommendation was modified to insure that the revenue source made available to each state was substantially equivalent to the costs of the functions to be assumed.[12] This was impossible to accomplish, and no further efforts were made by the committee to pursue its recommendations or to identify additional grant programs for transfer to the states.

Advisory Commission on Inter-governmental Relations (ACIR)

Over a period of years, ACIR has been concerned by the multiplicity of federal grant programs and the need to simplify grant administration. In 1967, the commission recommended that the number of separate grant authorizations be drastically reduced and proposed several methods for counteracting the fragmentation of grant programs. These included the consolidation of closely related categorical programs (by presidential submission of consolidation plans, subject to congressional disapproval, through a procedure similar to that used for reorganization plans) and the "packaging" in a single grant application of a number of interrelated projects

drawing on funds from more than one federal program.[13] Actually, the commission supported the enactment of legislation to authorize the latter procedure, known as joint funding simplification, that had already been proposed by the Johnson administration. Legislation had not been enacted authorizing the use of either of these procedures by late 1974. Much earlier, in 1961, ACIR had urged Congress to review grant legislation at fixed intervals to assure that programs are meeting current needs.[14]

On a more substantive level, ACIR has recommended separating the funding of certain functions by governmental levels primarily as a means of better matching program requirements with fiscal resources. The commission, in 1969, proposed federal assumption of full financial responsibility (but not direct federal administration) for public assistance, including Medicaid and general assistance, and state assumption of substantially all responsibility for the local share of public school costs.[15] Subsequently, the federal government took over the three adult public assistance categories previously supported by grants (aid to the aged, blind and disabled), but not the more controversial Aid to Families with Dependent Children program. Moreover, the states have continued in the direction of providing increased financial assistance to local schools, motivated strongly by court decisions favoring the intrastate equalization of school expenditures.

---

12. U.S., Congress, House Committee on Government Operations, *Federal-State-Local Relations, Federal Grants-in-Aid, H.R. 2533,* 85th Cong., 2nd sess., 8 August 1958, p. 29.

13. ACIR, *Fiscal Balance.*
14. ACIR, *Periodic Congressional Reassessment of Federal Grants-in-Aid to State and Local Governments* (June 1961).
15. ACIR, *State Aid to Local Government* (April 1969).

ACIR has also advocated strengthening the resources of state and local governments through federal revenue sharing[16] and through encouraging greater state use of the personal income tax—by permitting a substantial portion of an individual's state income tax payments to be credited against the federal tax.[17] To make the grant-in-aid system more flexible, the commission has endorsed a federal policy of using a combination of grant instruments. In addition to general revenue sharing, these include block grants for supporting established programs in broad functional areas and categorical grants to stimulate and support programs in specific areas of national interest.[18]

A recurring theme in ACIR reports is the principle that a healthy federal system requires strong local governments and that the states are primarily responsible for strengthening their general-purpose political subdivisions. In consonance with this principle, the commission has proposed channeling federal grants for urban development through the states if the states provide the appropriate administrative machinery and contribute a significant portion of matching funds.[19] It has also recommended that Congress increase the percentage of federal funds for those community development projects which the states "buy into" with their own money.[20]

16. ACIR, *Fiscal Balance.*

17. ACIR, *Federal-State Coordination of Personal Income Taxes* (October 1965).

18. ACIR, *Fiscal Balance.*

19. ACIR, *Impact of Federal Urban Development Programs on Local Government Organization and Planning* (January 1964).

20. ACIR, *Federal Approaches to Aid State and Local Capital Financing* (September 1970).

THE NEW FEDERALISM

The Nixon administration acted vigorously to implement a number of organizational and procedural changes in federal grant administration, including a greater decentralization of decision making to regional offices, establishment of common regional boundaries and Federal Regional Councils, standardization of grant program requirements, and enactment of joint funding simplification legislation. Efforts to accomplish the latter two objectives were commenced in the Johnson administration, and most of these administrative arrangements had been recommended by ACIR.

What is basically different about the New Federalism is its strong emphasis on broadening the discretion of state and local governments to make policy decisions in federally-aided programs. This objective is reflected in former President Nixon's statement that "Federal programs have all too often been accompanied by regulations and restrictions which have stifled innovation and initiative on the part of State and local officials, severely limiting the ability of those officials most familiar with problems at the local level to respond to local needs." To remedy this situation, the president said, "strengthening the resources and responsibilities of state and local governments . . . permits their policies and programs to reflect local needs more sensitively."[21]

The principal fiscal instruments chosen to promote government decentralization are general revenue sharing and special revenue

21. "The Budget Message of the President," *Budget of the United States Government, Fiscal Year 1975*, p. 14.

sharing—a type of block grant. The special revenue sharing concept, first unveiled in President Nixon's 1971 State of the Union Message, differs from the conventional block grant in several important respects. While both instruments are intended to consolidate related categorical programs into broader-purpose grants to permit the more flexible use of funds, special revenue sharing goes much further in reducing federal administrative involvement in how and where money is spent. It would distribute grant funds by a statutory formula that replaces detailed applications subject to federal agency approval (including state plans), and state and local governments would not be required to match grants with their own funds. None of the six special revenue sharing proposals made by the president in 1971—which would have combined a total of 130 categorical grants in the fields of education, law enforcement, manpower training, rural community development, transportation and urban community development—were approved by Congress.

In 1973, President Nixon again proposed special revenue sharing programs, this time in the fields of education, law enforcement, manpower training and urban community development. Congress took no action on the president's law enforcement proposal. Instead, it extended the block grant program administered by the Law Enforcement Assistance Administration with continued requirements for approval of state plans and the matching of federal funds—but at a reduced rate for most expenditure categories. In the manpower field, a bipartisan effort in Congress led to the passage of block grant legislation that consolidated a number of programs and gave state and local governments broad discretion in administering job training and community services activities.

As of July 1974, bills that would extend and amend existing programs for education and community development were well on the way to enactment. In both areas, Congress appeared to have rejected the special revenue sharing approach in favor of some program consolidation.

In essence, the New Federalism represents a reliance on general and special revenue sharing as instruments for greater decentralization, and a series of actions taken by the Nixon administration to simplify and streamline the management of assistance programs. While President Nixon advocated "sorting out appropriate governmental roles" and the decentralization of government, an exclusive federal responsibility for existing intergovernmental functions has been proposed only in the welfare field. That proposal, which resulted in nationalization of the three adult public assistance categories, must be viewed as a pragmatic step to impart greater equity and uniformity into an important income maintenance program and to improve management in an area that historically has been a state and local responsibility. It is noteworthy that nationalization has not been proposed for the grant-aided unemployment insurance program that is closely related to interstate commerce and, consequently, might more easily be justified as a federal responsibility.

Ends and Means

As indicated above, former President Nixon's proposals to combine categorical grants into special revenue sharing programs made no headway in Congress. This approach threatened the traditional congressional interest in targeting federal resources to more specific national objectives.

Over the years, Congress has authorized new grant programs for perceived needs which state and local governments were unable or unwilling to satisfy. Congress and past administrations responded to interest groups by enacting programs designed to encourage the performance of specific activities at the state and local levels.

The New Federalism, however, seeks to transfer resources with little or no specificity of purpose so that state and local governments will be relatively free to spend funds according to their own views of needs and priorities. It does not assume an identity of interest between the federal and other levels of government that will result in programmatic emphasis on the same problems and services as would occur under categorical grants. The assumption, rather, is that the other levels are as politically responsive to their constituents as is the federal government, and that Washington can disengage itself from intimate involvement in domestic social programs through forms of general assistance.

As was noted earlier, the Kestnbaum Commission cautioned against the use of broad subsidies on the grounds that they would not relieve pressures for federal action directed to specific objectives and would result in a piling of conditional grants on top of subsidies. This, in fact, has happened to a degree in the Partnership for Health program—the federal government's first experience with a block grant.

In response to a message from President Johnson decrying "an un-

necessarily rigid and compartmentalized approach to health problems,"[22] Congress enacted legislation in 1966 consolidating a variety of formula and project grants—including one general-purpose formula grant and 16 formula grants relating to particular diseases or other limited public health activities—into two broad programs:[23]

1. formula grants to states for comprehensive health services, with use of the funds to be determined by state priorities [Sec. 314(d)], and
2. project grants to direct funds to areas of greatest need or to stimulate initiative in developing new programs [Sec. 314 (e)].

Following passage of this legislation, both Congress and the administration acted to direct the use of Section 314(e) project grants for national objectives. When a bill proposing a grant program for rat control to be administered by the Department of Housing and Urban Development was rejected by the House in 1967, sponsors of the legislation succeeded on the House floor in increasing the authorization for Section 314(e) by $40 million, to be used for rat control projects. Similarly, the Public Health Service has earmarked project grant funds for such federally-conceived purposes as neighborhood health

22. Message to Congress on Health and Education, 1 March 1966.
23. Comprehensive Health Planning and Public Health Service Amendments of 1966 (P.L. 89-749). This act contained five broad grant programs designed to expand public health efforts in the states and create a Partnership for Health. Only two of these programs relating to formula and project grants for the delivery of health services are pertinent to this discussion.

centers and health maintenance organizations.

Furthermore, while the amount appropriated for formula grants under Section 314 (d) has remained unchanged, new grant programs have been created to deal with particular health problems. These include the Communicable Disease Control Amendments (1970), the Comprehensive Alcohol Abuse and Alcoholism Prevention, Treatment, and Rehabilitation Act (1970), and the Family Planning Services and Population Research Act (1970). This has occurred mainly because Congress, responding to pressures from professional and other health interests and to advocacy by influential members, has found it politically rewarding to support specific health goals that have public appeal in preference to more general programs that permit the discretionary use of funds.

When the Communicable Disease Control program was under consideration, and again when it was amended in 1972, the administration urged use of the Partnership for Health authority for achieving these purposes. Congress, however, indicated a desire to move more aggressively in combating tuberculosis and venereal disease and in providing immunization programs for children.

President Nixon's 1974 budget request for Section 314(e) grants included funding for six categorical areas: migrant health, family planning, family health centers, neighborhood health centers, lead-based paint and rodent control. In authorizing money for Section 314(e), the House Commerce Committee disallowed funding for migrant health and family planning on the grounds that these programs have adequate legislative authority of their own.

The committee provided separate money authorizations for these two categorical programs and amended Section 314(e) so that it could not be used to support any program for which an alternative authority was contained in the bill. This was done, the committee explained, so that the guidelines for the migrant health and family planning programs specified by Congress would be respected by the administration.

The committee also voiced concern that the Nixon administration strayed in recent years from the original intent of the project grant section by requesting funds for categorical programs but none to develop new and innovative demonstration programs of limited scope that could be absorbed by the states if successful.[24]

It should be noted that President Johnson, in whose administration the explosive growth of categorical programs took place, recognized the desirability of consolidating narrow-purpose grants in fields besides health. He stated in 1967 that the "Federal Government has a responsibility to examine and improve the grant-in-aid system, making it more flexible and responsive to State and local fiscal realities." Then, referring to the Partnership for Health and model cities programs, he added: "In the coming year we will examine other areas of Federal aid to determine whether additional categorical grants can be combined to form a more effective tool for intergovernmental cooperation."[25]

Along with his policy of decentralizing government by means of

24. U.S., Congress, *Health Programs Extension Act of 1973: H.R. 93-227 to Accompany H.R. 7806.*
25. "The Budget Message of the President," *Budget of the United States Government, Fiscal Year 1968,* p. 34.

revenue sharing, President Nixon indicated his intention to terminate ineffective grant programs. He sought to achieve this objective by impounding appropriated funds and by omitting budget requests for some existing programs. This raised questions in some quarters about the Nixon administration's basic goals, since general revenue sharing was intended by Congress to *supplement* the categorical grants paid to state and local governments.

Some insight on this matter was provided earlier this year when federal officials testified before Congress on President Nixon's budget. When asked whether he thought general revenue sharing would ever be discontinued, Treasury Secretary George P. Shultz replied:

My observation is that anything that starts is practically impossible to stop, and if it is good it is really impossible. Even if it is terrible, it is practically impossible to stop, and that is what most of this shouting about impoundment is really all about.

As you know, about once every 8 years you have the possibility of a President just reelected to a second term. If he is courageous and bold he can just put his foot down on all these crummy programs that we all talk about and can all point to and we all say should be cleaned out of the budget and just do it, and the way he has to do it is by impounding funds.

What this means is that if a President does that, you find on your hands somebody who is really trying to cut down the size of Government, and when that fact becomes clear around this city you have problems. In my opinion an awful lot of shouting that has been going on is exactly about that problem.[26]

26. U.S., Congress, *The Federal Budget for 1975: Hearings before the House Committee on Appropriations*, 93rd Cong., 2nd sess., p. 189.

Dr. Arthur F. Burns, chairman of the board of governors of the Federal Reserve System, was equally frank in stating his views on the basic objective of that program:

I have a confession to make. In 1969, when I served as counselor to the President, I persuaded the President, I think I can fairly say that, honestly say that— I am not proud of the fact; I am making a confession now—I persuaded the President that general revenue sharing would be a good thing. What I had in mind at the time was that general revenue sharing would become, to an increasing degree, a substitute for categorical grant programs.

What has happened is that we have kept those programs—in fact, we have enlarged them—and we have put general revenue sharing on top of it. If I had foreseen such a development, I would not have recommended general revenue sharing at the time. . . . I am making my sad confession to you, and at appropriate times I shall do penance.[27]

ACCOUNTABILITY

Intimately related to the form of federal assistance is the issue of accountability. The relevant questions in this connection are whether programs are serving their intended purposes and whether they are operating effectively to accomplish those goals. Accountability is obtained, in the final analysis, through the activities of Congress in reviewing program operations and results.

In recently recommending an extension on the Partnership for Health formula grants, which provide only about three percent of total state and local expenditures for health services, the House Commerce Committee said:

Evaluating the benefits produced by 314(d) funds is also complicated by the

27. Ibid., p. 312.

effect of what is described as "accounting convenience" in the records of State public health programs. In actual practice this means that funds under 314(d) are at times allocated in a bookkeeping and recordkeeping sense to those programs to which it is simplest to allocate them. Thus, for instance, 314(d) funds may have allowed States to expand their public health efforts beyond those provided when only categorical aid was available but instead of describing the 314(d) dollars as supporting the new programs, 314(d) funds may be recorded as going to old projects previously paid for with State dollars, which are now free to be spent on the other, new public health efforts. Because of these factors, it is presently difficult to evaluate how well the dollars have been spent, and often simply how they have been spent.[28]

The committee's remedy for this problem was to require a more detailed state plan, subject to approval by the secretary of health, education, and welfare, that "will be reviewed annually to insure that it, and the public health activities described in it, are up-to-date and appropriate."[29]

A similar concern for accountability is evident in the virtually condition-free general revenue sharing program. A recent survey of the views of members of Congress on the general revenue sharing program revealed a tendency on the part of many members to criticize priorities and spending decisions that do not conform to their own values.[30] Nearly half of the respon-

dents, for example, indicated they would regard the use of these funds for the purpose of constructing a public golf course as frivolous or undesirable, despite the fact that the law identifies recreation as a high priority category for local expenditures and places no restriction on the programs for which states may spend funds. Likewise, almost two-fifths of the respondents—including a majority of the Democrats—disapproved of the use of general revenue sharing for tax reduction or to avoid a tax increase, even though the law does not require the state and local governments to maintain their tax effort.

The members who responded were evenly divided on whether too much or too little use is being made of general revenue sharing in relation to other types of grants. By very large margins, however, the Democrats felt there is too heavy reliance on this program, while the Republicans felt there is too little. It is significant that a greater use of broad-purpose block grants was strongly favored by Democrats and Republicans alike.

There are practical disadvantages to assistance mechanisms that carry few or no conditions. The federal government may become locked into supporting ineffective and inefficient activities, and the information needed to evaluate programs becomes difficult or impossible to obtain. In discharging its responsibilities, Congress generally desires more than assurances of fiscal probity; it wants to know how well the money is spent and who benefits.

As a provider of resources only, the federal government would also give up leverage for effecting change in the way functions are performed. This is not to suggest that Washing-

28. U.S., Congress, *Health Revenue Sharing and Health Services Act of 1974: H.R. 93-1161 to Accompany H.R. 14214* (27 June 1974), p. 8.

29. Ibid., p. 9.

30. Intergovernmental Relations Subcommittee of the House Committee on Government Operations, *Replies by Members of Congress to a Questionnaire on General Revenue Sharing*, Committee Print, April 1974.

ton now knows how to solve problems and make programs more effective in fields such as education, health and community development. Rather, it is in a position to look at state and local programs with greater objectivity, to assure that adequate standards are met, and to help overcome resistance to change when innovative methods have been validated.

The conflict between categorical grants and general revenue sharing ultimately involves the issue of social priorities and who chooses them. While the consolidation of grants also enlarges the policy making role of state and local officials, their discretion is relatively limited, and the basic thrust of a consolidation is usually to minimize program duplication and to simplify grant administration.

CONGRESS, BUREAUCRACY AND INTEREST GROUPS

The legislative committees of Congress have been structured since 1946 by functional fields roughly paralleling those of federal departments, and subcommittees of the appropriations committees have been organized on the same basis. Because committees are specialized, their members become familiar with, and often experts on, particular programs and tend to develop close relationships both with organized interest groups and professional administrators in those fields. As a consequence, committee members sometimes serve as advocates or defenders of program interests. This alliance has operated to perpetuate categorical programs.

However, a new coalition of interest groups has been formed which may, in certain situations, operate to counterbalance the influence of organizations devoted to categorical program objectives. This new coalition of public interest groups, consisting of national associations representing the states, cities and counties, has emerged as a political force at a time when the associations have been greatly strengthened in organization and staffing.

General revenue sharing probably could not have been enacted without the effective and coordinated lobbying of public interest groups. They maintained very close contact with the House Ways and Means Committee and the Senate Finance Committee, as well as with the administration, and sought to extract commitments to support revenue sharing from candidates for Congress.

Although these groups are not natural allies on all issues, their interests coalesced on general revenue sharing. However, the municipal associations took the lead in this effort because the cities have been especially hard-pressed for funds. In this instance, no serious move to defeat revenue sharing was mounted by labor organizations and the other special interests which earlier had expressed opposition to the proposal. Consequently, the political clout of public interest groups was not seriously tested.

The municipal associations were also actively involved in support of a 1967 statutory amendment giving local governments more responsibility for local antipoverty programs. Prior to that time, the Office of Economic Opportunity had made frequent use of private, nonprofit organizations to administer community action programs, some of which had used their grants to "fight city hall." At the time of the amendment, about 80 percent of the community action agencies were under nongovernmental sponsorship.[31]

The Nixon administration also gained support from public interest groups for special revenue sharing, since governors, mayors and county executives stand to gain from programs that offer them more discretion in choosing priorities and administering grant funds, less federal direction, and the elimination of matching requirements. These groups could be expected to part company with the administration if the proposed programs were to result in a net loss of federal money.

PROSPECTS FOR GRANT REFORM

Whatever the future may hold for general and special revenue sharing, there can be little doubt that the demand for categorical grants will continue. It is essential, therefore, to improve the effectiveness of this basic form of assistance. Opportunities to do so exist primarily in the legislative process and secondarily in the executive branch, which has considerable authority for simplifying and standardizing administrative requirements.

Grant consolidation has been proposed as a means of rationalizing the very large number of federal assistance programs. Although desirable, this is often difficult to accomplish because grants in many functional fields are the legislative responsibility of more than one House and Senate committee. The realignment of committee jurisdictions presently under consideration in the House would help in this regard but would not eliminate the problem completely. Moreover, the dilution of

program visibility is often opposed by powerful interest groups.

Several other possible approaches exist for dealing with grant duplication and proliferation. One such approach, which received recognition in the Intergovernmental Cooperation Act of 1968, calls for congressional review of grant programs at regular intervals to ascertain whether they are meeting current needs effectively. An obvious related difficulty is that committees cannot be forced to review programs critically and in depth, and they may not be disposed to spend the time required for good program review when confronted with a heavy workload of new legislative proposals.

A more effective device would be the adoption of House and Senate rules applying the principle of the Ramseyer Rule to federal assistance legislation.[32] The Ramseyer Rule requires a committee reporting a bill that repeals or amends any statute to include in its report the statutory language affected and to compare the latter with the proposed amendment. The objective in this case is to require legislative committees to identify all assistance programs that are similar in purpose to any proposed new program and to specify how the latter would relate to the existing programs.

It would be helpful, also, if statutes authorizing grants contained clear and explicit statements of purpose for the guidance of federal administrators and grantees. However, grant legislation is often the product of political compromise that leaves program purposes ambiguous and diverse.

Resources for the public sector are not unlimited; there is and will con-

31. House Committee on Education and Labor, *H.R. 866 to Accompany S. 2388*, 90th Cong., 1st sess., pp. 22.

32. U.S., Congress, *Rules of the House of Representatives*, Section 745.

tinue to be competition for the available funds. This competition may well intensify in the future as Congress implements recently enacted legislation reforming the congressional budget process.[33] The new law provides a mechanism for setting an overall budget ceiling in relation to anticipated revenues and for making priority decisions by establishing expenditure levels for the budget's separate functional categories.

Due to their large labor costs, most grant-aided service programs have been relatively low in productivity and, consequently, have required continually increasing support. In public elementary and secondary education, for example, current expenditures per pupil increased almost 2½ times in constant dollars between 1950 and 1970.[34] A greater effort is evidently needed to develop and apply improved technology for education, and the federal government would appear to be in the best position to sponsor appropriate controlled studies for this purpose.

In light of the impressive growth of government expenditures during the past 20 years, one may ask if there is a level at which such spending becomes unacceptable. This, of course, is a judgmental question that is answered ultimately by the public's willingness to pay higher taxes in return for new or additional services. That the public sector in the United States accounts for a smaller proportion of GNP than in most industrialized nations is noteworthy. The general revenue collected by all levels of government amounted to 32 percent of GNP in 1969, as compared with 48 percent for Sweden, 39 percent for the United Kingdom, 38 percent for France and Germany, and 35 percent for Canada. Countries devoting less of their GNP to government activities than does the United States include Japan at 21 percent and Switzerland at 28 percent.[35]

As federal assistance costs grow, there is an increasing interest in learning which programs succeed in accomplishing their purposes. Congress has earmarked a small percentage of the authorized funds in certain programs for evaluation studies. Unfortunately, the art of evaluating human service programs has not developed to the point where it contributes significant help. In the long run, however, evaluation studies may prove to be a valuable tool for assisting governments at all levels to choose the most effective ways to deliver public services.

33. *Public Law 93-344.*

34. U.S., Department of Commerce, *Statistical Abstract of the United States, 1973,* (Washington, D.C.: Government Printing Office), table 183.

35. Organization for Economic Co-operation and Development, *National Accounts Statistics, 1953–1969,* part 5. Percentages for Canada and Sweden are for 1968.

Dimensions of Judicial Federalism

By JOHN W. WINKLE III

ABSTRACT: Distribution of power between national and subnational judiciaries is a significant yet often overlooked dimension of American federalism. Jurisdictional overlap between state and federal courts has long generated administrative and political tensions that strike at the heart of intergovernmental viability. Acute questions of intersystem equilibrium arise in the consideration of judicial federalism. The dual court configuration materially affects litigant behavior, judicial policy making, and court administration. Intersystem reconciliation assumes greater importance in light of modern demands of spiraling litigation. This article seeks to raise some of the myriad issues of judicial federalism.

John W. Winkle III, who recently completed his Ph.D. at Duke University, is Assistant Professor of Political Science at the University of Mississippi. He has an article on intergovernmental relations in criminal justice appearing in a 1974 issue of Policy Studies Journal.

I wish to thank Professor Peter G. Fish, Duke University, for his helpful comments on this manuscript.

STUDIES investigating federalism from the judicial perspective have traditionally focused on the United States Supreme Court's efforts to demarcate the ill-defined boundaries of state-federal relations.[1] Because the constitutional parameters of national and subnational powers are often ambiguous, political, economic, and social conflicts arise. Litigants in these controversies have sought judicial resolution when private negotiations failed. Beyond question, the Supreme Court as final arbiter of such disputes has long played an instrumental role in devising, justifying or popularizing various theories of federalism. Modern research has examined not only the impact of these decisions but also the degree of neutrality or partisanship that the Court displays in its adjudication.[2] While the Supreme Court's decisional role will continue to be critical for social science study, another less visible but equally significant aspect of the "judiciary and federalism" theme deserves attention.

Judicial federalism, the relationship between national and subnational courts, is a significant yet often neglected dimension of intergovernmentalism. Few writers in recent years have explored the dynamics of the dual system of courts.[3] Yet interjudicial linkages, with their impact on distribution of governmental authority and administration of justice, have important implications for political science. State and federal judiciaries not only resolve disputes but, with their overlapping jurisdictions, themselves engage in intersystem power struggles.

Within this framework, acute policy questions arise for administrators and scholars alike. To what extent, if any, does the dual court configuration affect litigants? Do special groups or sets of clients benefit more than others? Do intersystem conflicts disrupt judicial administration and thereby impair citizen confidence in the courts? Can policies be formulated to minimize friction and maximize coordination? Does the increasing trend toward centralization and the dissolution of state political autonomy have concomitant implications for judicial equilibrium? May a corresponding alteration in balance occur here or is it already subtly taking place? How long can current judicial resources withstand the demands imposed by separate court systems? As part of the contemporary reevaluation of American federalism, these questions deserve consideration. While this article by no means provides answers, it hopes to raise the issues of judicial federalism.

---

1. For a representative survey, *see,* David Fellman, "Federalism and the Supreme Court," *American Political Science Review* 36 (December 1947), pp. 1142–1160; John R. Schmidhauser, *The Supreme Court as Final Arbiter in Federal-State Relations, 1789–1957* (Chapel Hill: University of North Carolina Press, 1958); Loren P. Beth, "The Supreme Court and American Federalism," *St. Louis University Law Review* 10 (Spring 1966), pp. 376–391; Philip B. Kurland, *Politics, the Constitution and the Warren Court* (Chicago: University of Chicago Press, 1970), pp. 51–97.

2. Philip Kurland, for one, charges that the Supreme Court functions not as a neutral "umpire" of the federal system but rather as a "dam" regulating the power flow from states to nation. Kurland, *Warren Court,* p. 57.

3. Carl McGowan, *The Organization of Judicial Power in the United States* (Evanston: Northwestern University Press, 1969). Walter F. Murphy and C. Hermann Pritchett have devoted a chapter to judicial federalism in their new edition of *Courts, Judges, and Politics,* 2nd ed. (New York: Random House, 1974), pp. 98–121.

ORIGINS OF THE DUAL COURT SYSTEM

Parallel judicial systems are uncommon. Political, jurisdictional and administrative stress have discouraged most federations from implementing them. Despite this potential for disharmony, division of adjudicative responsibility is a fundamental presupposition of American federalism. To enhance unity while preserving state sovereignty, the Founding Fathers reasoned that federal courts, quite properly, should review issues of national concern while state tribunals were best suited to handle local matters.

Because of the deficiencies of isolated state courts, few delegates to the Constitutional Convention of 1787 even questioned the necessity of creating a national judiciary, especially a Supreme Court.[4] To define the nature and power of a federal subsystem, however, became an inconsonant task, as exchanges on the convention floor between nationalists and antifederalists reveal. Policy confrontations centered by and large on issues of federal encroachment versus state court incompetence and partisanship.[5] Compromises between the two factions ultimately led to the constitutional provision granting Congress the prerogative to "ordain and estab-

lish" inferior federal tribunals. The Judiciary Act of 1789[6] fulfilled the framers' designs by creating subsets of circuit and district courts, which together with the Supreme Court would insure a somewhat uniform application of the then small corpus of federal law.

Deference to state autonomy, however, resulted in jurisdictional restrictions upon the newly-organized judicial subsystem. While district courts under original jurisdiction could entertain diversity of citizenship cases if the suit met the threshold amount of $500, state tribunals more often served as courts of the first instance. Not until 1875, for example, did Congress invest United States trial courts with original "federal question" jurisdiction.[7] Until that time, states had assumed initial responsibility for suits arising under the Constitution or federal treaties and laws. Exclusive federal jurisdiction extended to these general categories: suits between states; cases involving the United States or a foreign nation as a party; and admiralty affairs. State judiciaries enjoyed concurrent jurisdiction over all other classes of controversies enumerated in Article III.[8]

Over time, however, a redistribution of judicial power between state and federal courts occurred as the once preeminent posture of state adjudication deteriorated. Through congressional legislation and court interpretation, the power of the federal judiciary increased enor-

4. Paul A. Freund, ed., *History of the Supreme Court of the United States*, 11 vols. (New York: Macmillan Co., 1971), 1: *Antecedents and Beginnings to 1801*, by Julius Goebel, Jr., p. xvii.

5. *See*, Max Farrand, ed., *The Records of the Federal Convention of 1787* (New Haven: Yale University Press, 1911), 1, pp. 124–125; 2, p. 46; John P. Frank, "Historical Bases of the Federal Judicial System," *Law and Contemporary Problems* 13 (Winter 1948), pp. 3–28; Alpheus T. Mason, *The States Rights Debate* (Englewood Cliffs, N.J.: Prentice-Hall, 1964).

6. Act of 24 September 1789, 1 Stat. 73.

7. Act of 3 March 1875, 13 Stat. 470.

8. For general reference, *see*, Norman J. Small, ed., *The Constitution of the United States of America: Analysis and Interpretation* (Washington, D.C.: Government Printing Office, 1964); Charles A. Wright, *Law of Federal Courts* (St. Paul, Minn.: West Publishing Co., 1970).

mously during the past century. Creation of new rights and expansion of federal political authority explain, in part, the accretion of national judicial power.[9] While subnational courts today still handle the preponderance of litigation, the national subsystem exercises an ever-widening control over the vindication of federal rights.

With this historical sketch in mind, one must now consider the impact of judicial federalism. In terms of outcomes, parallel organization and intersystem contact materially affect both litigants and courts. Because judiciaries allocate rewards and punishments, it might prove intriguing to examine first the strategies of litigants confronted with a two-tiered judicial structure. A consideration of the impact on state and federal courts will follow.

PRINCIPLES OF LITIGANT SELECTION

Dual court systems provide access options unavailable in countries with unitary judiciaries. Taking advantage of intersystem overlap, litigants may on occasion choose the initial forum, state or federal, for adjudication of their claims.[10] Diversity of citizenship suits, for example, that satisfy the current threshold jurisdictional amount of $10,000 may be instituted in United States district courts even if no federal ques-

tion is involved.[11] Through skillful maneuvering, plaintiffs and defendants alike may manipulate the judicial process in an effort to secure beneficial outcomes.

To gain tactical advantages is the chief motivation behind forum-shuffling. Usually, but not always, litigants select the national subsystem when they have the choice. Fear of local prejudice, whether real or imagined, has over time compelled certain sets of clients to turn to the allegedly more impartial federal forum.[12] Out-of-state individuals and corporations, especially during the nineteenth century, filed diversity suits in United States courts in order to sidestep partisan judges or biased juries.[13] During the 1960s, black defendants claiming civil rights violations frequently invoked removal procedures to avoid policy predilections of southern courts.[14] Because of increased social mo-

11. Congress in 1958 raised the jurisdictional amount necessary for suit in federal courts from $3000 to $10,000. Act of 25 July 1958, 72 Stat. 415. Litigants may also gain access to federal courts on subsidiary issues. Richard J. Richardson and Kenneth Vines, *The Politics of Federal Courts* (Boston: Little, Brown and Company, 1970), p. 84.

12. Because of selection and tenure of federal judges, among other reasons, national courts assumed a more disinterested reputation. American Law Institute, *Study of the Division of Jurisdiction Between State and Federal Courts* (1969), p. 100.

13. Mitchell Wendell, *Relations Between Federal and State Courts* (New York: Columbia University Press, 1949), pp. 78–79, 93.

14. 28 U.S.C. 1441-43; 42 U.S.C. 1983. *See*, Hervey M. Johnson, "Removal of Civil Rights Cases from State to Federal Courts: The Matrix of Section 1443," *Federal Bar Journal* 26 (Spring 1966), pp. 99–155. Litigants may be effectively shut out of the local system. *See*, Herbert Jacob, *Urban Justice: Law and Order in American Cities* (Englewood Cliffs, N.J.: Prentice-Hall, Inc., 1973), p. 9.

9. Consolidation of national authority is discussed in Henry M. Hart, Jr. and Herbert Wechsler, *The Federal Courts and the Federal System* (Brooklyn: The Foundation Press, Inc., 1953), pp. 727–730.

10. Litigants may at times select either courts or administrative agencies for conflict resolution. Glendon Schubert, *Judicial Policy Making* (Glennview, Ill.: Scott, Foresman and Co., 1974), pp. 68–69.

bility, however, most observers now minimize threats of localism.[15]

Forum selection strategies may be influenced by variations from one jurisdiction to another in the application of legal doctrine. Railroad companies in the nineteenth century sometimes sought relief in the federal subsystem to take advantage of the *Swift* v. *Tyson* doctrine.[16] In that 1842 decision, the Supreme Court ruled that national courts must apply state statutory, but not decisional, law. United States judges, as a result, enjoyed wide discretion in the application of federal common law principles when state statutes failed to cover a situation. In more recent times, imprecise residency requirements for diversity plaintiffs have permitted large corporations, foreign entrepreneurs and even commuters more flexibility in their selections.

While most transfers occur from state to national levels, it is not altogether uncommon for litigants to choose the state system. Variables such as docket congestion, geographical convenience of courts, variations in rules, and counsel familiarity with procedures often influence selection. While policy positions of judges are difficult to predict consistently, state courts are sometimes more receptive to certain types of claims than their federal counterparts.[17] The strategy, in sum,

is to pursue those initial options that maximize potential benefits.

Because of parallel organization and concurrent jurisdiction, litigants enjoy choices not just at the beginning but throughout the judicial process. The United States Supreme Court through appeal or certiorari routes may accept cases from state adjudication if a substantial federal issue is at stake.[18] This means that a defendant may have a second opportunity to present his claims. Litigants also may call upon federal courts to enjoin state prosecutions. In addition, state prisoners whose convictions have been affirmed by the system's highest appellate court may still seek federal habeas corpus relief. Present statutes permit separate and successive filing of these petitions.[19] While litigants often benefit from judicial federalism, courts and judges of the two systems do not.

DISCORD AMONG COURTS

Conflict is a characteristic feature of judicial federalism. Intersystem discord over time has stemmed from numerous friction points: diversity jurisdiction, federal common law doctrines, preemption and removal formulas, use of injunctions, state court noncompliance with federal judicial orders, three-judge panels and habeas corpus relief. Tensions reached such levels in the past two decades that judges and scholars alike pressed for reform of federal jurisdiction, but Congress has generally been unresponsive. To appreciate the dimensions of this controversy, the administrative and

15. Henry J. Friendly, *Federal Jurisdiction: A General View* (New York: Columbia University Press, 1973), p. 148.

16. Carl A. Auerbach, Lloyd K. Garrison, Willard Hurst, Samuel Mermin, *The Legal Process* (Scranton, Pa.: Chandler Publishing Co., 1961), p. 156. *Swift* v. *Tyson*, 41 U.S. 1 (1842), centered on the interpretation of the Rules of Decision Act (section 34 of the Judiciary Act of 1789).

17. Kenneth N. Vines, "Southern State Supreme Courts and Race Relations," *Western Political Quarterly* 18 (March 1965), pp. 5–18.

18. 28 U.S.C. 1257. *See*, Chief Justice John Marshall's classic defense of national judicial supremacy in *Cohens* v. *Virginia*, 19 U.S. 264 (1821).

19. 28 U.S.C. 2241-54.

political stresses that coincidence of jurisdiction has generated are highlighted.

At a time when spiraling litigation confronts judicial bodies, concurrent jurisdiction materially contributes to administrative burdens of federal courts by diverting judicial resources. Within the last decade, diversity jurisdiction, three-judge panels and habeas corpus relief have represented the most serious intergovernmental strains on federal judicial administration. Diversity suits are currently the single most numerous category of civil cases filed in district courts.[20] While once this jurisdiction enhanced the visibility and prestige of the national judiciary,[21] it now displaces judicial man-hours from more pressing concerns. Critics argue that the federal subsystem should concentrate not on these essentially local suits but rather upon cases in its exclusive jurisdiction or those in which it may "have greater expertise."[22]

Three-judge courts face similar charges. Created to insure greater deliberation and objectivity, these panels review injunction cases claiming the unconstitutionality of federal or state statutes.[23] In the past decade, hearings by these bodies have virtually tripled in number.[24] Reformers urge that increased workloads and disruptions of judges'

schedules justify immediate changes in this jurisdiction.[25]

No issue of interjudicial concern has commanded more attention since 1940 than federal habeas corpus relief. This historic writ provides the means by which judicial inquiry can be made into the legality of a person's detention or incarceration. State prisoners in recent years, although duly convicted by state processes, have inundated federal courts with petitions claiming violations of constitutional rights.[26] Most of these applications are "frivolous" or without a substantial federal claim. Studies indicate that less than two percent are meritorious. Losses in administrative efficiency to process the volume of petitions are indeterminable.[27]

Jurisdictional conflict has political repercussions as well. Antifederalist fears of national encroachment have echoed through succeeding centuries. Federal common law, interference in state proceedings, and habeas corpus have at one time or another upset the intersystem equilibrium. States, alarmed by federal jurisdictional expansion, often retaliated to regain lost power.

Because the real question in diversity suits is not which court system should hear the dispute, but rather whose law should be applied, federal common law assumes political importance. For almost a century, federal judges working under the *Swift* precedent drew from federal common law principles rather than

20. These are mostly insurance litigation, automobile accident cases and other personal injury suits. *Annual Report of the Director of the Administrative Office of the United States Courts, 1972* (Washington, D.C.: Government Printing Office, 1973), p. 113.

21. American Law Institute, *Division of Jurisdiction*, p. 101.

22. Friendly, *Federal Jurisdiction*, p. 141.

23. 28 U.S.C. 2281.

24. *Administrative Office Report*, pp. 181–186.

25. *See*, Harris S. Ammerman, "Three Judge Courts See How They Run!," *Federal Rules Decisions* 52 (April 1971), pp. 293–316.

26. For statistics, *see*, *Administrative Office Report*, p. 117.

27. *See*, George C. Doub, "The Case Against Modern Federal Habeas Corpus," *American Bar Association Journal* 57 (April 1971), pp. 323–328.

state decisional law. What some have called the "Copernican revolution" of interjudicial relations occurred in 1938 when the Supreme Court overruled *Swift*.[28] Despite *Erie* v. *Tompkins*[29] restoration of a sense of balance to federalism, debates still rage over the ill-defined guidelines that judges use to invoke federal common law.[30]

Judicial federalism is asymmetrical. While state judiciaries are expressly prohibited from enjoining federal processes,[31] United States courts may, within limits, interrupt state proceedings by issuing injunctions or declaratory judgments.[32] Overt interference has at times exacerbated an already uneasy political interplay. The scope of federal control over state prosecution remains somewhat unclear, as recent Supreme Court decisions indicate.[33]

Habeas corpus, as a collateral attack on state judgment, is the principal distributor of judicial power today. That one federal district judge may review decisions of a state's highest appellate court and order the discharge of prisoners has compelling force, especially to the conscientious state judge. While actual release occurs infrequently, this jurisdictional prerogative has only compounded the tensions for judicial federalism. With the enormous influx of petitions to federal courts during the past decades, the issue has assumed more sensitive dimensions. The Warren Court's incremental, yet systematic, incorporation of federally protected rights into the Fourteenth Amendment necessarily opened new grounds of substantive relief for state prisoners. Coupled with rules decisions expanding federal jurisdiction,[34] the Court's actions unquestionably contributed to increased writ-writing. While both state and federal judges, driven by considerations of political and administrative self-preservation, have for 25 years urged Congress to circumscribe federal jurisdiction, few legislative changes have been made.[35] As in other conflict areas of judicial federalism, Congress failed to provide necessary relief.

State courts, when they consider their power base jeopardized, enjoy few retaliatory options. On occasions, subnational courts will ignore or reinterpret Supreme Court rulings.[36] At times, they refuse to

28. *See,* Paul A. Freund, *On Law and Justice* (Cambridge, Mass.: Belknap Press, 1968), p. 224.

29. 304 U.S. 64 (1938). *See,* Kenneth Cole, "Erie v. Tompkins and the Relationship Between Federal and State Courts," *American Political Science Review* 36 (October 1942), pp. 885–895; Henry J. Friendly, "In Praise of Erie—And of the New Federal Common Law," *New York University Law Review* 39 (May 1964), pp. 383–422; *Wallis* v. *Pan American Petroleum Corporation*, 384 U.S. 63 (1966).

30. John Hart Ely and Abram Chayes debate the issue in *Harvard Law Review* 87 (February 1974), pp. 693–762.

31. *McKim* v. *Voorhies*, 11 U.S. 279 (1812).

32. 28 U.S.C. 2283; Act of 14 June 1934, 48 Stat. 955.

33. *Dombrowski* v. *Pfister*, 380 U.S. 479 (1965); *Zwickler* v. *Koota*, 389 U.S. 241 (1967); *Younger* v. *Harris*, 401 U.S. 37 (1971). *See,* "The Federal Anti-Injunction Statute and Declaratory Judgments in Constitutional Litigation," *Harvard Law Review* 83 (June 1970), pp. 1870–1886.

34. *Brown* v. *Allen*, 344 U.S. 443 (1953), *Townsend* v. *Sain*, 372 U.S. 293 (1963), and *Fay* v. *Noia*, 372 U.S. 391 (1963) illustrate well this development.

35. Act of 2 November 1966, 80 Stat. 1105.

36. Henry Robert Glick and Kenneth N. Vines, *State Court Systems* (Englewood Cliffs, N.J.: Prentice-Hall, Inc., 1973), pp. 103–105. *See also,* Donald E. Wilkes, Jr., "The New Federalism in Criminal Procedure: State Court Evasion of the Burger Court," *Kentucky Law Journal* 62 (1973–74), pp. 421–451.

comply with federal judicial orders. The most spectacular assertions of noncompliance occurred primarily in the nineteenth century. In land disputes,[37] Indian affairs,[38] and prisoner custody cases, state courts defied federal judicial demands. In the latter instance, accretion of national habeas corpus power alarmed some state judges to the extent that they asserted, in unprecedented fashion, the reciprocal prerogative of discharging prisoners in federal custody. Twice during a thirteen year span, the United States Supreme Court chastised Wisconsin courts for their interference.[39] In *Tarble's Case*, Associate Justice Stephen J. Field, in no uncertain terms, circumscribed state power. Neither government, he declared, "can intrude with its judicial process into the domain of the other, except so far as such intrusion may be necessary on the part of the National Government to preserve its rightful supremacy in cases of conflict of authority."[40] Such overt challenges for the most part are rare.

RECONCILIATION

Relations between state and federal courts are not altogether abrasive. Indeed, on a national basis, judges of the two systems indicate that they enjoy good working relationships.[41] Beyond that, judicially-devised restraints operate to minimize the friction overlap generates. Comity, abstention and exhaustion

of remedies are the principal tools of federal diplomacy.

Described as a self-imposed rule of judicial morality,[42] comity involves the exercise of mutual restraint in order to prevent collisions of authority in areas of concurrent jurisdiction. The Supreme Court in *Covell* v. *Heyman* converted this device of convenience and expediency into a principle "of right and of law, and therefore of necessity."[43] Years later, Chief Justice William Howard Taft expressed it in these terms:

It would be impossible for . . . courts to fulfill their respective functions without embarrassing conflicts unless rules were adopted by them to avoid it . . . The situation requires . . . not only definite rules . . . but also a spirit of reciprocal comity and mutual assistance to promote due and orderly procedure.[44]

Abstention and exhaustion of remedies are other frequently used restraints. Fashioned by federal judges to avoid unnecessary constitutional adjudication[45] and "needless friction with state policies,"[46] abstention permits national courts to postpone decision on cases pending trial at the state level. This gesture affords state systems opportunities, for example, to interpret unsettled statutes. Yet deference is not absolute. United States courts in recent years have declined to abstain when federal rights are involved or when

37. *Martin* v. *Hunter's Lessee*, 14 U.S. 304 (1816).

38. *Worchester* v. *Georgia*, 31 U.S. 515 (1832).

39. *Ableman* v. *Booth*, 63 U.S. 506 (1859); *Tarble's Case*, 80 U.S. 397 (1872).

40. 80 U.S. 397, 407 (1872).

41. Responses by state and federal judges to questionnaire surveys conducted by the author in 1972 and again in 1974 suggest this.

42. Small, *Analysis*, p. 711.

43. 111 U.S. 176, 182 (1884).

44. *Ponzi* v. *Fessenden*, 258 U.S. 254, 259 (1922).

45. *Specter Motor Service, Inc.* v. *McLaughin*, 323 U.S. 101 (1944). For discussion of contemporary trends, *see*, "The Abstention Doctrine: Some Recent Developments," *Tulane Law Review* 46 (April 1972), pp. 762–776.

46. *Railroad Commission* v. *Pullman*, 312 U.S. 496, 500–501 (1941).

any administrative delay might impair those rights. Abstention, moreover, suffers from uneven application, causing critics to demand either more clear-cut criteria or outright abolition of the doctrine.[47] Like abstention, the exhaustion of remedies principle requires litigants to seek relief first in the state system. Application of this rule has also stirred state animosity, however, especially in habeas corpus litigation.[48]

To stimulate intersystem communication and thereby reduce friction, Chief Justice Warren E. Burger in 1970 urged the creation of State-Federal Judicial Councils in each state.[49] Small groups of judges working jointly to solve problems is a basic step toward interjudicial reconciliation. While several states have not established these councils, those that have report that informational seminars and special projects have strengthened intergovernmental relations.[50] Mutual understanding of, and respect for, the duties and responsibilities that each set of judges must perform is essential for judicial federalism. How valuable this mechanism will be to

continued interchange between the two systems remains to be seen. Few councils today have sustained their original levels of energy.[51]

CONCLUSION

Commenting on the relationship between the state courts and the national government, Alexander Hamilton predicted, " 'Tis time only that can mature and perfect so compound a system, can liquidate the meanings of all the parts, and can adjust them to each other in a harmonious and consistent WHOLE."[52] Nearly two centuries later, observers are still pointing to the maladjustments and imbalance within the federal system. The development that Hamilton had envisioned for judicial federalism has yet to mature. This does not imply, however, that significant advances have not been made. It may suggest that within a federal arrangement there can be no fixed distribution of power. Judicial equilibrium may be as elusive as political balance.

Parallel judicial power is basic to American federalism. As long as state and federal courts exercise concurrent jurisdiction, however, an uneasy interchange will continue. While one should not overstate the conflict model of judicial federalism, the potential for disharmony remains. The question now is not whether friction is inevitable, but rather to what extent policies can minimize tensions and maximize cooperation. With the dismal record of congressional inaction, realistic solutions may be left to the creativity of the judicial branch and the com-

47. "Federal Question Abstention: Justice Frankfurter's Doctrine in an Activist Era," *Harvard Law Review* 80 (January 1967), pp. 604–622; "Abstention: A Case Against Forum Shuffling," *Journal of Public Law* 22 (Fall 1973), pp. 439–463. Representative court decisions include: *Younger* v. *Harris, supra; Wisconsin* v. *Constantineau,* 400 U.S. 433 (1971); *Mitchum* v. *Foster,* 407 U.S. 225 (1972); *Gibson* v. *Berryhill,* 411 U.S. 564 (1973).

48. *See, Brown* v. *Allen, supra.*

49. Warren E. Burger, "State of the Judiciary Address—1970" reprinted in *Congressional Record,* 92nd Cong., 1st sess., 24 September 1971, 117, p. 15012.

50. John W. Winkle III, "The Impact of Habeas Corpus on Judicial Federalism" (M.A. Thesis, Duke University, 1972), pp. 57, 63–65.

51. Responses to June 1974 questionnaire mailing indicate that several councils are virtually inactive.

52. *Federalist* 82.

mon willingness of state and federal courts to work toward joint resolution of sensitive issues.

Judicial federalism offers diverse research challenges. The dual court configuration raises fundamental questions of intergovernmental viability. It unfolds, moreover, tangential issues of litigant behavior, judicial administration and public policy making. By no means does this article pretend to set forth a comprehensive commentary on state-federal judicial relations. To the extent that it synthesizes the myriad issues of judicial federalism into a convenient framework, however, it may provide a useful springboard for further study. In decades to come, the issue of judicial federalism will increase in significance, presenting an ever-formidable challenge to American intergovernmental relations.

Federal-Local Relations and the Mission of the City

By Philip J. Rutledge

ABSTRACT: The administration's emphasis on New Federalism requires those concerned with governing to reexamine the complex intergovernmental system, and particularly the role of the city in that system. Traditionally, municipal government has been the level of government closest to the people and responsible for answering their needs. With the advent of World War II, however, the traditional roles reversed themselves to the point where, in 1944, federal government accounted for 89 percent of total government expenditures, whereas local governments expended only 6.4 percent of that total. The modern inclination to create "paragovernments" for special purposes has compounded the imbalance of the intergovernmental system. The current dilemma is to find a suitable split for governmental services, supported by a more equitable financial split. In resolving this dilemma, cities must be accepted as an integral part of the federal system. Local governments should have a clear voice in decisions in such policy areas as growth management, taxation, transfer payments and quality of life enhancement. The resources of cities should be conserved and fully utilized, and the mission of the city to create "a visible regional and civic structure, designed to make man feel at home with his deeper self and his larger world," should be implemented.

Mr. Philip Rutledge is Director, Office of Policy Analysis, National League of Cities, Washington, D.C., and formerly was Deputy Administrator, Social and Rehabilitation Service, Department of Health, Education, and Welfare. Prior to HEW, Mr. Rutledge served as Director, Department of Human Resources, District of Columbia. A graduate of the University of Michigan, Mr. Rutledge is Chairman, Committee on Manpower Revenue Sharing, National Research Council/National Academy of Sciences. He writes a monthly column for Nation's Cities magazine and contributes regularly to professional journals.

THROUGHOUT the history of the republic, the role of cities in the American federal system has been ambiguous. As the nation prepares to celebrate its 200th anniversary, with 70 percent of the population living in cities, it is a propitious time to reassess the mission of the once and future city in our intergovernmental structure.

One can not analyze fully the possible future alternatives for cities in the United States federal system without some appreciation of the role of the city in history. As Morton and Lucia White have pointed out, it has been a popular pastime historically for many American intellectuals and writers to disparage the city and its possibilities.[1] But this view has not been universal.

Lewis Mumford, for example, has written that "The city first took form as the home of a god: a place where eternal values were represented and divine possibilities revealed."[2] Scott Greer has reminded us that in medieval Europe, if a serf could escape from the manor and survive in the city for a year and a day, he was considered a free man.[3] Charles E. Silberman has characterized the "principal business and the principal glory of the American City" as one of "bringing people from society's backwaters into the mainstream of American life."[4] He went on to say that "Cities have always had to create their own stable, cultivate citizenry from whatever raw material lay at hand. Most of the huge middle class that dominates American life today was manufactured in the big-city slums of yesteryear."[5] Thus, any assessment of the future of the city in the American federal system must take into consideration its historic role as a converter of human resources and a weaver of the social fabric.

Under the shadow of Dillon's Rule[6] (discussed elsewhere in this volume), many have become accustomed to thinking of American cities as the creatures of state governments. However, cities existed in a more viable and self-conscious form than did the states prior to the American Revolution. Roscoe C. Martin has written:

1. Lloyd Rodwin, "American Intellectuals vs. the American City," *The Future Metropolis*, (New York: George Braziller Publishers, 1961).

2. Lewis Mumford, *The City in History*, (New York: Harcourt, Brace and World, 1961), p. 575.

3. Scott Greer, *Governing the Metropolis*, (New York: John Wiley and Sons, Inc., 1962), p. 7.

4. Charles E. Silberman, *Crisis in Black and White*, (New York: Random House, 1964), p. 19.

5. For a critical analysis of current malfunctioning of the city as a social converter, *see*, Jay W. Forrester, *Urban Dynamics*, (Cambridge, Mass.: MIT Press, 1969); and particularly, Louis Alfeld, John Miller, and Walter Schroeder III, "Urban Dynamics Applied to Lowell: Policy Recommendations," (Cambridge, Mass.: Systems Dynamics Group, Alfred P. Sloan School of Management, MIT); and Walter, Sweeney, and Rokeat, *Readings in Urban Dynamics*, (Cambridge, Mass.: Wright-Allen Press, 1974), ch. 4.

6. John H. Baker, *Urban Politics in America*, (New York: Charles Scribner's Sons, 1971), p. 45. Definition, Dillon's Rule: "It is a general and undisputed proposition of law that a municipal corporation possess and can exercise the following powers and no others: First, those granted in express words; second, those necessarily or fairly implied in or incident to the powers expressly granted; third, those essential to the accomplishment of the declared objects and purposes of the corporation—not simply convenient, but indispensable. Any fair, reasonable, substantial doubt concerning the existence of power is resolved by the courts against the corporation, and the power is denied."

A discussion of the American federal system which aspires to realism must begin with an understanding that local government was here first. The governments with which the colonists were first acquainted were the towns—local, home-grown, rural units close to the people. The colonial governments came next, the products equally of domestic recognition of the need for a unifying agency and of a companion but separate decision by a distant sovereign. The commonwealths were long establishing a stable base, and they spoke with an uncertain voice right up to the time when the issue of independence was resolved. The localities retreated slowly and grudgingly before this unifying trend, for even the watery prestate governments of colonial days were tolerated without enthusiasm. To this day, indeed, the state and its governments are regarded with suspicion in some quarters; Vermont, for example, is considered by its citizens to be a confederation of towns, and its state government is treated accordingly. It was from this stony soil that the Union grew.[7]

Indeed, the concept of the city, which originated over 5,500 years ago, pre-dates even the concept of the modern nation. Kingsley Davis and Gideon Sjoberg point out, however, that it has been only the past 100 years, since the industrial revolution, that the full potential of cities has been thrust upon us and their historic mission understood.[8] Certainly, at the time the American Constitution was being drafted, cities were not considered important enough by the Founding Fathers to be mentioned in that seminal docu-

ment. The irony is that, though our Founding Fathers displayed enormous foresight in so many other areas, they clearly did not anticipate the future growth in size and importance of cities in this nation. The fact that they envisioned an America which would remain enduringly rural is a burden that intergovernmental relations must bear today.

Federal-local relations, even with the role and functions of cities constitutionally clarified, would still strain the administrative systems capacity in 1974. Without such clarification, one of history's best mechanisms for social and human resources conversion has come close to being nullified. Rationalizing our intergovernmental system, however, can help restore its vitality.

CITIES AND THE STRUCTURE OF THE INTERGOVERNMENTAL SYSTEM

When one begins to think about federal-local relations, one is immediately struck by the fact that there are over 78,000 local governments with which the system of intergovernmental relations must cope. This number is down from 15 years ago when it was 102,000. The United States Census of Governments, in table 1, provides a concise picture of our complicated intergovernmental system.

A quick review of the data in table 1 shows two interesting trends over the last 15 years. The first is the tendency toward consolidation of school districts which has occurred during the last decade; the total number of school districts has decreased by almost 35,000 since 1957. The second trend is the increasing utilization of special districts to deliver local services; these districts

7. Roscoe Martin, *The Cities and the Federal System*, (New York: Atherton Press, 1965), pp. 21–22.

8. Kingsley Davis, "The Urbanization of the Human Population," and Gideon Sjoberg, "The Origin and Evolution of Cities," (cf. Hans Blumenfeld, "The Modern Metropolis"), *Cities*, ed. Scientific American (New York: Alfred Knopf, 1966).

TABLE 1

LEVELS OF UNITED STATES INTER-
GOVERNMENTAL SYSTEM,
NUMERICAL BREAKDOWN

TYPE OF GOVERNMENT	1972	1967	1962	1957
U.S. government	1	1	1	1
State governments	50	50	50	48
Local governments	78,218	81,248	91,186	102,341
counties	3,044	3,049	3,043	3,050
municipalities	18,517	18,048	18,000	17,215
townships	16,991	17,105	17,142	17,198
school districts	15,781	21,782	34,678	50,424
special districts	23,885	21,264	18,323	14,424
Total	78,269	81,299	91,237	102,390

SOURCE: "Governmental Organization," *1972 Census of
Governments* (Washington, D.C.: Government Printing
Office, 1972).

have increased in number from
14,424 in 1957 to 23,885 in 1972.

The structure of American local
government has been shaped principally by two dominant influences.
One influence, which could be characterized as forces of the open
market, stimulated people to move
about in search of better economic
and social opportunities. The other
influence has been government incentives either through direct grants
of land and/or cash or through national tax policies which rewarded
certain initiatives and penalized
others. These forces have combined
to create a situation in which 148
million persons, or 70 percent of our
population, now reside in 263
Standard Metropolitan Statistical
Areas.[9] These SMSAs, in the opinion of some, are replacing cities as
the centers of American life, and in
some respects are taking on the
characteristics of local governments
themselves.[10]

9. U.S., Bureau of the Census, *Statistical
Abstract of the United States: 1973*, 94th ed.
(Washington, D.C.: Government Printing
Office, 1973).
10. Norman Beckman, "Metropolitan
Area Trends and Developments," *The*

In any system of federal-local relations, the SMSA must be reckoned
with, for the mass of the nation's
wealth as well as its people is concentrated there. Sixty-eight percent
of the nation's civilian labor force
are located in the 263 SMSAs; 80
percent of the U.S. bank accounts
are there; and 75 percent of personal
income taxes are paid from there. It
is in the central cities of these
SMSAs that the burning social
issues of the nation still reside. In
these central cities are 60 percent of
the metropolitan area's poor, 62 percent of the elderly and 78 percent
of the metropolitan area's blacks and
other minorities. The central cities'
unemployment rate is two to three
times the rate in suburbia. This
peculiar clustering of the nation's
unresolved social problems in
SMSAs adds a different dimension
to what might otherwise be a logical
channel for federal-local relations.

In part, the efforts made by the
federal government—sometimes
consciously, sometimes inadvertently—to manage its relations with
the web of local governments created by free market forces and tax
incentives, has lead to the creation of
still another complex of local governments. The problems of the metropolitan area so often overlap legal
boundary lines that a series of
special districts has been created
to handle these situations. Special
districts today number between
24,000 and 25,000, depending on
how the count is made, and the number is still growing. The Advisory
Commission on Intergovernmental
Relations (ACIR) identified 24 federal programs in 11 different federal

Municipal Year Book 1974, (Washington,
D.C.: International City Management Association, 1974).

departments, as of 1972, which had resulted in the formation of some 1,800 regional or substate districts which handle special programs in a narrow functional manner. It further identified 4,045 such districts as having been funded or designated by the federal government.[11]

These regional and substate districts have added a new layer and a new dimension to federal-local relations. While seldom being clearly accountable to elected officials at any level of government, they are playing an increasingly important role in intergovernmental fiscal relations. As ACIR noted in 1973, while being funded at a level of 220.8 million dollars, the 24 substate districts ACIR identified then had a strong influence on how an additional 8.4 billion dollars in federal capital and operating funds were spent.[12]

The above discussion includes neither the many interlocal purchase of services arrangements which municipalities enter into on their own authority to improve efficiency of service delivery because of economies of scale, nor the 576 regional councils of governments which have varying degrees of authority to intercede with the federal government on behalf of local needs.

PARAGOVERNMENTS AS INSTRUMENTS OF NATIONAL PURPOSE

The accordionlike expansion and

contraction of local governments in the U.S. have been responses to changing thrusts in national policy and purpose. Each time a new problem or need is recognized, a new governmental structure is devised to carry it out. When a new regional, substate or local district is not established, some other form of "paragovernment" is. The issue of paragovernments has been defined as follows:

The term refers to the great number of ad hoc, quasi-governments spawned by the grant programs enacted in the 1960s, semi-public agencies that operate the local projects funded by . . . [categorical programs]. Typically, these agencies are nonprofit and operate independently of the general purpose local government.

Each locality's mix of paragovernments varies with the extent of its involvement with federal subsidies. But in the big cities troubled by a declining tax base and ever-widening poverty, congeries of paragovernments operate. The most commonplace are OEO-funded community action agencies, model cities-funded community development agencies, nonprofit sponsors of manpower training programs funded by the Labor Department, nonprofit sponsors of HEW-funded neighborhood health centers, and nonprofit sponsors of HEW-funded early childhood development centers operating under the Head Start Program. . . .

Operating almost entirely with federal dollars, and therefore free of most local budgetary controls, these semi-public bodies become, their critics claim, governments in their own right, albeit nearly invisible and unaccountable to the public. And they often conflict with the local general-purpose government and thereby drain its strength away, the critics say.[13]

11. ACIR, *Regional Decision-Making: New Strategies for Substate Districts*, (Washington, D.C.: Government Printing Office, 1973), pp. 168–219. [cf. ACIR, *American Federalism: Into the Third Century*, (Washington, D.C.: GPO, 1974) and *Unshackling Local Governments*, 24th Report by the Committee on Government Operations, (Washington, D.C.: GPO, 1968).]

12. ACIR, *New Strategies*, p. 170.

13. Timothy Clark, John Iglehart, William Lilley, eds., "The New Federalism: Theory,

Whatever the merits of the criticism directed against the so-called paragovernments, it would seem fair to say that federal policy in the past has encouraged their proliferation, thus further confusing the role of cities and municipalities in the federal system. The recent thrust of the so-called New Federalism, while counteracting the tendency to create new paragovernments, may have some unintended problems of its own as an effort to streamline federal-local relations.

IMPACT OF NEW FEDERALISM

While much recent rhetoric has tended to credit President Nixon's administration with the New Federalism, Jane Perry Clark, writing in 1938,[14] and Roscoe Martin, writing in 1965,[15] credit the concept to President Roosevelt's New Deal. As Martin put it, "the concept signifies the common sharing of public responsibilities by two or more 'levels' of government. The sharing may be national-with-state (or the reverse), national-with-state-with-local, state-with-local (though technically this is an intrastate rather than a federal matter), or federal-with-local."[16]

Whatever the recent origins of the New Federalism, it has refocused attention on the functions and responsibilities of local general purpose governments. Sorting out the roles, responsibilities and prerequisites of the different levels of government clearly offers a fruitful strategy for rationalizing federal-local relations in the intergovernmental system.

Municipal government has always been that level of government closest to the people and to which the people turned first when in need. The changing economic conditions of the country over the last half-century, and the fiscal policies initiated to deal with them, have thrown our intergovernmental system into a state of imbalance.

Until the late 1930s, functional and financial responsibilities were split within the federal system so that the federal governmental role was relatively restricted in comparison to local or state governments. Except during wartime periods, the burden of domestic activities fell to local governments and, to some degree, to the states. In 1902, the federal government was financing only 33 percent of the total governmental expenditures in this country. The primary source for governmental services devolved upon that level of government closest to the electorate—the local level. Local expenditures were 56 percent of the total expenditures in 1902, with state governments accounting for 11 percent.

However, with the advent of the depression years and World War II, the traditional roles reversed themselves. The federal government now assumed a number of far-reaching social, monetary and tax programs which expanded its activities enormously. On the other hand, the activities of local governments began to pale in relationship to the national problems then being encountered. By 1944, the federal government accounted for 89 percent of the total government expenditures, whereas local govern-

---

Practice, Problems", *National Journal*, Special Report, Government Research Corporation (March 1973), p. 48.

  14. Martin, *Cities*, p. 37; Jane Perry Clark, *The Rise of a New Federalism*, (New York: Columbia University Press, 1938).

  15. Martin, *Cities*, p. 37.

  16. Martin, *Cities*, p. 37.

ments expended only 6.4 percent, and states 4.6 percent, of the total.

Recently, the trend has been to return to a level somewhat more in line with the traditional functional splits. In fiscal year 1974, for example, total expenditures for all governments amounted to approximately $500 billion, with state and local governments expending nearly one-half—approximately $225–230 billion—of that amount. Further evidence of the rebalancing of governmental expenditures is the estimate that in 1975 federal aid to state and local governments is expected to total $52 billion.[17] Approximately 35 percent of the average municipal budget is now made up of intergovernmental transfer payments from the federal and state level. The concepts of New Federalism and revenue sharing seem to be expressions of this trend.

But in this movement toward a more balanced system, certain lingering national economic problems cannot be thrust upon local and state governments. Nor can there be a wholesale withdrawal of the federal role in treating social or ecological problems. Moreover, the federal government's preemption of the income tax as a revenue source has hobbled local governments in attempting to meet their growing expenditures. The current dilemma is to find a suitable functional split for governmental services which may be supported by a different, more equitable, financial split.

IDENTIFYING THE URBAN ROLE

To begin to sort out those func-

17. U.S., Treasury Department, *Special Analyses, Budget of the United States Government, Fiscal Year 1975*, (Washington, D.C.: Government Printing Office, 1973), p. 203.

tions that can best be performed at the local level, and to determine the most useful structure of local government that can carry out these responsibilities, is a task of immediate importance. One must start, of course, with the fundamental assertion that cities are and have always been an integral part of the federal system, whether they were recognized in the federal Constitution or not. Therefore, they are, and must continue to be, instruments in achieving the national social purpose. But it must also be borne in mind that, although they are important cogs in the federal wheel, municipalities also have a gestalt of their own.

The National Municipal Policy of the National League of Cities, for instance, describes this gestalt in the following manner:

In the federal system, municipal government is the only unit of government able to respond directly to the needs of persons wishing to govern themselves, flexible enough to adjust quickly to local needs and problems, and able to provide immediate availability and service to its citizens. To adequately respond to the pressures of changing population, technological revolution and rising public expectations, municipal government must be given greater power to self-organize and to act effectively to carry out its own policies and programs for the improvement and orderly growth of the urban, human environment. To be truly effective, municipal government should:

A. Be of such size that any service provided will be primarily beneficial and chargeable to its residents and that the cost of failure to provide a service will not be detrimental to other jurisdictions;

B. Be of such size as to secure economies of scale, minimize the unit cost of services, and allow effective performance of a function;

C. Have geographical and legal jurisdiction to cope with the problems that their citizens expect them to solve, including power to adjust governmental boundaries to meet changing social, economic, political and demographic conditions;

D. Be of such size as to reduce disparities among taxing units and facilitate raising adequate revenues equitably;

E. Be organized as general rather than single purpose units, with authority to determine its own organizational structure suitable to its individual needs; and

F. Be accessible to and controllable by the people and maximize opportunities for active citizen participation.[18]

The acceptance of cities as full partners in the federal system must be based on recognition of at least the following assumptions:

1. As the nation becomes more urban, the nature of public administration concerns must be redirected more to urban administration.

2. The social problems which afflict the nation's cities are the result of discontinuities in our national policy; therefore, the entire nation must share in the social and financial costs of their resolution.

3. The infrastructures, both social and physical, in the nation's cities represent over 200 years of continuous investment; therefore, with increasing scarcities in energy, dollars and other resources, the first priority must be urban conservation.

NEEDED FEDERAL CHANGES

In order to address adequately these remaining problems, both the legislative and the executive branches of the federal government must face up to them. One high order of business at the federal level remains an adequate organizational structure to respond to urban concerns. Congress still has no urban affairs committee of either house to provide appropriate oversight to urban legislative needs.[19] The Department of Housing and Urban Development is the putative advocate agency for the cities, but its authority and responsibilities are too limited to deal with the many scattered policies and programs that determine urban priorities. While there was at one time much hope for the Domestic Council (and its predecessor, the Urban Affairs Council), it seems to have been rendered inoperative. Thus, in spite of passage of the State and Local Government Assistance Act to provide some general sharing of revenues, attention given to the critical need for an effective financial support system of the nation's cities continues to be inadequate. Such a support system is the cornerstone of a productive federal-local relationship. Objectives for it are stated by the National League of Cities' National Municipal Policy as follows:

The federal financial support system is a critical tool in the design and implementation of the federal system. To achieve the goals of balanced urban growth, the support system must enhance the capacity of state and local governments to attack their pressing social, physical and economic problems. The financial support system should:

A. Strengthen local political institu-

18. National League of Cities, *National*

Municipal Policy, (Washington, D.C.: Government Printing Office, 1974), p. 57.

19. Hon. Herman Badillo, *Congressional Record*, 1 July 1974, p. E4410.

tions by recognizing the primacy of their responsibility to their citizens, and by encouraging local planning, by recognizing local priorities and by enhancing the capacity of local officials to coordinate and direct all the resources available for local problem solving. In particular, Congress should take action which supports the self-determination of local governments, and avoid taking action which forces cities to undertake projects they do not want in order to receive federal support, or to adopt unnecessary structural arrangements in order to secure federal resources;

B. Augment state and local fiscal resources through the continued development of an equitable and efficient intergovernmental fiscal system;

C. Provide a comprehensive set of national programs to eliminate disparities and inequities wherever they exist and are uncontrollable by any other level of government;

D. Aggressively encourage innovation and demonstration of new ideas and techniques through pilot programs;

E. Enhance environmental and human resources not controllable by states and local governments; and

F. Be accompanied by federal budgetary reform and multi-year budgeting to allow for local and state planning.[20]

In building this financial support system, care must be taken that policy encourages neither the proliferation nor the retention of units of local government which would not be viable otherwise. Some 38,000 of the 78,000 local governments in the nation are now receiving financial support from the $30.2 billion five-year general revenue

sharing appropriation. The local governments range in size from those like New York City, with populations in the millions, to tiny villages with populations of a few hundred.

Richard P. Nathan, one of the architects of general revenue sharing in the Nixon administration, recently observed that "Most of the 38,000 local governments to benefit in the program are very small. Half have less than 1,000 inhabitants and four-fifths have less than 5,000." He goes on to warn that:

A special problem in this regard is that some states have local governments called "general governments" but which actually have very limited responsibilities. Most of these "do-little" governments receive significantly more shared revenue in relation to their total expenditures than do larger jurisdictions. Particularly important is the fact that 13,000 midwestern townships (most of which do little more than provide town roads) receive shared revenue. In this case, and in several others, many believe, there are obvious needs—now that the revenue sharing program has been in effect for a year and a half—for the distributive formula to be changed if the program is extended beyond 1976.[21]

The intensity of the debate over the current distributive formula in revenue sharing prior to its approval does not pretend that this change will be an easy one. But it is essential nonetheless.

FEDERALISM AND URBAN CONSERVATION

The demands placed upon our national resources today—with worldwide inflation, an unstable

20. National League of Cities, *National Municipal Policy*, p. 46.

21. Richard P. Nathan, "Whither Revenue Sharing?" *New York Times*, 23 June 1974, p. 3.

international security situation and a revolution of rising expectations at home—mean that many identified needs can not be met in the short term, and some even in the long term. Local governments recognize this and are willing to go along with a deferred gratification policy, provided they have something to say about how the priorities for resource allocation are set. In the setting of priorities and determination of the economic policy from which resources flow, local government has rarely been at the conference table.

In an economy of abundance, everyone's needs might hopefully be touched through continuing expansion and growth. In an economy of scarcity, where competition is keener, it is essential that more actors be brought in on decisions. Therefore, it seems predictable that cities will demand to be brought in on national economic policy discussions with increasing fervor. In a time when even our most sophisticated leaders no longer know—if they ever did—when and how to stimulate or restrain the economy, local elected leaders will feel emboldened to demand a voice in economic policy making.

Thus it seems that a useful strategy for the nation to pursue in its future federal-local relations is to try to define a mutual national and local agenda for the intergovernmental system. If this can be done, then a policy and strategy for conserving and enhancing our existing urban systems—both large and small, suburban and central, intrastate and substate—could be one on which a majority might agree.

In order to do this, however, it would first be necessary to agree upon a theoretical framework that potentially would allow choices to be made which would support the enlightened self-interest of each partner in the intergovernmental system. Suppose that one could get the leaders at federal, state and local levels to agree that the primary purpose of governance is to improve the quality of life of citizens. The most confounding question would then be how to do it. Although improving the quality of life, or even defining it, for that matter, has been one of the most elusive goals of public administrators at all levels, the current state of the economy suggests that at least the following three factors be addressed:

1. Growth of our urban areas must be managed in a manner that maximizes the use of scarce resources.
2. National tax policies must be reexamined in such a way as to see that the decisions made about resource allocation and expenditures are conscious and not hidden.
3. The income transfer system must be examined more closely to determine the impact that increasing transfer payments to individuals will have on the underpinning of traditional institutions.

Calling attention to the above three areas is not intended to minimize in any way the importance of developing and refining further reforms in other areas of the intergovernmental system. Much of this has already been started through general revenue sharing, semi-block grant programs such as in law enforcement assistance, new comprehensive employment and training legislation, the pending housing and community development bill, and other initiatives directed toward giving local governments more discretion in the design and management of programs emanating from the federal level. It is assumed that this trend will continue. However, growth management, taxation, transfer payments and quality of life enhancement are policy areas in which local government concerns have not been adequately considered. In the last half of the nineteen seventies, these policy areas should move to the top of the agenda.

RESOURCES FOR MANAGING URBAN GROWTH

As Environmental Protection Administrator Russell Train said recently, growth management means learning to live within the limits of available resources. Along with Wilfred Owen, Train decries "accidental cities" which put "a premium on moving" because they offer "so little in the way of living."[22] With implicit support from federal policy, present local growth management strategy seems to be abandonment of existing urban investments, moving into the pasture land and building wholly new and competing infrastructures. Turning this policy around will require the keenest attention of federal policy leadership; but taking this step would strengthen greatly the capacity of local government to play a healthier role in the intergovernmental system.

Although little-noticed by most Americans and all but a few congressmen, the federal system finances urban programs from two budgets—one public, the other hidden. The appropriated federal budget for fiscal year 1975 contains approximately $52 billion in direct aid to state and local governments. This budget has been carefully reviewed by the ubiquitous Office of Management and Budget and intensely debated by members of Congress. But there is also available in FY 1975 a hidden tax expenditure budget, estimated at $80 billion, over which there has been no debate and few conscious priorities set. The "tax expenditure budget," as Stanley Surrey[23] has pointed out, is a system of tax expenditures under which governmental financial assistance programs are carried out through special tax provisions rather than through direct appropriations. It is made up of a complex of subsidies covering exclusions from income, exemptions, deductions, credits against tax, preferential rates of tax and deferrals of tax which serve ends very similar to those for which direct appropriations are made.

The force of the unharnessed priorities in the tax expenditure budget may often overwhelm decisions made by state and local governments for use of direct appropriations. The tax expenditure budget potentially plays havoc with the ability of central and suburban cities to manage their growth. In FY 1971, for example, the tax expenditure budget, without benefit of debate, contained some $20 billion for commercial and economic development. It is likely that local governments of all sizes were hurt by this hidden subsidy because most of the tax write-offs, investment credits and depreciation shelters probably spurred the exodus from central cities to suburbs, thereby causing growth management problems for

22. Russell Train, "The Quality of Growth," *Science*, American Association for the Advancement of Science, 7 June 1974.

23. Stanley S. Surrey, *Pathways To Tax Reform*, (Cambridge, Mass.: Harvard University Press, 1973).

both. At any rate, it would be useful to know consciously what trade-offs could have been made.

Meyers and Musial, for example, have offered some intriguing ideas for putting tax incentives to work in favor of urban conservation instead of against it. They suggest that urban incentive tax credits be authorized on the basis of an urban conservation need index.[24]

Fortunately, the recently adopted Budgetary Reform Act (S1541 and HR7130), if signed into law, will call for greater congressional review of the tax expenditure budget by 1976. Between now and then, both the executive and legislative federal partners should begin working with their local government partners to assure that a thorough review of all aspects of our national tax policy is possible.

INCOME STRATEGY AND URBAN DEVELOPMENT

Another area which should be high on the agenda for joint review in forging more healthy federal-local relations is the emerging, but almost equally hidden income strategy. The income security portion of the national budget has risen 165 percent since 1969, exceeding $100 billion, or approximately one-third of the 1975 federal budget. Included are such things as Social Security—up 70 percent since 1969 —public assistance, and unemployment and other forms of social insurance designed to provide some replacement of income for an individual during times of adversity. If all transfer payments in the fiscal 1975 budget were included, the total both in terms of percentages and

24. Edward W. Meyers and John J. Musial, *Urban Incentive Tax Credits*, (New York: Praeger Publishers, 1974).

actual dollars would be even higher. Transfer payments would include all tax and in-kind subsidies an individual receives that are not derived from current direct labor market participation. Examples of such subsidies would include, in addition to those mentioned above, veterans benefits, pensions, assistance to the disabled, housing, food and nutrition, education, health care and a host of other items—not all of which are directed primarily toward the disadvantaged.

This tremendous increase of income security and transfer payments to individuals during the last few years, if continued at the same rate, could bring about profound changes in the nature of the urban economy. Already this massive infusion of transfer payments has suggested some alternate ways in which an urbanized economy may be organized. The grant, or one-way transfer, is becoming of increasing interest to some economists as an instrument to integrate with the traditional two-way exchange as part of a modern complex economic system.

All signs seem to point to the conclusion that the Nixon administration intended to expand even further on its income strategy. If the Ford administration continues in like manner, the following trends seem probable:

—The Supplemental Security Income program, which federalized and placed a floor under the incomes of half the welfare cases in the country, will be further improved by legislation which would add an automatic cost of living adjustment to guaranteed income.
—If unemployment goes up, public service jobs (by some definitions a transfer payment also)

will be increased and unemployment compensation periods lengthened.

—Indications also are that any proposed reform dealing with the presently non-federalized welfare cases (families and children) would likewise feature an increase in direct cash payments rather than services. The income tax system is also likely to be used in this reform as well.

—Housing assistance to the poor is likely in the future to be provided through housing allowances rather than through public housing projects.

—Higher education student assistance will be provided more and more through direct cash grants and loans to individuals rather than through support to colleges and universities.

—Childhood and secondary education is likely to see more experimentation with vouchers to purchase learning on the open market than from the monopolistic neighborhood school.

Also, the debate is no longer over *whether*, but *how* universal health care will be financed through some form of social insurance with a high element of personal choice. These and other examples underpin the commitment to the income strategy of the New Federalism. They represent a massive shift in gross national product away from support of social institutions to the financing of individual choice and mobility.

The income strategy, while enhancing social mobility and personal choice on the part of individuals, has potentially sweeping effects on the social institutions of state and particularly of local government. The change in institutions brought

on by subjecting social programs to a market economy may be even more profound than the ultimate redistributive effects of the transfer payments system. In the last 25 years, neither the income tax nor the rise in transfer payments has changed the income gap between rich and poor very much. On the other hand, income security and transfer payments never existed on this scale before.

The ramifications of this strategy may be positive, but could be negative, depending on how well the transition is planned. The problem is that these decisions are being made with virtually no input from cities, yet this is where most beneficiaries of such programs reside and where institutions will be eroded.

Of necessity, urban administrators have concerned themselves more with managing those programs that a municipality directly controls than with analyzing the outcomes of programs and policies emanating from some other level of government. Thus, their overwhelming preoccupations are with urban renewal, local taxation and finance, public safety, transportation and the like. But if the income strategy is here to stay—and evidence suggests that it is—then federal and local leaders together must begin to assess the impact of this policy on the infrastructure of tomorrow's cities.

Finally, if it can be agreed that the primary purpose of government is to improve the quality of life of citizens, then a concerted joint effort should be launched by the federal, state and local partners in the intergovernmental system to quantify and measure life quality. Many millions of dollars have been spent on social indicators in the last 10 years, and at least a dozen bills have been introduced in Congress calling for the establishment of some national system of social accounting or some council of social advisers similar to the Council of Economic Advisers either in the White House or in Congress. Now that OMB has at least suggested some ground rules in its official publication, *Social Indicators*,[25] the stage at last seems to be set for movement in this important area. A set of benchmarks against which federal, state and local performance in our intergovernmental system can be measured may be established.

But to keep our goals in urban governance from becoming too mechanistic, federal and local policy makers should bear in mind those quality of life objectives which Lewis Mumford suggests were in the minds of the earliest founders of cities—that is, "to put the gods in their shrines." He says that "the task of the coming city is not essentially different: its mission is to put the highest concerns of man at the center of all his activities. . . . The chief mission of the city of the future is that of creating a visible regional and civic structure, designed to make man feel at home with his deeper self and his larger world, attached to images of human nurture and love. We must conceive the city, accordingly, not primarily as a place of business or government, but as an essential organ for expressing and actualizing the human personality. . . . "[26]

25. U.S., Treasury Department, Statistical Policy Division, Office of Management and Budget, *Social Indicators* (Washington, D.C.: Government Printing Office, 1973).

26. Mumford, *City in History*, p. 573.

Counties: the Emerging Force

By BERNARD F. HILLENBRAND

ABSTRACT: County government, the most universal form of local government, has risen to new prominence with the increasing demand for locally delivered public services. Today the people are calling for greater responsiveness from their government. The federal government has reacted to the needs of local government by enacting general revenue sharing and block grants, A-85 Review and Integrated Grant Administration. These programs are techniques or tools used by the federal government to increase local autonomy in a partnership for providing the best delivery of services to the citizen. This interaction of cities, towns, counties, states and federal government is called New Federalism. The process of placing increased responsibility on county governments dictates a continuing and expanding role for local government. Types of this expanded role would be participation in the development of the federal budget and increased general revenue sharing funds and block grants.

Bernard Hillenbrand has been Executive Director, National Association of Counties (NACo) since 1957. He also serves as Editor of the weekly newspaper County News. He has written numerous articles on local government for national publications and has taught special courses in local government at American University and Cornell University Extension Division. Before coming to NACo, Mr. Hillenbrand worked as Administrative Analyst, Budget Department, State of Wisconsin; as Deputy Director, Municipal Research, Syracuse, New York; and as Assistant Director, American Municipal Association. He served a one-year Administrative Internship with the State of New York Department of Taxation at Albany, New York.

THE most universal form of local governmental district in the United States is the county; yet for many years they were an ignored unit of government. Federal categorical grants often ignored the county. The model cities program provided several billions of dollars to approximately 150 cities, but only as an afterthought were approximately 10 counties added to the experimental program.

In recent years the county has become an increasingly visible and important governmental unit. Its role has expanded well beyond that ascribed to counties in 1854 by Chief Justice Taney of the Supreme Court, who wrote: "The several counties are nothing more than certain portions of the territory into which the state is divided for the more convenient exercise of the powers of government."[1] Today, counties manage airports and park services and provide services such as water, sewage, and fire and police protection, along with their typical role as assessors, judicial administrators and deed recorders. As their role has expanded, counties have been confronted with increasing financial woes and greater management difficulties. They have, as a result, been forced to turn to the federal government for increased assistance. For many years the federal government responded to the difficulties of local government by implementing categorical grants in response to immediate crises.

In 1968, talk began of New Federalism, the concept that decision making should return to local gov-

ernment, where elected officials have complete understanding of their citizens' needs. In the coming pages, the discussion will center on the components of New Federalism, their weaknesses, and areas counties feel are essential for the New Federalism to be a reality.

NEW FEDERALISM

The New Federalism is intended to be a response to the discovery that local units of government are better equipped to understand the needs and demands of the people in their locale than is a federal bureaucrat thousands of miles away in a Washington office building. Prior to this revelation, the federal government had provided financial assistance to other governmental units to execute programs designed and controlled by the federal government. The federal government was responding to citizens' needs in a crisis-oriented manner. The proliferation of grant-in-aid programs in the 1960s is evidence of crisis-oriented decision making. The result of categorical aid was confusion among local governments as to which of their projects could receive federal aid and from whom. Often one federal agency's prerequisites were contrary to another's. A county would frequently be confronted with the necessity of altering local priorities in order to receive federal aid. In an attempt to manage a comprehensive system of services to their citizens, county officials spent more and more time, not to mention money, pulling together dozens of federal programs and filling out federal forms for programs which only partially filled citizens' needs.

The New Federalism is purported to respond to these problems by returning decision making authority

1. Herbert S. Duncombe, *County Governments in America*, National Association of Counties Research Foundation (Washington, D.C.: Arrow Printing Service, 1966), p. 23.

and resources to local governments. Governmental activities should be as close to the people and as responsive to the people as possible, and the New Federalism, as embodied in revenue sharing and block grants, is a beginning on a long road back from federal domination, which peaked in the 1960s. There are two basic components of New Federalism: locally elected officials must be able to (1) determine local priorities within broad national goals and (2) design programs which will meet the needs of their citizens. This process cannot be complete unless local officials participate in setting national goals and priorities.

Revenue sharing

General revenue sharing is the key to the New Federalism. Under a complicated formula, the federal government allocates to local and state governments funds to be utilized as they deem appropriate within a framework of broad national goals.

Criticism of local governments' utilization of revenue sharing funds has raised the question of whether federal government continuance of the program is appropriate. Many areas have used the initial revenue sharing funds for capital expenditures rather than investing in long range programs. That should come as no revelation. County officials have seen numerous federal grant programs come to a sudden and unexpected demise, leaving them in the lurch with half-completed programs and no way to finance them out of their already badly expanded budgets. This is not true of capital investment which cannot be removed. Discussion about ending revenue sharing merely serves to prove those officials correct in their

fears about its future. It should be remembered, however, that delivery of social services depends on a facility, built with capital funds, to operate. Health care can not be delivered without a hospital; fire protection depends on fire engines.

Despite the uncertainty about whether the revenue sharing program will be continued, counties like revenue sharing. Many counties have reported that they have held public hearings about the use of revenue sharing funds. Many counties have used good, solid budget management techniques in planning the use of their revenue sharing funds, something they were unable to do with categorical grants because of the uncertainty of funding from year to year, or even from month to month.

Problems have resulted, however, from revenue sharing. Many counties have had to use revenue sharing funds just to fill the gaps in county services when funds for categorical programs were terminated. This is contrary to the initial administration proposal, which stated that revenue sharing would be in addition to categorical programs. Milwaukee's allotment for the first three entitlement periods was $16.5 million. Impoundments, freezes and cutbacks cost Milwaukee $75 million. Detroit got $57 million but lost $250 million. With the initiation of revenue sharing, the federal government has decreased the percentage of its domestic funds going to state and local governments, from 26.8 percent in fiscal year 1973 to a projected 24.7 percent in 1975. Revenue sharing cannot be meaningful unless the money the Internal Revenue Service collects from local units of government is returned to those units in greater amounts.

Integrated Grant Administration[2]

Today's public servicing problems cut across the lines of categorical grants. A county interested in developing a comprehensive program utilizing federal grants has to file separate applications, meet separate requirements, often receive funds at different times, and duplicate reports and audits for each federal agency. The Integrated Grant Administration (IGA) program is an innovative experimental program of the New Federalism enabling the packaging of related grants from different agencies. As such, it is a dramatic approach to cutting the enormous amount of red tape involved in gaining approval for federal aid. The January 1972 guidelines for IGA are a recognition of the meaning of New Federalism. For example: to provide a mechanism by which the state and local government can be given assistance in a timely and unified fashion, and to foster cooperation on the federal, state and local levels.

IGA presently handles 34 projects in planning and human services. This program saves administrative costs to both the county and federal agencies, freeing badly needed money for the program itself.

There are, however, problems with this program, as with all federal projects. A substantial amount of time is involved in coordinating all the agencies and receiving approval for the project proposal. Also, the problem of categorical grants is not eliminated, but only simplified. Counties still must apply for funds for a specific project and fill out innumerable forms on how and where every dollar is to be spent. IGA is an important step, but until the categorical system is simplified and unified, it can only ease the process and increase coordination and flexibility—certainly it can not ease all the red tape.

Special revenue sharing

Many argue that an addition to Integrated Grant Administration would be special revenue sharing or block grants. Presently, there has been talk of special revenue sharing in seven or eight different categories. Many of these programs have been killed in Congress. Education is an example of an attempt at forming a block grant program which failed before Congress. Health revenue sharing was given a great deal of publicity when the Partnership for Health Act, which consolidated seven single-purpose categorical grants into one general-purpose formula grant, became law in 1968. However, the health program [section 314(d) of the act] has not lived up to local officials' expectations. The present allotment is only $90 million yearly, and the authorization results in a fixed annual dollar allotment which is available to each state regardless of the different type, quality or geographic distribution of the services provided, or the size and adequacy of state and local funds contributed. Unless this program is greatly expanded and allocations distributed on a formula basis, the program cannot be deemed useful.

The other special revenue sharing programs are faced with many of the same problems: insufficient funding and inadequate distribution formulas. Special revenue sharing is better than categorical grants only if the sums allocated are large enough to have an impact. The 314(d) budget

2. *See,* Advisory Commission on Intergovernmental Relations, *Information Bulletin* (Washington, D.C.: Government Printing Office, July 1974), pp. 74–77.

covers only about 5 percent of the total federal, state and local monies spent on eligible 314(d) programs.

A bill with some potential is the Housing and Urban Development Act of 1974, which at the time of this writing was in conference committee in Congress. Unfortunately, the Senate-passed bill has no money allocated for the counties. Funds will go only to cities previously designated for urban renewal projects and model cities. The House version of the bill authorizes a new consolidated community development block grant program replacing existing urban renewal, model cities, water and sewer, open space and neighborhood facilities programs. Metropolitan cities (over 50,000) and urban counties (over 200,000 pop.) would be guaranteed an annual share of block grant funds based on an objective needs formula. Clearly, the counties are supporting the House version, which authorizes $8.05 billion for three years.

Special revenue sharing responds to two important criteria of the American governmental system. Congress can, through its allocations of funds, determine which issues it feels are of important national significance. Local governments can then best determine how to respond to the needs of their citizens within specific areas. One county's health care needs may be quite different from those of another county, yet both could benefit from federal funding for improvement of their health services. The same concept applies in other areas where revenue sharing has been considered.

A-85 review

One of the best tools for state and local input into program design and regulation preparation by the federal bureaucracy is the process outlined by Office of Management and Budget (OMB) Circular A-85. It provides chief executives of state and local governments acting through their national associations an opportunity to comment on major federal rules, regulations, standards, procedures and guidelines, on major interagency agreements concerning program operations, and on major organizational changes, any of which may have a significant and nationwide effect on state and local governments. The process also requires that, whenever possible, agencies consult with local and state governments well in advance of the formal development of regulations.

The counties are pleased with the A-85 process. However, neither the spirit nor the letter of the A-85 process have been followed by federal agencies. For example, OMB announced—with no prior consultation with state and local government—that federal aid to state and local pollution control agencies would be terminated. Another surprise federal government announcement was that major airports would be required to have round-the-clock security guards as an antihijacking measure. Local governments are consulted, if at all, only after the proposed regulations are virtually in final form. Almost no preconsultation occurs at an early stage of program design and regulation preparation so that states and localities may make their views known before federal agencies are committed to a certain point of view.

IMPROVING FUTURE INTERGOVERNMENTAL RELATIONS

Management assistance

OMB has said: "Federal, state

and local governments should cooperate in developing the necessary management, planning and evaluation skills that will enable all levels of government to manage more effectively and efficiently."

Management improvement is a vital ingredient of New Federalism. If power is to be returned to the people, counties and local governments must have efficient mechanisms to determine local needs and provide services which meet those needs. Very few efforts have been made by the federal government to assist local governments in developing management skills or even in making use of existing federal programs. For example, OMB Circular A-87 provides for federal government reimbursement of states and localities for certain central administrative costs of federally aided programs. This is a somewhat complicated and technical procedure with which few local governments have experience. Not only was no concerted federal effort made to assist and train local officials in the meaning and application of this circular, but also certain federal agency officials remain hostile to the concept and refuse to allow localities to make use of these provisions.

One program has been effective in upgrading the management skills of local government officials: the program established by the Intergovernmental Personnel Act, administered by the Civil Service Commission. This program has not only benefited personnel regulations at state and local levels, but also is now being used for management, stimulated through the efforts of the New County Center of the National Association of Counties (NACo).

In addition, the Advisory Commission on Intergovernmental Relations has developed a progressive position by realizing that in many areas counties should begin to function as regional entities. "Some counties already possess the geographic scope, regulatory powers, fiscal resources, and administrative capacity to occupy a pivotal position in areawide governance and service delivery."[3]

As the federal government delegates increasing responsibility to local governments to determine how best to use their limited resources, the need for improved management also increases. In previous years, the best management was on the national level within federal agencies administering categorical grants. It is time that the federal government aided the counties in sharing their expertise.

The counties have long recognized the need for administrative structures compatible with the type and extent of services they deliver. For this reason, the concept of county home rule has spread rapidly. With encouragement from the counties, 31 states have granted home rule or optional forms of government to counties. Other counties are modernizing their governments by clarifying the policy and administrative roles of county government through appointed administrators or use of the elected executive form of government.

NACo is also helping counties improve their management techniques by working with the state associations of counties' officers and NACo field representatives. The field representatives help identify management difficulties and assist counties in locating appropriate resources.

3. Advisory Commission on Intergovernmental Relations, *County Modernization: A Legislator's Guide* (Washington, D.C.: Government Printing Office, 1974).

Federal budget review

New Federalism cannot be complete without local government participation in outlining national goals and priorities. In many ways, federal and local government could be viewed as large and small gears. When the big gear turns just a little bit, by what it considers a minor policy decision, it can send the little gear spinning. This a truth quite apparent to the counties, but seemingly ignored by the decision makers in Washington.

Counties, other local governments and states firmly believe that they should participate in the federal budget process. During the early stages of federal budget preparation, consultation should be undertaken with appropriate state and local officials on major programmatic, fiscal and economic objectives to be achieved by the budget. If the idea of a New Federalism is to return decision making to state and local governments, then local and state governments, as program users, should be the major consultants on categorical programs, as far as their continuation, elimination or consolidation into block grant or revenue sharing programs is concerned.

The federal budget process should include in-depth analyses of intergovernmental fiscal and program impacts of new programs and any substantial modifications of ongoing programs. Those units of government involved in the daily planning and execution of federal programs are clearly those most knowledgable of the problems and the benefits of federal programs. Presently, local government has little input in determining the effectiveness of programs subject to cutback or termination.

Counties have been arguing for many years that appropriations for federal assistance programs should be requested on a multi-year basis, beginning with selected programs in fiscal year 1975 and moving toward multi-year requests for additional programs in subsequent budget years. Continual concern is that federal grants would be and often are abruptly terminated without forewarning. Too often, local governments are left in financial difficulties when the federal government suddenly decides that a program should no longer be funded. Rarely is a program completed within one year. Local governments should be given the flexibility to carry out a project from the planning stage to the implementation stage according to a pre-agreed time span.

In association with multi-year appropriations, the federal budget should insure adequate transition time and procedures for any major shift in funding or administration of a federal assistance program, particularly where shifts are from categorical to block grants or where they involve phase-out of an ongoing program. The reason for this proposal was the result of the introduction of revenue sharing, where, despite promises to the contrary, numerous categorical grants were suddenly ended.

Unless these proposals are implemented, New Federalism will be nothing more than an excellent idea on the books—without meaningful implementation.

CONCLUSION

The success of New Federalism will depend upon the strength of local governments—elected political leaders, administrators and planners. Local officials must press federal agencies to consolidate grants; encourage Congress to increase revenue sharing funds and develop special revenue sharing programs; demand management assistance; and reorganize their own governmental structures.

State legislatures must wrestle with local governmental reorganization. This will be a monumental struggle. However, New Federalism demands that counties occupy a position of strength in the governmental system. Counties must have the most effective form of government possible in order to handle adequately the increased responsibilities being placed on them as recognition that local problems must be handled on the local level grows. It is a struggle that the counties are prepared to handle, and handle well.

Intergovernmental Relations: a View from the States

By Brevard Crihfield and H. Clyde Reeves

ABSTRACT: Interstate relations can not be viewed apart from the broad concept of the American federal system. The utilization and viability of cooperative devices formally recognized by the Constitution of the United States, such as interstate compacts and agreements between states, are measurably offset by preemptive actions of the central government. There has been a vast increase in formal cooperative mechanisms among the states in past 30 years, accompanied by even greater changes in federal-state-local interrelationships. These changes have been accomplished without much regard for the theoretical framework in which decisions are made and functions are carried out. The authors describe states going about their business of rendering improved services to the people; of looking increasingly to each other for new and innovative approaches to problem solving; and of cooperating to increase their influence on federal policy. An emergent trend is discerned toward reversal of the theory that power is best exercised in the nation's capital. Circumstances indicate that the states today may take advantage of a golden opportunity to lead the way by working together to increase their individual and collective capacities.

Brevard Crihfield has viewed American government from the vantage point of the Council of State Governments for nearly 30 years. For the last 14 years he has been Executive Director and during this period has been associated with leading state and federal officials.

H. Clyde Reeves recently joined the staff of the Council of State Governments and is Director of Research and State Services. He has been a professor of political science at several universities and a long time official of the Commonwealth of Kentucky.

INTERSTATE relations cannot be viewed apart from the broad concept of the American federal system. For this reason the authors will touch upon facets ranging from interstate compacts to federal preemption; from history, to prognostics, to problem solving; and from substance to opinion. Many things, perhaps too many things, have happened since 1940 when THE ANNALS published a similar volume of essays. Nevertheless, the federal system has survived and has shown the necessary flexibility. In general, the subject matter to be treated in 1974 does not differ in kind, but rather in magnitude and methodology.

INTERSTATE COMPACTS

The most binding legal instrument to provide formal cooperation between states is known as the interstate compact or agreement.[1] Article I, Section 10, of the United States Constitution recognizes the device by declaring that "No State shall without the Consent of Congress . . . enter into any Agreement or Compact" with other states

1. Useful references to the background and utilization of interstate compacts include: Council of State Governments, *Interstate Compacts 1783–1970*, (Lexington, Ky., 1971); Frederick L. Zimmerman, and Mitchell Wendell, *The Interstate Compact Since 1925*, Council of State Governments, (Chicago, 1951); Council of State Governments, *The Law and Use of Interstate Compacts*, (Chicago, 1961); Council of State Governments, "Interstate Compacts," *The Book of the States*, vol. XX, (Lexington, Ky., 1974), pp. 267–270. Frederick L. Zimmerman, "Intergovernmental Commissions: The Interstate-Federal Approach," *State Government*, vol. XLII, no. 2 (Spring 1969), pp. 120–130; "The Role of the Compact in the New Federalism," *State Government*, vol. XLII, no. 2 (Spring 1970), pp. 128–135.

or with a foreign nation. Compacts actually pre-dated the Constitution, having been used mainly by the colonies for settlement of boundary disputes. Such boundary negotiations were almost the sole purpose of interstate compacts until 1920, and only 36 compacts were entered into during that first century and a quarter of the American union. Between 1921 and 1940, about 20 more compacts of various kinds were adopted; but between 1941 and 1970 over 100 additional compacts and agreements were negotiated. To depict the situation in somewhat more startling terms, more interstate compacts were developed after 1950 than during the entire period of American constitutional government to that date.

In relation to modern problems, two landmark compacts of the 1920s and one in the 1930s are outstanding. In 1921 New Jersey and New York created the Port of New York Authority for development of transportation, terminal and other physical facilities, as well as to promote commerce in the port area. This was the first interstate compact with powers to finance, build and operate public works. Later in the 1920s, the Colorado Basin Compact was designed to allocate water resources on a regional and inter-regional basis, with seven member states. This compact broke new ground both in function and in the number of participating states (all prior compacts had been bi-state agreements). In the mid-1930s, states joined in the first compact designed to meet pressing social needs. Under its terms, arrangements were made for cooperative supervision of parolees and probationers. The Parole and Probation Compact became subsequently the first interstate compact to be ratified by all 50 states.

The subjects now covered by compacts are myriad, including such varying fields as air and water pollution, bridges and tunnels, fisheries conservation, land and water resources, forest fire protection, mining practices, oil and gas conservation, corrections, juvenile delinquency, driver licensing, education, libraries, mental health, law enforcement, taxation, vehicle safety, navigation development, nuclear energy, pest control, planning and development, civil defense, disaster assistance, recreational parks, mass transit, and placement of children for foster care and adoption.

The newest, and perhaps most "intergovernmental" aspect of the compact approach, is exemplified in the Delaware River Basin Compact of 1961. Although this compact relates specifically to multipurpose development of water resources, the concept would be applicable to any activity in which all governmental jurisdictions must work together toward a common goal. In the Delaware River mechanism, the national government was made, by act of Congress, a full member of the compact body. This blending of state and national authority to meet a particular problem, utilizing existing agencies of the party jurisdictions wherever possible, was a unique and significant contribution to intergovernmental cooperation. Like the Tennessee Valley Authority (TVA), a completely national operation, the new federal-interstate compact combines management and planning. But unlike TVA, the compact coordinates and integrates the activities of state and federal agencies rather than displacing them. In sum, a joint body (1) melds legal powers of both governmental levels, (2) constitutes a single body of all interested governments, and (3)

does not preempt or displace existing functional entities. To meet the present crises that have developed with respect to energy shortfalls, the environment and land use planning —not to speak of the potential agony that these factors may yet cause in the remaining years of the 20th century—this positive, progressive device has great potential for the good of the nation and its people.

The Preemption Issue

Interstate cooperation can be no more viable than the viability of the 50 states that must work together and with the federal government. Weakening of the constituent units by a too-powerful central government can play havoc with any federal system of government, and the United States is not immune to that virus. Most observers are aware that Congress from time to time preempts state laws, but the concern at any given time tends only to affect one or another disparate group. The preemption issue has not been a subject of continuing attention or thorough analysis.[2] Preemption can occur in various forms, but its basic thrust is to deprive a state of jurisdiction over matters on which Congress acts. In some cases congressional action simply supersedes state law; in other instances states may be subject to forced compliance; and there are even complicated contingencies which specify what will happen if a governor acts, or if he does not act, or if his action is inadequate, as judged by a federal administrative officer or judge.

The variety of federal preemptive legislation is enormous. The object

2. For background information on the preemption issue, including citations, see, The Supersession of Sovereignty, Oklahoma Legislative Council, (Oklahoma City, May 1974).

may be an overriding national issue in the area of civil rights, or it may deal with such other matters as cigarette advertising, water quality, highway beautification, wheat allotments, noise control, egg products inspection or horse protection. Major preemptive legislation now pending in Congress, with pretty fair prospects of enactment, includes "no fault" automobile insurance and workmen's compensation, both of which involve regulation long considered proper for state supervision. Another preemptive development— one of serious concern to states—is the current trend of federal legislation containing "sanctions" whereby a state will, for example, lose highway or airport assistance under completely separate federal laws unless that state obeys guidelines that deal with land use controls. The issue of federal preemption carries significant overtones for the American governmental system.

This is not to say that Congress is always in the wrong when it embarks on a preemptive mission. But surely the gamut ranges beyond good sense and credibility when supersession becomes an indiscriminate habit. Regulation of everybody and everything is not necessarily the *summum bonum* of a legislative assembly, be it state or national. Legislative forbearance, like judicial restraint, has its place in the body politic. Congress is often urged to supersede state law as a means of promoting uniform applications throughout the nation, and on occasion the need will be manifest. On the other hand, interstate cooperative devices have shown their ability to achieve necessary uniformity and coordination in many areas of public concern. A federal system of government, by definition, envisions finer intergovernmental

tuning devices than does a centric doctrine.

The issues here raised deserve thoughtful consideration and meaningful efforts to utilize prescience in preference to preemption. Acts of force against governmental partners do not have a favorable record in the history of democratic commonwealths. Better and more productive means are at hand through imaginative development of interstate cooperation.

WHICH LEVEL CAN DO WHAT BEST

Scientific and technological change and rising expectations have produced a revolution in the functions of government, and in changing times the answers to questions highly relevant to the structure of government and the distribution of political power are not likely to be found by retreating into ways of the past. In recent decades, intergovernmental shifts in the distribution of power in the United States have been adopted characteristically in an atmosphere of urgency and under conditions responsive to political pressures. It can not be said that there were carefully considered general objectives or principles designed to enhance the effectiveness of government as a whole. Only recently have perspectives been developed that encourage the study of public programs and the methods by which they have impact on the governmental system. Preliminarily, this seems to be affirming some old conclusions and reaching some new ones.

The crux of any conclusions may well be keyed to a redefinition of the allocation of responsibility to levels of government. Prior to 1930, state-federal relations had typically settled into a pattern governed by strict construction of language in the Constitution. States, while asserting the legal right to define the structures, functions and powers of local governments, had delegated this authority, usually a little piece at a time, without much regard for the system being created. As the role of government began to expand in the days of the New Deal, all levels of government became involved, one way or another, in most governmental functions. For a while many deemed this to be the appropriate response. In more halcyon days Morton Grodzins described the American system of shared activities among governments as mildly chaotic, likened it to a "marble cake" and conceived it "as one government serving one people."[3] Later he observed that federalism "is a device for dividing decisions and functions of government."[4]

By the time the marble cake analogy had achieved general acceptance as a descriptive device, intergovernmental relations had become a major problem that consumed the energies of policy makers as well as bureaucrats. This was because public policy makers and administrators at all levels lacked a theoretical framework for decision making and functional responsibility.

How to make systems work in an industrial democratic society for effective delivery of services, broadly defined and on a large scale, is a principal concern of the public sector.

The elements of effectiveness change as problems change, and it might have been anticipated that the recent increase in government services would require very careful thought in the design of new models for implementing intergovernmental relationships. Unhappily, little thought has been given to adjusting a sturdy and well designed eighteenth century model to twentieth century conditions. As a consequence, a troubled nation is seeking, as never before and almost desperately, ways to make government more effective, more productive, more responsive and more accessible. The seeking is necessarily concerned with who is responsible and who is accountable. In a marble cake model the problem is horrendous.

Progress in better defining responsibility for actions of government can not have as its objective the simplistic model of a layer cake, but the model must involve a classification of functions. In any governmental organization, the nature and characteristics of a function have a bearing on where it belongs in the structural hierarchy. The underlying reason for this is especially important in the case of a federal system of government, because a function divided between levels of government must depend upon something in addition to legal authority to keep it alive.

In the American system, viable defining of responsibility relates to which government can do what best. Search the Constitution: this concept pervades it. Historically, legally, economically, and in common sense, any other approach to the allocation of responsibility among governments is imperious. Because many problems once considered private have become clothed with a public interest, value conflicts have

3. Morton Grodzins, "Centralization and Decentralization in the American Federal System," *A Nation of States*, ed. Robert A. Goldwin (Chicago: Rand McNally & Company, 1963), pp. 1–23.

4. Grodzins, "The Federal System," *Goals for Americans*, (Englewood Cliffs, N.J.: Prentice-Hall, 1965), p. 265.

multiplied and become involved in the allocation of governmental power. In the final analysis, it seems certain that improved working solutions to the allocation of power in the federal system will be hammered out in the political arena, with the states being very influential if they have a reasonable consensus about what their role should be. That role must be realistic in the light of generally accepted national objectives. A better and more common understanding about the mission of the states is essential to a truly new federalism.

For the central government to mandate or preempt the states frequently is the antithesis of federalism. For the states to act only out of political necessity, unregulated by generally accepted definitions of their responsibility, certainly passes the initiative to other levels of government and eventually will rob states of a significant role. How then may the application of constitutional principles be revised and updated to recreate a theoretical federal framework that will consume fewer resources in intergovernmental relations and provide more resources for improving service delivery?

In the 1960s, long range planning and choice mechanisms like the Planning-Programming-Budgeting Systems, were emphasized as governments experimented in these areas. In the 1970s, attention appears to be turning to the consideration of governmental capacity to deal with discrete problems. The outstanding example of this, of course, is revenue sharing, which is undergirded with the assumption that the federal government has a superior capacity for levying and collecting taxes. Revenue sharing may itself be the critical phenomenon, the catalyst, that enables objectivity in the allocating of

responsibility for many service functions of government. The inability to support a service and the desire of Congress to control the purse strings have powerfully influenced how things have been done in the United States. Some relief from the talons of financial necessity may enable American governments to do some things more wisely and economically than they would under a more conventional, Scrooge-like method of handling money. Many local programs involving state shared funds and the English experience with parliamentary support of borough budgets tend to validate this point of view.

Fortunately, other starts are beginning to be made in developing concepts that may be nurtured into powerful ideas on how best to organize governmental delivery of services. The economists, to analyze better the burdens and benefits of fiscal operations in the public sector, have classified government services in relation to their (1) marketability, (2) the ability of citizens to reject them, (3) the ability of government to exclude citizens from participation, and (4) the relation of price (or cost) to numbers served. This classification sheds light on the scope of the areal jurisdiction of the government entity best able to provide or administer the service.[5] The pure theory of economics of local government, spillover effects, and externalities are other economic concepts that may be useful in determining what government is best suited to do what.

Political scientists and public administrators have not yet grappled significantly with the problem of

5. See, Carl S. Shoup, Public Finance, (Chicago: Aldine Publishing Company, 1969), pp. 65–204.

rationalizing and disaggregating as well as integrating governmental power. However, this was clearly called for at the December 1973 Assembly of the States so that "we can turn to the real job of building delivery services through the respective governmental levels best suited to perform. . . . "[6] Some of the evaluative research currently being conducted by the Council of State Governments is concerned with the role of the states in various service delivery areas.[7] Governors and state legislators, representing the National Governors' Conference and the National Legislative Conference, are increasingly insistent that national laws, rules and guidelines reflect a realistic specification of the responsibilities of state and local governments. Academics "have just begun to reach for new tools"[8] to help develop a more viable theory of public administration and are beginning to deal with problems of centralization and decentralization of the federal system in terms of the values to be emphasized and the characteristics of the tasks.

HOPEFUL SIGNS

These were among the hopeful signs in late spring of 1974, when many observers of the American federal system were more than usually beset by misgivings. With the center

6. Council of State Governments, *Report of the Executive Director to the Governing Board*, (Lexington, Ky., 1973).

7. This implies equal concern for the roles of the federal and local governments. *See,* Council of State Governments, *The States' Roles in Solid Waste Management*, and, *A Place to Live: Housing Policy in the States,* (Lexington, Ky., 1973, 1974).

8. Peri E. Arnold, "Reorganization and Politics: A Reflection on the Adequacy of Administrative Theory," *Public Administration Review* (May-June 1974), p. 211.

of government laboring under the stress of Watergate, facing energy and environmental problems of great magnitude, and undergoing very severe inflationary inroads, there was no dearth of doomsayers about America's future. An American president, returning to office in early 1973 after an overwhelming victory at the polls, was at best the relict of a discredited administration and at worst a putative candidate for impeachment and conviction. Beyond that, in a period of only a few months, the governing authorities of nation after nation in the free world had toppled while the remaining democratic systems had reason to fear similar events. Indeed, the less democratic governmental forms were not in much better condition.

On the surface these are grim words in a grim world. Nevertheless, the authors are unwilling to accept a thesis that the United States, its federal system and its constituent states are doomed. The impeachment process, though rarely invoked, is a built-in provision of the Constitution. The governmental structure may sputter, but it will not grind to a halt. There is at least a fair prospect that positive reforms may derive from recent events. The separation of powers structure in the United States, despite its automatic invitation for abrasiveness between the executive and legislative branches, need be derogated no longer in comparison with parliamentary systems in Great Britain, Canada and Australia. The hiatus of ability to govern in those parliamentary nations can hardly be viewed as any improvement upon the American system. Things here may seem terrible, but the American political condition is not more parlous than elsewhere in today's world.

Perhaps standing aside to take the longer view may be appropriate, especially for those who believe in the doctrine that state and local governments should regain stature as equal partners in a cooperative federal commonwealth. In recent years the states have been thrust into the vanguard of governmental leadership. State governments, through determination, initiative and intelligent planning have been showing their capacity to cope with public burdens of immense complexity. This has repudiated very measurably the shibboleth that states are poorly endowed for service delivery and too feeble to survive.

To paraphrase a message delivered by Governor Marvin Mandel of Maryland, in his presidential address before the Council of State Governments' 1973 annual meeting, Americans should stand firm for the basic constitutional plan which (1) envisions a system of shared authority, (2) calls for harmonious cooperation without denigrating either side, and (3) seeks accomodation rather than conflict. While turmoil and confusion have reigned along the Potomac, the states have quietly been going about their business of providing worthwhile public services. The central government will not founder; hopefully, it will develop into a more responsible and responsive governmental partner. A trend is emerging toward reversal of the theory that power is best exercised in the nation's capital. Conversely, state and local officials should be less provincial and more interested in how their counterparts elsewhere are solving common problems.

Political scientists are now recognizing the validity of these new thrusts—new at least in the sense that such recognition has been sadly lacking in the past half-century. Daniel J. Elazar, director of the Center for the Study of Federalism at Temple University and a widely respected student of the art of government, has synthesized the current situation as follows:

Circumstances today have presented the States with their greatest opportunity in over a century to take the lead in serving the country. Not since the era of internal improvement that straddled the Civil War, when they were in the forefront of developing the groundwork of our industrial revolution, have the States been realistically offered such a chance to lead the way. The wherewithal to meet the challenges connected with this opportunity is now in the hands of state governments. . . .

In part, this is a function of the times. American political history has followed a consistent pattern at least since the Revolutionary era. Once in every generation there have been the right conditions plus sufficient public demand to stimulate a short period of intensive federal innovative activity . . . followed by a period of relaxation that has led to a rebalancing of intergovernmental relations. The present period, however, is more than simply another beat in the generational rhythm of American politics. Just as circumstances of the last decade have altered the federal government's role in economic and security matters so, too, have similar circumstances altered the potential role of the States. . . .

One of the great virtues of a federal system is the opportunity it allows for diverse responses to common problems. One consequence of this diversity has been an equal diversity in state interests. This, in turn, has kept the States from standing together on matters of common interest as fully as they should. Yet if the States are to be leaders, they must find ways to develop a common front on a wide variety of issues and to assist one another on a practical basis as well. Fortunately, the States already have a vehicle for doing so through the Council of State Governments and its associated organizations. . . .

Finally, and most importantly, the States must want to lead in building the Nation's future. Without the will, there is no way. In one sense, there is but little incentive for those aspiring to state leadership, whether political or administrative, to develop the will to lead. Monetary and career rewards will be just as great if they wait for others to lead, and the risks involved in seizing the initiative are not to be minimized. Why, then, should they do so? Only one answer can be given: because it will be good for the American people.[9]

Professor Elazar makes good sense. He is no so-called states' righter yearning for bygone days. He presents both a challenge and a viable opportunity for the states. He visualizes "a more perfect union" and a better nation, and he gives the best possible reason why state leadership—executive, legislative and administrative—should rise to the challenge: "because it will be good for the American people."

There is another hopeful signal on the horizon, potentially of very great significance, which can lead to more harmonious intergovernmental relations in the years ahead. States, counties and cities have all too often scattered their effectiveness at home and in the nation's capitol by bickering among themselves to their own detriment. But a great change has been emerging in the most recent decade. States no longer have the option to avoid involvement in the crisis problems of their political subdivisions; nor does the federal government have a viable choice to ignore the states in seeking remedies to local government malaise.

9. Council of State Governments, "A New Golden Age for the States: Do They Have the Will to Respond?" (Lexington, Ky., December 1973).

The states have shown their willingness to provide technical assistance to their local units of government by creating state departments of community affairs. Many states developed revenue sharing for their cities and counties well in advance of the federal government's first revenue sharing program. The number of state programs of direct assistance to local governments has increased vastly in recent years. In the enormously complex pattern of American intergovernmental relations the role of the states is pivotal. A nation the size of the United States cannot afford to go all the way down the path of unitary government. To ignore the values of the intermediate governmental level represented by the states is to invite administrative strangulation.

As never before in their history, the states, counties and cities are working together on common problems; and they are showing that joint action on a common front can wonderfully strengthen their voice in Washington. General revenue sharing would never have come to pass without the relentless and strongly united pressure that state governors and legislators, mayors and councilmen, and county executives and supervisors laid on Congress when the chips were down in 1972. All of the major associations of city, county and state officials now work closely together on an almost daily basis in considering their own initiatives as well as their responses to federal administrative and legislative developments. If this combination of state-local cooperation and mutual assistance can be continued and expanded, it will indeed be a formidable instrument. The time has passed for abrasiveness between statehouse, city hall and county courthouse. The stakes are simply too high.

New Directions in Interstate Relations

By THAD L. BEYLE

ABSTRACT: Despite their too often irrelevant boundaries and a long history of competitiveness, recent activities among the states suggest that they may be beginning to seek new ways of joint problem solving. There are several models of interstate cooperation available, and one, the interstate compact or agreement, is now very much in the forefront as a state-based vehicle to help states work with mutual problems. In the growth and development policy area, beginning with the stimulus of the federal-multistate efforts of the 1960s, new regional interstate organizations have been created to aid states and localities cope with unplanned growth and development. These new agencies do have problems of their own: a new manner of defining regions, a much greater expansion of roles than previous interstate agencies, and, importantly, an uncertain constituency base.

Thad L. Beyle is Director of State Services and Research for the National Governors' Conference. Currently on leave from the University of North Carolina at Chapel Hill, he also taught at Denison University and the University of Illinois at Urbana. He served in the Governor's Office of North Carolina, and has worked with the Appalachian Regional Commission, the Education Commission of the States, the Institute on State Programming for the 70s, the Southern Growth Policies Board and the Federation of Rocky Mountain States.

The author wishes to thank Tom Dark of the University of North Carolina at Chapel Hill for his considerable research and analytic skills, and the University Research Council for their financial support. Portions of this article were presented to the 1972 Conference of the American Society for Public Administration, New York, 24 March 1972.

THE STATES may be the least likely units of government in the American federal system on which to rely for the rational planning and controlling of future growth. There are 50 of them, many with boundaries having no relation to their problems, indeed many with boundaries artificially dividing those very problems. Each state has a unique identity, a set of peculiar political customs, and an individual governmental style. For years, the hallmark of interstate relations has been competition—each state trying to outdo or match sister states in development, while often trying to export or overlook problems.

This competition, while based on the American ethic, is not an unmixed blessing. The positive side sees the states leading in the development of the higher education system, as many states compete on the basis of achieving excellence in their institutions of higher education. As York Willbern notes, "A key element in the American dream, advancement and success by means of education and technical training, has always been associated with state governments. The state university is the one institution in which all citizens of the state, except those wealthy enough to send their children elsewhere, have a direct or potential interest."[1] Other examples, in such diverse areas as conservation, prison reform and mental health, vary from state to state, often depending on the idiosyncratic nature of the state, its political heritage and the type of leadership in state government.

But the diversity inherent in the accumulated strengths—and weaknesses—of the states has led them into competitive postures not always of a positive nature. For example, a perverse sort of reverse competition seems to obtain in the welfare system, whereby the least prosperous states, mainly in the South, continue grossly inadequate programs which virtually force those in need to seek help elsewhere. That elsewhere is well documented in the more affluent and urbanized states of the Northeast, Midwest and West. The welfare burden on these "recipient" states has become so great that attempts are being made by them to become unattractive for welfare seekers—and to call for federal assumption of the welfare burden.

Another type of competition lies in the drive of each state and its governor to attract new industry into the state, thereby creating more jobs, a larger economic tax base, and ergo, a more highly developed state. This has ranged from Mississippi's Balance Agriculture with Industry (BAWI) program; to Kentucky's and North Carolina's efforts to attract more research-oriented industries to their Spindletop and Research Triangle Parks; to former Ohio Governor James Rhodes' almost total emphasis on industry hunting and job creation. In fact, one careful observer of the gubernatorial scene suggests this may be one of the few major functions left to the governor in which he can have some sense of control and impact.[2] But too often a plan for rational growth in a state is overwhelmed once growth gets under way.

---

1. York Willbern, "States as Components in Areal Division of Powers," *Area and Power*, ed. Arthur Maass, (Glencoe: The Free Press, 1959), pp. 87–88.

2. Alan J. Wyner, "Governor—Salesman: Restrictions on Executives Have Caused Many to Focus on Industrial Promotion and Good Publicity," *National Civic Review* 56 (February 1967), pp. 81–86.

There are certain perverse effects here also. An attractive state to employers and employees is often one with lower taxes—hence the charge is made that states focusing on a strong economic development drive will be much less likely to impose new and broadened taxes, as they might scare away potential industry. While some suggest this to be a myth, it is probably more to the point to suggest that governors and legislators, taking due notice of peers who have had problems at the polls following tax raises, hesitate to impose new or expanded taxes in the first place, unless absolutely forced to. They can rationalize the lesser level of services obtained by a nontaxing decision by looking for an additional industrial base to provide government with more revenues and people with more jobs; or they can indicate that a reordering of priorities will allow for the necessary funds without having to resort to additional finances.

But in the 1960s problems overwhelmed the states, and new monies had to be raised. The concerted tax efforts in the states over the past decade ("in 1967, about one-half of the states raised taxes; in 1969, more than three-fourths took such action—an all-time record; and in 1971, the number of tax raises was second only to that of 1969,"[3]) placed taxation—be it repeal, reform or revolt—at the top of the list of citizen concerns across the states. Despite this activity, considerable variation in state tax structures still exists—and is played on to aid in developing a state's attractiveness to industry.

One further side effect of the comparative economic development approaches in the states is the "official" overlooking of the new industry's pollution potential. In the tradeoff between new industry, new jobs and additional sources of revenue versus possible pollution, the toss seems to go to more pollution.

Therefore, obvious and very possibly debilitating reasons exist for not counting on the states in approaching the problems of planning regional growth.

REASONS FOR MULTISTATE REGIONALISM

To think of bypassing the states by creating regions to fit current problems would certainly be more rational. One scholar recently suggested a "Thirty-Eight State U.S.A." to overcome the mismatch between state boundaries and problems.[4] Another says, "the main argument for regional organizations is that they are needed to respond to the problem of scale that arises when functions spill over state boundaries without, however, requiring nationwide attention."[5] But regionalism faces some hard realities, especially the pivotal position of the states in the federal system.

The power base of the states lies on a four-sided foundation: their constitutional role as "keystones of the American governmental arch;"[6] their administrative role in authoriz-

3. Leon Rothenberg, "Recent Trends in State Taxation," *The Book of the States,* 1974–75 (Lexington, Ky.: Council of State Governments, 1974), p. 224. *See also,* Deil S. Wright and David E. Stephenson, "The States as Middlemen: Five Fiscal Dilemmas," *State Government* (Spring 1974), for a more systematic review of recent tax activity among the states.

4. *New York Times,* December 1973, p. 24.
5. Martha Derthick, *Between State and Nation* (Washington, D.C.: The Brookings Institution, 1974), p. 6.
6. Daniel J. Elazar, "The States and the Nation," *Politics in the American States,*

ing, if not being major participants in, carrying out most of the programs in the federal system; their political role placing them "in the warp and woof of our national political fabric;"[7] and the notion held by many that although boundaries are oft-times artificial, the states are thought of or felt to be communities with certain aspects of their political life style tied to this sense of community. The first two sides of the foundation are structural and underscore the importance of the states in the intergovernmental system. The latter two are political, in that they lie in the views and votes of citizens. To those who call for the realigning of state boundaries so that more rational regional units might provide better governmental services, the sources of state power suggest not only that there would be serious conflicts on a constitutional and statutory basis, but also that politically such an approach is unthinkable—both for those calling themselves political leaders and, more importantly, for the citizenry who are socialized or attach themselves to the states as communities.

Therefore, the argument for regionalism, and the operational definition of it, must include the states—no matter how irrational this may seem to some and regardless of how fragmented an approach it may appear to others. Despite the problems involved, discussion of subfederal regionalism must be prefaced by the understanding that such regionalism must be multistate in character. To do otherwise is to miss the point of the American federal system and to show a lack of awareness of what is possible or not possible.

MODELS OF MULTISTATE REGIONALISM

Several models of multistate regionalism are available for review, and likewise various vehicles are being used. For years the series of regional Governors' Conferences have served, at first blush, as foci of regionalism in the states. However, this has always been more apparent than real, as they are more like gatherings than conferences. With few states, an historical concept and identity and some common problems, the New England Governors' Conference has become a major policy agency—other Governors' Conferences have not been as fortunate. This model is an entirely state-based and energized effort and can cover as broad and deep a range of policy as the governors in the particular conference wish. The governors come together based on the commonality of their governmental positions—not necessarily their states' problems or the proposed solutions.

The Appalachian Regional Commission (ARC) approach, along with the Title V multistate efforts, presents another model: a joint, multistate and federal endeavor to tackle the problems of development, or lack of development, in certain portions of the country. These commissions attempt regional development planning and are, in fact, a nuance of the federal grant-in-aid system. They are primarily concerned with expending more rationally certain joint federal-state programs, and thus must be considered part of the delivery system or, as one official of the ARC suggested, "sophisti-

ed. Herbert Jacob and Kenneth N. Vines (Boston: Little, Brown and Company, 1965), p. 449.

7. Terry Sanford, *Storm Over the States* (New York: McGraw-Hill, 1967), p. 7.

cated pork barrelling." (However, only the ARC, of these efforts, has had sufficient funding to meet even minimal goals).

While these regional commissions have strengths and weaknesses, there are at least two main drawbacks: (1) they take only a partial view to their planning, which is tied to the programs they are delivering (that is, 79 percent of the initial ARC monies were earmarked for highways), and (2) they too often have only parts of states within their bounds, which can lead to potential regional antagonisms and a fragmented statewide approach within these states. While the New England Regional Commission does not suffer from this, the state of North Carolina has the Appalachian Regional Commission in the west and the Eastern Coastal Plains Regional Commission in the east, and continual efforts must be made to achieve balance between these—as well as between them and the rapidly developing middle portion, the Piedmont. That these three regions have political meaning in North Carolina only exacerbates the problem of the partial approach. Vice President Agnew indicated to the February 1972 National Governors' Conference that steps were being taken to overcome the latter problem—but this remains to be accomplished, especially as these commissions are being phased out of existence.

A third approach is the ad hoc arrangements that states make to overcome particular problems. These range from joint agreements to work on a certain situation, to the more formal legal agreement or interstate compact. The compact mechanism has been used in many ways, from creating the Port of New York Authority in 1921, to the nation-wide Compact for Education in 1965. It has been called on to help deliver services, to resolve disputes, to regulate certain behavior, to provide mutual aid and to study and recommend courses of action.[8] "Authorities on the compact device appear to be in agreement that it is applicable for coping with legal and narrowly-conceived administrative problems that are in a sense caused by the federal system of government and that cannot be handled without involving the compacts in continuous political decision-making."[9] "They [have] never [been] used to shape and administer complicated and intricate problems of far reaching state social and economic policy."[10] With this limitation, compacts are "now clearly emergent" as devices of interstate relations[11] and appear indeed to be moving beyond their former constraints.

The compact has served a regional purpose especially well in New England, where "in the summer of 1966 the New England states adhered to forty-three compacts, ten of which had to do with boundaries. In one of their most successful ventures, these states coordinated their work in higher education under the New England Board of Higher Education, a compact agency established in 1955."[12] The southern states have been likewise well

8. Marian E. Ridgeway, *Interstate Compacts* (Carbondale: Southern Illinois University Press, 1971), pp. 17–18.

9. Welden V. Barton, *Interstate Compacts in the Political Process* (Chapel Hill: University of North Carolina Press, 1967), pp. 3–4.

10. Ridgeway, *Interstate Compacts*, p. vii.

11. Frederick Zimmerman and Mitchell Wendell, "Interstate Compacts," *Book of the States: 1974–75*, (Lexington, Ky.: Council of State Governments, 1974), p. 267.

12. Sanford, *Storm*, p. 112.

served by the Southern Regional Education Board (1949), as have 13 western states by the Western Interstate Commission on Higher Education (1951).

These mechanisms are not without problems, however. Marian Ridgeway lists 10 negative attributes after studying four interstate compact agencies from the perspective of the state of Illinois. These are: they are proliferating without sufficient proof of their worth; they are not being adequately evaluated; they are being used in improper areas (as a political expedient); they are inadequately policed; they are separatistic from the public and the states that created them; they are undemocratic and unrepresentative; they are often unresponsive to the general public but highly responsive to special interests; there is little gubernatorial control over them; and they soon come to be controlled by specialists.[13] However, as Ridgeway notes, some of these negative aspects apply to many parts of the federal system—not just interstate compacts.

But the potential strengths of the interstate compact or agreement are of greater interest to us—they can bring multistate political and governmental leadership together, focus it on a common problem, and, with the help of the specialists, undertake the action they were chartered to do.

All three of these models—the regional conference, the regional commission and the interstate agreement or compact—can be and have been called on to alleviate various problems in the states. The point of this article is that they are increasingly being used by the states,

and to attack broader ranging and more volatile problems—a change from their past use. One area of state concern—growth problems and policies—will be focused on to show how the states are attempting to use these interstate devices for the goal of more rational growth policies.

INTERSTATE RELATIONS AND STATE GROWTH

The federal government must be viewed as a critical actor in this surge of interstate activity. Most examinations of interstate compacts stress that interstate cooperation is often a response to a feared federal intrusion into a policy area traditionally left to the states. "The interstate compact agencies have provided a new dimension for state power. They permit the states to take continuing cooperative action in fields where they cannot act effectively or do not wish to act alone, fields which might fall by default to the federal power if not occupied through the initiative of the states."[14]

The establishment of the Education Commission of the States, by over 40 states in the mid-1960s, was looked upon by some observers as just such a "states' rights" effort, coming just as the federal government was moving into all levels of the educational system with grants, programs and guidelines. The fact that the Education Commission had the support of the United States Commissioner of Education, several so-called liberal national foundations, and major educational

13. Ridgeway, *Interstate Compacts*, pp. 295–6.

14. Richard H. Leach and Redding S. Sugg, Jr., *Administration of Interstate Compacts*, (Baton Rouge, La.: Louisiana State University Press, 1959), p. 6.

leaders, did not alleviate this fear.

Although many interstate agreements are still explained best with this anti–federal government rationale, the interstate activities concerning us and the potential new directions they are exploring can be traced in great part to the federal regional activities of the Johnsonian "Great Society." The economic development approaches formulated under the ARC, the Title V regional commissions and the Title II river basin commissions did much to broaden the states' perceptions of the potential uses of interstate mechanisms.

While these commissions must be considered as parts of the federal service delivery system, the notion that interstate agencies could enter a wide variety of policy fields almost certainly can be traced to the new actors and arrangements brought into the regional picture during the mid-1960s. An Advisory Commission on Intergovernmental Relations report talked to this point:

To overcome the defects of traditionally narrow approaches to economic development and water resources management, the commissions generally have been given broader program mandates than had been the case with earlier efforts. All involve the participation of more than one level of government and thereby benefit from a broader intergovernmental input. Economic development is not viewed as limited to public works, but includes health, education programs, and other human resources activities. Water resources management is viewed as having multiple concerns, including water supply and quality, waste management, watershed and flood plain management, power plant siting, recreation, and other water related land uses.[15]

Whether the regional commissions actually are fulfilling their multifunction mandate is not the most important question here. What is critical to the new directions interstate relations have taken is that the federal-multistate agencies serve as starting points for state-initiated and state-oriented organizations in policy areas broader than ever before. The states may have learned from the federal efforts' successes and mistakes, and the results are only beginning to be felt in state activities.

There is one further way that the federal government has been influential in the development of two recent interstate regional agencies, the Federation of Rocky Mountain States (FRMS) and the Southern Growth Policies Board (SGPB), both of which are interested in growth policy for their regions. The FRMS, formed in 1966 as a partnership between state government and industry in six western states, "initiates, stimulates, and supports commercial, scientific, technological, economic, civic, cultural and educational activities necessary to the orderly development of the region." The SGPB, formed in 1971 by the executive order of nine southern governors, is to "employ regional resources in planning and implementing public policy by identifying and analyzing regional influences, problems, and opportunities."

Here the decision was not to follow the model established by the federal government, nor was it to respond to federal initiatives in the development of more rational growth policy. In fact, the federal government was perceived (1) as part of the problem, with its myriad

15. Advisory Commission on Intergovernmental Relations, *Multistate Regionalism*, (Washington, D.C.: Government Printing Office, 1972), p. 210.

of programs, grants and guidelines tugging the states and their local governments in many directions—the least of which is a rational growth policy, and (2) as unable to formulate an adequate example of a rational growth policy, let alone coordinate its own activities in the states and regions of the country. Thus it is the vacuum of growth policy at the federal level which calls upon the states to act—however they wish to define that action.

The problems of growth policy formation or the management of orderly regional development are not the exclusive tasks of these interstate organizations—all levels of government are grappling for meaningful solutions. However, from the experience of the ARC and the regional commissions has come an increased awareness of the potential powers and uses of interstate approaches and new confidence that the states acting together can indeed make their impact felt. As the states begin moving in these new directions—stimulated by both federal activity and inactivity—the federal government may begin to change its view of these interstate devices. "In the past, Congress and federal agencies often urged the use of interstate compacts. This is not as true today. . . ."[16]

NEW APPROACHES TO INTERSTATE RELATIONS

Two major differences separate the "new" approaches to regional activities from their predecessors: (1) a different manner of defining region, and (2) an expansion of role for interstate agencies.

For most of the interstate agreements and compacts adopted over our governmental history, the problem of how to define an appropriate and useful interstate region was not critical. The boundaries of a region seemed natural to those devising interstate answers to the particular problem at hand. As long as interstate relations could be described primarily in terms of boundary disputes, river basin management or the bi-state operation of public facilities, the meaning and importance of the interstate region's composition was less relevant than they are today.

Now the very meaning of region in the context of interstate relations has expanded. "Starting as a geographic concept, it gradually was regarded as having economic and social qualities. Thereby, regionalism came to exhibit a composite quality which proved useful for a variety of political, administrative, and planning purposes."[17] Issues are being raised—and responded to—which transcend geography or traditional regional cultures.

For example, in neither the FRMS nor the SGPB, "is there any reason inherent in the subject matter to include precisely the states which in fact participate nor to exclude the next adjoining tier of states."[18] However, that growth policies or development strategies are no respecters of state boundaries is certain, but the question of which areas or states should compose a "growth region" is much less clear. The answer to which states are in or out of these particular interstate agencies is political—the governor and the state legislature decide whether they are a part of a particular region. Obviously, regional definitions are subject to the va-

16. Zimmerman and Wendell, "Interstate Compacts," p. 267.

17. ACIR, *Multistate Regionalism*, p. 1.
18. ACIR, *Multistate Regionalism*, p. 138.

garies of shifting political winds and the problems currently faced. That a new governor or a newly constituted legislature may demur from a prior decision is obvious. This suggests that such new interstate agencies may suffer from less political security than their predecessors have, especially with the changing role these agencies are undertaking.

The second major difference—that of role change—flows in part from the dilemmas facing the federal-state regional commissions over the past decade. There are markedly different options open to an interstate agency:

It may be a lobbying organization whose main function would be to lobby projects from the region through the Washington bureaucracy; or it may be an industrial development organization, selling the region to business and industry as an extension of state economic development agencies. A third role may be that of a research-information agency engaged in a continuous series of studies on regional problems, producing information and recommendations for others to act upon. Or it could be a public investment coordinating agency.[19]

To categorize, the newly emerging interstate agencies have chosen the study and recommendation option, with some passes at the other options available. They may in time be able to fill a pressing need in our society—what Frederick Hayes called "bridges between research and action."[20] In fact, there were

19. Edward F. R. Hearle, "Regional Commissions: Approach to Economic Development," *Public Administration Review* 28 (January/February 1968), p. 16.

20. Ralph R. Widner, "Regional Institutions for Improving the Public Utilization of Technology," *Technology and Social Institutions*, ed. Kan Chen (Proceeding of an Engineering Foundation Conference, Institute of Electrical and Electronics Engineers, Inc., 1974), p. 39.

National Science Foundation grants to both FRMS and the SGPB to inventory regional research capabilities, assess regional research needs in the public sector, identify barriers between these capabilities and needs, and then build bridges between "research providers and research users."

Of course this track poses the traditional problem of the planner or the planning agency—how are results of successful planning demonstrated and how can they hold political support? These questions are especially poignant for new agencies operating in a changing interstate political milieu. The time frame always seems just wrong: long term planning results for short term political actors, and actors from several states at that. Simultaneous satisfaction appears to be impossible; yet the very quick and enthusiastic support by the political actors involved in these two agencies at least suggests that a need is being addressed, and hopes are still being held that such an interstate role will be performed elsewhere.

PROBLEMS OF CONSTITUENCY

The most important problems which must be faced by these new types of interstate agencies relate directly or indirectly to the question of constituency: with whose support and for whose benefit are these new interstate relations conducted? Interstate agencies in the traditional sense have usually been able to identify at least a portion of their so-called relevant public—those counterpart agencies and professionals in each of the states who can be relied on to provide backup and impetus to their efforts. (Of course, many interstate agencies can be "captured" by these relevant publics, so the interstate effort loses its basic reason for being, becoming almost a lobbying force for these agencies and professionals.)

Such clear-cut constituencies are simply not a function of issues like growth management or development policy, as they are for river basin agreements, park commissions or bridge authorities. The consequences of this fact are far-reaching and must be considered in the context of these so-called new directions.

The nation's experience in the field of interstate relations would indicate that a truly regional constituency is unlikely in any case. "Despite the fact that most of the compacts set up a geographical district within which the agencies are authorized to operate, the party states have not regarded the compact agencies as regional units distinct from themselves. They plainly regard them as instrumentalities of state power which enable the states to work together in reaching particular goals . . . rather than for regional action philosophically conceived."[21] The result is that each state's political and administrative structures must be looked at in search of a constituency for these new agencies. This presents both strength and problems.

These agencies must rely on state governors and legislators as their principal sources of support. However, gubernatorial leadership in interstate relations is a two-edged sword. With active involvement of governors, the agency not only becomes subject to the political winds within the states described above, but also the agency can become

part of a particular governor's attempts to develop a constituency larger than his own state.

There is also the problem of attention span, and ARC's experience is instructive on this:

After the first crucial decisions following passage of the Appalachian Regional Development Act, gubernatorial participation in Commission decisions was delegated down further and further into the bureaucracy of many of the Appalachian states. This occurred because of the basically non-controversial nature of the program; governors of necessity spent their energy on crises and the most urgent issues of governance. But the lower the level of representation the less the capability to exact cooperation from state agencies other than the home agency of the state representative himself.[22]

Remember, the Appalachian program delivered tangible goods and services; these new interstate agencies do not have that role initially. Therefore, maintaining gubernatorial involvement is that much more difficult. However, without gubernatorial involvement, these new study and recommendatory agencies have no effective voice in state government.

The planning dimension of the new agencies would suggest state planning agencies would form a natural constituency for the new agencies. This does overlook the political realities of state planning today. The state planning process is not sufficiently developed in most states to form a basis for regional activities. Although the state planning process is rapidly being pressed into significant performance, it is

21. Leach and Sugg, *Administration*, p. 216.

22. Ralph R. Widner, "Transport Investment and Appalachian Development," *Public Administration Review* 33, (May/June 1973), p. 233.

still too early to determine the potential of planning agencies in regional concerns. The involvement of the state planning agency in the interstate arena is, however, a welcome alternative to the tradition of looking no farther than the state line when evaluating policy alternatives.

The lack of a visible and solid constituency throughout the states forces these agencies into the game of interstate constituency building. "Stroking" may be a psychological concept, but it certainly is apropos for describing what these agencies must do vis-à-vis governors and state legislators. A new breed of professional interstate actors exists—actors who build support for these agencies through very low-keyed stroking of the relevant political actors in each state. They carry the word back and forth between agency and state legislature, accentuating the positive and maintaining support levels in both directions.

Another effect of this lack of constituency is felt in the types of tasks undertaken by these agencies. Their agendas are no longer the traditional "once-and-for-all" solution to an otherwise intractable problem, but must be a continuing flexible search for approaches to some of the stickiest problems facing the states and the nation. Ralph Widner warns, "The danger inherent in many present efforts to assist in regional innovation is that, in attempting to prove useful to those they serve, they may be reduced to 'projectitis' and be deterred from providing the help which regional decision-makers need to evolve the large framework of social policy within which innovation must occur in the future."[23] The early decisions

23. Widner, "Regional Institutions," p. 43.

are the hardest, when the choice is between short term tangible results and longer range possible impacts.

Finally, it must be noted that this lack of a natural constituency places an even greater burden than usual on agency staffs. It is the staff which must seek out support, projects, direction, constituency and political leadership. Weakness in staffing capabilities and capacities can undo promise and potential.

Political leadership is the crucial factor in the success of interstate organization—since political leadership must provide the means for implementing the recommendations offered by the interstate agencies. While the problems faced by these agencies may appear immense, they can be ameliorated to a large extent by the presence of a few public officials—governors and legislators—who are willing to take the time and make the political effort necessary to lead these new agencies. In the absence of a well-defined constituency, particularly committed individuals and leaders are critical to the formation and effectiveness of these interstate study and recommendatory agencies.

CONCLUSION

Over the past decade, the states have raised their horizons, addressed controversial subjects, and refined techniques through interstate approaches. The interstate organization is now viewed, albeit cautiously, with new hopes. But as much as the interstate approach has changed, the interstate agency must change too. No longer can those interested in interstate cooperation focus their efforts on the agreement itself or on the category into which it falls. What happens after the agreement is signed is a field of study promising to be as broad as is the subject matter of the agreements themselves. Pinpointing the exact effects of individual decisions is not possible, but the pattern which emerges may prove useful as a guide to the new directions of the next decade.

To recognize the critical role of leadership, the importance of project selection and the necessity of guber-natorial involvement is one thing. The challenge is to determine the necessary combinations which mean the difference between effective-ness, mere self-maintenance, or oblivion. Whether the states' work-ing together can indeed make a dif-ference in these new and important arenas is still open to debate. The organizations discussed—the new directions in interstate relations—may indeed provide an answer.

Dillon's Rule Reconsidered

By John G. Grumm and Russell D. Murphy

ABSTRACT: Dillon's Rule has been a guiding doctrine in the constitutional relations between state and local government for more than a century. Simply stated, it declares that local jurisdictions are the creatures of the state and may exercise only those powers expressly granted them by the state. Historically, this doctrine represented a response to the revolutionary changes of the latter half of the nineteenth century and was part of the struggle to control and reconcile the often conflicting demands of the old and the new. Though not always at a steady pace, state centralization mounted during this period. Eventually a countermovement emerged, identified with the proponents of home rule. The latter, however, had only a minor impact in arresting the erosion of local autonomy. In the face of the overwhelming political, economic and social forces of the twentieth century fostering centralization, the constitutional controversy originating with Dillon's Rule became less relevant as a determinant of state-local relations. The kind of centralization that eventually emerged was one in which power was concentrated in functionally-defined bureaucracies which essentially transcended geographically-defined levels of government. The recognition of this development fostered new home rule movements aimed at weakening the grip of professional bureaucracies and returning greater discretionary authority to the *political* officials at the local level. Such programs as the war on poverty, model cities and revenue sharing represent the attempts to diminish the influence of bureaucracies on local policy.

John G. Grumm received his Ph.D. from the University of California at Berkeley and is presently Chairman, Government Department, Wesleyan University. He has been research director for the Citizens Conference on State Legislatures and staff director for the Federal Advisory Committee on Higher Education. He is author of A Paradigm for the Comparative Analysis of Legislative Systems *(1974),* A State Agency for Local Affairs *(1961) and* Metropolitan Area Government *(1959).*

Russell D. Murphy received his Ph.D. in political science from Yale University in 1968 and is currently an Associate Professor of Government, Wesleyan University. His book, Political Entrepreneurs and Urban Poverty, *is an analysis of New Haven, Connecticut's efforts to establish a prototype program for the national war on poverty.*

DESPITE its venerable heritage, Dillon's Rule remains a source of confoundment to laymen and specialists alike—as well, one suspects, to more than a few members of the bar and the bench. On the face of it, the Rule seems sufficiently straightforward, to wit, there is no common-law right to local self government and, as creatures of the state, localities may exercise only those powers expressly granted them. The Rule, however, is deceptively simple and of limited value to those hoping to understand state-local relations, past or present.

That the Rule is a source of confoundment is hardly surprising, for lurking behind its apparent simplicity is a variant of an old and troublesome philosophical question, "who should govern?" This, obviously, is not a matter that can be resolved by general rules or the deductive method alone, at least not in a democratic society. Indeed, the more cynical might conclude that the Rule is less useful in predicting such matters as the degree of centralization in state government or the outcome of court cases than is, for example, a table of random numbers.

A second and equally important difficulty exists. Debate and discussions of the Rule are usually framed in terms of the center and the periphery, of state versus local authority. This is unfortunate, for the more interesting question, quite often, is not whether state or local government is responsible for a given function, but rather what state-local functional alliance prevails. The state government is an appellate arena where those who lose locally, or expect to lose there, can press their case anew.[1] This is as much a reality

today[2] as it was during the late nineteenth century, when the Rule formulated by Judge John Forrest Dillon of the Iowa Supreme Court first gained currency.[3]

THE CONSTITUTIONAL HERITAGE

Historically, Dillon's Rule was part of the groping that marked the nation's efforts to adjust to the generally nonviolent but nonetheless revolutionary changes of the nineteenth century. Philosophically and institutionally, as well as physically, the nation was largely unprepared for what Adna Weber termed "the most significant social phenom-

---

of the reverse. An example is low income public housing. Most states had passed enabling legislation prior to the enactment of the federal Housing Act of 1949, when public housing was less a controversial policy. Rather than seeking reversal of the enabling legislation itself, opponents sought, and in some states obtained, legislation requiring local referenda approval before any public housing could be built. See, Leonard Freedman, *Public Housing: The Politics of Poverty* (New York: Holt, Rinehart and Winston, Inc., 1969), pp. 40–45.

2. This political reality is recognized by the courts and often serves as justification for judicial intervention to "protect" local "minorities" from local "majorities." See, Note, *City Governments in the State Courts*, 78 HARVARD LAW REVIEW 1596 (1965). One difficulty in any policy to protect local minorities is, of course, the choice of which minority to protect. This is especially true if local politics are characterized less by permanent or stable "majorities" and "minorities" and more by fluid and shifting coalitions, themselves consisting of various and diverse minorities.

3. Dillon enunciated his Rule in *City of Clinton* v. *The Cedar Rapids and Missouri River Railroad*, 24 IOWA LAW REVIEW 455 (1868). The case involved the city's challenge to a state statute granting the railroad the right to seize, without compensation, as much of the city's streets as the railroad needed to complete its lines.

---

1. While such appeals are usually from the local to the state arenas, there are instances

enon of the century," urbanization.[4] The years between 1830 and 1900, especially, were years of rapid growth in the population of cities, of extensive immigration and internal migration, and of intense economic activity. They were years, also, in which new demands confronted local governments, when both the scope and the stakes of local politics expanded dramatically, causing alarm to some and opportunities for others.

The alarm, in part, was the alarm experienced and expressed during any period of rapid social change that endangers familiar and established patterns and statuses. It was intensified, moreover, by the great and novel experiment of the day, namely, universal manhood suffrage. This experiment, coupled with the on-going demographic revolution, threatened to swamp existing political institutions and transform the composition and character of local leadership. At very best, urban democracy was an uncertain matter, particularly for previously dominant local elites.

It was within this setting that Dillon's Rule gained currency. This is not to say the struggle between established and emerging elites was the only factor. Other powerful forces, in commerce, industry and transportation, for example, were demanding centralization, standardization and uniformity. Nor was it the case that Dillon's Rule marked the invention or even discovery of the principle of state sovereignty and state supremacy. This had long been acknowledged, although earlier applications of the principle seem generally to have been free of the

latter-day conflict—in large measure, one suspects, because the society was more homogeneous and because there were fewer opportunities for loss as well as for gain. With the growth in opportunities, however, and with the shift in the composition of the urban electorate,[5] the principle of state supremacy acquired new and expanded operational meanings.

In the legislative arena, this principle was translated into increased state intervention in so-called local affairs. During the latter half of the century, there was a dramatic rise in the instances of special—as opposed to general— local legislation. Through these, legislatures acted to shift authority from one local faction to another, for example, by mandating capital projects to be financed by city monies and more generally by assuming what at times amounted to administrative responsibility for city affairs.[6] At times the intervention was reasonable and fair; at times it was excessive and unwise; at times it was even humorous, at least in retrospect. But whatever its merits, or lack thereof, state intervention was sufficiently disruptive of political and economic power that it occasioned intense opposition and challenge.

4. Adna Weber, *The Growth of Cities in the Nineteenth Century* (New York: Columbia University Press, 1899), p. 1.

5. To cite one notable example, New York City's budget rose from $676,000 (1830) to $87,020,000 (1903). In 1800 the city was spending 1.7 times as much as the state; in 1880, 13.3. In 1830 the foreign born population was only 9 percent of the city's population. By 1855 this had risen to 52 percent. By 1900 approximately 75 percent of the population was either foreign born or of foreign or mixed parentage.

6. While some of these special acts are chronicled by turn-of-the-century reformers, most remain "lost" in the statutes—a rich and as yet untapped source on the evolution of the nation's political and governmental institutions.

One arena for challenge was the court, and as state intervention mounted, so too did the instances of litigation. In the main, the outcomes were disappointing, at least for champions of local self government. There were dissenting voices, to be sure,[7] but generally speaking federal and state courts legitimated state intervention in pronouncements that at times were both sweeping and near intimidating. According to Justice William H. Moody of the United States Supreme Court, for example:

The number, nature and duration of the powers conferred upon [municipal] corporations and the territory over which they shall be exercised rests in the absolute discretion of the State . . . The power is in the State and those who legislate for the State are alone responsible for any unjust or oppressive exercise of it.[8]

Or, in the words of John Forrest Dillon some 39 years earlier:

Municipal corporations owe their origins to and derive their powers and rights wholly from the legislature. It breathes into them the breath of life, without which they cannot exist. As it creates, so it may destroy. If it may destroy it may abridge and control. Unless there is some constitutional limitation on the right, the legislature might, by a single act, if we can suppose it capable of so great a folly and so great a wrong, sweep from existence all of the municipal corporations in the State and the corporations could not prevent it . . . They are, so to phrase it, mere tenants at the will of the legislature.[9]

The growth in legislative initiative, while the most dramatic, was but one of the new and expanded meanings given the general doctrine of state supremacy. There was another application as well, one that proved a far greater challenge than direct state intervention to the interpretive skills of judges, local officials and private citizens. This was the so-called doctrine of expressed powers. In brief, local governments were conceived as convenient administrative devices created by legislatures to implement state policies. As such, they were delegates of the state, and the exercise of any delegated authority was to be both scrutinized closely and construed narrowly. Only those powers "granted in express words [or] necessarily or fairly implied in or incident to the powers expressly granted [or] . . . essential to the accomplishment of the declared

---

7. The most instructive, in the sense that it represents an opinion quite distinct from that which eventually prevailed is *People ex rel. LeRoy* v. *Hurlbut*, 24 MICHIGAN LAW REVIEW 44 (1871). At issue was a Michigan statute ordering the Detroit Commissioners of Water and Sewers to vacate their office—which at the time controlled substantial city tax and bond revenues—in favor of a State Department of Public Works. In ruling for the city, Judge Thomas Cooley invoked a number of familiar themes, among them that local governments pre-dated the states and hence were entitled to self-government, a right they previously had enjoyed and had not relinquished under statehood. In addition, Cooley argued, local governments were essential to the decentralization of power, which in turn safeguarded citizens against the despotic tendencies of centralized state governments.

8. *Hunter* v. *Pittsburg*, 207 UNITED STATES 161, 178 (1907). In the Hunter case, the Supreme Court upheld a Pennsylvania annexation statute which delegated the annexation decision to a combined rather than a concurrent majority of Pittsburg and Allegheny. Plaintiffs from the smaller community, Allegheny, alleged this constituted a denial of due process in that their

property tax rates would be substantially altered by the change.

9. *City of Clinton* v. *The Cedar Rapids and Missouri River Railroad*, 24 IOWA LAW REVIEW 455, 462–463 (1868).

objects and purposes of the corporation" were to be allowed.[10]

While qualifications such as "fairly implied" and "essential to the declared objects" were not self-defining, the effect of this judicial guideline was to impose the burden of proof on the locality. Unlike the state, unless a locality could convincingly demonstrate otherwise, the presumption was that it had acted *ultra vires*. In practice, this doctrine, along with permissive state provisions for taxpayers suits,[11] proved a powerful resource for those opposed both to the expansion of the regulatory or service state or to particular local administrations, whether machine dominated or not. Actual or threatened court challenges came to be a factor in the policy making calculus,[12] as did the choice as to whether local officials wished to don their supplicants'

robes and endure the vagaries of seeking explicit state authorization, in some instances from representatives who were their own hometown political rivals.

The doctrine of expressed powers fueled state initiatives and provided legislators a political as well as constitutional rationale for intervening —their actions, they could argue, were both judicially sanctioned and responsive to local "requests." Thus frustrated in the judicial as well as the legislative arenas, champions of local self-government turned to yet another arena, that of constitutional politics.

The continual legislative interference in purely local matters, "Frank Goodnow noted in 1895," has caused us to resort to the remedy to which we had resorted before, in order to protect the sphere of freedom of private individuals. We have incorporated into most of our later state constitutions, provisions which limit very largely the power of the legislatures to interfere with the affairs of municipal corporations.[13]

At the time, the movement to provide constitutionally for some degree of local autonomy was well underway. What came to be known as the Home Rule Movement combined, like most political movements, diverse interests and pursued a variety of strategies and objectives. One objective was the prohibition of special legislation. To this end, some proponents of home rule pressed for constitutional mandates banning such legislation, on the assumption that state legislatures would exercise greater restraint if required to deal with localities collectively rather than individually. Others sought a more direct remedy, one requiring

10. John Forrest Dillon, *Municipal Corporations*, vol. 1, 5th ed., 1911, pp. 448–449. Quoted in Terrance Sandalow, *The Limits of Municipal Power Under Home Rule: A Role for the Courts*, 48 MINNESOTA LAW REVIEW 643, 654 (1964), p. 650, note 26.

11. In terms of standing in the courts, localities are far more vulnerable to judicial scrutiny than are either the state or federal governments. Since the mid-nineteenth century, citizens as taxpayers, even though not otherwise directly "harmed" by the action of municipal governments, have been granted the right to obtain judicial review. For a discussion of this constraint on local governments *see*, Note, "Taxpayers Suits: A Survey and a Summary," 69 YALE LAW JOURNAL 895 (1960).

12. As Terrance Sandalow notes, this may have a cautionary influence on local officials or be used by them as an excuse for not acting. *See*, Terrance Sandalow, *Limits of Municipal Power*, p. 656. At the same time, more entrepreneurial local officials may capitalize on the very uncertainty surrounding grants of authority to innovate. Moreover, while the burden of proof rests on the localities, the burden of initiation rests on the plaintiff and these costs may be sufficient to deter litigation.

13. Frank Goodnow, *Municipal Home Rule: A Study in Administration* (New York: Columbia University Press, 1895), p. 56.

local concurrence before special legislation could go into effect.

As defensive perimeters around local government, constitutional restrictions on special local legislation were all too easily breached. For one thing, most of the limitations, then and since, applied typically to a limited range of issues—charter adoptions, the appointment of officials, annexation and consolidation, and franchises.[14] Second, the adoption of these constitutional provisions gave rise to evasive legislative tactics that once again demonstrated the richness of the political imagination and the elasticity of the law. The most familiar of these was the classification of cities and the technique of framing legislative acts applicable to all localities with a given characteristic rather than to a specifically named city. This technique, sanctioned by the courts, often allowed legislatures to circumvent constitutional prohibitions on special local acts. A general law, applicable, for example, to all cities with populations over one million, is in fact, if not in name, a special local act in a state that has but one such city.[15]

Whatever their limitations, constitutional restrictions on special legislation did provide a rallying point for early advocates of local autonomy and the organizational basis for subsequent efforts. By contrast, these efforts were concerned less with curbing legislative abuses and more with loosening judicial constraints on local initiative. Over the years this has become the predominant concern of home rule champions, as they have searched for and experimented with various formulas to counter the effects of the expressed powers doctrine.

Of the formulas devised, the most successful in terms of adoptions has been the constitutional provision granting local control over the organization of municipal corporations. Although these provisions vary from state to state, generally they grant localities broad, though not exclusive, authority over their charters, including their design and adoption and the allocation of responsibility and authority among municipal officials.[16]

---

14. Frank Goodnow, *Municipal Home Rule*, pp. 45–63, lists a number of the earliest restrictions. Individual state constitutions should be consulted for more contemporary data. An extremely useful source for these is the "Index Digest" included in *Constitutions of the United States: National and State*. This constitutional compendium is the work of the Legislative Drafting Research Fund of Columbia University (Dobbs Ferry, New York: Oceana Publications, Inc., 1974). *See also*, Citizens Conference on State Legislatures, *State Constitutional Provisions affecting Legislatures* (Kansas City, Mo.: Citizens Conference on State Legislatures, 1967), pp. 35–37.

15. Like most remedies, moreover, constitutional restrictions on special legislation had undesirable and perhaps unforeseen side effects. As Sandalow notes: "The task of

obtaining authorizing legislation [as required under the express grant doctrine] may be most difficult for the municipality when the legislature is restricted by an effective prohibition on local legislation. Although the authorization may eventually be forthcoming, the necessity of drawing legislation generally applicable throughout the state means that enactment may have to await crystallization of opinion on a statewide basis . . . Often, too, the strength of the opposition to the municipality's proposal may be increased by the required application of the legislation to areas where the problem is less acute, or, perhaps, non-existent." Terrance Sandalow, *Limits of Municipal Power*, p. 654.

16. These powers extend to such matters as the executive budget, veto, and length of term in office. Charter reform, of course, has been an enduring feature of American local politics and the occasion of intense political battles, particularly over the city manager plan.

In itself, of course, control over the charter is meaningless if municipalities lack constitutional or statutory authority over substantive matters. Securing this authority proved more troublesome. Early constitutional assurances that municipalities had jurisdiction over so-called local affairs, for example, were of limited value, given their lack of specificity. Moreover, neither legislative history nor case law provided much in the way of guidance. After reviewing numerous cases of the day, Frank Goodnow concluded, somewhat dolefully one suspects: "the decisions do not reveal any definite conclusion as to what are corporate or municipal or internal . . . affairs." Indeed, with such assurances municipalities were only slightly less vulnerable—if even that—to the doctrine of expressed powers.

Efforts to specify, by way of enumeration, the scope of local affairs were somewhat more effective. But even these, it turned out, left municipalities vulnerable to the doctrine of expressed powers. Given the complexities of any political system, it is difficult to catalogue each and every municipal responsibility and even more so to anticipate and provide for each and every eventuality. Whether for practical, political or epistemological reasons, therefore, enumerations were characteristically incomplete, and any attempt to infer other powers from those already granted was often frustrated by the doctrine of expressed powers.

While most operative home rule provisions are of the sort discussed above, some few have, as it were, turned the doctrine on its head.

17. *See*, Columbia University Legislative Drafting Research Fund, "Index Digest," *Constitutions of the United States: National and States* (Dobbs Ferry, New York: Oceana Publications, Inc., 1974), p. 15.

Again the precise wordings differ, but the formulas generally stipulate that localities have the power to adopt and amend laws not inconsistent with the constitution and general laws of the state. This variant on the Tenth Amendment to the United States Constitution is the most direct contravention of Dillon's Rule thus far devised. Though by no means universal, the formula has been adopted, *inter alia*, in New York, Pennsylvania, Alaska, Colorado and Maryland,[17] as well as by the National Municipal League in its 1964 Model State Constitution.

While this variant on the Tenth Amendment avoids the ambiguities and semantic difficulties of other home rule provisions, it nonetheless leaves localities very much the so-called creature of the state. Constitutionally, the states remain sovereign, and the exercise of this sovereignty continues to have important implications for the management of local affairs. Though courts are perhaps more permissive in home rule jurisdictions, the formally decentralizing provisions of state constitutions seem to have had little bearing on the overall balance between state and local governments. For one thing, there is considerable state by state variation in the extent of local autonomy, but none of this, as shall be shown presently, appears to be associated with the constitutional or statutory status of home rule. Moreover, most measures seem to indicate a steady erosion of local autonomy, despite the increase in the number of states with constitutional home rule provisions designed to eliminate or minimize the effects of Dillon's Rule.

CENTRALIZING TENDENCIES

A key factor in maintaining and even increasing state power over localities is the almost universal imposition of state restrictions on local fiscal powers. Home rule does not mean fiscal autonomy, and this, of course, is crucial. It is meaningless to grant local governments broad authority over substantive issues if they at the same time lack the fiscal capacity to act. But such, in fact, is often the case. Fiscal constraints, mandated either constitutionally or statutorially, include limits on local taxation, bonding and expenditures.

Few states, the most permissive home rule states included, provide local units of government much flexibility or discretion over revenues, even over those commonly defined as "revenues from own sources." Generally, what sources may be tapped is subject to explicit state approval. Until recent years the most productive of these sources was, of course, the property tax. This productivity is influenced, however, by both the private market and state regulation. Many states limit the yield on this major source of local revenue by imposing a ceiling, usually in terms of a maximum percentage of assessed valuation, on the amount that can be raised.

State limits on local bonded indebtedness are equally stringent and at times far more detailed. At least two-thirds of the states have constitutional limits on some, if not all, local debts. As in the case of the property tax, these limits usually are specified in terms of assessed valuations. A number of states limit the tax rate that may be levied for debt service, and most require municipalities to submit bond proposals to referenda.

Despite the limitations and restrictions, local government revenues are extensive, and compared to their late nineteenth century coun-

terparts, contemporary local public officials probably have greater discretion in allocating these public monies. Still, there are state-imposed restraints even here: both constitutionally mandated minimum expenditures for such public functions as education, libraries or zoological gardens[18] and statutory requirements that one unit of local government appropriate funds to support programs administered by another.[19] More indirectly, most states have enacted general laws governing civil service, collective bargaining, and retirement for public employees, and increasingly these are having an expansive effect on municipal expenditures. Conversely, some localities are prohibited from allocating public funds for private or nonpublic purposes. Historically, many of these restrictions date from the mid-nineteenth century and were imposed to curtail the at times reckless municipal investments in internal improvements, railroads included. Today

18. Legally, education is a state function, and even in those cities where major fiscal responsibility is lodged with the general institutions of government, members of a board of education are "officers of an independent corporation separate and distinct from the city, created by the state for the purpose of carrying out a purely state function." *Lanza* v. *Wagner*, 97 AMERICAN LAW REPORTS 2d 344, 351. Moreover, the general institutions of government, despite their fiscal responsibility, have limited discretion over educational expenditures. Though permitted to cut education budgets, mayors and councils often are prohibited by state law from specifying where the cuts should occur.

19. Chicago, for example, is required to provide funds for public aid programs administered by the Cook County Department of Public Aid. Boston is responsible for funding the government functions of Suffolk County, a county which includes, in addition to Boston itself, three surrounding communities.

these same limitations often pre-
clude municipal grants to private,
nonprofit corporations of the sort
that gained popularity in the war on
poverty.

Whatever the constitutional or
statutory limitations, there are other
realities, more fundamental perhaps, that restrict still further the
fiscal policies of localities. Not the
least of these is the greater fiscal
capacity of state—and federal—
governments. In large measure this
is a function of territory—the more
inclusive a unit of government, the
greater its taxing and bonding potential[20]—and increasingly this potential is being realized. As a result,
there has been a shift in the shape of
fiscal federalism, and this has a major
bearing on efforts to modify the effects of Dillon's Rule.

The shift is reflected, albeit imper-
fectly, in the distribution of state-
local revenues. Measured in these
terms, the balance of power has
altered dramatically in favor of the
states. At the turn of the century,
localities were clearly the dominant
of the two—in 1913, for example,
close to eighty percent of combined
state-local revenues were raised
locally, from local sources. In the
course of the century, however, local
preeminence declined, and by 1970
the relative standing of the two had
been almost completely reversed, as
shown in table 1.

These are national averages, however, and like all averages they con-
ceal important variations among the
states. Interestingly, these variations
seem unrelated to constitutional
home rule. Of the five states with
the highest level of state centraliza-

20. See, among others, William Riker,
Federalism: Origin, Operation, Significance
(Boston: Little, Brown & Co., 1964).

TABLE 1

STATE-LOCAL FINANCIAL RESPONSIBILITY
FOR SELECTED YEARS

	1913	1932	1957	1970
Percent of state-local revenues raised locally	79.4	61.6	44.8	38.1
Percent of state-local revenues raised by states	20.6	38.4	55.2	61.9

SOURCE: G. Ross Stephens, "State Centralization and
the Erosion of Local Autonomy," Journal of Politics 36
(February 1974), p. 58.

tion[21]—that is, those in which more
than 70 percent of state-local revenue in 1969 was collected by the
state—three have constitutional
home rule and two do not. In this
respect, at least, home rule provisions seem to have little bearing on
the relative standing of state and
local governments.

To an extent, the rise in state revenues corresponds to an expansion of
traditional state functions. This is
not the only factor, however, for increasingly states have assumed direct operational responsibility for
functions previously delegated to
localities. Even in the most permissive home rule states, local authorities generally must yield to this exercise of sovereignty, and as the scope
of state functions expands, the range
of laws "not inconsistent with the
constitution and general laws of the
state" contracts.[22]

21. The five states are: Hawaii, Alaska,
West Virginia, New Mexico and Vermont. As
this suggests, the most centralized states seem
to be the least populous and the least
industrialized.
22. The relationship is not always, however, entirely straightforward. While state
laws often preempt local ordinances and
regulations, ambiguities nonetheless remain. Such has been the case, for example,
when localities enact ordinances that are
more stringent than statutes regulating the
same behavior or activity. For a discussion of
this general issue, see, Note, Conflicts Be-

One indication of this general contraction is the decline in the number of public functions for which state and local governments share fiscal responsibility. Between 1957 and 1969, according to G. Ross Stephens, these functions declined in nearly all states. More to the point here, as the number of shared functions declined, the number of state dominated functions increased.[23]

Programmatically, the increase in state activity bears on a range of contemporary concerns, few of them as publicized or as potentially far-reaching as the environment. Environmental pollution, in all its sensible manifestations, seeps readily across local boundaries, and this seepage has had, as it were, a corrosive effect on them. To control spill-outs, state governments have increasingly imposed general policies and standards on localities, thus curbing further the effective exercise of home rule. There have been similar state initiatives in the closely related area of land-use planning. In Colorado, Vermont, Florida and Maine, comprehensive state land-use programs have been developed to which local authorities must, in varying degrees, conform.[24] In California, Delaware and Washington, coastal zone management programs largely determine usages in these areas, and in Connecticut and New Jersey, the states have, in effect, assumed control over both the use and development of wetlands.

Even in those areas of traditionally shared—or predominantly local— functions, state participation has broadened markedly. An example is the long neglected area of mass transportation, where states, particularly on the eastern seaboard, have accepted greater responsibility for financially hard-pressed transit systems.[25] More generally, the level of state participation has increased in virtually all areas of local public policy—in education, police, corrections, highways, public welfare, health, hospitals and housing. The magnitude of this change is suggested by the shift in the sources of local revenues. Historically, these were derived almost exclusively from local sources, particularly the property tax. In 1902, for example, 94 percent of local revenues were from these sources, and as recently as 1955 close to three fourths were

---

tween State Statutes and Municipal Ordinances, 72 HARVARD LAW REVIEW 737 (1959).

23. G. Ross Stephens, "State Centralization and the Erosion of Local Autonomy," Journal of Politics 36 (February 1974), pp. 59–61. Stephens classifies functions by revenue source. State financed functions are those in which 60 percent or more of state and local expenditures are provided by the state; locally financed functions are those in which local units provide 60 percent or more. The remainder are defined as shared functions.

24. If the recommendations of the Douglas Commission are adopted, the federal government would encourage the development of comprehensive state land-use programs by denying some federal aid to those states

without them. See, President's Commission on Urban Problems, Building the American City (Washington D.C.: Government Printing Office, 1968), pp. 237–238. At present there is no such federal policy though a number of congressmen, led by Representative Morris Udall (D, Az.), are pressing for a greater federal voice in this general area.

25. In this regard, half the states now have departments of transportation or enabling legislation to create them. Council of State Governments, The Book of the States, 1974–1975 (Lexington, Ky., 1974), p. 350. In New York, Massachusetts and Maryland, the state governments have attempted, with varying degrees of success, to extend state subsidies for both operating and construction costs. In Maryland, the state recently assumed sole responsibility for public transportation in the Baltimore metropolitan area.

still of local origin. Throughout the century, however, local revenues from local sources have declined as a proportion of total local revenues, despite their steady increase in absolute, constant dollar terms. As local sources diminished in relative importance, state support increased, and although there are variations from state to state—and indeed within states from locality to locality —the historical trend has been toward greater state financial support for local government functions.[26]

For the most part, this support has been channeled through categorical grants-in-aid, and while states are free of the constitutional impediments that condition federal grants, they nevertheless have relied on them as instruments of state policy. Politically, of course, this so-called outside money has its attractions. Few voters are concerned about the redistributive implications of state taxing and expenditure policies—or so it would seem, since this is far less a grass-roots issue than are spiraling local tax rates. But such is the human condition that nothing is entirely free, and in policy terms state support has its price, if not in limiting local discretion, then at very least in determining who, *locally*, will govern.

THE VERTICAL INTEGRATION OF PUBLIC FUNCTIONS

The discussion thus far may evoke the image of mayors and councilmen

26. In fiscal year 1971–72, state transfers accounted for 30.7 percent of total local revenue, compared to 5.7 percent in 1902. Though more publicized, *direct* federal aid to localities has risen more modestly, from 0.4 percent in 1902 to 3.3 percent in 1971–72. This does not include, however, federal monies that "pass through" the states to localities.

losing much of their autonomy to governors and legislators—who in turn are yielding more and more to presidents and congressmen. In actuality, centralization of this sort is less important than is the functional concentration of authority in professional bureaucracies. Stated somewhat differently, discretionary authority has shifted less *among* political officials than it has *from* them to bureaucratic experts and professionals.

Of the various and varied bureaucracies, the most influential, perhaps, are those in the field of health, education and welfare. If so, they are hardly unique. Nationally, bureaucratic power has expanded steadily during the twentieth century, and today professionals and experts are probably the most important participants in such diverse areas as law enforcement, housing, urban and environmental planning, and transportation.

Whether this development has favored federal bureaucracies more than state or local ones is debatable, but the question is relatively less important with respect to these organizations than it is with respect to political officials. The professional and programmatic commitments of bureaucrats typically lessen their identification with any level of government. As a result, bureaucracies are generally well-integrated across, and largely transcend, geographical boundaries.

Paradoxically, the rise in the power of functional experts was fostered in part by local political officials themselves. Since at least pre–New Deal depression years, these officials have pressed vigorously for increased state and federal support, particularly for new and expanded grant-in-aid programs. These programs, however, typically earmark funds for general program areas. More to the point, local bureaucrats, along with their federal and state counterparts—and often in alliance with them—have a major voice in determining how, within broad legislative guidelines, these funds will be spent.

The widespread bureaucratization of public policy prompted what might be loosely termed a modern-day home rule movement. This, at least, is one perspective on many recent political experiments, particularly those that gained popularity during the 1960s and early 1970s. The experiments are diverse and at times tenuous—police review boards, community planning boards, community school boards, community action programs and model cities. But generally speaking, they have one common thrust, namely, the curbing of bureaucratic power or, at the very least, the expansion of participation in bureaucratic policy making.[27] Moreover, there is irony in at least some of these. In seeking federal and state support for such programs as the war on poverty, model cities and Law Enforcement Assistance Administration (LEAA), local political officials are in a real sense searching for ways to counter the effects of the bureaucratic alliances fostered by their former efforts to elaborate the grant-in-aid system.

Similar broad objectives underlie federal revenue sharing. Since this money is distributed automatically on a formula rather than a grant basis, is administered by the Treasury

27. For an analysis of one of the earliest experiments of this type, see, Russell D. Murphy, *Political Entrepreneurs and Urban Poverty: The Strategies of Policy Innovation in New Haven's Model Anti-Poverty Project* (Lexington, Mass.: Heath Lexington Books, 1971).

Department rather than by program-oriented agencies, and is provided with relatively few strings attached, it has the potential of enhancing the discretionary authority of local political officials. As yet, however, its impact has probably been limited. For one thing, the authorized level of expenditure, $6.0 billion annually, must be distributed among 50 states and some 33,000 local governments. Moreover, it is still too early to determine how local officials will treat these funds. It is unclear, for example, whether they will see an opportunity to make local policy more responsive to local constituents, and, if so, whether this response will alter the policy thrust of the grant-in-aid programs; on the other hand, local officials might treat these funds, as some critics of LEAA maintain, as a windfall for which they will not be held accountable and which, therefore, they can squander.

CONCLUSION

While Dillon's Rule may have some effect at the margins, political and socio-economic considerations are far more important factors in shaping intergovernmental relations. Similarly, attempts to reverse the Rule by means of various constitutional home rule provisions have achieved little in the way of practical results. Generally, local governments in states with such provisions fare no better or no worse in maintaining local autonomy than do those in other states.

In the final analysis, the most significant trend in federal-state-local relations is not the geographical centralization of power, but rather the concentration of power in functionally-defined bureaucracies at all levels. Constitutional-legal issues involved in either Dillon's Rule or home rule are not particularly relevant to this development. It can only be reversed, assuming one wants to reverse it, by returning some discretionary authority to political officials at each level of government. As far as state and local jurisdictions are concerned, this means lessening the role of conditional grants from higher levels of government and an expansion of local sources of revenue or, at least, an increase in the unconditional sharing of revenues between governments.

The Metropolitan Area Problem

By Joseph F. Zimmerman

ABSTRACT: Intergovernmental service agreements, transfer of functional responsibility to the county and state levels, establishment of regional special districts and state-controlled public authorities, and federal preemption during the past fifteen years have combined to effect major changes in the metropolitan governance system. Available evidence suggests that few metropolitan governments will be created by popularly approved charters during the next decade and the ones created probably will be located in the South. The upward transfer of functional responsibility, however, will incrementally transform a number of counties into metropolitan governments. The failure of charters creating area-wide governments to win voter approval and the growing seriousness of metropolitan problems have been responsible for state and federal initiatives seeking solutions for the problems. The most important state initiatives have been the establishment of the Twin Cities Metropolitan Council and the creation of state-controlled public authorities in New York. The federal initiative has taken the form of promotion of interlocal cooperation and exercise of preemptive powers. Whereas interlocal cooperation has failed to solve the major problems of the metropolis, partial federal preemption of the right to regulate air and water pollution abatement has enhanced the quality of the environment.

Joseph F. Zimmerman is Professor of Political Science at the Graduate School of Public Affairs, State University of New York at Albany, and formerly served as Director of the school's Local Government Studies Center and Chairman, Department of Political Science. He currently serves as Research Director, New York State Select Legislative Committee on Transportation, and as a Contributing Editor of the National Civic Review. His publications include The Federated City: Community Control in Large Cities and The Massachusetts Town Meeting: A Tenacious Institution.

METROPOLITAN problems since the turn of the century often have been attributed to jurisdictional fragmentation on the local government level, and numerous campaigns have been launched to establish areawide governments with sufficient powers to solve the problems. Voters in most areas, however, have not been convinced of the need for a comprehensive reorganization of the local government system. During the past 27 years, the concerned electorate have approved only 11 charters consolidating the central city and the county, and one charter establishing a two-tier system with a strong upper tier—Metropolitan Dade County, Florida.[1] Available evidence suggests that in the near future voters only occasionally will ratify a charter establishing a major areawide government, and an affirmative vote is most apt to be cast in the South because of a number of relatively unique factors.[2]

Significant changes in the unrestructured metropolitan governance system nevertheless have occurred during the past 15 years as the result of a sharp increase in the number of intergovernmental service agreements, the upward shift of responsibility for functions to the county and state levels, establishment of locally-controlled regional special districts, creation of state-controlled public authorities, and federal preemption.

SERVICE AGREEMENTS

Pressures for a major restructuring of the metropolitan governance system have been lessened by the increasing use of formal and informal agreements for the provision of services to local governments by other local governments, the state, and private firms. Several reasons account for the growing popularity of such agreements—a municipality may be able to obtain a service or a product which it can not provide itself, the quality of the service may be higher and costs may be lowered, agreements do not seriously impede the freedom of action of the parties to the agreements, and the structure of the local government system is not altered in a fundamental way.

Of 2,248 municipalities over 2,500 in population responding to a 1972 questionnaire, 1,393, or 61 percent, reported they were receiving services under provisions of formal and informal agreements.[3] The tendency to enter into agreements is positively correlated with the size of a municipality and its form of government, with larger municipalities and council-manager ones having the greatest propensity to enter into agreements for the receipt of ser-

1. For details on the politics of metropolitan reorganization, see, Vincent L. Marando, "Voting in City-County Consolidation Referenda," Western Political Quarterly (March 1973), pp. 90–96; Joseph F. Zimmerman, "Metropolitan Reform in the U.S.: An Overview," Public Administration Review (September/October 1970), pp. 531–43; and Joseph F. Zimmerman, "Mergers Reviewed for Local Units," National Civic Review (September 1972), pp. 417–19.

2. Zimmerman, "Metropolitan Reform," pp. 535–39.

3. See, Joseph F. Zimmerman, "Meeting Service Needs through Intergovernmental Service Agreements," The Municipal Yearbook: 1973 (Washington, D.C.: International City Management Association, 1973), pp. 79–88; Joseph F. Zimmerman, "Intergovernmental Service Agreements for Smaller Cities," Urban Data Service Reports (January 1973); and Joseph F. Zimmerman, "Intergovernmental Service Agreements and Transfer of Functions," in Substate Regionalism and the Federal System, ed. Advisory Commission on Intergovernmental Relations (Washington, D.C.: Government Printing Office, 1974), vol. 3, pp. 29–52.

vices. Cities, towns and villages enter into agreements most frequently with counties—61 percent —and other municipalities—40 percent. State governments and public authorities also are major providers of services—28 percent of the respondents receive services from the state and 16 percent receive services from authorities.

Only 13 percent of the agreements call for the provision of a package of services. Most agreements involve only two governments and one service, and the services provided— fire and police mutual aid, jails, civil defense and water supply— tend to be relatively noncontroversial. The small number of package agreements can be explained by the fact that few local governments have the ability and the desire to provide several services to another local government.

Although many municipalities had received more than one service from another local government prior to 1954, the concept of a contract providing for a large number of services did not originate until 1954 when the newly incorporated city of Lakewood, California signed a formal contract with Los Angeles County to have it provide all municipal type services to Lakewood citizens.[4] All 32 cities incorporated in that county since 1954 have contracted with the county for a package of services.

A typical service package includes animal regulation, election services, emergency ambulance services, enforcement of city health ordinance, engineering services, fire and police protection, library, planning and zoning, street construction and maintenance, and street lighting. Certain services—animal regulation, for example—are financed by fees. Other services—fire protection, library, sewer maintenance, street lighting—are financed by means of special tax districts administered by the county. All other services are financed by direct reimbursement of county costs by the recipient cities.

Seventy-seven cities in the county currently are parties to contracts for the receipt of services.[5] All 77 receive election services under contracts, all except Vernon have contracted for state health law enforcement, and all but Santa Monica have contracted for the maintenance of city prisoners in the county jail. As the result of the package contracts, Los Angeles county provides a sizeable number of services on an areawide basis.

With a few exceptions, the reason checked by respondents for entering into service agreements was to take advantage of economies of scale rather than to improve the quality of services. Municipalities generally are satisfied with service compacts if dissatisfaction is measured by resort to discontinuance— only five percent of the municipalities had terminated agreements.

The use of agreements to provide services and products may be viewed as a limited and temporary form of function consolidation with

4. See, California Government Code § 51301 and Los Angeles County Charter § 56 ½.

5. Considerable bargaining takes place between the county and the municipalities, as each municipality has several alternatives to entering into a contract with the county. A municipality can purchase services from another city, produce its own services, obtain services from a private firm or join a special service district. See, Robert O. Warren, Government in Metropolitan Areas: A Reappraisal of Functional Political Organization (Davis: Institute of Governmental Affairs, University of California, 1966), pp. 224–33.

policy making decentralized and administration centralized. Closely related to the use of agreements is the shift of functional responsibility.

UPWARD SHIFT OF RESPONSIBILITY

The growing magnitude of a number of metropolitan problems, particularly environmental ones, and failure to muster sufficient voter support for the creation of an areawide government have combined in some states to promote interest in the upward shift to the county and state levels of responsibility for functions perceived to be best performed on a broader geographical basis.[6] Eleven states—Alaska, California, Florida, Illinois, Michigan, Missouri, New York, Ohio, Pennsylvania, Tennessee and Virginia— have specific provisions in their constitutions authorizing functional transfers. In several other states, the legislature has authorized functional transfers.

The achievement of economies of scale, more even service provision throughout the entire area, and a more equitable system of financing the service are the principal arguments advanced in favor of an upward shift of functional responsibility. It should be pointed out that partisan considerations may be at least partially responsible for a transfer. Economies of scale may not result from a transfer, even though

unit costs generally tend to decrease with an increase in output, because diseconomies of scale may be encountered as output continues to increase.[7] Whether efficiency and equity will be improved depends, of course, on the upper tier unit's quality of service and method of financing, compared to the quality of service and method of financing employed by cities, towns and villages. Unfortunately, few studies have been conducted to determine whether the transfers have achieved their objectives.

Relatively few data are available on the extent of voluntary and involuntary transfers and the reasons therefor.[8] Questionnaires returned by state municipal leagues, state association of counties and state agencies for local affairs in 1974 reveal that responsibility for few functions has been transferred upward to the state level. The most major transfer occurred in 1960, when Connecticut abolished organized county governments and transferred county functions to the state level. In 1965, responsibility for district courts, public schools, hospitals, and burial of indigents in Hawaii was shifted from counties to the state government.[9] Rhode Island assumed responsibility for public health in 1966, and public welfare was transferred to the state level in Delaware and Massachusetts in 1968. Twelve states have

---

6. There has been little state interest in a comprehensive reallocation of functional responsibilities. However, Governor Ronald Reagan of California in 1972 inaugurated a Local Government Reform Program which, among other things, will determine the proper assignment of functions to the various levels of government.

7. Advisory Commission on Intergovernmental Relations, "Size Can Make a Difference—A Closer Look," *Information Bulletin*, 16 September 1970.

8. A national survey of incorporated municipalities will be conducted by the author in 1974 to collect data on the frequency of transfers, reasons for the transfers, and the impact transfers have had on the perceived need for subcounty special districts, a modernized county government, a multicounty regional service agency, and a council of governments (COG). The results will appear in an Information Bulletin to be published by the Advisory Commission on Intergovernmental Relations.

9. *Hawaii Laws of 1965*, Act 97.

laws making the state responsible for the regulation of coastal lands and wetlands. In November 1972, for example, California voters approved Initiative Proposition 20, creating the Coastal Zone Conservation Commission and mandating preparation by 1976 of comprehensive growth plan for a five-mile-wide area along the 1,000-mile coastline. Until the plan is prepared and adopted, all proposed development in a 1,000-yard-wide strip along the shoreline requires the approval of one of six regional commissions, composed of citizens and public officials, with the statewide commission authorized to veto any proposed development. Construction of buildings which would obstruct the view of the ocean from shoreline highways are prohibited, and homeowners must obtain a permit for additions costing in excess of $7,500.

Functional transfers from the municipal to the county level appear to be occurring with increasing frequency. In a number of instances, the transfer is statewide, as in Florida, where property tax administration has been shifted to the county level, and in New York State, where welfare has been shifted to the county level.[10] More commonly, a function is shifted from one or more municipalities to the county. In New York, since 1947 the following functions have been transferred from municipalities to Monroe County: airport operation, civil defense, public health, major parks and the public safety laboratory. In addition, the city of Rochester and the county jointly are responsible for planning, the civic center, the port authority, the youth board, human relations, probation, vital statistics, consumer

protection, and library, museum and public defender services. As one would anticipate, counties with home rule charters usually are responsible for more functions than are noncharter counties. In New York, charter counties on the average provide 35 services compared to 21 services provided by noncharter counties.

The Metropolitan Dade County charter authorizes the Board of County Commissioners or a city council to hold a referendum on the question of transferring a function to the county and also empowers a city council by a two-thirds vote to request the county to assume responsibility for a service.[11] Although voters in 1968 disapproved a proposed charter amendment consolidating all police and fire-fighting functions on the county level, Florida City and North Miami, in 1968 and 1969 respectively, turned over responsibility for fire protection to the county. Thirteen other municipalities have voluntarily transferred fire protection responsiblity to the county. In addition, library programs and voter registration have been surrendered to the county by seventeen and nine municipalities respectively.

A most interesting development is the adoption of home rule charters by Dade County and Volusia County in Florida, partially preempting responsibility for functions. The Dade County charter, adopted in 1957, authorizes the Board of County Commissioners to "set reasonable minimum standards for all governmental units in the County for the performance of any service or function."[12] If a municipality fails to com-

---

10. *New York Laws of 1972* (McKinney, 1972), ch. 28.

11. *Metropolitan Dade County Charter*, art. 1, § 1.01 A 18 (b).
12. Ibid.

ply with the standards, the county "may take over and perform, regulate, or grant franchises to operate any such service."

The Volusia County charter, approved in 1970, grants the county the power of preemption with respect to protection of the environment.

County ordinances shall prevail over municipal ordinances whenever the County shall set minimum standards protecting the environment by prohibiting or regulating air or water pollution or the destruction of the resources of the County belonging to the general public.[13]

THE STATE ROLE

The states have played one or more of three roles—inhibitor, facilitator or initiator—relative to the formation of general purpose metropolitan governments. In several states, the formation of such governments is impeded by constitutional requirements. The New York State Constitution, to cite only one illustration, requires the separate approval of voters of cities as a unit and voters of towns as a second unit within a county before a function can be transferred by a city or town to the county.[14] The transfer of a village function to the county is more difficult since a triple concurrent majority—separate affirmative votes in referenda by city voters, town voters and village voters—is required.

State legislatures have facilitated the creation of general purpose metropolitan governments by establishing or authorizing the establishment of study commissions and

by passing enabling legislation for the creation of areawide governments. The appointment of commissions to study the local government system in metropolitan areas was a popular response by state legislatures to growing areawide problems in the 1950s. In the 1960s, however, conditions attached to various federal grant-in-aid programs resulted in a significant change in the number and nature of surveys. There was a sharp rise in comprehensive land use and transportation studies, while the number of studies concerned with governmental organization declined from 40 in 1960 to 34 in 1966 and 29 in 1967. Thirty-six such studies were launched in 1968.[15] A national survey of study commissions has not been conducted since 1968, yet it is apparent that the number of commissions concerned with reorganization of the local government system in metropolitan areas is small today.

More than four-fifths of the states also have attempted to facilitate the resolution of regional problems by enacting statutes authorizing, and in some cases encouraging, intergovernmental agreements and cooperation. Currently, 42 states have a general interlocal contracting law. In 29 of these states, local governments may cooperate with neighboring units in other states.

Three-fourths of the municipalities responding to a 1972 questionnaire indicated active state government encouragement of intergovernmental provision of services. Forty-eight percent reported that the state provided incentive grants-in-aid, 42 percent mentioned financial assis-

---

13. *Volusia County Charter*, § 1305.
14. *Constitution of the State of New York*, art. IX.

15. Joseph F. Zimmerman, ed., *Metropolitan Surveys* (Albany: Graduate School of Public Affairs, State University of New York, 1966–68).

tance, and 56 percent reported technical assistance. One hundred nine municipalities, however, reported that state statutes impeded their ability to enter into service agreements. Two provisions in many interlocal cooperation acts restrict the ability of local governments to enter into compacts. A power may not be exercised in 32 states unless each local government possesses the power. This means that a city and a town can not provide a service jointly if only the city possesses the authority to provide the service. The general interlocal cooperation statute in 13 states further restricts the ability of local units to enter into agreements by stipulating that an individual statute authorizing cooperation in a specific functional area is not superseded by the general statute. In New Jersey, there are approximately 200 specific statutes.[16]

Although Rhode Island lacks a joint exercise of powers act, the state has a general law specifically authorizing cities and towns to establish councils of governments (COGs) which "may, by appropriate action of the governing bodies of the member governments, exercise such other powers as are exercised or capable of exercise by the member governments and necessary or desirable for dealing with problems of mutual concern."[17] No COG has yet been authorized to exercise a power capable of exercise by a member government.

To facilitate the solution of particular metropolitan problems, state legislatures have enacted laws authorizing voters to decide in a referendum whether to form a single or multipurpose metropolitan special district. Currently, there are 900 such districts in the United States. To cite only one example, the Oregon Metropolitan Service District Act of 1969 authorizes the holding of a referendum on the question of the formation of a metropolitan district with authority to provide four services—sewage treatment and disposal, solid waste disposal, public transportation, and flood control. Creation of a district was authorized by the electorate on May 26, 1970 in the Portland area—Multnomah, Clackamas and Washington Counties.

States have sought to solve environmental problems by totally or partially preempting responsibility for a regulatory function. Rhode Island has forbidden cities and towns to enact air pollution control ordinances and bylaws, whereas Delaware allows local governments to establish standards higher than those established by the state air pollution control agency.[18]

Massachusetts and New York in the nineteenth century directly initiated the establishment of metropolitan governments as numerous towns were annexed to the city of Boston by mandate of the General Court, and New York City was formed in 1898 by a legislatively directed amalgamation of all local governments within a five-county area. Despite the precedent of direct state action, no other major consolidation of local governments was ordered by a state legislature without provision for a referendum until the Indiana Legislature in 1969 enacted a law merging Indianapolis and Marion

16. *Joint Services—A Local Response to Areawide Problems* (Trenton, N.J.: County and Municipal Government Study Commission, 1970), p. 38.

17. *Rhode Island General Laws Annotated*, §§ 54-43-3.

18. *Rhode Island General Laws Annotated*, § 23-25-19 (1968); *Delaware Code Annotated*, tit. 7, § 6207 (Supp. 1968).

County.[19] This merger must be viewed as an isolated one resulting from special circumstances in a state lacking a home rule tradition. It is highly unlikely that a state legislature will mandate another major consolidation within the next decade. The more likely prospect is that state legislatures in northern states will facilitate the establishment of a federation within large cities with a citywide level and a neighborhood level.[20]

The most important state-initiated organizational response to growing areawide problems during the past decade is the metropolitan council established for the seven-county Twin Cities area in 1967 by the Minnesota Legislature without a referendum.[21] The council's chairman, who serves at the pleasure of the governor, and 16 other members are appointed by the governor for overlapping six-year terms with the advice and consent of the Senate.

The Twin Cities model of metropolitan governance is a federated one with powers divided between the metropolitan council, counties, municipalities and metropolitan special districts. The council is the comprehensive areawide planning agency and possesses the power to review and suspend plans indefinitely of each metropolitan special district in conflict with the council's development guide, to review and suspend for up to one year proposed projects of local governments, to act as a housing authority, and to appoint the Metropolitan Sewer Board. The Metropolitan Reorganization Act of 1974 authorizes the council to appoint members of the Metropolitan Transit Commission and changes the name of the Sewer Board to the Waste Control Commission, effective January 1, 1975.[22]

The 1969 legislature created a Metropolitan Park Reserve Board to operate a park system and provided for its appointment by the council. The board's role as an operating service body was terminated in 1970 by a Minnesota Supreme Court ruling invalidating laws passed on the 121st day (one day past the constitutional limit of the 1969 legislative session).[23] The council has retained the board—renamed the Metropolitan Parks and Open Spaces Commission—as an advisory body, but reenactment of the original Park Reserve bill has been blocked by opposition from the Inter-County Council and the Hennipin County Park Reserve District. Regional parks and waste disposal facilities will be operated by the counties.

The distinguishing characteristic of the Twin Cities model is the separation of policy execution from policy making, with the council determining policies to be carried into execution by service boards appointed by the council. In theory, it can devote its full attention to broad policy making for the region and leave routine administrative problems to the service boards.

Several highly favorable accounts have been published about the council,[24] yet the Twin Cities gov-

---

19. *Indiana Acts of 1969*, ch. 173.

20. *See*, Joseph F. Zimmerman, *The Federated City: Community Control in Large Cities* (New York: St. Martin's Press, 1972).

21. *Minnesota Statutes*, ch. 473B (1971).

22. *Minnesota Laws of 1974*, ch. 422. The act has been codified as *Minnesota Statutes*, ch. 473B (1971).

23. *Knapp* v. *O'Brien*, 179 N.W. 2d 88 (1970).

24. Stanley Baldinger, *Planning and Governing the Metropolis: The Twin Cities Experience* (New York: Praeger Publishers, 1971); "Twin Cities Metropolitan Council Anticipates and Supplies Orderly Growth," *Urban Action Clearinghouse*, Case Study No.

ernmental system remains a fragmented one suffering from three major weaknesses. First, the most important problems generally are being attacked on a piecemeal basis, and the legislature continues to play a major referee role between competing regional bodies and interests. Political fragmentation on the regional level is responsible for a second and related weakness of the model—deadlocks arising between various regional entities as they fail to operate on the basis of comity. The council twice exercised its power to veto indefinitely a new jetport site proposed by the Metropolitan Airport Commission, yet the council lacks the power to order the commission to construct the jetport at a council-selected site. The 1974 legislature strengthened the control of the council, effective in 1975, by authorizing it to appoint members other than the chairman of each regional commission with the exception of the Airport Commission. Chairmen of commissions, except the Park Board, will be selected by the governor. The council is required to prepare and adopt policy plans for the commissions, and each commission must prepare a development program to implement the policy plans subject to council approval. Parts of the commissions' budgets relating to capital improvements also are subject to council approval.

The possibility of disputes between the council and its service boards is a third and inherent defect of the Twin Cities model. The council and the Sewer Board engaged in a major dispute relative to the board's 1971 construction program.

The Minnesota Legislature in 1971 took another action to reduce metropolitan problems by enacting the Metropolitan Revenue Distribution Act, which authorizes a partial sharing of the growth in the commercial-industrial property tax base in the seven-county Twin Cities area.[25] The purpose of the act is to reduce gross fiscal disparities among municipalities by providing that the revenue produced by 40 percent of new nonresidential construction be deposited in the Municipal Equity Account in the state treasury and distributed to municipalities according to a need and population formula. Whether the act will reduce or eliminate fiscal zoning remains to be seen, since each municipality retains 60 percent of its new nonresidential tax base, and the revenue produced may provide a sufficient incentive for municipalities to employ fiscal zoning.[26]

New York State in the 1960s took a different approach to the solution of regional problems by establishing both statewide and regional state-controlled public authorities for special purposes: Urban Development Corporation (UDC), Environmental Facilities Corporation (EFC), Job Development Authority (JDA), Metropolitan Transportation Authority (MTA), Niagara Frontier Transportation Authority, Capital District Transportation Authority,

25. *Minnesota Statutes*, ch. 473F (1971).
26. Fiscal zoning often is loosely defined. It is used here to refer to the adoption by a municipality of zoning and other codes designed to keep low income persons from becoming residents and to encourage certain types of commercial and industrial development requiring relatively few municipal services and producing substantial property tax revenue.

20 (Washington, D.C.: United States Chamber of Commerce, 1971); and John Fischer, "The Minnesota Experiment: How to Make a Big City Fit to Live In," *Harper's* (April 1969), pp. 12, 17–18, 20, 24, 26, 28, 30, 32.

Central New York Regional Transportation Authority, Rochester-Genesee Regional Transportation Authority and 23 others.

The creation of state-controlled authorities on an ad hoc basis has produced fractionalization of responsibility on the regional level and a nearly total neglect of essential coordination of authorities' activities with those of regional planning commissions and local governments, inasmuch as these authorities are independent of each other and of local governments in terms of planning, financing and programming.[27] To reduce the fragmentation problem within a metropolitan area, the device of the interlocking directorate can be utilized, as it has been employed in the New York City area since 1967 to coordinate transportation authorities. The board of the newly created MTA was made the *ex officio* board of directors of the Long Island Railroad, New York City Transit Authority, Manhattan and Bronx Surface Transit Operating Authority, and Triborough Bridge and Tunnel Authority.[28] The MTA board also is the *ex officio* board of the more recently created Staten Island Rapid Transit Operating Authority, Metropolitan Suburban Bus Authority, and Stewart Airport Land Authority. The interlocking directorate model in the New York City area appears similar to the Twin Cities model, but differs in that the metropolitan council has no direct operating responsibilities.

Finally, state governments since 1965 have been playing a more im-portant role in the metropolitan governance system as the result of partial federal preemption of responsibility for solving environmental problems.

THE FEDERAL ROLE

Not until Congress enacted the Federal-Aid Highway Act of 1962 did the federal government become involved in more than a very minimal way in the solution of metropolitan problems. In that year, the federal government began to place heavy emphasis upon regional planning as a mechanism for promoting interlocal cooperation as a device for solving areawide problems, and in 1965 it began to preempt partially the authority to abate environmental problems.

The ecumenical approach

By 1965, Congress reached the conclusion that metropolitan planning had been largely ineffective because the planning commissions were not directly under the control of local elected officials. To improve the effectiveness of the commissions, a provision was added to the Housing and Urban Development Act of 1965, making organizations of public officials in metropolitan areas eligible to receive federal grants for the preparation of comprehensive areawide plans.[29] In 1966, Congress added another incentive for integrating metropolitan planning with local decision making by enacting a requirement—popularly known as Section 204 review—that all local government applications for grants and loans for 30 specified projects be submitted for review to the organi-

27. *See, Strengthening Local Government in New York, part 2: Services, Structure and Finance* (New York: New York State Temporary Commission on the Powers of Local Governments, 1973), pp. 83–86.

28. *New York Laws of 1967* (McKinney) ch. 717.

29. *Housing and Urban Development Act of 1965,* 79 STAT. 502, 40 U.S.C.A. § 461 (g), (1965).

zation responsible for areawide planning "which is, to the greatest practicable extent, composed of or responsible to the elected officials of a unit of areawide government or of the units of general local governments."[30] This requirement promoted the formation of numerous COGs and regional planning commissions composed of local elected officials.[31]

Two other acts—the Intergovernmental Cooperation Act of 1968 and the National Environmental Policy Act of 1969[32]—further enhanced the importance of metropolitan planning. Parts of these two acts and Section 204 are implemented by United States Office of Management and Budget Circular A-95, which broadens the coverage of the review of grant applications by the planning agency to 155 programs currently and extends review to nonmetropolitan areas and the state level.

The ecumenical approach, as epitomized by planning agencies and COGs, has been unable to solve the major problems of the metropolis.[33] While promoting interlocal co-

operation, Congress increasingly began to exercise its powers of preemption to help solve metropolitan problems.

Preemption

By the mid-1960s, Congress decided that a number of areawide problems—particularly environmental ones—could not be eliminated by reliance upon state and local governmental action encouraged by the "carrots" of federal grant-in-aid. Enactment of the Water Quality Act of 1965[34] and other acts has had great significance for metropolitan America. The Water Quality Act required that each state adopt "water quality standards applicable to interstate waters or portions thereof within such state," as well as an implementation and enforcement plan. The secretary of the interior, now the administrator of the Environmental Protection Agency (EPA), is authorized to promulgate interstate water quality standards which become effective at the end of six months in the event that a state fails to establish adequate standards. The federal role has since been strengthened by other enactments, particularly by the Federal Water Pollution Control Act Amendments of 1972.[35] The governor of each state is directed by the 1972 amendments

30. *Demonstration Cities and Metropolitan Development Act of 1966*, 80 STAT. 1255, 42 U.S.C.A. §§ 3301-314 (1966).

31. The federal government since the early 1960s also has spawned, via grant-in-aid conditions, 481 Law Enforcement Planning Regions, 419 Cooperative Area Manpower Planning System Councils, 195 Comprehensive Areawide Health Planning Agencies, 115 Economic Development Districts, and 165 Resource Conservation and Development Districts. *See*, Advisory Commission on Intergovernmental Relations, *Substate Regionalism and the Federal System* (Washington, D.C.: Government Printing Office, 1973), vol. 1, *Regional Decision Making: New Strategies for Sub-State Districts*.

32. *Intergovernmental Cooperation Act of 1968*, 82 STAT. 1103, 42 U.S.C.A. §§ 4201-243 (1970); *National Environmental Policy Act of 1969*, 83 STAT. 852, 42 U.S.C.A. §§ 4321 and 4331-332 (1972).

33. *See*, Melvin B. Mogoluf, *Governing*

Metropolitan Areas: A Critical Review of Councils of Governments and the Federal Role (Washington, D.C.: The Urban Institute, 1972); Joseph F. Zimmerman, "Metropolitan Ecumenism: The Road to the Promised Land?" *Journal of Urban Law* (Spring 1967), pp. 433–57; and Joseph F. Zimmerman, "The Planning Riddle," *National Civic Review* (April 1968), pp. 189–94.

34. *Water Quality Act of 1965*, 79 STAT. 903, 33 U.S.C.A. 1151 *et seq.* (1969).

35. *Federal Water Pollution Control Act Amendments of 1972*, 70 STAT. 498, 33 U.S.C.A. §§ 1151 *et seq.* (1972).

to identify areas suffering water quality control problems and designate "a single representative organization, including elected officials from local governments or their designees, capable of developing effective areawide waste treatment management plans" for each area. EPA issued regulations on September 14, 1973 giving governors until March 14, 1974 to designate or nondesignate such areas and agencies.[36] On April 11, 1974, the EPA administrator approved the first gubernatorial area and agency designations —the Triangle J Council of Governments in the Raleigh-Durham, North Carolina area.

Space limitations allow comments on only one of the other fields totally or partially preempted by Congress. In 1967, Congress completely preempted the right to establish automobile exhaust emission standards for 1968 and subsequent model vehicles.[37] The Air Quality Act also partially preempts other air pollution abatement activities of state and local governments by following the general procedure embodied in the Water Quality Act of 1965. Municipal, metropolitan, state and interstate air pollution abatement programs are encouraged, provided they meet minimum federal standards; federal enforcement action is authorized in the event of state inaction.

The Clean Air Amendments of 1970 represent a sharp break with the earlier approach to air pollution abatement, which relied upon state and local governments to provide the necessary leadership and took into consideration the economic and technical feasibility of abatement

controls.[38] Direct federal action to protect public health was made national policy, and explicit dates for adoption of standards and abatement plans by states were specified.

The amendments stipulated that 1975 model automobiles must achieve a 90 percent reduction of the 1970 standards for emissions of carbon monoxide, hydrocarbons and nitrogen oxides.[39] In contrast to earlier ones, the new standards were mandated without considering the economic and technical feasibility of pollution abatement systems. On April 18, 1973, the EPA administrator granted the automobile industry's request for a one-year extension to meet the standards established in the amendments for automobile emissions of carbon monoxide and hydrocarbons.

Of particular importance to metropolitan areas is the provision directing the administrator to publish in the *Federal Register* within 90 days a list of categories of stationary sources of air pollution subject to the performance standards established under the amendments. He was given an additional 120 days following publication of the list to include in the *Federal Register* proposed regulations establishing federal standards for new sources of air pollution. Each state was authorized to submit to the administrator a procedure for implementing and enforcing standards of performance for new sources located in the state, and the administrator was empowered to delegate authority to each state to implement and enforce the standards for other than new United States-owned sources. On February 25, 1974, the administrator pub-

36. 38 *Federal Register* 25681 *et seq.*
37. *Air Quality Act of 1967*, 81 STAT. 485, 42 U.S.C.A. §§ 1857-1857(L), (1969).

38. *Clean Air Amendments of 1970*, 84 STAT. 1676, 42 U.S.C.A. §§ 1857 *et seq.* and 49 U.S.C.A. §§ 1421 and 1430. (1970).
39. Ibid., §§ 1421 and 1430.

lished final regulations for reviewing the air quality impact prior to construction of new facilities—labeled indirect sources—which may generate significant amounts of automobile traffic.[40] The regulations become effective January 1, 1975.

The 1975 automotive emission standards and the regulation of new major sources of air pollution—electric power generating plants, factories and shopping centers, for example—have major land-use implications. If stationary source controls, combined with new motor vehicle emission controls, can not ensure the attainment of statutory ambient air quality standards within an air quality control region, transportation controls must be adopted. Such controls will force significant life style changes of residents of the region.

A decision portending important consequences for metropolitan America is the four-to-four decision of the United States Supreme Court, on June 11, 1973 to let stand a district court decision forbidding states to permit significant deterioration of existing air quality.[41] Since the Supreme Court's decision was without opinion and the district courts did not elaborate upon its ruling,[42] EPA has been forced to execute a non-degradation policy without judicial guidelines.

To implement the courts' decisions, EPA proposed that four steps be taken, including the establishment of clean air and polluted air zones. Although pollution levels would not be allowed to exceed federal standards in either zone, only minor increases in the degree of

pollution would be allowed in the former zones, whereas larger increases would be allowed in the latter zones. Any further growth of so-called Spread City will be ruled out if this proposal is implemented, since development would not be allowed in fringe areas if it would degrade the areas' existing air quality. Allowable growth may have to be accommodated within developed areas. States are required to submit air quality maintenance plans to EPA by June 18, 1975.

Conclusions

Critical problems in most metropolitan areas during the next decade will be alleviated or solved by intergovernmental tinkering rather than by a comprehensive reordering of the local government system. COGs will promote interlocal cooperation, but will not play an important role in the governance system because they lack the power to control land use and to reallocate resources. Service agreements, often arranged on a trade-off basis, frequently will be entered into by municipalities with other governmental units, and responsibility for a troublesome function occasionally will be shifted upwards to the county or state level or to a newly created unifunctional regional special district.

The continuing proliferation of service compacts may have three disadvantages. First, the average citizen may experience greater difficulty in understanding a local government system made more complex by the widespread use of multilateral agreements and he may be unable to pinpoint responsibility for failures in the system. Second, agreements may reinforce the existing fragmented governmental system in the typical metropolitan area

40. 39 *Federal Register* 7271 *et seq.*

41. *Fri* v. *Sierra Club,* 41 U.S.L.W. 4825 (1973).

42. *Sierra Club* v. *Ruckelshaus,* 344 F. Supp. 253, 4 ERC (D.D.C. 1972).

and reduce the pressures for creation of an areawide government with adequate powers to solve metropolitan major problems. A third and related disadvantage is the possible promotion of additional political fractionation and fiscal disparities. The Advisory Commission on Intergovernmental Relations is correct when it says:

Under certain conditions such contracts can only further fragment unnecessarily the metropolitan tax base. The presence of nonviable "paper" communities, incorporated under highly permissive state legislation and sustained by interlocal contracting arrangements, undoubtedly creates extremes of fiscal capacity or incapacity within certain areas.[43]

The facts that not all governmental problems lend themselves to solution by means of service agreements, and that the potential of intergovernmental cooperation is limited principally to the solution of relatively minor and noncontroversial problems involving a small number of local governments, must not be overlooked.

The county will be converted incrementally into a metropolitan government by the upward shift of functional responsibility in many of the 112 single-county Standard Metropolitan Statistical Areas (SMSAs). Public works-type functions are the ones which most commonly will be shifted upwards, since it is reasonable to assume that lower tier units will seek to retain control of the more politically sensitive functions, such as land use control, housing and alcoholic beverage control licensing.

No state has initiated action to "rationalize" what has been labelled a "dysfunctional system of local government" in metropolitan areas, and no state is likely to do so during the next decade. It may be anticipated, however, that regional special districts, created or authorized by state legislatures, will play a more important role in multicounty SMSAs in many states. The urbanized states undoubtedly will become more deeply involved in solving areawide problems through direct state action and standard setting. In part, the enlarged state role will be attributable to prodding by the federal government as it continues to rely upon the states to develop and implement programs meeting federal environmental standards.

Although the National Commission on Urban Problems proposed that revenue sharing be utilized as a catalyst to encourage small local units—those under 50,000 population—to consolidate,[44] Congress enacted the State and Local Fiscal Assistance Act of 1972 without considering seriously the impact of federal revenue sharing upon the governmental system of metropolitan areas. Revenue sharing, unless modified, will help to perpetuate the atomistic government of the metropolis by enabling many small units to survive and other units to perform functions better performed on an areawide basis, thereby delaying formation of metropolitan governments. Congress would have chosen a more desirable course of action had the revenue sharing law contained a clause providing incentives for the formation of a two-

43. Advisory Commission on Intergovernmental Relations, *Fiscal Balance in the American Federal System: Metropolitan Fiscal Disparities* (Washington, D.C.: Government Printing Office, October 1967), vol. 2 p. 15.

44. National Commission on Urban Problems, *Building the American City* (Washington, D.C.: Government Printing Office, 1968), pp. 378–82.

tier system of local government in SMSAs.

In any event, increasing metropolitan scale and the development of megalopolises will generate additional pressure for the transfer of functional responsibility to the state and federal levels.

Conflict in Metropolitan Areas

By Henry W. Maier

ABSTRACT: The dichotomy between the central city and its suburbs is more pronounced than the more traditional conflict between rural and urban areas. Central cities contain the concentrations of the poor in the metropolitan area because of the lack of low income housing outside the city. The basic conflict arises from the contention for resources between the "have" suburban communities and the "have-not" central cities. Unless the suburbs are opened up to lower income residents, central cities will become even more impoverished. Conflict arises as suburbs fight to maintain the housing status quo, as cities fight to prevent expressways from destroying additional housing and tax base and to attain greater emphasis on adequate transportation, as heavy reliance on the property tax leads central city and suburb to compete for the same industry. In general, voluntary intergovernmental groups have not been responsive to central city needs in the metropolitan area. What is required is a basic change in the system which separates resources from need and provides both greater fiscal equity and a metropolitan-wide sharing of the burden of social problems.

Henry W. Maier has been Mayor of Milwaukee, Wisconsin since 1960. He has been prominent as a national leader in urban affairs, having served as president of both the National League of Cities and the United States Conference of Mayors. He was the first chairman, National Coalition for Human Needs and Budget Priorities, an organization of 100 groups concerned about the neglect of domestic programs in the president's 1973 budget message, and is presently chairman, National Conference of Democratic Mayors. He has also served as a consultant to a study of housing in the metropolitan plan by the National Association of Housing and Redevelopment Officials, and is the author of Challenge to the Cities: an approach to a theory of urban leadership.

IN THE nearly 35 years that have passed since THE ANNALS devoted its first volume to intergovernmental relations, the dichotomy between city and suburb has taken on a classic dimension in the literature of urban affairs, replacing in many respects the historic contention between urban and rural interests.

In 1940, this metropolitan conflict was little noted, largely because the Golden Age of Suburbia was yet to come, and the cleavages were not so sharp.[1] Much of the change that has taken place within metropolitan areas since that time has involved much more than simply the numerical growth of suburban populations. The city of Milwaukee's percentage of the population of Milwaukee County, for instance, dropped merely from 76 percent to 68 percent from 1940 to 1970. During that time, however, the city's nonwhite population increased fifteenfold, to 16 percent of its total, while the proportion of nonwhites outside the city is less than seven-tenths of 1 percent, not far removed from the four-tenths of 1 percent counted in 1940. While the value of the suburban house was only 30 percent higher than the city house 35 years ago, today it is 50

percent higher. While in 1940 the number of upper income professional and managerial workers was about equal in city and suburb, today there are nearly twice as many in the suburbs as in the city.[2] In 1974, as was not the case in 1940, the conflict between central city and the wealthier suburb is one of the basic facts of metropolitan life.

The purpose of this paper is to point out some of the underlying factors in this conflict, to portray the conflict as it manifests itself in the particular areas of housing, transportation, and economic and fiscal competition, and to make some observations on the future.

Whether what is said here will still be pertinent in another 35 years remains to be seen. Perhaps a way will be found to end the concentration of the poor in the central city and to open the gates for widespread low income housing outside the city. Perhaps there will be a metropolitan sharing of the responsibility for social problems, social and economic equity will prevail in all corners of the metropolis, and the lion of the city will at long last lie down peacefully with the lamb of suburbia.

However, in 1974 that great day has not yet arrived, and in a sense this paper is a report from the battlefield by a central city mayor who has long been involved in the fight for resources for the central city, which in many instances has meant involvement in the melee of metropolitan conflict. No doubt, bias in favor of the central city will be evident, but hopefully it will be accepted as a sign of long-held concern for the central city, and a strong belief that the health of the metropolis as a whole is dependent upon the health of the city at its heart.

1. See, Victor Jones, "Politics of Integration in Metropolitan Areas," and J. B. Shannon, "County Consolidation" Annals, American Academy of Political and Social Science 207 (Jan. 1940). Jones discussed briefly suburban opposition to the central city in the context of city-county integration. Shannon observed that suburbanization was "blurring distinctions" between rural and urban government. What was not foreseen was that large-scale suburbanization would sharpen the distinctions between central city and suburban government.

2. Statistics based on United States Census data compiled by the City of Milwaukee's Department of Intergovernmental Fiscal Liaison.

Basic Differences between City and Suburb

Municipalities differ in many respects, of course, within metropolitan areas as well as across the nation. Central cities vary, as do their suburbs. Newer cities often do not share the same kinds or degrees of problems as do older cities. There are residential and industrial suburbs and others with specialized functions. Some are, in effect, satellite cities. Suburbs vary in age and in the average income of their residents. While keeping these variations in mind, it is still possible to make some generalized comparisons between the suburb and the central city.

The 1970 census showed that 13.4 percent of central city residents were living below the poverty level; the figure outside central cities within Standard Metropolitan Statistical Areas (SMSAs) was 6.3 percent.[3] In other words, central cities on the whole are twice as poor as their suburbs, and, of course, in some instances the percentage of the poor in the central city is much higher than the national average.

In addition, a large percentage of central city residents can be counted among the near-poor. Using the Bureau of Labor Standards "moderate" budget for a family of four as its standard for an adequate income to meet normal needs, a recent study by the Council on Municipal Performance showed that in the 31 central cities surveyed, the proportion of residents who are deprived in the sense that their income fails to meet this standard ranges from 41 percent to 64 percent.[4] The implication is that much of the burden of paying the costs of poverty in the central city falls on the near-poor.

In addition to housing a larger concentration of the poor and the near-poor, central cities compared to their suburbs have proportionately more older persons, more older housing, higher crime rates, more money spent for social services and less money for education.

These contrasts in the city-suburban economic and social composition suggest that the root of much of the conflict within the metropolitan area is a variation of the traditional confrontation between the "haves" and the "have-nots." At stake are the resources to provide a good urban environment for all citizens of the metropolitan area. This metropolitan area becomes, as described by Norton Long, "a battleground . . . for the conception of people with unequal incomes desiring to spend those unequal incomes on a quantity and quality of public goods they do not wish to share with others of lesser income."[5]

While these divisions within our metropolitan areas were abetted by laissez faire metropolitan policies, they were also the result of pressures from outside the areas. It is true that the most dramatic developments in American cities have been witnessed within the past two and a half decades. During that period two caravans passed on the urban highway: the Cadillacs of the rich, heading for the green fields of

3. See, Norman Beckman, "Metropolitan Area Trends and Developments," The Municipal Yearbook 1974 (Washington, D.C.: International City Management Association, 1974), p. 12.

4. The Wealth of Cities, Municipal Performance Report 1:3 (New York: Council on Municipal Performance, April 1974), p. 8.

5. Norton Long, The Unwalled City (New York: Basic Books), p. 102.

suburbia, passing the jalopies of the poor, heading for the hand-me-down housing of the central city.

But while the effects of these migrations were looked upon as local phenomena, they were also expressions of national actions: such things as an agricultural policy which helped to drive the marginal worker off the farm and into the city, a federal housing policy which promoted the building-up of suburban tracts, and a federal highway program which not only bulldozed vast areas of the central city, but also made it easier for the suburbanite to live at a greater distance from his job in the city and facilitated the movement of industry from the city to the industrial suburb. Unfortunately, a national urban policy to provide for the growing needs of the central city did not—and does not—exist.

The rise of many inequities within our metropolitan areas can be noted. In many cases, the child who lives on the city side of the municipal boundary is denied an education equal to that of the suburban child who lives just across the street. Often the house on the city side is taxed at a much higher rate than the house across the way, and yet its owner picks up the tax for many tax-free city institutions and tax-paid services enjoyed free of charge by his suburban neighbor.

On some occasions the areas of conflict, while seemingly distinct, are actually related. While the surface issue may be an expressway, from the viewpoint of the central city the issue can be related to housing, public transportation and the city tax base. Housing and fiscal problems are related to the overriding issue of the concentration of metropolitan area poor within the central city, which imposes an overload on the city's resources.

THE CONFLICT OF HOUSING

Anthony Downs, recognizing the "forced concentration" of the poor as "one of the main causes of big-city maladies," argues convincingly that to continue to build new housing in suburbs without opening it up to the poor will lead to the spread of central city poverty areas as housing "trickles down" from city middle class residents moving into newer suburban housing. He further argues that the benefits of unwalling what he calls the "crisis ghetto" in the city so that lower income persons have entry into all areas of the metropolis would include not only a more viable central city, but also might represent one of the best opportunities to break the cycle of poverty which traps many of the poor. According to Downs:

There is a crucial difference in scale and intensity between the poverty that suburbanites would encounter if they opened up their communities as I am suggesting and the poverty in central cities from which they have often fled. In many central-city neighborhoods, poverty and deprivation are overwhelming because of their dominance of the local environment. But opening up a prosperous suburb to a relatively limited influx of low- and upper-income households would produce an entirely different context for poverty. The middle- and upper-income character of the community would remain dominant. Relatively well-off suburbanites could become personally, governmentally, and fiscally involved in helping the poor without being overwhelmed by the immensity and intransigence of the poverty they faced. Thus, diluting urban poverty by spreading it over a much broader landscape might produce qualitatively different—and much less forbidding—problems than concentrating urban poverty in a few highly deprived areas.[6]

6. Anthony Downs, *Opening up the Suburbs* (New Haven: Yale University Press, 1973), p. 41.

Downs accompanies his analysis with a strategy and tactics for opening up the suburbs, but while his words evoke a ready "amen" from the already converted—such as mayors of larger cities—it remains to be seen whether they will strike the hearts of the recalcitrant. Personal experience has shown that there is a "metropolitan hypocrisy" which sets one standard for the central city and another for its suburbs.

In the wake of Milwaukee's civil disorder of 1967, the city was the scene of many marches and rallies in favor of an open housing ordinance which would apply only to the City of Milwaukee. The marchers included a number of suburban sympathizers, and the local newspaper, whose editors largely live in the suburbs, actively crusaded for passage of the ordinance. I opposed it, arguing that a city-only law would only lead to further enrichment of the suburbs at the city's expense. I proposed, instead, either a state or county law that would include all the municipalities in the area, and I stressed the need to provide low and moderate income housing in the suburbs.

Shortly thereafter, federal law provided the umbrella of equity that I had favored, and the city backed it up with the passage of its own open housing ordinance. Since then there have been no marches and no newspaper crusades for low income housing in the suburbs. In fact, after expressway construction had destroyed more than 6,000 homes in Milwaukee, and I had reached an agreement with the Governor and the County Executive that new freeway construction would not be undertaken until provision was made to build 2,000 low income housing units outside the central city, the howl went up from freeway proponents that the mayor of Milwaukee was halting the construction of highways much needed by suburban residents.

Given the abandonment of the central city by the programs of the present administration in Washington, a significant federal push towards opening up the suburbs is unlikely. There was a time when former Housing and Urban Development (HUD) Secretary George Romney's movement in that direction seemed to offer promise, but that hope was scuttled by the Nixon administration. Housing quotas proposed by some of the metropolitan planning agencies may offer a start in the right direction, but they are not likely to work without large housing subsidies of one kind or another.

In the final analysis, it seems that opening up the metropolitan areas will require meeting the issue in a larger arena than the local level—by either state or federal action employing a "carrot and a stick" approach.

THE CONFLICT IN METROPOLITAN TRANSPORTATION

As previously indicated, another source of conflict stems from decisions regarding metropolitan transportation. Long ago, Lewis Mumford warned of some unplanned deleterious effects on cities that were likely to result from congressional passage of the 1957 federal highway program. In addition to destroying housing and neighborhoods, Mumford foresaw expressways increasing rather than decreasing traffic problems in cities as they tempted people who were previously using public transportation. Mumford continued:

So a clamor arises to create other similar arteries and to provide more parking garages in the center of our metropolices; and the generous provisions of these facilities expands the cycle of congestion without any promise of relief until that terminal point when all the business and industry that originally gave rise to the congestion move out of the city, to escape strangulation, leaving a waste of expressways and garages behind them. This is pyramid building with a vengeance: a tomb of concrete roads and ramps covering the dead corpse of a city.[7]

While the city has not yet become Mumford's predicted necropolis, nevertheless central city residents are not as likely to envision expressways as highways to happiness as are those who live outside the central city. The uprooting of homes, neighborhoods and small businesses, together with a loss of tax base and the burden on the vast numbers of older and poorer residents of the central city who do not own automobiles, are costs which are not borne by those from outside the city who share the benefits. Another cost to the central city resident is that emphasis on expressways is likely to mean a de-emphasis on public transportation, and in city after city, bus and transit systems have been caught in the self-defeating cycle of decreased ridership leading to increased fares leading to the loss of even more passengers.[8] Meanwhile, those who depend on public transportation are saddled with higher fares of which they are the least capable of paying, creating a demand for local subsidies.

Small wonder, then, that central city officials sometimes find themselves accused of fighting progress when, in fact, they are fighting to protect their own citizens, gain reparations for past losses, avoid future losses, and gain a recognition that past transportation plans may no longer be appropriate and should certainly be modified and strengthened.

The central city feels at times that the expressway program has been thrust upon it by forces entirely beyond its control, particularly when the commission responsible does not include proportionate central city representation. To correct this unfair situation, when I proposed a four-county metropolitan transportation authority to take over all expressway and public transportation planning and operations in the Milwaukee area, I specified that Milwaukee County's representation on the authority should contain a percentage of City of Milwaukee representatives proportionate to the population.

While in principle, no doubt, most persons in the metropolitan area favor a balanced transportation system, many of the decisions necessary to attain it require what may well be a controversial reallocation of resources. On the federal level, a greater proportion of funds would go to public transportation rather than to highways. On the metropolitan area level, there is the question of who pays for the local share of operating subsidies or for public take-over of privately-owned facilities. There is also the question of raising money; reliance on sales and property taxes means that lower in-

7. Lewis Mumford, *The Highway and the City* (New York: Harcourt, Brace and World, 1963), p. 238.

8. Between 1955 and 1973, bus fares on Milwaukee's privately owned bus system rose from 20 cents to 50 cents. During the same period, annual ridership decreased from 130 million to 49 million.

come residents pay a larger percentage than higher income residents.

However, the lack of a viable transit system remains a covert or potential source of conflict, largely because the issue continues to evoke an apathetic yawn from wealthier, non–bus riding suburbanites and, even more importantly, from suburban-based opinion makers.

Moreover, the transportation conflict is often expressed in terms of opposition rather than advocacy. Citizens become more vocal as expressways become a concrete threat to their neighborhoods and are no longer merely abstract lines on a map. There has been no organized grass-roots advocacy of expressways by suburban residents in the Milwaukee area, but then, none was needed because the ball was being carried for them by planners, the local press monopoly, and other establishment actors, including the suburban officials who comprise the Intergovernmental Co-Operation Council for Milwaukee County.

There are also more remote causes for transportation conflict. Much of the conflict stems from national programs unrelated to a national urban policy, such as a highway policy without a transportation policy related to central cities' needs. Indications now are that the bloom is off the highway rose. The energy situation, the high cost of new housing, and new environmental and relocation requirements have all combined to force many metropolitan areas to take another look at their expressway mania, and perhaps they will force federal action requiring a more balanced approach to metropolitan transportation needs.

THE FISCAL CONFLICT

While the transportation problem within the metropolitan area has been a source of conflict in itself, it has also contributed to other conflicts over fiscal and economic resources as middle and higher income residents and some central city industry followed the freeway to suburbia. The result has been the separation of the metropolitan area resources from the needs of the central city. In many areas, property taxes in the central city remain much higher than in adjoining suburbs where incomes are higher. The regressiveness of the local property tax is felt most keenly by lower income residents, who pay a much larger percentage of their income in property taxes—either as renters or as homeowners—than do the higher income residents outside the city.

As a central city mayor, I have long fought for the reduction of the burden of the local property tax with both state and federal assistance, particularly for a reordering of national priorities to meet domestic needs. The property tax is overburdened because it pays for many functions for which it was never intended, and it has long been my contention that the property tax per se should primarily be used to support property related functions, such as fire, waste disposal and portions of police costs. Other functions should be financed out of user fees—auto fees for functions attached to automobile use, for instance—or by the income tax, which I believe is the most appropriate source of funds for social overhead costs such as education, health and the costs of poverty.

However, as long as municipalities rely so heavily on the property tax, there will be continuing conflict over fiscal and economic matters. As an example, for many years in Wisconsin the system of state-shared taxes returned a portion of the income tax to the municipality where the taxpayer lived. The area with the highest income residents would receive the highest proportion of state-shared taxes, although in many cases the actual income was gained within the central city. Although the tax was collected according to the progressive principle of ability to pay, it was not distributed on the basis of need.[9]

When the City of Milwaukee began its campaign to change this system, it naturally ran into strong opposition from surrounding suburbs. The suburban lobbying effort in the state legislature was intense, and the first attempts were defeated. The opposition preyed on the traditional rural fears of the Big City of Milwaukee. But in this case, the old conflict between city and rural areas did not prevail. We were able to show that some 1,500 municipalities in Wisconsin—cities, as well as rural villages and towns—would benefit from the proposed reform; only the richer communities, where a minority of the population lived, would suffer losses. Out of this grew an urban-rural Have-Not Conference of leaders of labor, farm groups, municipalities and civic organizations from across the state which eventually won the campaign for tax reform.

9. One critique of the Wisconsin system of that time stated: "Wisconsin is known for sharing funds with local governments; yet this generosity is upside down from the standpoint of equalization: The rich industrial communities get $314 per capita, the high income suburbs get $161, and Milwaukee proper is low man with $88. It would be hard to devise a more perverse effect on local government financing—and the direct result is interlocal balkanization and ferocious fiscal zoning." John Riew, "Fiscal Disparities in the Milwaukee, Wisconsin, Metropolitan Area," *Fiscal Balance in the American Federal System*, vol. 2 (Washington D.C.: Advisory Commission on Intergovernmental Relations, 1967), p. 278.

Whether the kind of coalition brought about on this one issue can be transferred to other issues remains to be seen. But the example does suggest that there are certain areas in which central city-rural interests coincide more than do suburban-central city interests, and that there are cases where the central city can help resolve its conflicts with the suburbs by appealing to rural allies.

THE COMPETITION FOR INDUSTRY

Because of the fiscal impact, central cities are greatly concerned about their economic health and have resorted to a number of approaches to maintain it: land banks, industrial revenue bonding, industrial promotion and a professionally-staffed economic development department. At the same time, the areas outside the city have been active with their industrial parks, tax breaks and recruiting efforts to compete aggressively, often for the same industries—particularly those forced to abandon old, outmoded plants in the central city.

The tragedy of all this, at least in Milwaukee's case, is that the metropolitan area should be competing as a region instead of playing industrial musical chairs within the region. Like it or not, the Milwaukee region is in competition for industry with other regions of the nation, and increasingly, with other regions of the world.

Because of my belief in this approach, I have proposed that within the region we pool our recruiting efforts and also share new industrial tax-base.[10] However, I believe that

10. A version of regional sharing was approved by the Minnesota legislature in 1971. New and improved nonresidential tax base in the Minneapolis-St. Paul region is shared

this kind of sharing should also be coupled with a regional sharing of low income housing.

CONFLICTS IN "COOPERATION"

Naturally, regional recruiting and sharing would require some degree of intergovernmental cooperation between the municipalities of the region. The history of intergovernmental cooperation in the Milwaukee area thus far fails to indicate that matters of substantial importance to the central city are likely to win approval by a *voluntary* intergovernmental council.

The Intergovernmental Cooperation Council for Milwaukee County, brought together by the county executive, has long pointed a critical finger at the mayor of the central city for his refusal to join the county executive and 18 suburban officials in the council. However, it has not addressed itself to the reason for this refusal. Although a majority of the citizens of the county live within the city, its mayor's vote would weigh no heavier than that of the head of the tiniest suburb, a direct contravention of the principle of "one man, one vote." The central city would even face difficulty in placing matters of its own serious concern on the agenda, since that requires the vote of the majority of the members.

The Milwaukee experience with intergovernmental councils is probably not unique. A 1970 study by the Metropolitan Fund of 103 regional councils of elected officials came to the conclusion that "the general impression is that COGs

[councils of government] have not related very well to the central city and its problems.[11] The study also noted that most central cities are seriously underrepresented in the councils of government from the standpoint of population.[12]

The study was also critical of COGs for avoiding the serious social problems of cities, pointing out that "the main areas of COG programs are the non-controversial or least controversial areas such as joint purchasing, air and water pollution programs, regional library systems, joint park and recreation projects, solid waste disposal systems, water and sewer systems, police training, etc."[13] In other words, the services which suburbs need but cannot afford to pay for individually.

It is doubtful that councils of government have the capacity to meet on a voluntary basis many of the main issues that face the central city. It is unlikely, for instance, that any voluntary groups would have met the need for room for residential and industrial expansion that faced so many central cities in the fifties and sixties. What voluntary efforts there were consisted largely of the banding together of suburban interests to prevent the city from expanding. Once legislation was obtained which placed an "iron ring" around the central city, the main voluntary effort was to make sure the poor stayed in their place in the central city.

Nor is it likely that suburbs will voluntarily take up the costs of

---

on the basis of 60 percent to the locality in which the facility is located, 40 percent to the other jurisdictions within the metropolitan area.

11. *Regional COGs and the Central City* (Detroit: Metropolitan Fund, Inc., 1970), p. 25.
12. *Regional COGs*, p. 27.
13. *Regional COGs*, p. 25.

city-owned facilities their citizens often use. This is a basic conflict. In Milwaukee the conflict has been expressed by the rebuffs of attempts to transfer the city-owned museum to the county with a fair return to city taxpayers for their equity in the facility. While attendance records show a high percentage of suburban use of this municipal facility, suburban voters have twice voted against negotiations for transfer while the transfer was overwhelmingly favored by the voters of the city. More recently, county supervisors turned down a move to set up a county-wide assessment system, even though state assistance would substantially underwrite the cost if assessing were performed by the county rather than by the individual municipalities.

CHANGING THE SYSTEM

The people of the metropolitan area are not so much at fault as is the system which generates conflict. After all, many of the people who live outside the city now are the same people who lived inside it a few years ago. Many of the poor confined to the central city have the same aspirations that motivated their metropolitan neighbors to move to the suburbs. There are also some for whom the green fields of suburbia have lost their charm and who are migrating back to the city. Of course, central cities are encouraging this movement.

But it is the system which is the cause of conflict within metropolitan areas—a system that separates resources from needs. The system must be changed so that there is more sharing of the social responsibilities of metropolitan areas. In recommending a metropolitan social

district to take responsibilities for financing and meeting social problems, I pointed out that we have put water, sewers, and even the animals in the zoo on a metropolitan basis—so why not the problems of people? Similarly, we need a metropolitan school district to equalize educational opportunity, a metropolitan transportation authority to balance both public and private transportation, and, as I have suggested, a regional economic development vehicle.

At the heart of changing the system is finding a means of opening up the suburbs to low and moderate income housing to reduce the concentration of poor in the central city and also, as Downs suggests, of making it more possible to cure the cycle of poverty itself. This is not likely to happen without a strong federal hand, possibly one which would withhold funds for other kinds of municipal needs unless a housing plan exists which includes low income housing.

At the same time, it is essential that the property tax be relieved of much of its responsibility for non–property related functions by switching to a functional tax system and by placing a greater emphasis on domestic needs in the federal budget.

Perhaps much of the conflict witnessed in metropolitan areas in recent decades is a reflection of the revolutionary changes in technology and social conditions that have made the urban world of 1940 a quiet and quaint village compared with today's city. If this is so, as much thought and ingenuity must be used in providing a metropolitan system that will resolve conflict as was used in developing the technology that has helped to produce the conflict.

Interlocal Relations: Cooperation

By WILLIAM C. SEYLER

ABSTRACT: The persistence of large numbers of local governments in the United States emphasizes the continuing need for interlocal cooperation. In the American federal system, where local units are the creatures of the states, it is the states which must play a key role if the service needs of the 1970s are to be met by local governments. It appears that the states are increasingly recognizing this key role by granting local governments broader powers of home rule, by empowering them to enter into agreements among themselves to provide badly needed services, by extending some state powers—such as purchasing—to local units, and by devising revenue sharing programs which have the effect of strengthening local governments. Although the federal government undoubtedly has a greater impact on interlocal cooperation than it did in the pre–New Deal days, it would appear that the early results of the federal revenue sharing program do not reflect the hopes of those who saw the program as a great stimulant for localities to become more innovative and more cooperative with each other, particularly when the early record of the program seems to show a net loss in resources for the local units.

William C. Seyler is Assistant Vice President and Secretary at Temple University. He has served with the Commonwealth of Pennsylvania as Director of Program and Policy Research in the Governor's Office and as Deputy Secretary of the Department of Internal Affairs. Educated at the University of Pittsburgh and at Duke University, he has taught at both of those institutions and at Temple University. He has also served on task forces in Pennsylvania dealing with the reorganization of state government and the preparation of a master plan for higher education.

ABOUT a decade ago, a speaker at the annual meeting of the National Municipal League made an impassioned plea for greater cooperation among local governments. To illustrate the kind of cooperation which he felt was essential, he told the story about a man trudging down a backwoods Arkansas road, lugging along a pig, a chicken and a wooden tub. He came upon a very attractive farm girl whom he asked about directions to the Smith Farm. The girl paused a moment and then replied that the best way to reach the Smith Farm was through the woods just adjacent to the roadway. The traveler glanced at the dense woods, reminded the young lady that he was a stranger in the area, and asked if she might accompany him to his destination. She replied that she would like to help him but, after all, he was a stranger, and he might take advantage of her. The traveler smiled his most reassuring smile, telling her that he understood her fears, but he really felt she was in no danger because he was already fully occupied with the pig, the chicken and the wooden tub. Responding with a degree of cooperation not expected, the young lady said, "You could put the pig on the ground, put the tub over it—and I could hold the chicken."

LARGE NUMBERS OF LOCAL GOVERNMENTS

Students of interlocal relations might well hope for the kind of all-out cooperation illustrated by the above tale, especially when note is taken of the massive numbers of local governments in existence in the United States. Between 1962 and 1972, the total number of local governments was reduced by some 11,000 (from about 91,000 to about 80,000), but the only real progress in

reducing the number of units came about through school district consolidations. These consolidations resulted in 19,000 fewer school districts in 1972, as compared with the number in 1962; but this progress was offset by increased numbers of municipalities (500 more), townships (1900 more), and special districts (5600 more).[1] The large numbers of local units and the tendency of these units, with the exception of school districts, to increase in number in the past decade emphasize the importance of cooperation among local governments if the service needs of the 1970s are to be met.

FRAMEWORK FOR INTERLOCAL COOPERATION

Because local governments in the American system are essentially creatures of the state, one must look to state constitutions and to state statutes for an understanding of the framework for interlocal cooperation. A survey of the 50 state constitutions in 1967 disclosed a wide range of approaches to interlocal relationships: (1) some state constitutions, including most of those in the New England states and those in Delaware and Iowa, were silent about local governments and/or their inter-relationships; (2) some, such as those in Pennsylvania and Maryland, were silent except for provisions directed to specific situations (the consolidation of the city and county of Philadelphia, for ex-

1. U.S., Bureau of the Census, "Governmental Organization," *Census of Governments: 1962* (Washington, D.C.: Government Printing Office, 1963), vol. 1, pp. 11–12; and "Governmental Organization," *Census of Governments: 1972* (Washington, D.C.: Government Printing Office, 1973), vol. 1, pp. 12–13.

ample); (3) some, such as those in
Kansas and Hawaii, contained brief
general authorizations to establish
local governments and to prescribe
their relationships with one another;
(4) some, such as those in Alaska,
California, Missouri and Florida,
authorized a wide range of interlocal
relationships, including such features as city-county consolidations
and separations, intergovernmental
transfers of powers, regional governments, special purpose districts or
authorities, and intergovernmental
cooperation; and (5) some, such as
those in Tennessee and Hawaii, had
isolated references to specific types
of interlocal relationships.[2] In general, then, state constitutions do not
inhibit interlocal cooperation.

As far as state statutory provisions
relating to interlocal cooperation are
concerned, the Committee of State
Officials on Suggested State Legislation of the Council of State
Governments in 1957 drafted a
Model Inter-Local Contracting Act,
which was endorsed by the Advisory
Commission on Intergovernmental
Relations (ACIR) in 1961, and 42
states have enacted all or part of the
act.[3] A survey of more than 2,200
municipalities in 1972 showed that
only two percent of the reporting
units indicated that the state constitution prohibited them from entering into agreements for the provision
of services or inhibited their ability
to enter into service agreements. In
addition, 75 percent said that the

state government actively encouraged the intergovernmental provision of services, and 47 percent
said that the state provided incentive
grants-in-aid.[4]

ROLE OF THE FEDERAL GOVERNMENT

Although the legal framework for
interlocal cooperation is provided by
state constitutions and state statutes,
the federal government, particularly
since the New Deal era, has come to
play an increasingly important role.
When THE ANNALS dealt with
intergovernmental relations in 1940,
the contributor who covered federal-
municipal relationships pointed out
that most of the pre-New Deal
federal-municipal relationships
were casual and incidental, with aid
being in the form of statistical, research, informational, and advisory
services; but he described the
emerging relationship as follows:

The new and more intimate relationship of municipalities to the Federal
Government has been one of the most
significant developments of the present
decade. Officials—both local and Federal—are just beginning to realize that
this new relationship, born of the depression, is likely to be permanent. The
depression, the growing complexity of
society, and an expanding concept of
civic needs have imposed new demands
upon every level of government, the
satisfaction of which has forced the
adoption of new channels for intergovernmental cooperation.[5]

By 1965, when THE ANNALS
again dealt with intergovernmental
relations, the executive director of
ACIR wrote that "The number of
direct federal-local programs has in-

2. *Local Government—Reference Manual
No. 4*, Prepared for delegates to the Pennsylvania Constitutional Convention 1967–
1968 by the Preparatory Committee (Harris-
burg, Pa.: Commonwealth of Pennsylvania,
1967), pp. 201–202.

3. Joseph F. Zimmerman, "Meeting Service Needs through Intergovernmental
Agreements," *Municipal Year Book—1973*,
p. 79.

4. Ibid., pp. 85–86.

5. Raymond S. Short, "Municipalities and
the Federal Government," THE ANNALS
207 (January 1940), pp. 44–53.

creased over recent years to the point that a significant proportion of current federal aid flows directly to local governments."[6]

A 1972 survey of municipalities showed that only 28 out of 1,859 local governments felt that federal statutes or regulations restricted their ability to enter into agreements for services with another governmental unit. Forty-eight percent said that federal statutes and regulations actually encourage intergovernmental cooperation and contracts, and they specifically mentioned federal incentive grants-in-aid for cooperative and regional water and sewer projects.[7]

IMPACT OF FEDERAL REGIONAL ORGANIZATIONS

The federal government's increasing involvement in grant-in-aid programs in the early 1960s led the deputy director of the Bureau of the Budget to tell Congress in 1966 that the federal government was filling "a role in many communities and most States which did not exist 10 or even five years ago: it acts as a catalyst for joint attacks on common problems—environmental pollution, rural and urban development and regional economic growth—and in many cases becomes an active partner in these cooperative programs, through the common effort of several Federal agencies on a specific project within an individual community."[8] These circumstances

eventually culminated in the establishment, by executive orders, of 10 Federal Regional Councils (FRCs), composed of the top regional officials of the major domestic agencies of the federal government. Although the Office of Management and Budget early stressed the job of FRCs as being the better coordination of federal programs at the regional level, later it began to stress the need to respond to state and local governments. That FRCs have not performed very effectively in the latter role is the conclusion of a recent study:

State and local officials, knowing that councils do not have power to make program decisions or to resolve those intrafederal conflicts that they might like to have resolved, such as the dispute in St. Louis between the community action and model cities agencies, will not bring such matters to the councils. And even if the councils' authority was [sic] enlarged, state and local officials would not bring them those intrafederal conflicts that it is not in the local interest to resolve. Chaos in the grant system is not all bad from the local point of view: the more sources of funds the better. If HUD and OEO, without each other's knowledge, are both giving money to a legal services project, as was the case in Denver, local sources are not likely to lodge a complaint.[9]

AGREEMENTS AND CONTRACTS AS COOPERATIVE DEVICES

One of the oldest and most persistent forms of interlocal cooperation is the agreement device, which is usually entered into by two or more adjacent units. In 1958 the Pennsylvania Department of Inter-

6. William G. Colman, "The Role of the Federal Government in the Design and Administration of Intergovernmental Programs," THE ANNALS 359 (May 1965), pp. 23–34.

7. Zimmerman, "Meeting Service Needs," p. 86.

8. Quoted in Martha Derthick and Gary Bombardier, Between State and Nation

—Regional Organizations in the United States (Washington, D.C.: The Brookings Institution, 1974), pp. 158–159.

9. Ibid., p. 180.

nal Affairs, through its Bureau of Municipal Affairs, surveyed some 780 municipalities in the state to determine the scope of cooperative agreements. Of the nearly 650 responding municipalities, 617 cooperative arrangements, involving 1,784 municipalities in the joint performance of government services, were reported. The most numerous local government activities covered by the agreements were water supply, fire protection, sewer services, tax collection, recreation, and health and hospitals. Additional agreements covered such areas as airports, comfort stations, county municipal buildings, garbage collection, police, public safety communication networks, purchasing and libraries. The author of this Pennsylvania survey felt that the major advantages of cooperative agreements included financial savings, increased efficiency of service, needed regional action and retention of community identity. It was felt that the principal disadvantage was the dependence of such agreements upon the willingness of elected or appointed officials to continue the arrangements.[10]

A 1972 national survey of nearly 6,000 incorporated municipalities (cities, villages, boroughs and incorporated towns) revealed that "of the 2248 responding municipalities, 1393, or 61% have entered into formal or informal agreements for the provision of services to their citizens by other governmental units or private firms. Formal agreements tend to relate more to water supply, sewerage treatment, and joint facili-

ties. Informal agreements deal mostly with mutual aid and maintenance of highways and bridges."[11]

Another device which has been used to achieve interlocal cooperation is the so-called Lakewood Plan under which several incorporated cities in Los Angeles County have voluntarily entered into contractual arrangements with the county government to receive, in exchange for a fee, such services as fire and police protection, street maintenance and construction, building inspection and library services. There are 77 incorporated municipalities within the boundaries of Los Angeles County, and they have more than 1,650 separate service contracts with the county covering such services as those listed above.[12] Although the legal authority for the Lakewood Plan exists in several states, its use is somewhat limited.

CITY-COUNTY CONSOLIDATION

Advocates of city-county consolidation maintain that this form of interlocal cooperation promotes greater efficiency in the provision of services, promotes economies of scale and coordination of services, reduces the amount of governmental fragmentation, permits an area to bring together the resources of the central city and the surrounding area, and reduces the need for the creation of special districts or authorities. There are 21 consolidated city-county jurisdictions in the United States, with four of these having been approved since 1969. Twelve of the 13 consolidations approved since 1947 have been the result of referenda, and the remain-

10. Martin J. Kelly, Jr., "617 Agreements Link 1,794 Municipal Units in Cooperative Action," *Department of Internal Affairs Bulletin* 26, no. 7 (July 1958), pp. 1–9, 28.

11. Zimmerman, "Meeting Service Needs," p. 79.

12. Rodney L. Kendry, "Trends in County Government," *Municipal Year Book—1974*, pp. 43–46.

ing one (Indianapolis—Marion County, Indiana) resulted from state legislative action.[13]

REGIONAL COUNCILS

A recognition of the need for a regional, as contrasted with a state or a local, consideration of the problems of the 1970s is the rapid growth of regional councils. These councils include councils of governments (COGs), regional planning commissions, economic development districts and certain other voluntary, multijurisdictional and multifunctional organizations representing local elected officials. The 1972 Membership Directory published by the National Association of Regional Councils lists more than 600 such councils, as compared with only 142 three years earlier. Staff members of ACIR attribute the growth of these regional councils to the following factors: (1) expansion of the federal "701" comprehensive planning assistance programs in 1965 to include regional councils as eligible recipients of funds; (2) implementation of requirements for review and comment of applications for certain federal and federally-assisted projects for conformance with regional plans contained in Section 204 of the Demonstration Cities and Metropolitan Government Act of 1966 and Title IV of the Intergovernmental Cooperation Act of 1968; and (3) a propensity among several federal agencies for using areawide bases for formal planning and grant administration.[14] The executive director of ACIR told the 1973 annual conference of the International Personnel Management Association that "administrators at all levels will have to get used to a new layer of governments at the substate regional level, thanks to the growth of areawide special districts, federally encouraged regional units (1800), state substate districts (488 in 40 states), and regional councils (600)."[15]

The need for a device such as a COG is especially great in a state such as Pennsylvania where there are more than 2,600 units of local government. This local government fragmentation, second highest in the nation, makes it very difficult to solve regional problems and to provide services more economically and efficiently. It is not surprising, therefore, to find that as of 1973 there were 39 COGs operating in Pennsylvania, covering a total population of nearly two and one-half million people and involving more than 400 member municipalities. Typical of the work of these COGs is the Centre Region Council of Governments, which has programs in the areas of recreation, planning, code enforcement and landfill operations. An estimated annual savings of $75,000 is realized by the Bucks County Regional Cooperation Council through its regional joint-purchasing program. A full-time director is supported by the Mid-Monongahela Council of Governments, and through his professional guidance 18 municipalities in three separate counties have been able to implement several regional programs of common interest to the area. The Commonwealth of Pennsylvania, along with several other states, en-

13. Kendry, "Trends."

14. Jean M. Gonsel and Carl W. Sternberg, "Regional Council Performance: The City Perspective," *Municipal Year Book—1973*, pp. 63–76.

15. William MacDougall, "Future Trends in Public Administration—Predictions and Dreams," *ASPA News & Views* 24, no. 1 (January 1974), p. 6.

courages the formation of COGs by providing technical assistance to interested local governmental officials.[16]

INTERLOCAL COOPERATION IN SEWAGE DISPOSAL TREATMENT

The field of sewage disposal and treatment lends itself very well to cooperative action among local governments because of the high costs of constructing the necessary facilities and also because in many instances the natural drainage in an area virtually dictates cooperation. One of the earliest and most complex techniques for getting interlocal cooperation in this field was the Allegheny County Sanitary Authority, which was created in March 1946 under the Pennsylvania Municipal Authorities Act of 1945. The authority was formed for the purpose of handling the collection, transportation, treatment and disposal of sewage and industrial wastes in Allegheny County, which was a maze of 129 municipalities, comprising one second class city (Pittsburgh), three third class cities, 81 boroughs and 44 townships. In addition, the authority had to negotiate with 21 different water supply agencies to obtain periodic water meter readings for the purpose of calculating sewage charges. Within a few years after its giant sewage treatment plant began operation in the spring of 1959, the authority was handling sewage disposal for the city of Pittsburgh and 71 surrounding municipalities having a combined population of 1.4 million

people. The authority has entered into municipal and industrial agreements, forming the basis for sewage charges which will yield about $9.5 million annually to amortize the authority's $100 million of bonds, and to operate its sewage collection, transportation, treatment and disposal facilities.[17]

Recent examples of cooperative efforts in the sewage treatment field are California's establishment, in 1972, of the largest intergovernmental sewage treatment management agency in the nation for nine San Francisco Bay Area counties and all the cities in the area,[18] and approval by voters of Portland, Oregon in 1970 of the formation of a metropolitan district to provide regional sewage treatment and disposal and flood control services in a three-county area.[19]

COOPERATIVE PURCHASING BY LOCAL GOVERNMENTS THROUGH STATES

In 1972, the Arkansas legislature enacted a law to permit cities to purchase supplies at state contract prices.[20] In Pennsylvania, under 1971 legislation, political subdivisions or authorities created by political subdivisions were authorized to purchase materials, supplies and equipment from purchase contracts entered into by the Common-

16. Jae Chung, "Intergovernmental Cooperation—New and Effective Way to Make it Work," *Pennsylvania Department of Community Affairs Reports* 3, no. 8 (October 1973), pp. 13–14.

17. William C. Seyler, "Municipal Cooperation in Action in Pennsylvania," *Department of Internal Affairs Bulletin* 29, no. 8, pt. 1 (August 1961), pp. 6–9; 29, no. 9, pt. 2 (September 1961), pp. 8–15.
18. Don Benninghoven, "Significant State Actions Affecting Local Government," *Municipal Year Book—1973*, p. 8.
19. George S. Blair, "State Local Relations in 1970–71," *The Book of the States, 1972–1973*, p. 281.
20. Benninghoven, "Significant State Actions."

wealth Department of Property and Supplies. By the spring of 1973, nearly 1,400 municipalities in the state were participating in the program, taking advantage of some 270 state purchase contracts available to them. Most frequently used contracts are those covering tires and tubes, fuel oil, gasoline, steel office furniture, traffic zone paint and electric typewriters. Although motor vehicles are not under an annual contract, since many municipalities indicated an interest in them, the Department of Property and Supplies, in making a vehicle purchase, asks the successful vendor if he will extend the price to local units for a specified time. Until the spring of 1973, 81 vehicles were purchased by local governments through this commonwealth program, with a reported savings of more than $60,000.[21]

GRANTING HOME RULE AUTHORITY TO LOCAL GOVERNMENTS

Although the granting of home rule authority to local units does not necessarily stimulate interlocal cooperation, it can, and frequently does, have that effect. It is encouraging, therefore, to find widespread home rule actions by the states in recent years. In 1972, all cities in Iowa were granted complete home rule authority in all areas except finance; Colorado strengthened its procedure for adoption of municipal home rule charters; progressive home rule constitutional amendments or statutes were adopted in Missouri, Montana and Pennsylvania; in addition, study commissions designed to make local governments more effective were created

in Florida, Ohio and California.[22] In 1973 the trend continued, with constitutional amendments providing for municipal home rule being adopted in Wyoming and South Dakota. In addition, the Massachusetts Supreme Judicial Court ruled in favor of a broad interpretation of home rule powers, and decisions in Indiana and New Hampshire allowed cities all powers not expressly denied by law.[23]

STATE ACTIONS IN THE FINANCE AREA

Although much recent attention has been centered on the revenue sharing program of the federal government, one should not lose sight of the most important role which the states play in the fiscal fortunes of local governments. State payments to local governments in fiscal 1970 amounted to $28.9 billion, or $143 per capita. The 1970 sum was up $4.1 billion, or 16.6 percent from the 1969 amount. In 1957, the total was $7.4 billion, or $44 per capita. But other state expenditures were going up at a similar pace, so that the proportion of total state general expenditures represented by payments to local governments was changed relatively little—37.3 percent in 1970 and 35.3 percent in 1957.[24]

The states in recent years have been developing revenue sharing programs of their own. In 1972, for example, Alaska enacted a State Revenue Sharing Act which made $7.8 million available to local units.

21. "Cooperative Purchasing Act," *Pennsylvania Department of Community Affairs Courier* 4, no. 5 (27 March 1973), p. 3.

22. Benninghoven, "Significant State Actions," pp. 5–6.

23. Don Benninghoven, "Significant State Actions Affecting Local Government," *Municipal Year Book—1974*, pp. 3–5.

24. "State Aid to Local Governments in 1970," *The Book of the States, 1972–73*, pp. 283–290.

Wisconsin completely revised its Shared-Tax System, with greater emphasis being given to local tax effort, and it abandoned the distribution of funds according to source. Florida passed the Revenue Sharing Act of 1972, providing for distribution of $132 million to eligible cities on the basis of weighted population, sales tax collections and ability to raise local revenues. Perhaps one of the most significant pieces of legislation passed by the states in 1972 in the fiscal field was the New York statute creating the Intergovernmental Fiscal Advisory Board within the State Office of Local Government. The board is charged with making studies and recommendations in the areas of coordination of state and local debt and taxing powers, home rule powers, the state aid system, the role and control of public authorities, joint intergovernmental cooperation, and the re-allocation of functions between the state and local governments.[25]

In 1973, the states continued to encourage interlocal cooperation by providing expanded revenue sharing programs. Ohio, one of several states with revenue sharing programs, revised its sharing formula. It now allocates 3.5 percent of collections from the state sales tax, personal income tax and corporate franchise tax to the Local Government Fund, in place of the fixed monthly allocation formerly used. Florida reenacted its 1972 State Revenue Sharing Act. In 1973, four states granted cities and counties the authority to establish separate agencies with the powers of taxation and assessment. By constitutional amendment in Georgia, and by statute in Maine, Pennsylvania and

Maryland, two or more local governments in those states may now agree to exercise joint powers to fund and operate a program attractive to one or the other, or to both. Local debt limits in Pennsylvania were also revised so as to be based on average annual revenues rather than on assessed valuation.[26]

IMPACT OF THE FEDERAL REVENUE SHARING PROGRAM

Although it is probably too early to evaluate the federal government's revenue sharing program as to whether it will encourage greater cooperation among local governments, the early signs appear to be on the negative side. Under the general revenue sharing bill, the State and Local Fiscal Assistance Act of 1972, automatic payment is authorized to eligible governments in a five-year program. Approximately $30.2 billion has been appropriated from general United States Treasury funds attributable to the federal individual income tax. The appropriations for the 1972 calendar year amounted to about $5.3 billion. For each subsequent year, the total figure will be increased by $150 million. For 1972, of the $5.3 billion allocation, $1.8 billion was distributed among state governments, and the remaining $3.5 billion was divided among local governments.[27]

One-third of a state revenue sharing allocation will go to the state government, and the remaining two-thirds will be distributed among local units of government. In Penn-

25. Benninghoven, "Significant State Actions," (1973), p. 8.

26. Benninghoven, "Significant State Actions," (1974), pp. 6–11.

27. The information about the general revenue sharing program is based on "Revenue Sharing for Local Government," *Pennsylvania Department of Community Affairs Courier* 3, no. 26 (11 December 1972), pp. 1–2.

sylvania, for example, for the first year, the state received about $91 million and all local governments received about $183 million. Funds received by local governments may be used only for expenses which are "ordinary and necessary," including reduction of taxes. Revenue sharing funds may be spent for operating and maintenance in the following categories: (1) public safety (including police and fire protection, and building inspection); (2) environmental protection (including sewage disposal and garbage collection); (3) public transportation (including transit systems and streets); (4) health; (5) recreation; (6) social services for the poor and the aged; (7) financial administration; and (8) libraries.[28]

In spite of this broad range of purposes for which funds from revenue sharing may be spent, including areas which would appear to be more than ready for imaginative interlocal cooperation (such as sewage disposal, public transportation systems and garbage collection), a leading authority on local government and its administration, Dean Alan K. Campbell of the Maxwell School at Syracuse University, has expressed doubt about the success of the program:

My own reservations about the use of revenue sharing as a means of dealing with the fundamental problem of fiscal inadequacy at the state and local level is that it will cast in concrete the present state-local governmental system. It constitutes a step away from regionalization and reinforces the present distribution of responsibilities between state and local government. It will thereby perpetuate the current maldistribution of state resources. Since those resources now flow in response to political power, rather than need, the result of revenue

sharing will be simply a continuation of disparities between cities and suburbs, as well as between high, middle, and low-income suburbs. It may be that these disparities will exist at a generally higher level of expenditures, although even that is not certain, but it will not eliminate the inequities which now exist.[29]

Dean Campbell's misgivings appear to be supported by one of the early studies of revenue sharing, where it was shown that most cities have spent their initial revenue sharing checks in very few policy areas, and that most of these funds have not been used to initiate new programs or activities; rather, they have been used to supplement and extend existing programs. The study also showed that most cities tended to spend their funds in similar fashions. Finally, the great majority of officials responding to the survey reported that they support the revenue sharing concept, although a large proportion believed that revenue sharing would mean a net loss of federal funds for their city.[30]

28. Ibid., pp. 3–4.

29. Alan K. Campbell, "Old and New Public Administration in the 1970s," *Public Administration Review* 33, no. 4 (July/August 1972), pp. 343–347. It has also been pointed out in the article cited in footnote 33 that "the arbitrary one-third State, two-thirds Local division of the sharing monies roughly approximates the State/Local division in terms of the level that ultimately spends State and Local monies for public services. It does not take into consideration the variation among the states where you have the State level in Hawaii spending directly 77% of the State/Local total and New York only 23%. Nor does it take into account the State/Local distribution of financial responsibility (which level pays for public services). For fiscal 1971 the average State paid for 62% of the State/Local package of services with a range from 47.3% in Ohio to 82.5% in Alaska. Differences of these magnitudes need to be included in the formula used to divide monies between state and local governments."

30. David A. Caputo and Richard L. Cole, "Initial Decisions in Revenue Sharing," *Municipal Year Book—1974*, pp. 95–102.

This fear of a net loss of federal funds was also reflected in a letter which the governor of Pennsylvania sent in the spring of 1973 to all county commissioners and mayors of cities having a population of 50,000 or more. The governor urged these local officials "to use a portion of your Federal revenue sharing to pick up a fair share of the costs of continuing essential programs in your county that the Federal government is cutting." The governor wrote that the state government was trying to do its share by proposing in its 1973–74 budget increased financial support for county governments, including an additional $31 million to pick up direct court costs. He concluded as follows:

I have recommended that the State pick up a portion of the Federal cutbacks in programs to aid our senior citizens and for day care programs that are now operating in most counties. Many additional cutbacks are proposed in the President's 1973–74 Budget that will affect people in your county. The State cannot assume this burden alone. Our preliminary estimates indicate that the loss of Federal funds to support programs at all levels of government in Pennsylvania will exceed $350 million. I am, therefore, urging that local governments put some of your Federal revenue sharing funds to use along with State funds to assure that vital programs continue.[31]

Another paradox of the federal revenue sharing program, pointed out by an astute observer of the state and local scene, is that the program has arrived at a time when the national government is running large deficits and the states and local units are in better financial condition than at any time since the end of World War II. Professor G. Ross Stephens points out that "State and Local

revenue surpluses approach $3 billion in fiscal 1970, $5 billion in 1971, $11 billion in 1972, and are estimated at $17 billion in 1973, with the estimate for 1974 being about $24 billion." In the March 1974 issue of *State Government News*, the Council of State Governments reports that 22 states are anticipating surpluses for fiscal 1973–74, ranging alphabetically from Alaska, with a surplus of $151.7 million, to Wisconsin, with $54 million. On the deficit side, four states—Delaware, Missouri, Vermont and Virginia—and Puerto Rico will be looking for revenues to balance their 1973–74 budgets.[32] One of the reasons for this improved fiscal position of the states is, of course, that new and increased state taxes enacted over the past five or six years are beginning to produce substantial amounts of revenue at the same time that many states and local units are reducing some of their obligations. As Professor Stephens indicates, however, unfortunately this happy state of affairs does not apply to all state and local units. It should also be emphasized that some of this so-called surplus is somewhat misleading because it includes monies which are not really available for other programs since they are needed for funding public employee retirement systems. Finally, it should be noted that states and local governments are not immune from the inflationary pressures which apply to the goods and services they must purchase.[33]

As suggested earlier, although the federal government's revenue sharing program has a very brief history, there is little to suggest that the impact of the program will in any

31. Letter quoted in *Pennsylvania Department of Community Affairs Courier* 4, no. 6 (3 April 1973), p. 2.

32. Cited in *ASPA News & Views* 24, no. 5 (May 1974), pp. 10–11.

33. G. Ross Stephens, "State and Local Public Administration in 1973," *ASPA News & Views* 33, no. 2 (February 1973), pp. 4–6.

way encourage interlocal cooperation; and the early signals appear to show that it may have a negative impact, particularly if the net effect is to reduce federal expenditures to assist local governments in carrying out service programs.

SUMMARY AND CONCLUSIONS

This survey of the state of interlocal cooperation in the 1970s shows that the great number of local governments is not declining substantially, especially in the non–school district segment. This circumstance continues to emphasize the need for cooperation among local units. Despite new terms which have been invented to describe the American federal system, the overriding factor governing interlocal cooperation is the fundamental concept that local governments are creatures of state governments. It is encouraging to note that the states, through constitutional and statutory devices, are extending a greater degree of home rule to municipalities, are developing revenue sharing programs of their own, are extending the advantages of the state's purchasing programs so that municipalities can benefit from them, and are granting broader powers to local units so that they can enter into service agreements among themselves where that appears to be most beneficial.

Although the federal government has had an impact on encouraging interlocal cooperation through its grant-in-aid programs, early assessment of the federal revenue sharing program is not encouraging to those who looked upon revenue sharing as a device to unleash the imaginations of local officials so that they would seek new solutions to the nagging problems of the 1970s.

Perhaps local government officials interested in making interlocal cooperation more effective might take the advice of a very effective protagonist of the Tennessee Valley Authority, David E. Lilienthal, who wrote as follows:

Why is it that the "water control", the "save the soil" and the "unified program of land and water" aspect of TVA is such a sad failure, so far as capturing the general public imagination is concerned? And why has the power program, from the time Senator Norris used that issue, years ago, been such a success, so far as public interest and concern goes?

Isn't the answer that all the eloquence about land and water omits two factors almost essential to wide public interest of a lively kind, to wit, emphasis upon human beings and a fight? In my activities "crusading" on the power issue, when we were surrounded by a "ring of steel" and the getting of a market presented a problem indeed, I sensed the crucial importance of stressing the human factor, the concrete picture of men and women benefiting from low electric rates, etc. . . . And, of course, the utility companies furnished the "fight" element.[34]

It appears to this writer that the states and the federal government have provided local governments with a wide variety of tools to accomplish effective interlocal cooperation. If additional tools are needed, then local officials should take the initiative to persuade state legislators and governors to provide them, keeping in mind the importance of Mr. Lilienthal's first principle of "stressing the human factor." Little effort will be needed to bring into play his second principle, the importance of a good "fight."

34. *The Journals of David E. Lilienthal*, vol. 1, *The TVA Years, 1939–1945* (New York: Harper and Row, 1964), p. 107; quoted in Derthick and Bombardier, *Between State and Nation*, p. 26.

Intergovernmental Relations in Canada

By J. E. HODGETTS

ABSTRACT: Intergovernmental relations in Canada have tended to be viewed in light of the paper distribution of powers contained in the British North America Act, and, as a result, debate and research have focused on judicial interpretation and amendment as means of adapting inter-governmental relations. The tremendous augmentation of governmental functions (and spending) at all levels has necessitated the creation of extra-constitutional mechanisms for providing the flexibility required to meet the contemporary trend toward the merging and blending of jurisdictions that had been thought to exist in relatively watertight compartments. What is unique about the processes termed executive federalism is the way in which adjustment of regional and local relations tends to move to the top for resolution in a species of diplomatic conferences. While the new procedures have injected a realistic flexibility into the system, a high price is exacted in terms of Canada's capacity to arrive at an overall set of national policies.

J. E. Hodgetts is Professor of Political Science at the University of Toronto, Canada. Between 1967 and 1972 he served as Principal and then President of Victoria University in the University of Toronto. For 20 years he taught at Queen's University, Kingston; he served for three years as editorial director of the Royal Commission on Government Organization, and has written widely in the field of Canadian public administration, his latest book being The Canadian Public Service: A Physiology of Government, 1867–1970.

FIFTEEN years ago, the editor of this issue of THE ANNALS called to the attention of Canadian scholars the "strong tendency [in Canada] to regard all intergovernmental relations as comprised within Dominion-Provincial relations." From his particular point of concern at the time this attitude had resulted in the "failure to see interprovincial relations as a separate aspect of Canadian federalism." Professor Leach might well have added that the myopia also extended to federal-local and provincial-local relations. Indeed, so persistent has been this narrower conception that the term "intergovernmental" itself has only in the past decade become a familiar word in the vocabulary of Canadian students and practitioners and in the lexicon of Canadian organizational manuals. Failure to use more comprehensive terminology, as Professor Leach's pioneering article on interprovincial relations revealed, did not mean that wider relations had not been developing; however, it was probably an indicator of the limited focus of Canadian scholarly attention pretty well up to the second world war.

THE "PAPER CONSTITUTION" AND THE JUDICIARY

Historically, that focus has been on the written document, the British North America Act of 1867 (BNA Act), which was a charter for new nationhood, a contract between two founding "races" (French and English), and a reasonably explicit assignment of jurisdictional responsibilities to the national and provincial governments. The fact that the paper distribution of functions made no reference to interprovincial relations—as does the United States Constitution to interstate compacts

—and the fact that municipal institutions were legally regarded as creatures of the provinces may account in some measure for the "strong tendency" to which Professor Leach called attention, that is, to view "all intergovernmental relations as comprised within Dominion-Provincial relations."[1]

In any event, it is the allocation of functions found in the BNA Act that provides the starting point for any discussion of intergovernmental relations in Canada. Insofar as the original allocation of functions was soon deemed to be inappropriate for changing times and requirements, attention was directed to the possibilities of achieving change by amendment and by judicial review of the paper distribution. Both processes raised the question of Canadian nationhood, for the BNA Act was (and remains) an Imperial Statute, formally amendable by the British Parliament, while the final judicial interpretation of the act, until 1949, was also in the so-called alien control of the British Judicial Committee of the Privy Council.

During the 1930s, the nationalists' criticism of the Judicial Committee was apparently vindicated when the judiciary struck down the federal government's legislation designed to cope with the effects of the depression—action that was all the more distressing in the wake of prior decisions on broadcasting and aeronautics that had been favorable to the central government.[2]

1. Richard H. Leach, "Interprovincial Cooperation: Neglected Aspect of Canadian Federalism," Canadian Public Administration 2 (June 1959), p. 84.
2. For these and other cases see, Peter H. Russell, ed., Leading Constitutional Decisions, Carleton Library No. 23 (Toronto: McClelland and Stewart Limited, 1965).

The apparent judicial rejection of the national government's claim to legislate for a national crisis under the ostensible residual powers of the BNA Act—"peace, order, and good government"—gave further credence to the nationalists' claim that the intervention of a so-called outside agency, so obviously out of touch with the domestic situation and so intent on a literal reading of the BNA Act, must be abolished.

Ironically, by the time this step was taken in 1949 and the Supreme Court of Canada was made final arbiter over such questions as the powers, or *vires*, of the federal and provincial governments, the judicial branch began to lose its central position as the mediator and arbitrator of intergovernmental relations. In part, this trend was fortified in the 1960s by the vigorous assertion of the "two nations" theory promoted by the francophone Province of Quebec. From this perspective, the Supreme Court itself became suspect as the ultimate defender of a federation which was coming to be viewed, to use the descriptive term of Arend Lijphart, as a "consociational democracy."[3] From Quebec's point of view, as D. V. Smiley has recently written, "the Court operates entirely under federal law and because its members are appointed by the federal cabinet a neutral and objective interpretation of the constitution is impos-

sible."[4] This challenge to the Supreme Court as a domestic source of legal finality in adjudicating the competing claims to jurisdiction asserted by the provinces and the federal government is a somewhat special argument that sees the Court as one of a number of institutional pawns to be deployed by French Canada in its efforts to avoid checkmate by the central government.

Even without this special attack on the Supreme Court, most acute observers of the federal scene agree in concluding that the judicial branch, since 1945, has been much less influential than in the past in determining the ground rules and the parameters within which intergovernmental relations are conducted.[5] F. R. Scott, one of those who had long promoted a final domestic court of review, wrote in 1961 that "the emergence of fiscal and monetary policy [since 1945] as economic regulators [is] so important a factor today as almost to make us forget the question of legislative jurisdiction. . . The lawyers are moving out and the economists are moving in."[6]

Another long-time student of Canadian federalism, J. A. Corry, assessing postwar trends, observed in 1958 that the gathering of powers and programs into the center originally precipitated by World War II

See also, Professor Russell's useful review of "The Supreme Court's Interpretation of the Constitution Since 1949," in *Politics: Canada*, 1st ed., ed. Paul Fox (Toronto: McGraw-Hill Co. of Canada, Ltd., 1962), pp. 64–80.

3. Richard Simeon's recent study, *Federal-Provincial Diplomacy: The Making of Recent Policy in Canada* (Toronto: University of Toronto Press, 1972), pp. 232, 291, calls attention to the relevance of the Lijphart terminology and mode of analysis to Canada.

4. Donald V. Smiley, *Canada in Question: Federalism in the Seventies* (Toronto: McGraw-Hill Ryerson, Ltd., 1972), pp. 25–26. See also, Peter H. Russell's special study, *The Supreme Court as a Bilingual and Bicultural Institution*, Documents of the Royal Commission on Bilingualism and Biculturalism (Ottawa: Queen's Printer, 1969).

5. For example, Smiley, *Canada in Question*, p. 25, and authorities cited there.

6. F. R. Scott, "Our Changing Constitution," *The Courts and the Canadian Constitution*, ed. W. R. Lederman, Carleton Library No. 16 (Toronto: McClelland and Stewart, Ltd., 1964), p. 27.

but prolonged for postwar reconstruction purposes, had created such a reliance on the use of powers by the central government—especially an assumed spending power for objects within the exclusive legislative competence of the provinces—"that prudent men hesitate to take steps that might wipe it out."[7] In addition to offering this practical explanation as to why "no spectacular cases challenging federal legislative power have recently come to the Supreme Court," Professor Corry concluded that "a political process [was] replacing, or at any rate supplementing more extensively than in earlier years, the judicial process."

More recent commentators have confirmed this conclusion, even though the tide that was flowing so heavily toward the national government has, in the last decade, most obviously ebbed back toward the provinces.[8]

Although intergovernmental conflicts over jurisdictional issues are now more likely to be negotiated through political processes rather than arbitrated by the courts, the judiciary's ultimate role as arbitrator can not be dismissed. One should observe, for example, the unique power conferred on the Supreme Court to render advisory judgments on matters referred to it by the federal or provincial governments. On the other hand, less weight seems to be attached to such advisory decisions, perhaps best exemplified by the general refusal of the provinces to accept an advisory decision of the Supreme Court in 1967 which favored the federal government in a disputed claim of jurisdiction over offshore mineral rights. Similarly, sporadic threats on the part of disgruntled provinces to invoke judicial intervention by way of a reference to the Supreme Court have, in recent years, not been followed up.[9]

Should there be a judicial challenge waiting in the wings, it would most likely be addressed to the assumed federal spending power; but even here the complex negotiating arrangements developed especially to cope with intergovernmental fiscal issues have operated with sufficient give-and-take that the contestants may never have the occasion to place this issue before the courts.[10] Granting the importance of such negotiating procedures for coping with intergovernmental problems, as W. R. Lederman has observed, the courts still must be there to answer the question of who has the power; and the kind of bargain that is struck between governments is influenced by the participants' perception of what the courts have said in the past or their anticipation of what they might say in the future about respective powers and jurisdictions.[11]

THE PAPER CONSTITUTION AND AMENDMENT

As noted above, the conceptualization of intergovernmental rela-

---

7. J. A. Corry, "Constitutional Trends and Federalism," reprinted in *Canadian Federalism: Myth or Reality*, 1st ed., ed. J. Peter Meekison (Toronto: Methuen, 1968), pp. 51–64, at p. 62.

8. *See*, Smiley, *Canada in Question*, pp. 26f and chapter 3; *see also*, Simeon, *Federal-Provincial Diplomacy*, pp. 29–30; and J. R. Mallory, *The Structure of Canadian Government* (Toronto: Macmillan's of Canada, 1971), ch. 10.

9. For examples, *see*, Smiley, *Canada in Question*, p. 26.

10. *See*, Corry, "Constitutional Trends," pp. 62–63.

11. *See*, W. R. Lederman, "Some Forms and Limitations on Cooperative Federalism," *Canadian Bar Review* 45 (September 1967), pp. 409f.

tions in terms of dominion-provincial relations directed attention to the distribution of powers set out in the BNA Act. Resolution of conflict between governments over this distribution was to be achieved either through mediation of the courts or by way of amendment. The substantial decline in the role of the judiciary as arbiters of intergovernmental relations, even after this role was transferred from the Judicial Committee of the Privy Council to the Canadian Supreme Court, has been noted. It is now pertinent to observe how the amendment of the BNA Act became not so much a technique for adapting intergovernmental relationships to meet changing conditions but, in effect, became itself one of the prime and as yet unsolved problems in the arena of intergovernmental debate.

Even more than was the case with judicial review, Canadian nationalists were intent on eradicating the demeaning remnants of colonial status by "repatriating the Constitution" so that the British Parliament would no longer have to be involved in formal amendments. During the 1930s, the active search for an amending formula produced agreement that different components of the BNA Act would need to have different amending procedures and that those matters having to do with the rights of minorities, the use of English and French languages, and the fundamental relationships between the provinces and federal government should be entrenched in the constitution.[12]

In order to counteract the obvious inflexibility produced by entrenching certain key aspects of intergovernmental relations in the constitution, proposals in the 1960s centered on a formula to provide for delegation of authority from one level of government to another. By a happy quirk of political party fortunes, first a Progressive Conservative and then a Liberal Minister of Justice were able to endorse a federal proposal that came to be known as the Fulton-Favreau formula, one important element of which was the provision for mutual delegation of authority. (It is perhaps worth noting, in light of the comments from the previous section, that nothing less than a constitutional amendment would permit delegation of legislative responsibilities because the Supreme Court had denied this possibility.)[13] In 1964 it appeared that concurrence in this formula had been achieved and that the centennial project of repatriating the constitution was in sight. However, the project foundered when Quebec failed to approve and began to pursue with renewed intensity its claim for a special status —a claim that was seen to be inconsistent with the spirit and intent of the Fulton-Favreau formula and, indeed, on the more extreme separatist scale of values, inconsistent with the survival of the union itself.

Constitutional reform, despite this setback, continued high on the agenda of dominion-provincial con-

12. For an excellent brief analytical review of the question of constitutional amendment, see, Mallory, The Structure of Canadian Government, pp. 371–86.

13. On this point, see, Ronald I. Cheffins, The Constitutional Process in Canada (Toronto: McGraw-Hill Co. of Canada, Ltd., 1969), pp. 40–42, where the court's verdict against delegation is queried in a Nova Scotia case, Attorney-General for Nova Scotia v. Attorney-General for Canada 1951 S.C.R. 31.

ferences, at least as recently as the meeting in Victoria, British Columbia, in February 1971. During the last two or three years, however, all governments have shown diminished enthusiasm for a comprehensive approach to the problem. It now seems clear that a number of provinces were willing to give the issue high priority if, by so doing, the special claims of Quebec could be sufficiently placated to retain her uneasy allegiance to the federation. But with each rejection by Quebec—including the proposals in the so-called Victoria Charter of 1971—it began to appear that nothing less than a root-and-branch alteration of the constitution would meet Quebec's theoretical position—and thus far none of the other provinces go. Meanwhile, all governments—including the province of Quebec—were faced with urgent questions that revolved around such practical issues as money, energy resources and transportation; each of these required hard-nosed bargaining through a pragmatic, piecemeal process in which there was little room for, and small patience with, a consideration of comprehensive constitutional revision.[14]

In retrospect, it would appear that the intense though sporadic efforts to find a domestic amending formula that would satisfy all participants were not generated from a conviction that ability to change power distribution would improve the capacity of all governments to adapt to changing system requirements. In fact, only two amendments have had a direct bearing on the paper distribution of powers contained in

the BNA Act: the listing of unemployment insurance as an enumerated federal legislative power (Section 91, 2a) in 1940, and the inclusion of Section 94A in 1964 to enable the Parliament of Canada to legislate "in relation to old age pensions and supplementary benefits, including survivors' and disability benefits," but not so as to deprive the provinces of the right to occupy the same field. The existence of these amendments proves that failure to secure agreement on a domestic amending process has not prevented governments from using this formal technique for making specific additions to the functions listed in the act. However, the infrequency of such amendments does suggest that speedier and more direct ways have been discovered for adjusting the functions of all levels of government to contemporary pressures for change. The anxious debate over constitutional amendment appears, then, to have been occasioned less by the expectation of practical benefits in managing intergovernmental relations and more by the urge to secure symbolic release from old colonial bonds that implied the possession of less than full nationhood. Unfortunately, this last urge has more recently been caught up in Quebec's formulation of status symbols of its own which, if they were to be fully met, would make such demands on the constitution as to raise serious doubts about the federation's capacity to survive. Out of fear, boredom, or the more immediate urgency of practical issues, constitutional revision appears to have been temporarily set aside; yet, like Banquo's ghost, it will continue to hover over the participants in most intergovernmental negotiations, no matter what specific matter is on the agenda.

14. *See*, Professor Smiley's conclusions, *Canada in Question*, pp. 51–52.

INTERGOVERNMENTAL RELATIONS THROUGH EXTRA-CONSTITUTIONAL MEANS

The inherent limitations of both judicial arbitration and of formal amendment in providing the mechanisms for viable intergovernmental relations only came to the fore when governments were obliged to expand their activities to meet the forces of change and mass demands for economic regulation and social intervention. Intergovernmental friction remains latent, even where jurisdictions touch or overlap, as long as neither governmental party is called upon to press outward on its assigned powers. When, as was the case in the mid-thirties, the problems caused by the depression could be met only by full deployment of the central government's powers, friction was immediately generated by the courts' invoking of the classical notion of so-called watertight compartments in determining that the only government in a position to deal with the crisis was denied the legal competence to do so. During the second world war this conclusion was set aside when, for all practical purposes, Canada became a unitary state, and intergovernmental relations were effectively put in abeyance. The immediate postwar period found the federal government riding high: its civil service had not only swollen enormously but had become highly competent; it had acquired great confidence in its capacity to regulate the economy through fiscal and monetary policies; and this same confidence, fortified by the prevailing Keynesian wisdom, was to be applied to the task of postwar reconstruction without recession and pledged to the maintenance of full employment. This centralizing momentum carried through pretty well up to the 1960s, coinciding until 1957 with the not-unrelated fact that the Liberal party monopolized the powers of the federal government.

Though the period began with the federal government playing the game of intergovernmental relations as if it had *droit du seigneur* over the provinces, very quickly the larger provinces dug in their heels on the federal package of postwar proposals. As far as the barter terms of trade between the two levels went, the provinces could lean on the legal position, well sustained by the courts, that the bulk of the social service and welfare proposals clearly lay within their jurisdiction; they could also continue to balk at amendments that might alter the legal balance. On the other hand, the federal government, with its unlimited legal right to tax (the provinces being restricted to direct taxation), was in the usual dominant position of one who controls the financial levers and has access to taxable sources, unconstrained by the territorial limits imposed on the provinces. The need for money to meet costs of programs was becoming more significant in those programmatic fields of health, education, welfare and highways—all lying within provincial jurisdiction —which now had the highest priority on provincial budgets. They were also functions for which it was highly desirable, both in practical terms of preserving a meaningful union and in human terms of achieving equity, that minimum standards of service be preserved. Yet how could this be done as long as each province had the legal right to mount the programs but varied enormously in its capacity to extract tax revenues to pay for them?[15]

This conundrum had been the prime focus of the Royal Commission on Dominion-Provincial Relations, whose report and supporting studies appeared in 1940. Its proposals for adjusting revenue resources to programmatic responsibilities were overtaken by the war, but its analysis—particularly of intergovernmental adjustment of public finance—has become a classic and has had a profound influence on the extra-constitutional mechanisms for adjustment that such so-called fiscal federalism generates. However, the Royal Commission's stress on preserving a balanced federation by emphasizing the financial and administrative independence of the provincial and dominion governments did not survive the challenge of the centralizing trends mentioned above. Only in the 1960s was this trend reversed, but not because of a simple pendulum-swing back to the provinces, reinstating the royal commissioners' 1940 version of balanced but relatively autonomous units. Rather, as a consequence of the heavy accretion of programs, there occurred what amounted to a total obliteration of those neat legal compartments into which the duties of each level of government had been consigned and doggedly protected by the courts. Now, the permeation and interpenetration of the walls surrounding respective jurisdictions over the main policy arenas led to a species of functional osmosis, in which boundary maintenance or adjustment by courts and constitutional amendment were increasingly irrelevant. In brief (retaining the classical vocabulary for describing what had been happening), nearly all functions had become "concurrent" in practice, even though in constitutional form only agriculture, immigration and old age pensions (Sections 95 and 94A, BNA Act) were so designated.

Nowhere was this intermingling trend more prominently displayed than in the field of fiscal relations. Here the Royal Commission's recommendations of 1940 have left an indelible mark on the substantive measures that have been negotiated to produce fiscal equalization based on fiscal need, as well as a legacy of intergovernmental negotiating mechanisms that such interdependent policies were bound to bring in their wake.

Beginning in 1941 with the pre-emption by the federal government of lucrative sources of direct taxation, which in effect the provinces rented in return for off-setting payments, a scheme of tax and revenue sharing was inaugurated. It has followed such a convoluted trail ever since that it would require many pages of labored prose to guide a visitor through the undergrowth. For present purposes, it is enough to point out that the need for regular revision of these financial terms of intergovernmental trade and their extraordinarily technical, as well as politically sensitive, nature have brought into being negotiating committees of the chief financial officers of all governments at the highest political and bureaucratic levels. It is also pertinent to observe, without getting immersed in the detail, that changes in the nature of these

15. The intricate and technical issues raised with respect to fiscal issues are brilliantly dealt with in Smiley's *Canada in Question*, in a chapter aptly entitled "The Political Economy of Canadian Federalism".

agreements have—over time but with increasing clarity in the past decade—drastically altered the initial overwhelming power of the federal government. Through the concession of tax abatements to the provinces, beginning with the agreement of 1957–62 and, in 1965, with the opportunity afforded the provinces to "contract out" of certain conditional grant programs (receiving fiscal equivalents in compensation), the provinces were rapidly moving into a position where the federal government was being relieved of such significant portions of its classical leverages on the economy that its earlier commitment to a national policy of full employment and stable economic growth could be seen to be jeopardized. From the viewpoint of the larger and more well-endowed provinces (with Quebec's special pleas adding further urgency to the case), their cry for more so-called tax room and their desire to contract out of shared costs rose from a newly found feeling of potency in relation to matters such as education, health and welfare that were of vital concern to their own residents. Buttressing these demands to go it alone was the virtual revolution that had occurred in provincial bureaucracies, which had led to their overnight modernization and placed them on a par with the federal bureaucracy that had undergone the same transformation, largely under the impact of wartime demands.[16] Thus fortified with competent manpower and with increasing freedom to engineer their own spending priorities, the larger provinces especially became less enchanted with having the federal government's priorities thrust upon them, sugarcoated in the form of conditional grants or shared costs which they— and particularly the less wealthy provinces—could ill afford to reject.

The endless intergovernmental negotiations required to achieve a moving equilibrium with respect to the basic financing of the federation, have been duplicated in a great many of those functional arenas which, as noted above, have come to be literally fields of concurrent jurisdiction. The term applied to this entire complex of processes was cooperative federalism, but the expression coined by Professor Smiley, executive federalism, is much more apt and accurate.[17] Possibly the most severe testing of executive federalism in the seventies will be the issue of planning and development. As an example, a recently created federal Department of Regional Economic Expansion is attempting to ameliorate regional imbalances in economic growth by the injection of federal aid and incentives into regional constructs of the federal government's own making. At the same time, a province like Ontario has embarked on a regional development program of its own which involves the re-centralizing of municipal governments by incorporating them into larger regional entities to which both the former powers of allegedly inviable local units and certain provincial powers will devolve. Needless to say, pro-

16. For a quick sketch of these changes, see, J. E. Hodgetts, "The Public Service: Its past and the challenge of its future," *Canadian Public Administration* 17 (Spring 1974), pp. 16–25; for the explosion in size of provincial (as well as local) governments' public services, see, J. E. Hodgetts and O. P. Dwivedi, "The Growth of Government Employment in Canada," *Canadian Public Administration* 12, (Summer 1969), pp. 224–38.

17. See his chapter with this title in *Canada in Question*, pp. 55–74.

vincial regional constructs which are now both administrative and legislative (the latter by delegation) do not coincide with new federal regional constructs whose purposes are set within a totally different hierarchy. In a situation where many provinces are using their legislative supremacy over local authorities to modify quite drastically their historic status as relatively autonomous, so-called self-governing municipalities, a new and still unstable set of intergovernmental relationships is emerging.[18] Insofar as the federal government—unlike its counterpart in the United States—has not developed direct relations with local authorities, federal initiatives in regional development have had to be taken in relative isolation from provincially-inspired local government reform plans which also hinge on a regional approach. And, despite the growing importance of large urban governments as regions in their own right, insistent cries for representing the so-called third level of government in such formal gatherings as the Dominion-Provincial Conferences have been ignored.[19] One of the most recent federal creations, a Ministry of Urban Affairs, has sponsored a rather tentative experiment with tri-level mechanisms which may ultimately help create the conditions for the kind of coordinated negotiation so urgently required for joint development of policies in such areas as housing, land use planning and land banking, and environmental pollution.

The current state of intergovernmental affairs also demonstrates how prophetic the Royal Commission on Dominion-Provincial Relations was when, in 1940, it opposed conditional grants on the score that differences over them would rise to the top for adjustment, rather than be resolved quietly by specialists at the administrative level. The high visibility of intergovernmental relations anticipated by the Royal Commission has been analyzed recently by Richard Simeon in a book significantly entitled *Federal-Provincial Diplomacy*. Going beyond the limited case made by the Royal Commission, Simeon makes the persuasive point that the national legislature, the federal cabinet and bureaucracy, and the Canadian party system are all inadequate in fostering regional accommodation. As a consequence, governments are compelled to negotiate directly with each other and, on the larger issues, to negotiate almost as foreign powers meeting regularly in Dominion-Provincial Conferences.[20]

Unquestionably, the procedures described by Simeon as diplomacy, and by Smiley as executive federalism, exact a high price for the undoubted benefits conferred on the system.[21] Most negotiations are conducted in an atmosphere of closed

18. The most recent reform proposals for Nova Scotia were contained in a three-year royal commission (the Graham Commission) study that was tabled in the provincial legislature on June 27, 1974. The Toronto *Globe and Mail*, 28 June 1974, reported that the recommendations "include takeover by the provincial Government of all responsibility for education, health, social services, housing, and administration of justice, and a redrafting of the county boundaries."

19. Illustrative of the jealousy with which the provinces guard their constitutional rights in the area of local government was their unanimous opposition to a federal Municipal Loan Fund which the federal government planned to administer itself; instead, the provinces insisted on administering the program on behalf of the federal government.

20. Simeon, *Federal-Provincial Diplomacy*, ch. 2 especially.

21. *See*, Smiley, *Canada in Question*, pp. 66–72, for his balancing of the liabilities and assets of executive federalism.

politics; there is discontinuity, an exaggeration of divisive regional claims in which "the West" now joins Quebec as odd-men out; and, above all, the impression is that negotiations lean heavily on the incrementalism characteristic of bureaucratic policy making, and that a national policy—such as on energy—is a highly unlikely outcome from an accumulation of piecemeal bargains arrived at pragmatically and often opportunistically. Short of a reversion to the old classical form of federalism in which governments were seen to operate out of separate compartments, Canadian intergovernmental relations in the seventies may well develop along the international relations path suggested by Professor Simeon's analogy to the diplomacy of federal-provincial negotiations. In that case, Canadians may witness—on the analogue of the United Nations—the emergence of tri-level secretariats, joint aid to the underdeveloped, the contracting out of a service or a program by one level of government to another level, or even the assignment of a program to a private group. Fanciful as these notions may seem, there are already embryonic exemplars to prove that ingenuity, imagination and the will to survive as a union will be deployed to meet the perennial challenges posed by intergovernmental relations in Canada.

Intergovernmental Relations in Britain

By G. W. JONES

ABSTRACT: Intergovernmental relationships in the United Kingdom are more confused and uncertain than they have been for a long time. The recent reorganization of local government has made more complex relationships between the tiers of local authorities, especially in the cities where a single-tier system had prevailed. The establishment of new functional agencies for water and the health services, distinct from local authorities, has further fragmented local power. To work the new system, elected members and their staffs will require diplomatic skills to relate their own authority with tiers both above and below and with other public agencies involved in providing services in their area. Local authorities are not so dependent financially on the central government as is sometimes alleged, and although the center has many devices available to it to influence local government, the use made of them varies between the departments, and the response to them varies again between the local authorities. Regional devolution is advocated by nationalist movements in Wales and Scotland, and by some in England who want to reduce the power of the center and involve the public more in government. Seven models of devolution are currently under discussion. Ulster remains a thorny problem. Complications to intergovernmental relationships are introduced by pressure for popular participation in community councils and by Britain's entry into the European Economic Community.

G. W. Jones, M.A., D.Phil., is Senior Lecturer in Political Science at the London School of Economics and Political Science. Educated at Jesus and Nuffield Colleges, Oxford University, he is author of Borough Politics, co-author of Herbert Morrison: Portrait of a Politician, and contributor to Political Quarterly, Political Studies, and Public Administration. He served as Secretary of the Political Studies Association of the United Kingdom.

INTERGOVERNMENTAL relationships in the United Kingdom appear at the moment to be in such a flux that it is hard to believe Britain is a unitary state or to guess what pattern of interaction between government institutions will form in the future. Relationships between the national government and local authorities in England and Wales have not yet settled down after the upheaval of a major reorganization of local government in April 1974, and Scotland undergoes a similar process in May 1975.[1] The new system of local government covers the country with a two-tier structure of counties (regions in Scotland) and districts, thus subjecting the cities, which up to now have enjoyed the single-tier county borough form of all-purpose government, to a hierarchy of tiers that fragments local governmental authority. Beneath these local authorities there is a growing movement for popular participation in parish, community and neighbourhood councils, both to provide a few services to their localities and to channel public views to higher authorities. Complexity at the local level has been further increased by the establishment of new public agencies, distinct from local government, for water and sewerage functions and for the health services.[2]

At the level between local government and the national government, major changes are under consideration. In Scotland and Wales, nationalist movements urge a considerable devolution of power to governments in Edinburgh and Cardiff, and in England there is pressure for the establishment of provincial or regional councils to which would be handed a range of services at present controlled from London or by the various ad hoc functional authorities that operate at the regional level. Proposals for regional devolution are being considered by the government, which in March 1974 set up in the Cabinet Office a team of constitutional advisers, headed by Lord Crowther-Hunt. Their starting point is the report of the Royal Commission on the Constitution, the Kilbrandon Report of October 1973, which recommended wide-scale devolution.[3] In June 1974 the first results of the work of Lord Crowther-Hunt appeared in the form of a consultative document, to stimulate public discussion, on the implications of devolution, primarily to Scotland and Wales.[4] Firm government proposals are promised for later in the year.

The Kilbrandon Commission also examined relationships between the United Kingdom and the Crown dependencies of the Channel Islands and the Isle of Man, as well as the problem of Northern Ireland. In May 1974 a strike of Ulster Protestants brought down the power-sharing executive so painfully constructed in 1973. Northern Ireland, for the time being, is under the direct rule of London, and the government faces the seemingly intractable task of devising a system of government for Ulster that can command the support of both the Protestant majority and the Catholic minority. Increasingly, voices are heard urging that the United Kingdom withdraw from Ireland and leave the two Irish nations

1. Local Government Act 1972; and Local Government (Scotland) Act 1973.

2. Water Act 1973; and National Health Service Reorganization Act 1973.

3. Royal Commission on the Constitution 1969–73, vols. 1 and 2, Cmnd. 5460 (London: Her Majesty's Stationery Office, 1973).

4. Office of the Lord President of the Council, Devolution Within the United Kingdom (London: H.M.S.O., 1974).

either to reach an accommodation between themselves or to fight it out.

Britain's entry into the European Economic Community (EEC) in January 1973 added another dimension to intergovernmental relationships, since its activities impinge directly not only on the national government, but also on local authorities and on many functions that may be devolved to any new regional institutions.[5] The future is unpredictable, for the Labour government is pledged to renegotiate the terms of entry, and a large section of the Labour party is in favor of Britain's withdrawal.

Finance bedevils discussions of intergovernmental relations. Britain's contribution to the EEC budget is a bone of contention. A stumbling block to schemes of regional devolution is the difficulty of working out a viable system of financing regional authorities; local government's only tax, the rate, comes under mounting criticism, while the growth of central grants to local government is said to be undermining its freedom of action and transforming it into a mere agent of the center.

Intergovernmental relations in the United Kingdom, therefore, seem never to have been so complex and so confused, and their future development so uncertain.

The Local Level

Local government has been simplified to some extent by the recent reorganization.[6] In England—ex-cluding London's 34 authorities— 1,210 local authorities have been reduced to 377, in Wales 181 to 45, and in Scotland 430 to 65. But the two-tier structure introduces to the cities a new problem of intergovernmental relationships. The government's decision to adopt the two-tier system was a repudiation of the recommendation of Lord Redcliffe-Maud's Royal Commission on Local Government in England, which between 1966 and 1969 had conducted a searching inquiry. It criticized the division of functions among tiers, outside the county boroughs, for so confusing the citizens that they found it hard to comprehend which authority performed which function and to take an active interest in their local government, whereas the county borough was "local government in its simplest, most understandable and potentially most efficient form."[7] Accordingly, the commission recommended that over most of England there be 58 so-called unitary authorities. Arguments in favor of the unitary approach emphasize the disadvantages of the two-tier system that now prevails:

---

5. R. A. W. Rhodes, "The European Community and British Public Administration: The Case of Local Government," *Journal of Common Market Studies* 11 (June 1973), pp. 263–275; and "Anaemia in the extremities and apoplexy at the centre," *New Europe* 2 (Winter 1973–4), pp. 61–77.

6. For the new system, *see*, Peter G. Richards, *The Reformed Local Government System* (London: Allen and Unwin, 1973); Richard Buxton, *Local Government*, 2nd ed. (London: Penguin, 1973); Lord Redcliffe-Maud and Bruce Wood, *English Local Government Reformed* (London: Oxford University Press, 1974). For two critical assessments, *see*, G. W. Jones, "The Local Government Act 1972 and The Redcliffe-Maud Commission," *Political Quarterly* 44 (April–June 1973), pp. 154–166; and R. A. W. Rhodes, "Local Government Reform: Three Questions—What is Reorganisation? What are the Effects of Reorganisation? Why Reorganisation?" *Social and Economic Administration* 8 (Spring 1974), pp. 6–21.

7. *Royal Commission on Local Government in England 1966–1969*, vol. 1, Cmnd. 4040 (London: H.M.S.O., 1969), para. 253.

1. By ending the fragmentation of local government, the unitary authority would be comprehensible and likely to interest and involve the public.

2. Services which increasingly impinged on one another would be considered together by a single authority. Housing, for instance, is closely linked to land use and transport as well as to the personal and social services. Combining them all in a unitary authority would allow an integrated approach to the totality of local government services.

3. A unitary authority would enable the directly elected representatives to assess the needs of their area, to draw up a set of priorities, and to allocate resources for that mix of services most appropriate for their area. This power to control the development of the community would make choices of voters at local elections really meaningful.

Thus, the unitary system would be both democratic and efficient.

The commission, however, destroyed the arguments by advocating a two-tier structure for the three conurbations of the West Midlands, Merseyside and Greater Manchester. Without any evidence, it concluded that a unitary authority of more than a million would present organizational and managerial problems and be too massive for a viable system of local democracy. The commission thus provided ammunition for its opponents who were supported by Derek Senior's memorandum of dissent, which advocated a two-tier structure for the whole country,[8] and by Lord Wheatley's Royal Commission on Local Government in Scotland, which also proposed a two-tier structure.[9]

Although the Labour government adopted Redcliffe-Maud's approach, it was defeated at the general election of 1970 before it could implement the changes. The new Conservative government, which drew more political support from the counties and districts than did Labour, which commanded more the loyalty of the county boroughs, overturned the Labour plans and adopted a two-tier system which was eventually enacted as the Local Government Act of 1972.

The two-tier system is not uniform throughout the country. Slight differences exist in the distribution of functions between the tiers in England, Wales and Scotland. In the six English metropolitan areas of the West Midlands, Greater Manchester, Merseyside, South Yorkshire, West Yorkshire, and Tyne and Wear, the functions are allocated between the tiers in a quite different way from the rest of the country. In brief, in the metropolitan areas the lower tier has the most functions; in the nonmetropolitan areas the top tier has the most. For example, counties in both have land use and transport planning, police and fire services, and in the nonmetropolitan areas they have education, libraries and the social services as well; but in the metropolitan areas the latter three functions are the responsibility of the districts. Outside the metropolitan areas, districts have relatively few functions: housing,

8. *Royal Commission on Local Government in England, 1966–1969*, vol. 2, Cmnd. 4040-1 (London: H.M.S.O., 1969).

9. *Royal Commission on Local Government in Scotland, 1966–1969*, Cmnd. 4150 (London: H.M.S.O., 1969).

local planning, local transport and environmental services.

Intergovernmental relations have been made complex because functions have not been allocated on a clear-cut basis. Instead, the same function has been split between the tiers. For example, in land use planning the county draws up the structure plan, which outlines broad uses of land, while the districts devise local plans in more detail and operate development control, all within the framework of the structure plan. A further complication is that the county, in consultation with the district, draws up the development plan scheme which designates whether the county or a district will in fact prepare a local plan.[10] Counties plan the provision of public transport, but districts provide the facilities; some roads are the responsibility of the county, others of the district; garbage is collected by the district, but disposed of by the counties; complaints about food hygiene are handled by the districts, but complaints about misleading trade descriptions or inadequate weights and measures are handled by the counties.

Services which are closely linked with others are carried out by different tiers. In the metropolitan areas, housing, as the responsibility of the districts, is severed from the land planning and transport functions of the counties; in the non-metropolitan areas, housing is separated from the social services as well. Such divisions are a repudiation of two authoritative reports. The Seebohm Report on local authority social services concluded that the provision of social services to families would not be fully effective unless the social service department and the education, health and housing departments were the responsibility of the same authority;[11] Redcliffe-Maud's Commission stated that housing, as a major instrument of land planning policy, needed to be linked intimately with decisions on development, redevelopment, conservation and transportation.[12]

Complexity and scope for dissension between tiers are also encouraged by the devices of shared and concurrent powers—for instance, with museums and art galleries, swimming baths, parks and open spaces, aerodromes and health education—and are further confounded by the so-called agency concept, whereby one authority may arrange for another to carry out a particular function, but not education, social services or the right to levy a rate. For example, a county might arrange for a district to provide libraries.[13] Already the tiers have squabbled over agency arrangements and have drawn in the central government to arbitrate.

Such a complex distribution of functions may be seen as a challenge to the counties and districts to cooperate on a variety of joint committees and working parties. But the more likely consequence is friction,

---

10. *See,* Department of the Environment, *Local Government Act 1972, Town and Country Planning: Co-operation Between Authorities,* Circular 74/73 (London: H.M.S.O., 1973).

11. *Report of the Committee on Local Authority and Allied Personal Social Services,* Cmnd. 3703 (London: H.M.S.O., 1968), paras. 676–681.

12. *Royal Commission on Local Government in England 1966–1969,* vol. 1, Cmnd. 4040 (London: H.M.S.O., 1969), paras. 244–247.

13. Department of the Environment, *Local Government Act 1972, Sections 101 and 110, Arrangements for the Discharge of Functions ("Agency Arrangements"),* Circular 131/72 (London: H.M.S.O., 1972).

since each authority, directly elected and with its own full-time bureaucracy, will develop its own concept of what is in the best interests of its own area; the tension between the tiers will be increased when, as may often happen, the county is controlled by one political party and the district by its rival. In any case, the citizen is likely to find it more difficult than in the past to know which local authority is responsible for which service.

Fragmentation exists not only by tier, but also by function. Water, sewage disposal and some sewerage functions have been removed from local government and handed to 10 appointed regional water authorities, thus hindering the task of tackling pollution, since local government remains responsible for environmental health. But personal health services, including home nursing, midwifery, child care, family planning, health centers, health visiting, ambulances, vaccination and immunization, and school medical and dental services, have all been removed from local government and allotted to 14 regional and 72 area appointed health boards. Thus the health services have been splintered from the social services, and interlocking problems will not be able to be dealt with comprehensively. Elected members and bureaucrats will have to devote much more time to negotiating and bargaining across administrative boundaries. New skills of diplomacy will have to be acquired by members and staff if they are to work the new system successfully.

It is ironic that at the very time when a planning-programming-budgeting system (PPBS), corporate management and community planning were becoming fashionable in British local government, a new structure was erected that raised obstacles to their achievement.[14] Although a recent report on the internal organization of local authorities observed that local government has within its purview the overall economic, cultural and physical well-being of the community,[15] the fragmentation of power inherent in recent reforms inhibits local government from being an effective community planner. The county boroughs, especially, have been damaged, since they once had responsibility for water, health and all local government functions, and had developed corporate planning on a wide scale.[16]

It is not too fanciful to suggest that the new system reflects Conservative ideology: where Labour is committed to planning and emphasizes coordination, Conservatives stress decentralized decision making, partisan mutual adjustment and a system of administrative competition similar to the classical market economy.

CENTRAL-LOCAL RELATIONS

Lord Redcliffe-Maud's commission advocated fewer, larger, and

14. Tony Eddison, *Local Government: Management and Corporate Planning* (Aylesbury: Leonard Hill Books, 1973); and J. D. Stewart, *Management in Local Government* (London: Charles Knight, 1971).

15. *The New Local Authorities: management and structure* (the Bains Report), (London: H.M.S.O., 1972), para. 2.10. *See also*, for Scotland, *The New Scottish Local Authorities: Organisation and Management Structures* (the Paterson Report), (Edinburgh: H.M.S.O., 1973).

16. R. Greenwood, A. D. Smith, and J. D. Stewart, *New Patterns of Local Government Organisation* (Birmingham: Institute of Local Government Studies, Occasional Paper No. 5, Series A, 1971); Richard C. Lucking, Keith Howard, and Michael J. Greenwood, "Corporate Planning and Man-

stronger authorities to enable local government to check increasing central control. The center would then have no justification to remove functions from local government, services lost in the past might be regained, and a host of petty irritating controls could be relaxed. If there were only one type of local authority, the unitary, then at the center there would be only one pressure group for local government. A single local authority association would replace the four which had represented county boroughs, counties, urban districts and rural districts, had engaged in battles among themselves, and had thus allowed the central government to divide and rule. But the creation of the tiered structure has produced three associations, the Association of County Councils, the Association of District Councils and the Association of Metropolitan Authorities, each defending the interests of its constituent authorities. Local government still does not speak with a single voice to the central government.

In the new system of local government there has been a small relaxation in some of the 1,254 statutory controls operated by central departments over local government; for instance, local authorities are more free to decide what committees to appoint or what officials to employ, but they must still appoint a number of officials, including a chief education officer and a director of social services.[17] Although the government has not adopted the Redcliffe-Maud suggestion that local authorities be given a general competence to do anything not specifically excluded by Act of Parliament, it has widened their scope by empowering local authorities to incur expenditure up to the product of a two-penny rate on anything which in their opinion is in the interests of their area, any part of it, or all or some of its inhabitants. However, there is little sign that the center is ready to allow local authorities much greater discretion than in the past. Since 1970 it has removed functions from local governments, at the very time it was supposed to be strengthening them, and has created new curbs on local authorities' freedom: for instance, by preventing local authorities from determining the rents of council houses, threatening recalcitrant authorities with centrally appointed housing commissioners, stopping the provision of free milk to children over the age of seven, and dictating the form of secondary education.

Redcliffe-Maud subscribed to the view that local government was becoming a mere agent of the center because of the weakness of local government structure, a national insistence on uniform and high standards of service, and the need for national restriction of the level of capital and current expenditure (in the interests of serving the economy as a whole and of managing demand for economic resources). Another major factor encouraging central control was said to be the inadequacy of local government's only tax, the rate, which provides insufficient finance for the needs of local government, causing it to be even more dependent on central grants— and with central grants comes central control.[18] A number of aca-

agement: A Review of their Application in English Local Government," *Town Planning Review* 45 (April 1974), pp. 131–145.

17. *Local Government Act 1972*, Section 112.

18. *See*, W. A. Robson, *Local Government in Crisis* (London: Allen & Unwin, 1966), pp. 47–68.

demics, however, are skeptical of the view that there is tight central control and that this central control flows from central grants.[19] It is often pointed out that central grants cover an increasing proportion of local expenditure. In England and Wales, of current expenditure considered for grant purposes, rates cover about 40 percent, and grants 60 percent. But these figures are averages for the whole country and do not show the variations in the proportions of grants to individual local authorities, some of which receive as much as 80 percent, and others only 30 percent. Also, it has not yet been proved that those authorities receiving the highest grants are the most tightly controlled. In any case, the bulk of the grant, about 90 percent, is given through the Rate Support Grant, a general grant which allocates a block sum to a local authority without attaching conditions as to how it should be spent. Financial dependence does not necessarily lead to close central control. Also, the degree of financial dependence has been exaggerated, since the ratio of 60 to 40 for grants and rates relates only to net expenditure considered relevant for grant purposes. It does not cover all expenditure, and omits income from local charges, fees, rents and trading services. When these incomes are considered, grants provide 45 percent of total local authority income, rates 35 percent, and miscellaneous items 20 percent.[20]

Central government has many ways other than the grant system of exercising influence over local government. It can obtain statutory authority for issuing policy directives; through its power to approve loan sanction for specific projects of capital expenditure in the most important services, it can influence local authority provision, modifying and even rejecting what local authorities seek to do; its approval is needed for a number of local authority plans for the long term development of their services, such as land planning, education and the social services; and, through the issuing of guidelines, model schemes, circulars of advice, and such informal contacts as meetings at the ministry, sessions with inspectors and even phone conversations, it can seek to persuade and cajole local authorities. Central government also exercises an appellate function when a citizen is in dispute with his local authority about an application for planning permission or the compulsory purchase of his property.

Although this battery of controls and inducements seems formidable, the use made of them varies between departments, and even between divisions within departments, some of which are more interventionist than others, depending on the tradition of the department, the nature of the service, the personalities of the ministers and leading civil servants, and the state of public opinion. The center is no monolith.[21] Local au-

19. Noel Boaden, *Urban Policy-Making* (Cambridge: Cambridge University Press, 1971); John Dearlove, *The Politics of Policy in Local Government* (Cambridge: Cambridge University Press, 1973); K. Davey, "Local Autonomy and Independent Revenues," *Public Administration* 49 (Spring 1971), pp. 45–50; O. A. Hartley, "The Relations between Central and Local Authorities," *Public Administration* 49 (Winter 1971), pp. 439–456.

20. The statistics have been provided by the Chartered Institute of Public Finance and Accountancy, and my L.S.E. colleagues, Richard Jackson and Maurice Perlman.

21. J. A. G. Griffith, *Central Departments and Local Authorities* (London: Allen and Unwin, 1966).

thorities vary in their reactions to central attempts to control them. Some are docile; others are more responsive to the needs of their areas and more assertive and skillful at using the financial, legal, administrative and political resources at their disposal to pursue an independent line. Local authorities vary accordingly in their willingness to accept control, with the result that significant variations exist between authorities in patterns of expenditure, levels of service provision, and policies adopted over a wide range of important services. Central control, therefore, is an inappropriate description for the relationship between central departments and local authorities; interaction is the more apt term. Collaboration and partnership are words used at times to describe the relationship, and they rightly convey the notion that the relationship is not dominated by one side.

THE REGIONAL LEVEL

Between the national government and local government is a confusing mixture of public agencies. Most central departments have regional outposts to handle parts of their administrative responsibilities. Coordination between them in England is through interdepartmental committees, mainly the Regional Economic Planning Boards, chaired by the regional directors of the Department of the Environment. No English region has a counterpart of the Scottish or Welsh Office and their secretaries of state—that is, an organization and a minister with a number of domestic, executive and administrative (and to some extent policy making) functions which cover the responsibilities of more than one of the central departments. All of the regional outposts are re-

sponsible to their ministers, who are in turn responsible to the national Parliament in London. At the regional level, too, are a variety of ad hoc functional boards. Some have taken over duties previously performed by local government; some were set up to deal with central responsibilities. Some are commercial and industrial, some provide personal or social services, and some are mainly advisory. Approximately 50 such authorities cover the whole of Britain and are involved in public utilities such as gas, water and electricity, in the provision of the national health service, and in running the coal and steel industries, the post office and the advisory Economic Planning Councils. Such authorities are composed in various ways: by ministerial appointment, by interest group nomination, by indirect election from local authorities, but never by direct election. Their boundaries rarely coincide.

Critics of this tangle of so-called intermediate authorities emphasize the need to rationalize the jungle of boundaries, to create a central focus of authority in each region so that a single regional strategy for the development of public services can be followed, and to make regions democratically accountable to a directly elected regional council. Such a new tier of government might be allocated functions presently carried out by the central departments and their regional outposts, thus relieving the center of a great work burden while involving local people more intimately in governing themselves.

Regional devolution was the main concern of the Kilbrandon Royal Commission on the Constitution (1969–1973).[22] The occasion for es-

22. *See,* note 3 above. Assessments of the report are John P. Mackintosh, "The Report

tablishing the commission was the increase in support for the Scottish and Welsh nationalists, who in 1966 and 1967 won Parliamentary by-elections and surged ahead in local elections. Their advance came at the same time as the Channel Islands' concern about the impact on them of British entry into the EEC, and as the Ulster situation deteriorated. At the 1970 general election, the nationalist tide seemed to have receded. They won slightly more than 11 percent of the vote in Scotland and in Wales respectively, and only one Scottish seat. When the Kilbrandon Report was published in October 1973, devolution seemed irrelevant, but it was put to the forefront of the political agenda by the general election of February 1974, when the Scottish nationalists won nearly 22 percent of the vote in Scotland and seven seats, and the Welsh nationalists won nearly 11 percent in Wales and two seats, missing a third seat by only three votes. Britain's new minority Labour government found itself needing to woo the nationalists, and so it instituted consultations on regional devolution, publishing in June 1974 a discussion document which outlines the various schemes proposed in the Kilbrandon Report and sets forth some questions concerning their implementation.[23]

The Kilbrandon Commission rejected separatism, the transfer of sovereignty in all matters, because it would damage prosperity in the various countries and because the vast majority of the people did not want it. Federalism, too, was repudiated as awkward and impracticable, appropriate only for states coming together to form a single unit, damaging to Britain's economy, and presenting a major obstacle in the devising of financial arrangements between the federal and provincial governments. But on what was desirable the commission was divided. It presented seven different schemes, which are now the subject of debate in Britain:

1. Legislative devolution was recommended for Scotland by eight of the 13 members of the commission, and for Wales by six. Responsibility for legislating on specifically defined matters in the domestic field would be transferred from the Westminster Parliament to directly elected Scottish and Welsh legislatures. The ultimate sovereignty of the Westminster Parliament would be preserved in all matters, but it would be a convention that it would not legislate for Scotland and Wales on a transferred matter without the agreement of the Scottish or Welsh government. In exceptional cases it could veto a bill passed by the Scottish or Welsh legislature. Scotland would have devolved to it slightly more functions than would Wales, and both would see their representation in the Westminster Parliament in proportion to population reduced to be the same as for England;

of the Royal Commission on the Constitution," *Political Quarterly* 45 (January-March 1974), pp. 115–123; Editorial, "The Royal Commission on the Constitution," *Public Administration* 52 (Spring 1974), pp. 1–12; Eric M. Barendt, "The British Constitution," *Round Table* 254 (April 1974), pp. 173–184; R. A. W. Rhodes, "Anaemia in the extremities and apoplexy at the centre," *New Europe* 2 (Winter 1973–4), pp. 61–77; and Jeffrey Stanger, "Nationalism, Regionalism and the British System of Government," *Social and Economic Administration* 8 (Summer 1974), pp. 42–63.

23. *See*, note 4 above.

thus, Scottish MPs would fall from 71 to about 57 and the Welsh from 36 to about 31. An independent appointed Exchequer Board would allocate each government a "fair share of United Kingdom resources."

2. Elected assemblies in Scotland, Wales and the English regions were supported by two members. The Westminster Parliament would be responsible for the framework of legislation and major policy on all matters, while the assemblies would be responsible for adjusting United Kingdom policies to the special needs of their areas and for implementing them. The assemblies would assume control of the regional outposts of central government and of some ad hoc agencies, and would exercise a supervisory responsibility over the industrial and commercial authorities. They would also have a residual competence to act for the welfare and good government of their areas, and possess some independent revenue raising powers.

3. Executive devolution for Scotland, Wales and the English regions was recommended by two members. It is a less radical version of the scheme presented immediately above. The United Kingdom Parliament and government would be responsible for the framework of legislation and major policy, but wherever possible it would transfer to assemblies the responsibility, within that framework, for devising specific policies and executing them.

4. A Welsh Advisory Council was recommended by three members. The secretary of state and the Welsh Office would continue in their present form, but a directly elected Welsh Council would have the duty to advise the secretary of state and to scrutinize the operation of government policies and agencies in Wales.

5. A Scottish Council with advisory and legislative functions was recommended by one member. Like the Welsh Council above, it would have advisory functions, but in addition it would have some powers in relation to Scottish legislation. It would take the second reading, committee and report stages of Scottish bills referred to it by the House of Commons.

6. Regional coordinating and advisory councils for the English regions were recommended by eight members. This scheme is based on the view that the English region should not be given any legislative or executive powers now exercised by the central government, and that it would not be sensible, after the recent reorganization of local government, for regions to take over powers from local government. But there is scope for more cooperation between local authorities and a need for more discussion about those matters affecting the region, which are decided by central government and the ad hoc authorities. To meet these objectives, and to give advice to the central government on regional problems, there would be regional councils; four-fifths of the members would be elected by local authorities in the region, and the rest would be nominated by the central government to secure representation from industry

and commerce, trade unions, education and other interests.

7. Regional coordinating committees of local authorities in England were recommended by one member. This scheme is based on the view that the best way of devolving power from the center is to concentrate on strengthening the new local authorities. At the regional level, therefore, all that is required is to coordinate the planning activities of local authorities. Each committee would consist of indirectly elected representatives of local authorities, and it would be mandatory for local authorities to submit their plans to the regional committee and to obtain its comments before submitting them for ministerial approval.

The government has posed so many important questions about each of these proposals that it is clear that the country as a whole will be even more divided than the commission. Sufficient political will to embark on any major constitutional change is hard to envisage. Finance presents a major difficulty, since it will be nearly impossible to give Scottish, Welsh and English regional governments a sufficient degree of financial independence to make full use of powers devolved to them, while preserving economic unity and leaving the United Kingdom government with fully adequate economic and financial powers to discharge its responsibilities for demand management, the balance of payments and the control of inflation. It is also unlikely that a majority would agree to much devolution in trade, industry and employment. Distribution of industry policy and industrial incentives needs to be controlled on a United Kingdom basis, especially with international obligations, through the EEC for example. Additionally, it would be unacceptable to drop as a goal broad equality between different parts of the country and to allow a wide divergency of policies on housing, health, education, and town and country planning.

Local authorities are likely to oppose regional devolution, since it would bring a controlling authority closer to them and might threaten to remove more of their functions, as well as erect a barrier between them and the central government. Major political difficulties can be foreseen when regional governments are of a different political complexion than the United Kingdom government. The English would reject the idea that, while the United Kingdom Parliament would not in general be able to legislate (under scheme 1) for Scotland and Wales in matters of health, education and local government, Scottish and Welsh MPs at Westminster would participate in legislation for England on those topics. Furthermore, the people of Scotland and Wales are hardly likely to welcome a reduction in the number of their MPs, and minorities in various regions may be anxious that regional governments might be dominated by a single political party that might hold such a monopoly as that which has brought Ulster to its tragic plight.

The future is uncertain. But the government's consultation paper makes clear the difficulties of implementing any scheme of regional devolution. The Conservative and Labour parties are not eager to weaken the authority of the central government and the United Kingdom Parliament, but they may decide that it is a political necessity to try to appease those voting nationalist by conceding elected councils with some limited functions to Scotland and Wales. It is, however, very much an open question whether that would satisfy the Scottish nationalists or merely whet their appetite, since at the moment they are vociferous in demanding extensive devolution, a federal system, and even separation. Their enthusiasm is fueled by the prospect of such great wealth flowing into Scotland from offshore oil fields that they can go it alone. The government, however, will try to prolong discussions, hoping that the next election will reveal a considerable reduction in nationalist support, so that it can put aside consideration of thorny constitutional matters and turn to tackling the major economic and social problems facing the whole country.

193a

Kindly mention THE ANNALS *when writing to advertisers*

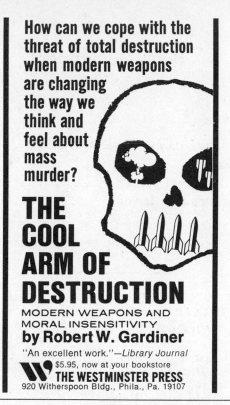
INDUSTRIAL AND LABOR RELATIONS REVIEW

Announcing: Two Special Issues

Plus, in each issue, other articles on current issues in the field of industrial and labor relations, book reviews, recent publications, and research notes.

Published quarterly by the New York State School of Industrial and Labor Relations, Cornell University, Ithaca, New York 14850.

Annual rates: $10.00 (domestic) $11.00 (foreign)
Single issues: $ 2.75 (domestic) $ 3.00 (foreign)

Kindly mention THE ANNALS *when writing to advertisers*

Book Department

INTERNATIONAL RELATIONS AND POLITICAL THOUGHT

HENRY J. ABRAHAM. *Justices and Presidents: A Political History of Appointments to the Supreme Court.* Pp. vii, 310. New York: Oxford University Press, 1974. $10.00.

Well known as a writer about courts and constitutional law, Professor Henry J. Abraham of the University of Virginia now offers (1) a useful historical summary of the processes of appointment to the Supreme Court of the United States and (2) a textual chronology of the politics of each of the appointments and, at least briefly, of the impact of the appointee in the development of American jurisprudence. The first of these two objectives covers for the Supreme Court, but more succinctly, what Harold W. Chase's *Federal Judges: The Appointing Process* (University of Minnesota Press, 1972) accomplishes for the lower Federal judiciary.

Particularly for the modern period, and always for the great justices, Professor Abraham brings to life the character and vicissitudes of his subjects. He does not hesitate to make his own judicious appraisals both of jurists and appointing presidents. For example

(p. 87), "It is a pity that the Taney Court has not only been widely misunderstood but even maligned." Harding, he thinks (p. 172), was the "crassest failure" in the presidency, but two of his four appointees to the Court (p. 173) "have generally been given high ratings."

Professor Abraham praises judicial experience but suggests (p. 49) that raising it to a requirement "would render a distinct disservice to the Supreme Court." He believes (p. 272) that the Court should "shun prescriptive policy-making" but adhere to its better role of saying "yes" or "no" to the government.

The book is written with brevity, superb powers of selectivity, and maximal interest for the general reader. It is marred by a few unrevised textual aberrations. Among them the late Senator Henry F. Ashurst, "Mr. Arizona," is identified (p. 39) with an adjoining state; Mr. Justice Curtis's middle name (p. 101) is confused with that of Cardozo; President Wilson (p. 181) is said to have left foreign policy to Charles Evans Hughes. The level of excitement is not that of David J. Danelski's story of the inadequate Pierce Butler in *A Supreme Court Justice Is Appointed* (Random House, 1964). But Professor Abraham has followed a broader theme, supplementing it in his initial chapters with statistical and chronological tables. He has made a permanently useful contribution.

FRANKLIN L. BURDETTE
Bureau of Governmental Research
University of Maryland
College Park

IVAN BERNIER. *International Legal Aspects of Federalism.* Pp. vii, 308. Hamden, Conn.: Shoe String Press, 1973. $15.00.

MICHLA POMERANCE. *The Advisory Function of the International Court of Justice in the League and U.N. Eras.* Pp. xvi, 440. Baltimore, Md.: The Johns Hopkins University Press, 1973. No price.

Both of these books deal with an important aspect of the problem of world order, that of the interrelationships among increasingly interdependent and diverse and complex political authorities. The time when the global political system could be conceived solely in terms of a set of unitary, territorially defined political units that related to one another mainly on the battlefield is long past, if it ever existed. The present global system is extremely complex, encompassing a huge number of unitary states, but also several federal states as well as an increasing number of international organizations, some of which have taken on supranational characteristics, and the scope of international relations has expanded enormously.

Classical international law treated all states as unitary authorities, and paid little attention to the problem of federalism. As the subject matter of international relations expanded, however, practical accommodations had to be made to federalism, and Ivan Bernier's book is a welcome comprehensive survey of how federal states are treated in international law. The first part deals with the broad issues of international personality, international responsibility and international immunity. Each section contains a thorough

survey of the views of publicists and a detailed examination of the opinions of domestic and international courts. Particular attention is given to cases involving Canada, the United States, Switzerland and Germany. The second part analyzes how international law has dealt with the problem of the divided competence of federal states and the extent to which international law has copied practices adopted within federal states. If current regional integration schemes are forerunners of federal unions and if federalism is increasingly adopted as a way of allowing regional diversity, the importance of the issues treated in Bernier's book will grow. Bernier treats the European Community in this perspective.

When the Permanent Court of International Justice was created, in addition to being given jurisdiction to deal with disputes among states, it was also given authority to render advisory opinions on legal issues on the request of the Council or the Assembly of the League of Nations. When the Permanent Court was succeeded by the International Court of Justice, this authority was continued and the right to request advisory opinions was extended beyond the Security Council and the General Assembly to other organs and agencies of the United Nations. In her book, Michla Pomerance analyzes how the advisory function has been utilized. Although the book is basically an examination of cases, attention is focused on the procedures leading to requests for advisory opinions, on the Court's view of its advisory function, and on the reception of advisory opinions, rather than on the substantive issues that were involved. A chapter on "stillborn" requests effectively makes the point that in delineating the utilization of the advisory function it is as important to understand abortive attempts to make requests as well as those that succeeded. In brief, her thesis is that while during the League era the advisory function was frequently and successfully used to facilitate the settlement of interstate disputes, in contrast during the UN period it was used less extensively and mainly in relationship to organizational issues. This thesis is substantiated through cleverly designed comparative sections that conclude the major substantive chapters. Pomerance's preference for the former purpose unfortunately results in her understating the significance of the latter, yet in the long run, in a system of organizational complexity, it could be the more important.

Neither book is easy reading. Both are works of patient and painstaking legal scholarship, and are detailed and dry. The specialist, however, will find each rewarding.

HAROLD K. JACOBSON
The University of Michigan
Ann Arbor

BERNARD BRODIE. *War and Politics.* Pp. vii, 514. New York: Macmillan, 1973. $8.95.

This is an important book by an important author on an important subject. A writer of international renown on military strategy for more than a quarter of a century, Dr. Bernard Brodie is one of the most eloquent and enlightened bearers of the message contained in that famous but often misrepresented dictum of Karl von Clausewitz: "War is a continuation of policy by other means." "War," as Brodie explains, "takes place within a political milieu from which it derives *all* its purposes." In the conduct of war, therefore, "the question of *why* we fight must dominate any consideration of means" (pp. vii, 1–2).

In the informed judgment of Dr. Brodie, and to the great tragedy of mankind in the past, such an "absurdly simple theme has been mostly ignored, and when not ignored usually denied" (p. vii). It is to remind the world of this "absurdly simple" message that the author has undertaken to reexamine four major wars of this century involving the United States—World War I and II, Korea, and Vietnam (Chapters 1–5). He also covers such key topics on the questions of war as the changing attitudes toward war, various theories of war causation, the idea of "vital interests," the strategic functions of nuclear weapons, and the decision-makers of strategy (Chapters 6–10). The resulting work in a mixed bag of histories, opinions, and generalizations is a testimony to the author's uncommon insight, balanced judgment, and above all, sensitive appreciation of human suffering in war rarely found among the writers of strategy.

The central theme of the book, of course, is simple enough. War which entails wanton destruction of human lives and their sustenance could hardly be regarded as a game to be played for the sake of winning. At the heart of the problem of strategic decision-making, thus, is the temptation to view war as a contest to be won for its own sake while the original reason for fighting or the cost of winning is cast aside. The military profession in general, because of special training and discipline oriented toward effective fighting in battle, is particularly vulnerable to this vision of war. The civilian control of the military, therefore, is absolutely necessary, not in the least in time of war.

These are familiar themes of discourse on the civil-military relationship among the students of national security. The special merit of the book, accordingly, is not so much in bringing out these points as in giving us in the process some of the most readable and erudite accounts of the wars and crises of the past and of our time. In fact the Clausewitzian message would have had little concrete meaning except in such well-defined though diverse contexts of political-military issues of war as the author provides here.

If a criticism must be made of the book, one might note that its author is a wise judge of events and decisions but not a particularly imaginative builder of conceptual schemes to explain them. Dr. Brodie, like many of us, is a believer in accidents and mistakes in history (see, especially, pp. 130–144), and is understandably impatient, for instance, with any suggestion that some "knaves" in public office, acting in behalf of particular "interests," might have gotten us involved in the Vietnamese War. But to point out, as he does, that the United States military intervention in Vietnam was really a result of mistakes by some "stupid" men in high public office (see, for example, pp. 298–300) is merely to characterize an unfortunate situation rather than to explain it.

Dr. Brodie prefers to analyze events largely in terms of the series of decisions and quite correctly is sensitive about the differences that exist in individual decision-makers. But he seems to be overly critical of those who adopt analytical schemes that do not make such a fine distinction in personalities. Thus, he charges "depersonalization" of decisions by "a strong movement in academia bent on creating a 'theory' of international relations in which events conform to models that have the virtue of being simple" (p. 127). He calls it "the triumph of ideology over evidence" when Leslie H. Gelb and Daniel Ellsberg of the Pentagon Papers develop a thesis which is characterized by him as claiming that each President "was intent simply on avoiding blame for losing South Vietnam to Communism and did what he construed to be the minimum necessary for passing the burden on to his successor" (p. 129). He also mocks at "something called the 'New Left'" for allegedly trying to "wipe out *any* distinction between Lyndon Johnson and his 1964 electoral opponent Senator Barry Goldwater" (p. 131).

What Brodie is implying here is the crudity of analysis, if not intellectual dishonesty, by some of his colleagues. A part of the problem, however, seems to stem from his fundamental intellectual confusion between efforts to evaluate, as he does in the book, particular decisions in terms of choices made by particular individuals at particular times and the other kinds of analyses that seek to find out "nondecisional"—social as well as institutional—constraints which more or less determine the effective range of choices open to individual decision-makers. One

could point out other blemishes in the book, to be sure, but none would seem serious enough to cast doubt on its being a major contribution in the literature of war and politics. It is hoped only that everyone will read this book, especially those who may someday find themselves confronted with decisions affecting hundreds of thousands of human lives.

SUNG HO KIM

Ohio University
Athens

FRANCIS DVORNIK. *Origins of Intelligence Services.* Pp. 334. New Brunswick, N.J.: Rutgers University Press, 1974. $15.00.

As the author says in the preface, this book is a by-product of his continuing research, especially in Byzantine and Slavic history and its ideological background. Long years of research, expressed in a two-volume work, *Early Christian and Byzantine Political Philosophy* (Washington, D.C.: Dumbarton Oaks, 1966), were its springboard. Furthermore, the author's preparation in a symposium, held in the international Congress of the Slavists in Moscow in 1970, on *Greek and Western Missions in the East,* led him to the study of Chinese and Mongol history and Catholic missions in the Far East, which began in the thirteenth century. This completed his historical perspective, which he so firmly held in Slavic and Byzantine studies, and which he expressed so well in his definitive works. Furthermore, the author was curious to find out by which means different regimes and empires were able to survive, often for centuries, although they generally neglected the social and economic welfare of their peoples, which led him to the conviction that their survival was largely due to the efficient organization of intelligence services.

The book is divided into six chapters, following the development of intelligence services chronologically. The first chapter, "Intelligence in the Ancient Near East" (pp. 3–47), reveals that the idea of intelligence services is an old one and that its origins may be found in Egypt, perhaps in the *Tell-al-Amarna* documents of the period of Amenhotep III (14th century B.C.). Intelligence services led to the establishment of thousands of miles of road networks with fortified way stations and post systems, complete with draft mules, relay riders on horseback, and carriages used as "stage coaches," controlled by the vizir. The Hittites, Babylonians and Assyrians perfected this system, which the Persians further enhanced with the amazing subtlety of a police service, and the Greeks with a kind of telegraphy.

The second chapter, "Intelligence in the Roman Empire" (pp. 48–120), reveals that Scipio Africanus was the first to adopt the Persian system and introduce the State post—*cursus publicus*—and the private road for merchants, speculants, and exporters. Augustus made it *regular* and Diocletian made it *efficient*. Dvornik insists that there is a certain analogy between the Roman agents called *frumentarii* and the German *Gestapo*, namely that both institutions were founded on the military basis to exercise and to deal with espionage.

The third chapter, "Byzantine Intelligence Service" (pp. 121–187), reveals how Byzantines accepted the Roman system and reorganized it by putting imperial agents called *verendarii* under direct control of a high official, later called *Logothete*, which lasted till the 14th century. The Emperor had also his bodyguards and the Palace guard, but the agents of state post were charged with a secret police. In the 17th century the military intelligence was reorganized under the leadership of *Domesticus* and Commander *Strategus*. Because of frequent invasions of Arabs, a special corps of guards called *Akritai* was placed on the borders, and under the emperor Constantine VII, espionage and counterespionage services were introduced. Perhaps interesting was the circumstance that the Empire did not have a Ministry of Foreign Affairs and all contacts abroad had been, since 740, the responsibility of *Logothete* and of a state ceremonial, as a chief of protocol, who was charged with the receiving of envoys and with the bureau of interpreters. All agreements were deposited in state archives and originals in imperial archives.

The fourth chapter, "Intelligence in Arab-Muslim Empires" (pp. 188–261), shows how the Arabs had diplomatic and political shrewdness, full of intrigue and clandestine activities. Especially the Abbasid Empire, representing the strength of Islam, made a maximum effort to concentrate all channels of the Intelligence Service in their new capital, Baghdad. Numerous ingenious systems were devised—optic, fire and smoke signals—by which information could be relayed across the whole vast empire within hours. Even carrier-pigeon post services, possibly imported from China by Arabic traders, provided swift communications. The Caliphs had many spies, informers and agents in their services, and the whole intelligence system was very complex, so much so that Al-Mamun even had about 1700 women employed in the bureaucratically structured intelligence center in Baghdad, which had such great dimensions that it could be seen as a kind of historical precedent of the colossal Central Intelligence Agency (CIA) headquarters at Langley, Virginia. The Arabs were industrious in intelligence and information services and, in certain aspects, became pioneers of medieval geography. Their geographical reports became important historical sources, as one can see in Yakut's *Geographical Dictionary* of the 13th century.

The fifth chapter, "Intelligence in the Mongol Empire" (pp. 262–299), reveals how the vast intelligence network (*jami*) established by Jenghiz Khan (d. 1227) in his Mongol Empire, which extended from the Pacific Ocean westward to the heart of Central Europe, was perhaps the supreme accomplishment of its time. The famous traveler, Marco Polo, who visited China in 1275, described the intelligence service in detail, saying that there were about

10,000 state stations, with 200,000 horses in their use. Another Chinese writer, Yule in 1350, insists that besides the *jami* system, there were towers called *kargüs*, built in the roads for the transfer of optic signals throughout the Empire. In 1311, the emperor Jen-Tsung concentrated all intelligence services under the leadership of the Ministry of the Army.

The sixth chapter, "The Intelligence in the Muscovite State" (pp. 300–316), illustrates that Russians were the first nation in Europe with the well-established system of State stations and intelligence services throughout the State. Because of this, the Muscovite state, profitting from the Mongols and from the cumulative experience, expanded from a small principality to the immense Empire of Ivan IV, who introduced a secret police to insure the empire's survival. This perhaps was the ominous precedent of present Communist Russia, whose survival is maintained only by ill-famed Secret police as well.

This book by Dvornik is richly informative and educational as well, since it shows that while the good use of intelligence services is a means of guaranteeing the security of any nation, its abuse can become a threat to peace among the nations and to individual freedom and democratic society. The book is replete with 21 illustrations and 18 maps and provided with a detailed index and it can be read with a complete confidence. It is warmly recommended to the common reader as well as the learned public, for the great benefit of both; it can serve as a handbook to students as well.

LUDVIK NEMEC

Rosemont and Chestnut Hill
   Colleges
Pennsylvania

LLOYD JENSEN, *Return from the Nuclear Brink*. Pp. vii, 150. Lexington, Mass.: Lexington Books, 1974. $12.50.

The Nuclear Non-Proliferation Treaty (NPT) occupies, at least occasionally, the headlines of American newspapers, and more frequently earns mention on inner pages. One suspects that the Treaty enjoys a general if vague support from the American public (who, after all, would oppose limitations on nuclear weapons?). Yet, the nature of the Treaty's provisions, let alone its larger ramifications for the international political system and the complexities of achieving wide ratification, are little known even to the interested lay public. Professor Jensen's book has rendered a service in providing this concise and readable account of the NPT from 1961 to date.

Not surprisingly, Jensen finds concern for national security to be the primary consideration in the ratification decisions, but as he also demonstrates, "security" is a protean word; its meaning is very different to the great powers than to Belgium or Switzerland. Even ignoring the problem of effective inspection (which is becoming more difficult to insure due to engineering advances such as the breeder reactor), "security" concerns must also consider alliance relationships, umbrella guarantees of the superpowers, possession of uranium deposits, conventional armaments, use of "nonnuclear" soil as bases or storage depots by nuclear nations, and progress of more general arms control efforts such as SALT. Economic considerations of the "peaceful atom," while distinctly secondary to security interests broadly construed, are further complicating factors, especially within regional nuclear pact nations such as those of Euratom.

Jensen makes it clear that current NPT provisions are distinctly favorable to established nuclear powers, and this suggests that the "threshold nations" (Jensen lists twenty) are the category crucial to the immediate future of the treaty. Under what circumstances, he asks, can they be expected to accept the risks of forgoing nuclear status? The question is an ominous one to NPT advocates for several reasons, not least because it is increasingly difficult to envision a satisfactory set of inducements. There is, Jensen notes, a certain bandwagon effect that can come to play on the threshold nations, and the impetus of recent weeks seems to be running toward proliferation rather than control. After India's nuclear explosion and America's pledge to supply reactors and technicians to Egypt, the pressures to "go nuclear" must surely increase upon Israel; and with India, Egypt, and Israel in the club, can Japan long remain outside? The genie would seem at present to have little to fear from the bottle, and in this respect, Professor Jensen might as well have entitled his book, Return to the Nuclear Brink.

PAUL F. KRESS

University of North Carolina
Chapel Hill

WERNER LEVI. International Politics, Foundations of the System. Pp. 285. Minneapolis: University of Minnesota Press, 1974. $11.00.

Werner Levi's herculean effort to add sociological and psychological dimensions to his analysis of international politics is, indeed, laudable. While this methodological approach is most interesting, the end-product is distressing since the author avoided the central political element in his paradigm—that is, the foundations of a future international political system.

As a realist, Levi acknowledges certain realities—namely, that "politics" permeates all social action; that nationalism remains the "highest value"; that a "sense of insecurity" overshadows all international behavior; and that, therefore, "survival" continues as the primary objective in the resultant "struggle for power and prestige." The author admits that moral norms are of "secondary concern" to the "primacy" of the national interest with the consequence that force remains the "single, major tool of power."

As a theorist, Levi valiantly attempts to extrapolate selected perceptions and modalities from domestic societies and communities and projects these variables into a nascent international society with vague assertions that "the ideal of separate states is giving way to the ideal of cooperative states." Yet, the scenarios he inserts are so broad and general as to suggest exhortation rather than scholarly exploration, especially when measured against the author's voluminous "Notes" (pp. 241–250)— that is, a distillation of behaviorist studies on socio-psychological attitudes.

Levi's basic thesis—"the functional nexus"—is commendable, but requires more rigorous analysis. He hypothesizes that the development of economic growth and welfare through interdependence will result in a "sense of community and functional relationships" that will displace nationalism. Similarly he asserts that "habits" for peace through "functional cooperation" will result in a "metamorphosis of mankind from a conglomerate of states to a global society."

Yet, he fails to scientifically examine the European Community as an extant model, or the several United Nations Agencies with their emerging functional programs. The euphoric statement that "as the borderline between internal and external affairs of a state becomes blurred, as linkages increase, not only will controls geared more to the maintenance of an international social order impose themselves upon states, but the greater exposure of more people to the international society directly will also make controls more acceptable" reveals both the author's confusion and evasion as well.

What "controls," by whom, and how? Levi avoids examining these crucial questions: the central "power" dimensions, the "political" factors, the institutions of power, and the "conflict" dilemmas within the entire spectrum of human behavior. The resultant intellectual lacuna, wherein the author jumps from reality to fantasy, is most distressing, albeit interesting.

ALFRED J. HOTZ

Augustana College
Sioux Falls
South Dakota

JERRY S. MILSTEIN. *Dynamics of the Vietnam War: A Quantitative Analysis and Predictive Computer Simulation.* Pp. vii, 254. Columbus: Ohio State University Press, 1974. $12.50.

Systems analysis potentially encompasses, using a performance model of sequential phases, evaluation of performance as well as predictive criteria (a) for goal oriented actions and (b) for behavioral alterations to actions dysfunctional to goal and sub-goal achievement. Building upon standard S-O-R and S-R models Milstein attempts to devise a quasi systems analysis of the cost effectiveness, phenomenologically and objectively based, of the Vietnam war from the perspective of goal structures of elites in Washington, Hanoi and Saigon as well as of the "masses" in America and North and South Vietnam. Relying upon graph analysis, correlations and serial correlations, regression analysis and computer simulation on a monthly basis, he articulates performance potentials vis-à-vis sundry goals for each major group of participants. He presents a provocative commentary upon themes of Washington's calculated versus miscalculated premises concerning probable outcomes and trade-offs in the Vietnam encounter. While providing many interesting findings based upon unobtrusive measures, trends and statements—all correlated with actual and statistically predicted behavior of participants, and usually supporting my own biases based upon evaluations of other forms of data—Milstein also presents three dilemmas. First, any variant of the "calculated" thesis assumes policy makers are depending upon criteria for their predictions inconsistent with the "objective" data Milstein utilizes—data readily available to such elites. Second, despite sophisticated usage of regression analysis, the chicken-egg problem cannot be resolved. Finally viable systemic predictions invariably are a function of validity of indicators. Though Milstein's operational measures are useful, his indicator for popular support in South Vietnam (reliable for what it measures) of piastre value is an indicator so weighed solely to Saigon as to be less than useful as a general indicator in his articulated model.

Nonetheless, Milstein's imaginative attempt to utilize public data as indicators to test hypotheses of diverse orientations constitutes a valuable tool for "calculated" attempts at decision making and policy formulation. Further, his findings concerning the total disillusionment of South Vietnamese on all sides with the militant postures of all principal parties—a militancy whose costs they have borne regardless of which party initiated which specific actions or strategies—detail succintly the tragedy of the war in Indochina. These data also provide witness to the helplessness of affected publics in initially determining policies based upon their readiness to sacrifice for goals determined by others, although providing evidence of such publics' potential ability, at very high costs, to influence policy alterations and to influence shifts in goal hierarchies. But such evidence is solely for extremely gross stresses and cannot spell out the inevitable weakness of disparate interests demanding policy alterations consistent with their own survival requirements but inconsistent in the goal substitutions they demand.

CHARLES A. JOINER
Temple University
Philadelphia
Pennsylvania

RICHARD ROSE, ed. *Electoral Behavior: A Comparative Handbook.* Pp. xii, 753. New York: The Free Press, 1974. $29.95.

This is a useful, attractive, and expensive collection of essays and data summaries dealing with the electoral systems of twelve western democracies. Students of elections, political parties, and democratic theory should find this handbook a helpful source for basic material on electoral history and structure, party systems, and the role of various demographic and social vari-

ables in determining partisan preferences in the twelve rather arbitrarily
chosen countries.

These clearly written essays are arranged in a comparable format, each
with an analysis of the role of religion,
region, education, occupation, sex, and
social class in influencing electoral
choices (as expressed in survey interviews). There is less material on the
structure of political belief systems or
regime legitimacy. The country essays
and their authors are: "Belgium: Political Change in a Segmented Society" by
Keith Hill; "Germany: Continuity and
Change in Electoral Politics" by Derek
W. Urwin; "Italy: Religion and Class in
Electoral Behavior" by Samuel H.
Barnes; "The Netherlands: Continuity
and Change in Voting Behavior" by
Arend Lijphart; "Finland: Party Sup-
port in a Fragmented System" by Pertti
Pesonen; "Norway: Conflict Structure
and Mass Politics in a European Pe-
riphery" by Henry Valen and Stein
Rokkan; "Sweden: The Social Bases
of the Parties in a Developmental
Perspective" by Bo Särlvik; "Australia:
Class Politics in the New World" by
Don Aitkin and Michael Kahan; "Brit-
ain: Simple Abstractions and Complex
Realities" by Richard Rose; "Canada:
Canadian Voting Behavior" by Mildred
A. Schwartz; "Ireland: Politics Without
Social Bases" by J. H. Whyte; and
"United States: The Politics of Hetero-
geneity" by Walter Dean Burnham.

The brief efforts at a systematically
comparative approach to electoral systems (found in essays by Rose and
Converse) are the most intellectually
intriguing aspects of a volume organized around individual countries.
Particularly helpful is a comparative
analysis of the effect of social structure
upon partisanship across countries.
That analysis is based on Sonquist and
Morgan's method for detecting interaction effects. The method is used here in
an effective but somewhat mechanical
way to allocate variance rather than to
find interaction effects.

Finally, the country essays make one
appreciate how modest and parochial
are considerations of electoral reform in
the United States. All the other democracies examined in this handbook have
managed, for example, to develop voter
registration systems that are virtually
cost-free to citizens—and, as a consequence, turnout generally runs about
twenty percent higher than in the U.S.
Or, with respect to campaign and party
finances, consider that in Sweden in
1970, public grants in political parties
were the equivalent of $12 million (or
$1.50 per citizen). Such a level of
public financing in the U.S. would be
over $300 million!

EDWARD R. TUFTE
Princeton University
New Jersey

WILLIAM M. ROSS. *Oil Pollution: As an
International Problem.* Pp. iii, 279.
Seattle: University of Washington
Press, 1973. $12.00.

ROBERT A. SHINN. *The International
Politics of Marine Pollution Control.*
Pp. vi, 200. New York: Praeger, 1974.
$16.50.

Two timely additions to a relatively
sparse field of literature should be
welcomed. Both books are based on
beliefs impossible to dispute: that a
politically divided world is an environmental unity whose current problems cannot be measured only in
economic terms or solved unilaterally;
that existing laws and practices are
hopelessly inadequate for combatting
pollution of the oceans internationally;
that nations have pursued national security, economic development, and doctrines of "freedom of the seas" rather
than policies for ecological protection;
and that without a drastic change of
attitudes among decision makers the
world is threatened by a crisis which
well may overwhelm it. Both books
adopt a scholarly rather than a polemical approach in stressing the seriousness of the problems. The data they
provide should dispel any complacency
that the oceans have a limitless capacity
to absorb the wastes of industrial civilization and still regenerate life which
can help feed the increasing population

of the earth. Yet both authors appear to suggest that if new international institutions with broad powers could be created it would be possible to continue to exploit the oceans for food, petroleum and other resources, carry on military and mercantile shipping across them, and simultaneously reduce the impact of pollution. This seems an over optimistic view of the probabilities of international conduct; both books show evidences that the authors are aware of incompatibilities between objectives.

Ross' study of oil pollution in the salt water estuary of Puget Sound and the Strait of Georgia is a well written and admirable effort. By focusing on a particular region and its most potent cause of marine pollution (oil), he illustrates the general problem of tackling an ill perceived environmental threat through traditional and diverse management organizations. The study region is well chosen not only because the potential for oil spillage is increasing, but because the two countries involved, Canada and the United States, enjoy cordial relations and have mechanisms for dealing with pollution problems. Ross describes their respective responses to the question of oil spillage and finds both domestic and international legislation inadequate, lacking in stringency, and influenced by transportation and oil interests. He suggests an alternative organization for prevention and control of oil pollution. This would take the form of a regional joint international commission functioning like river basin authorities, having means of preliminary control, capability of delineating responsibility, a special fund, and powers to respond to the largest of spills. He feels that through such a partial surrender of national sovereignty, Canada and the United States could go a long way towards meeting the crisis at hand. Besides, if these two countries are unable to reconcile demands for higher consumption with rights to a clean environment, the prospects for resolving the global crisis are bleak indeed.

Shinn attempts to cover a vast field of study, and, perhaps for that reason, it is difficult to sustain interest in his writing. His summary of the different types, sources, and effects of marine pollutants and his summaries of the international laws and organizations bearing on the subject certainly convey the complexity of the problems, especially since various contending "interests" dominate the field. But a more outspoken analysis of these interests and the actual politics of international decisions—or non-decisions—or marine pollution would be welcome. Shinn gives valuable critiques of major ocean regime proposals made in the last decade. While each addresses ecological considerations, security and economics remain dominant. The Maltese draft ocean space treaty of 1971 was an exception, but Shinn finds it "too comprehensively good to be true," and bound to failure because it runs contrary to Soviet and US military interests. He rightly describes international environmental efforts as rhetorical, having neither consolidated old organizations including those of the United Nations, nor established new forums with comprehensive capability. Given the present day crises of energy, inflation, and population, one cannot help but feel that Shinn's hope for international agreement on ocean governance "that will conform to the welfare of the whole world community without being inconsistent with the short term perceived interests of the most important nations" will not be brought about at the forthcoming Laws of the Seas Conference. Only a dramatic increase of international awareness of environmental problems will make cooperative efforts fruitful in the future.

SURJIT MANSINGH
Washington, D.C.

GEORGE SCOTT. *The Rise and Fall of the League of Nations.* Pp. 432. New York: Macmillan, 1974. $9.95.

The Rise and Fall of the League of Nations critically examines the personalities, politics, ideals and imperfections which gave birth to the League of Nations and procured its demise. The central theme of the author, George Scott, a British writer and broadcaster, is that the League was not destroyed by the depression of 1929, the rise of fascism in Germany and Italy, the failure of disarmament efforts, the Sino-Japanese or Italo-Ethiopian wars; it was killed by the weaknesses of the dominant personalities of the day.

Scott acknowledges that events can twist and shape human experience; but he contends that "great men can dominate circumstances . . . if their will and their dedication to an avowed principle is determined enough and is matched by their capacity to light up the imagination with their words" (p. 402). Woodrow Wilson, with a capacity to "light up" the imagination with ideals, was the chief architect of the League, but his overbearing conceit also occasioned the U.S.' failure to join it—a grave blow; Poincare ensured France's economic health, but his commitment to Germany's permanent impotence beclouded his vision of the League's ideals and caused the "invasion" of the Ruhr; and Lloyd George was too uncertain of his dedication to the League's ideals.

True, during the tenure of Britain's Austin Chamberlain, France's Aristide Briand, and Germany's Gustav Stresemann, the League's emergence as the champion of minorities evinced signs of its developing into the strong institution its founders envisioned. But these very leaders were so incapable of committing themselves and/or their states *in toto* to the ethos of collective security, that they resorted to extra-League, multilateral ties and relationships reminiscent of the nineteenth century. And, when any development threatened the integrity of the League or its ideals and those relationships, the powers gave the latter priority—a most virulent phenomenon which plagued the world and proved most significant in undoing of the League.

Although the author's account is based on interviews with participants at various Geneva conferences, quotes from important debates and cabinet decisions, scholars will find the almost total absence of footnotes and supporting bibliography disturbing. Yet, it should be read by all who believe that man's survival lies in collective security and especially those who would inadvertently destroy the United Nations by foregoing its machinery, as a means to solve issues threatening to world peace, in preference for efforts bottomed on bilateral and multilateral relationships.

WINSTON E. LANGLEY
Boston State College
Massachusetts

JOHN G. STOESSINGER. *Why Nations Go to War*. Pp. 230. New York: St. Martin's Press, 1974. $8.95.

Why do nations go to war? Conventional wisdom, says John G. Stoessinger, attributes the causes of war to "bloodless abstractions" such as nationalism. Such explanations miss "the human essence of the problem. After all, wars were begun by men."

Stoessinger proposes to illuminate this neglected dimension by selecting six case studies and focusing on the personalities and perceptions of individual national leaders at the critical " 'moment of truth' when leaders crossed the threshold into war." The studies are of the major international wars of the twentieth century: "the two world wars, Korea, Vietnam, India and Pakistan and the Arab states and Israel."

When Stoessinger's methodology works, it works very well indeed, as in his discussion of the German, Austrian and Russian leaders on the eve of World War I. Although ostensibly in contact with each other, they passed like ships in the night, doomed by their illusions, prejudices, rigidities, and incapacities for empathy.

The methodology does not always work, however, because Stoessinger does not apply it consistently. As he proceeds chronologically he broadens his time frame and muddies his focus. By the time he gets to the India-Pakistan conflict, for example, he is no longer focusing on threshold periods just prior to resorting to force; he is discussing the entire independence period, 1947 to 1971. And he is no longer looking for causes primarily in the perceptions of national leaders. He is attributing the basic cause of the conflict to one of those "bloodless abstractions" he originally proposed to avoid, in this case, religion. Similarly, he broadens some of his final conclusions beyond the capacity of the data to support them. Eloquent as is his assertion of "a slow dawning of compassion and of global consciousness over humanity's bleak skies in our generation," it simply does not follow from the case materials.

Shortcomings pale, however, before the significance of Stoessinger's undertaking, the lucidity of his prose, and the controlled passion of his humanitarian concern. (A World War II refugee himself, Stoessinger is a distinguished scholar of international politics and director of the political affairs division of the United Nations.)

In this volume, Stoessinger returns to a theme he introduced in *The Might of Nations:* the gap between perception and reality in international relations. His provocative conclusions point the way for future studies. "The case material reveals that perhaps the most important single precipitating factor in the outbreak of war is misperception." Critical misperceptions involve "a leader's image of himself" as well as distorted views of his adversary, especially his adversary's power. "Thus, on the eve of each war, at least one nation misperceives another's power. In that sense, the beginning of each war is a misperception or an accident. The war itself then slowly, and in agony, teaches men about reality."

JOY MILLER HUNTLEY
Ohio University
Athens

CLAUDE E. WELCH, JR. and ARTHUR K. SMITH. *Military Role and Rule: Perspectives on Civil-Military Relations.* Pp. v, 294. North Scituate, Mass.: Duxbury Press, 1974. $4.95. Paperbound.

ZEB B. BRADFORD, JR. and FREDERIC J. BROWN. *The United States Army in Transition.* Pp. 256. Beverly Hills, Calif.: Sage Publications, 1974. $10.00.

The authors of *Military Role and Rule* first develop a number of hypotheses concerning military behavior and conditions related to military involvement in politics. Those general propositions are then tested and demonstrated with specific case studies from various countries. And finally, the theoretical and concrete material is united to form the beginnings of a theory in the field of civil-military relations.

An important theme developed by Welch and Smith is that military rule marks the decline or collapse of political institutions—that is, *political legitimacy* is the most significant single factor affecting the possibility of military intervention. This is one of some twenty propositions stated and reviewed in light of actual experiences in Thailand, Nigeria, Egypt, Peru, and France. It is indeed this effort to relate theory to practice that constitutes the most valuable contribution of the study. The bulk of recent writings on civil-military relations have concentrated on "third-world" or undeveloped nations with the consequent result being a climate of opinion which too often sees military rule confined to the "new" nations or those with an immediate revolutionary past.

The cases studied here represent a broad spectrum of experience in at least two ways. First, they illustrate the whole range of military involvement from complete exercise of governmental authority to acceptance of civilian control. At the same time, different kinds of societies—modern-industrial, partially industrialized, and traditional-rural—are analyzed. *Military Role and Rule* thus has a broader scope and a more thoroughly explored theorical framework than most other similar efforts.

Among the numerous general ideas formulated by Welch and Smith is the concept of "boundary" to describe the place of the military in relation to the larger social environment. Armed forces with strong corporate identities, with structures that are highly institutionalized, have integral boundaries. Their relationships with the other institutions of society are directed by well established rules and procedures. Other military establishments that are less institutionalized, whose interchanges with society are numerous and unregulated, have fragmented boundaries. As boundaries are fragmented, institutionalized civilian control of the military becomes more difficult and the roles, values, and expectations of both become confused.

Intriguing to Americans in light of the Vietnam experience was the role of the French army during the Algerian war. During that conflict, military boundaries were blurred, political institutions lost their vitality and legitimacy, and the army failed to appreciate the depth and nature of popular feelings about the war.

It is partly the fragmentation of boundaries in the American condition that Zeb B. Bradford, Jr. and Frederic J. Brown, in *The United States Army in Transition*, address themselves.

Bradford and Brown are both career army officers (West Point) with considerable experience, including service in Vietnam. Their book is a reasoned, well argued case for the extensive reshaping of the American Army. Both believe that the army must be restructured for several reasons: to meet changed international conditions, a new social and economic environment within the United States, and to reinvigorate the army as a profession.

The authors call the changed world conditions affecting American defense policy "coalition security." The principal theme here centers around the realization that international politics is no longer the sole province of two super powers but, rather, a complex situation requiring a more flexible military establishment.

While international realities form the general environment for *Army in Transition*, much effort is devoted to the actual reorganization of the ground forces in light of economic pressures, the impact of Vietnam, and the constraints imposed by an all volunteer force. A number of far reaching proposals are advanced to deal with these developments. Among the more significant is a recommendation to, in effect, divide the army into two forces—a ready combat army and a support service.

The new volunteer combat force would be characterized by heavily equipped, highly trained persons who would be well paid, rapidly promoted, and retired early. These troops would function in a traditional military atmosphere of authority, discipline and rigorous duty, spending as much as fifty percent of their time in field exercises.

Service units would approximate the type of service much publicized in current army advertising—that is, technical specialists working under conditions, and with a life style, paralleling civilian employment.

The plausible claim is made that these as well as other changes will result in a smaller but much more effective army. Along with this structural overhauling, Bradford and Brown are equally concerned with values. And here they stress re-emphasizing, especially for the officer corps, the traditional military values of honor, duty, and integrity. It is at this point that *Army in Transition* and *Military Role and Rule* converge. The Vietnam war wrecked much of the army's corporate sense and the various proposals advanced in *Army in Transition* are aimed at restoring that identity as well as eliminating specific, internal abuses. There is ambivalence, however, when Bradford and Brown discuss values and here one must raise some questions.

Is it really possible, in an open society, to construct the kind of military force suggested in *Army in Transition?* Has the fragmentation of civil-military boundaries, caused as much by the "military-industrial-complex" as Vietnam, proceeded to the point where genuine civilian control is impossible? Welch and Smith have demonstrated that higher levels of professionalization in armies do not necessarily encourage

Let's bring government documents down to size.

By that we mean make them more manageable and accessible through microforms.

Take, for example, THE CONGRESSIONAL RECORD. Our new subscription service can provide not only each month's issues of the RECORD on microfiche, but also a hardcopy *Monthly Index and Guide to the Congressional Record*. This Index is the first comprehensive, easy-to-use guide to the RECORD ever published — making the RECORD more accessible than ever before.

Thousands of other documents are available from our microform collection, including many that are out-of-print or difficult to obtain. Among these are *The Catalog of U.S. Census Publications, 1820-1945* ... *Congressional Hearings* from 1839-1954 ... *The Annals of Congress* for the 1st through 18th Congresses, 1789-1824 ... *Session Laws* for all states and territories prior to 1900 ... and *The Monthly Labor Review,* 1915-1972.

We also offer many non-governmental source materials, including a tape cassette series on the structure of American government, and thousands of doctoral dissertations about the government.

To size up our resources, write our Literature Services Department for information on the government materials you're interested in.

XEROX

Xerox University Microfilms

300 North Zeeb Road
Ann Arbor, Michigan 48106   XEROX® is a trademark of XEROX CORPORATION.

Kindly mention THE ANNALS *when writing to advertisers*

acceptance of civil authority—are there, then, any such implications to be considered in the professionalism advanced by Bradford and Brown?

These are only a few of the many important questions raised by two well-done and thought-provoking books.

DON LEFAVE

Yuba College
Marysville
California

ASIA AND LATIN AMERICA

IDE ANAK AGUNG GDE AGUNG. *Twenty Years of Indonesian Foreign Policy, 1945–1965.* Pp. 640. The Hague: Mouton, 1973. f. 69.

Commencing the period of these memoirs as Interior Minister, then Prime Minister of the State of East Indonesia while still in his twenties, Anak Agung's career proceeds through several ambassadorships and a tour as Foreign Minister and ends up with four years in Soekarno's jails. Today, ambassador once again, Anak Agung has good reason to look back in some bitterness, even hatred, at the man who was responsible for his plight. Indeed, rancor does come through, but the volume is nonetheless a well-reasoned, exceedingly detailed, account and forms another essential contribution among what hopefully will become a long list of personal accounts of principals of the last several decades of Indonesian politics.

Anak Agung dwells upon his own participation only when pertinent to specific events, but these experiences clearly shape his analytic perspective on the entire era. It is a perspective which, though shared by many prominent Indonesians, has been severely underplayed in existing literature. One might hazard to characterize it as the perspective, highly variegated in manifestation, of non-Javanese statesmanship, particularly of those individuals who did not become absorbed into, or contrarily, were banished from, Soekarno's immediate bureaucratic family

as the 1950s pushed on to Guided Democracy.

Anak Agung is most interesting, for instance, with regard to statesmanship during the Revolution and with regard to the politics of the West Irian issue then and later on. He argues convincingly, from the vantage point of a former head of state, that "national conscience was not only a living reality among the leaders of the Republic. . . ." Indeed, at the Round Table Conference, the delegation from the State of East Indonesia, according to Anak Agung, stood virtually alone in its intransigence against compromise on the West Irian issue. Politics at Istana Merdeka and the postures of Soekarno in the advent of Guided Democracy brought general disparagement of the bona fides of an important segment of nationalist figures, such as Anak Agung, Hatta and Sjahrir. The balance is somewhat redressed as persons like Anak Agung, in their recaptured intellectual freedom, undertake the arduous task of providing their own analyses of events.

While there are lengthy treatments of Belgrade, Afro-Asian diplomacy, and Indonesia's relationships individually with the U.S., U.S.S.R., China, India, Australia and other Southeast Asian nations, the author's heaviest post-Revolution attention is given to West Irian and to other ramifications of international politics attendant to Indonesian evolution into Guided Democracy. He adds new grist to the litany of horror stories concerning Dulles diplomacy. He speaks not unsympathetically to the reasons for the development of Soekarno's political *konsepsi*, notwithstanding a deep antipathy to the resulting authoritarianism. And he effectively counters the image, so widely broadcast in the West, of the conquest of West Irian merely as an ingenuous feature of Soekarno's megalomania.

One may object vociferously to Anak Agung's interpretation of many issues. And it must be said that the book is frequently repetitious and occasionally tediously detailed. But in sum, it will undoubtedly stand as one of the principal source books on Indonesian foreign policy.

ROGER K. PAGET
University of Colorado
Boulder

ROBERT J. ALEXANDER. *Agrarian Reform in Latin America.* Pp. 118. New York: Macmillan, 1974. $5.95.

Another book on our Latin American neighbors by Professor Alexander is always to be enthusiastically welcomed, and this one does not disappoint. It is elementary in conception and tone; it leads us through the jungle of opinion on the vital process of land distribution and helps us understand the revolutionary movements which have occurred in Latin America since the Mexicans started it in 1915. It states clearly why they were necessary, what happened and their meaning to the nation involved. But Alexander does not stop there; he is interested in the advance of democracy throughout the world and he points out how agrarian reform strengthens it. In fact, he begins with a revealing quote about land distribution during the American Revolution, incidentally by confiscation now so frowned upon by the U.S. Department of State.

Although land reform laws have been placed on the books of almost all Latin American countries, only six have actually carried them out "far enough to bring about a fundamental change in the economy and society" (page 108): Mexico, Bolivia, Venezuela, Cuba, Chile and Perú. (Columbia has made a good start.) The first four of the six are examined in some detail in regard to: Who gets land and how; what happens to the former landlords; economic and educational support for agrarian reform; and the organization of rural workers. There is a concluding evaluative chapter, "The Results of Agrarian Reform," the last sentence of which can be taken as the key note of the book:

It is an essential part of the process of "modernization" transforming a hierarchical, rigidly stratified society with a relatively unproductive agricultural economy into a much more socially mobile, economically diversified, more wealthy, and hopefully, more democratic, society.

Alexander explains why hope for a "more democratic society" has not been fulfilled in Cuba; it has been betrayed by the dictatorship established by Castro. Unfortunately, he does not deal with the shortcomings of Allende's brief tenure in Chile.

Some day, I hope, someone will point out as well as Alexander does for Latin America, how much our land tenure arrangements need improvement! Since 1936 thousands of our small independent farmers have gone out of buiness: 36,000 in 1973 alone. And federal subsidies to help farmers are paid overwhelmingly to big producers.

The book is a worthy addition to Macmillan's new Latin American Series, edited by Alexander's colleagues at Rutgers, Samuel L. Bailey and Ronald T. Hyman. Bailey took the photographs which illustrate some of the points made by the author.

CLARENCE SENIOR
Inter American University
Hato Rey
Puerto Rico

A. DOAK BARNETT. *Uncertain Passage: China's Transition to the Post-Mao Era.* Pp. ix, 387. Washington, D.C.: The Brookings Institution, 1974. $3.95.

To be both cautious and daring at the same time is no easy task, but that is precisely what the author of this book—perhaps in the spirit of the book's protagonist, Mao Tse-tung— attempts. It is daring to predict any country's future, even when limiting oneself to the 1970s; it is triply daring to predict the future of a land whose course has veered so erratically in recent years that even the best-informed experts have been fooled time and again, and a land that is on the eve of what the author believes to be the beginning of a new era. Barnett, having gone far enough out on a limb to write a book about China in the 1970s, then declines to place his full weight on the outermost branches; he examines the issues as carefully as he can from a safe distance, meticulously inventories the possibilities, but gives the reader only small guidance as to probabilities and likelihoods. Since this is exactly what he declares his purpose to be in writing the book, perhaps no more need be said. But in fact he does both more and less. The book contains ample history, especially on post-1949 China; it has a great deal of information on what China looked like at the time of writing (1972–73) when Barnett had a chance to visit the country and compare what he saw then with what his research revealed and with what he had seen on earlier visits twenty-four and more years ago; and it has a rich body of footnotes that provides non-specialists with an excellent starting bibliography on modern and contemporary China. The book is broadly conceived: in addition to the predictable chapters on values, institutions and the leadership, there are lengthy chapters on China's military, economy, and international relations. Indeed it is in this sense that more becomes less, because so much is touched upon that depth is sacrificed for breadth and the relative importance of many issues is blurred. This may trouble the non-specialist reader for whom the book seems to be intended (specialists will find little that is new), especially since the writing is unremittingly ponderous. But as a compendium of information on China from 1949 to 1973 and as a survey of the range of possible development for the remainder of the 1970s, this is a thorough and reliable work.

Some will surely question Barnett's point of view, especially his tendency to associate Maoism with irrationality. While he concedes the appropriateness for China of much that Mao has attempted to do, he cannot really accept the idea that a country that is serious about modernization can also be serious about conducting a social revolution. Success, he seems to assume, always requires stability, order, and compromise, all of which he tends to subsume under terms like "pragmatism." This is only one of many issues that the book raises but does not pursue. Still, it is informative and suggestive, and many readers will welcome it even if few will be delighted with it.

MICHAEL GASSTER

Livingston College
Rutgers University
New Brunswick
New Jersey

HAROLD BOLITHO. *Treasures Among Men: The Fudai Daimyo in Tokugawa Japan.* Pp. 278. New Haven, Conn.: Yale University Press, 1974. $12.50.

This mean-looking little volume, with its plasticized, mud-colored binding and its narrowly monographic title, will transcend that cover very quickly and go on to become one of the important works of the decade on Tokugawa Japan. Focused on the fudai daimyo, those personal vassals of the Tokugawa whom one of the family designated "treasures among men," the book is quite a lot of them and a great deal more, too, for as Mr. Bolitho understands well enough, no group exists in a vacuum. To alter our understanding of the fudai daimyo's segment of Tokugawa Japan is to demand reappraisal of the Tozama daimyo and of the Bakufu itself. In documenting his thesis that the traditionally supremely-loyal fudai daimyo became more diamyo than fudai as the years passed, and became, too, important agents in the decline of Tokugawa power, the author has revised a good many standard western and Japanese interpretations of those daimyo and has limned out where further revision is needed.

Mr. Bolitho demonstrates that the fudai daimyo filled the "treasure" role which tradition and modern scholars have assigned them only up until the mid-seventeenth century. Then their loyalty began to evaporate into a hollow myth of loyalty, impressive in the frequency with which it was proclaimed, but without substance. Increasingly conscious of their daimyo status and inevitably influenced by the local interests of their own vessals and fiefs on one hand, on the other, they monopolized key Bakufu offices. Caught for a time in ambivalence between the decentralizing pull of their own landed interests and the absolutist thrust of the shogunate, where the rewards of office-holding were rather slight, they opted finally against centralism, and through their Bakufu positions helped arrest Japan's progress toward absolutism. The great failure of the Tokugawa was in drawing their counselors from among a landed group whose interests necessarily dragged them out from the center and erased the personal bond of feudal loyalty. The fudai daimyo, the author shows, far from superloyalists, were in fact the prime factor in keeping the Tokugawa from achieving the Japanese equivalent of absolute monarchy on the European pattern.

Mr. Bolitho's evidence is extensive, varied and impressive. Studying national, local, and family archives, memoirs, and a host of other materials, and culling a wide range of statistics and data concerning, for example, marriage patterns between fudai and tozama diamyo, he has sifted out an enormous amount of evidence about the fudai daimyo which has enabled him to focus on them from a nearly full-circle of perspectives. The evidential bases of his arguments go far past the older political platitudes to encompass the social realities and the economic uncertainties as well. Certainly not least important, Mr. Bolitho has a rare control over the language and an infectious joy in it. One can only hope that he keeps probing Tokugawa Japan and that he keeps writing. Whether he does or not, others will have to, in response to this book.

R. KENT LANCASTER

Goucher College
Baltimore
Maryland

SRIPATI CHANDRASEKHAR. *Abortion in a Crowded World: The Problem of Abortion with Special Reference to India.* Pp. 184. Seattle: University of Washington Press, 1974. $6.95.

Abortion in a Crowded World is a book about the population problems of India and the successful drive to liberalize the abortion law in India through the democratic process. After several years of debate, India replaced its old restrictive abortion law dating from the 1800s with the Medical Termination of Pregnancy Act of 1971 which allows abortion on many grounds, including the mental health of the mother. Chandrasekhar expresses the hope that the mental health clause will be interpreted to mean that abortion on demand will be a reality in India.

With the sole exception of Catholicism, Chandrasekhar argues that religious and governmental opinion about abortion have been very slowly adjusting to the new realities of world-wide overpopulation and undersupply of food. Classical Hinduism was opposed to abortion, for example, but Radhakrishnan seemingly would allow abortion under certain circumstances. The conclusion is that, like governmental and social attitudes, the Hindu view of abortion has never been static. On a practical side, regardless of official views, Chandrasekhar estimates the actual number of abortions in India to be five million a year. He arrives at this figure by taking the highest estimate from the various surveys he quotes and applying it to the country as a whole. The estimate may be high, but good survey data on the issue are not available.

Population pressure provided one important argument in favor of passage of the liberal abortion bill. Chandrasekhar believes that India, with 2.4 percent of the world's land area and 14 percent of the world's population, is the cutting edge of the Malthusian dilemma. Universal (and early) marriage combined with a near-successful attack on malaria and tuberculosis have made rapid growth a problem in the past twenty years. As minister of health and family planning, Chandrasekhar began the process of abortion reform in 1969 by drafting a model bill. After getting detailed responses from all the states, a few changes were made and the modified bill passed. This book makes very clear that wide ranges of opinion were sought before the final decision was made. Reducing the maternal mortality rate from five million illegal abortions was also one of the stated reasons for passage. Appendix seven gives verbatim many newspaper editorial comments about abortion reform before final passage of the new act.

But will abortion reform help solve India's population problems? Chandrasekhar looks to the recent history of Japan and Hungary for examples. As a careful demographer, the author avoids the easy (but misleading) statement that abortion alone "caused" the sharp decline in births in Japan after World War Two. Rather, abortion is the most certain of birth control measures and was adopted by a country otherwise ready for a sharp decline in births. Whether abortion will work out in India therefore depends largely on increasing medical facilities and upon sufficient motivation among the population. At best, given facilities and economic pressure (or incentives), a reduction in the birth rate might be possible in a developing society. At the least, the new reform bill will remove the legal barrier to safe abortions for those wishing them. The portrait of an illegal abortion clinic operating before the new law (appendix 4) provides a vivid example of the kind of situation the new law might be realistically expected to change. While Chandrasekhar at times is a little too strong in his advocacy of the benefits of abortion on demand in India, and sometimes relegates very important issues to the footnotes, all in all the probable effects of the new law are clearly outlined.

This is a very useful book. Students of politics in India will find it of interest, as well as those interested in population problems. Teachers of courses on India will welcome this volume, for it puts India's population problems in perspective by comparison with other countries. It is short—the text actually runs 90 pages—and the issues are clearly outlined. This book is a welcome addition to the literature on the sociology of population and politics in India.

GEORGE H. CONKLIN
Sweet Briar College
Virginia

MICHAEL CURTIS and MORDECAI S. CHERTOFF, eds. *Israel: Social Structure and Change.* Pp. 443. New York: E. P. Dutton, 1973. $8.95.

YUVAL ELIZUR and ELIAHU SALPETER. *Who Rules Israel?* Pp. vii, 342. New York: Harper & Row, 1973. $8.95.

Serious books on Israel inevitably arouse questions in the minds of modern scholars that are rarely raised in their more conventional academic pursuits. A small country, in a hostile environment, off the beaten path; yet continuously reasserting its determination to survive, to fulfill its "mission," to safeguard its social gains and make additional large strides towards seemingly utopian goals. Whence comes the passionate hostility of the Left, both the "old" and the "new," and the seemingly hysterical response of the Arab world, dating from long before the emergence of wars and refugees? How does one explain modern Zionism, the Nazi Holocaust and the post-war messianism, all of which are tied together in the birth of Israel and its present development?

These questions go largely unanswered in the two books under review, which set for themselves much more limited and manageable goals, dealing with the issues of modern Israel as if it were "just another state." For the larger questions, one is logically referred to the growing literature that deals with Israel's historical and ideological development.

Israel: Social Structure and Change brings together a remarkable collection of papers that seek to fill the need to provide substantial scholarly materials in the English language to students seeking to understand the broad contemporary challenges faced by Israeli society. It follows Eisenstadt, Patai, Fein, Lipset and others, who have begun in recent years to make such basic research studies available to the western scholarly world.

This volume includes comprehensive analyses of Israel's urban development, ethnic relations, educational issues, economic progress, the Kibbutz, and social change. Inevitably, the 27 essays are of mixed quality, with considerable duplication, ranging from the strikingly original and the profoundly academic, to the superficial restatement and the propagandistically partisan. A casual skimming through the collection will readily disclose which is which. The editors obviously had their reasons for making the selections they did, and are by and large to be complimented.

A theme that runs through the entire collection is the central commitment of Israel's leadership to the "quality of life" of its citizenry. For this reason, close to half of the papers feel moved to comment on the brief "Black Panther" demonstrations in 1970–71, as indicative of Israel's major social challenge —the ethnic gap between the western and oriental Jews, and how to bridge it. Several of the contributors regard the gap as widening (Remba, Toledano), and others sense that it is narrowing (Avineri, Elazar, Pelled). Patai, after years of studying these matters, summarizes his findings thusly:

Genetically, the Oriental Jewish population of Israel is rapidly absorbing the Ashkenazi Jews of the country, while culturally it is the Ashkenazi Jews who are absorbing the Oriental Jews (p. 307).

Who Rules Israel? is motivated by the conclusion "that it is enough to know one hundred, perhaps one hundred and fifty or at most two hundred, people in Israel in order to know who is responsible for decision making in the political and military spheres, who makes the wheels of the economy turn and who molds public opinion" (p. vii). It then proceeds, along the lines of Stephen Birmingham and society columnists, to describe the politicians, scientists, soldiers and businessmen that comprise Israel's leadership. What emerges is a highly informative and engrossing survey of Israel's modern development.

The poor timing of the book (early 1973) must, of course, be forgiven. When repeatedly discussing the diminishing prospects for war, they obviously could not foresee the general attack on Israel launched in October 1973. When conjecturing on the heirs apparent to Golda Meir's office, they simply could not anticipate that most of the logical candidates would be rendered unacceptable within six months because of the war developments, and therefore did not even mention the eventual winner, Yitzhak Rabin, as a dark horse.

In any such subjective study, there are bound to be exaggerations on the one hand and understatements on the other. The notions of "protekzia" and inter-locking directorates of the "elite" are not as uniquely Israeli as the authors seem to believe; nor is the bureaucratic red tape. They are the rule, rather than the exception, in most developed countries. A more serious miscalculation, probably reflecting the author's personal biases, is the singular lack of attention, a mere two pages (140–42), devoted to Israel's religious establishment. Both its opponents and its defenders would agree that it is a major political force to be reckoned with, however unspiritual it may at times appear.

Both books, therefore, are useful additions to the growing literature on modern Israel. The first will be of primary interest to the social scientist, and the second to the student of general background material on Israel's present leadership.

HERBERT ROSENBLUM
Hebrew College
Brookline
Massachusetts

JOHN N. HAWKINS. *Mao Tse-tung and Education*. Pp. 260. Hamden, Conn.: The Shoe String Press, 1974. $10.00.

Western interest in Chinese education varies directly with our enthusiasm for the economic and political successes on the mainland. Somehow (the argument goes) those schools must have contributed to the inculcation of attitudes and skills which seem to work. For Americans this is not only an exciting but also an urgent problem and it comes as somewhat of a disappointment that Hawkins does not deal with it at all. Instead he sets himself the more modest goal—one which he achieves remarkably well—of detailing whatever Mao has said about education in the last half century. This is no easy task since Mao has not only written little on education but what he has written is of a general nature and must be understood in the context of Marxist theory generally and the changing pressures on the Chinese Communist Party from the Kiangsi period through Yenan and finally to Peking. The author is aware of the problem and has sought a solution in separately discussing topics easily recognizable to schoolmen such as Goals, Curriculum, Administration, Students, and the like. Each chapter is then divided neatly into periods such as 1928–1934, 1935–1949, and 1949–1973. The expected result might be wooden and mechanical but is surprisingly readable and informative. The reason for this, apart from an attractive style, is probably the obvious feel and "sympathy" the author demonstrates for his material. He was in China in 1971, although I could not discover from reading the book how long he spent there. He extensively quotes Chinese and Japanese sources, but again usually accessible only through translations so far as I can gather from the recorded credits.

Despite its limited scope and obvious shortcomings, the book fills a need in bringing together in a careful and organized manner the many fragmentary remarks by the Chairman on schools, youth and education. Since many of these are of certainly more than passing interest in Western countries, the book should be well received by scholars and laymen alike. One may argue about whether Mao alone could have swayed a nation as the author sometimes implies when he reads pronouncements from the leader's pen as equivalent to accomplished social fact, or how—if Mao's thoughts were so dominant and all pervasive—could things have deteriorated to a point where only the Great Cultural Revolution could bring China back to revolutionary purity; but these do not seriously detract from the work. Compared with other texts on the same subject, Hawkins is more in the tradition of Stewart Fraser's *Chinese Communist Education*, a collection of important documents on education than R. F. Price's *Education in Communist China* which describes his experiences while teaching in China. We of course need both approaches but combined with the kinds of insight demonstrated in the Wingspread Report, *Education in the People's Republic of China*. My severest criticism I would reserve for the numerous unnecessary photographs quite unrelated to the text and containing the almost embarassingly simple-minded captions such as "Peasants, teachers, and students discuss textbook compilation" (p. 103), or "Mao chats informally with students" (p. 117). On page 96 "local control" is transliterated as *min-pan* and on page 86 as *min-ban*.

JOSEPH E. DiBONA
Duke University
Durham
North Carolina

LARRY D. HILL. *Emissaries to a Revolution: Woodrow Wilson's Executive Agents in Mexico*. Pp. ix, 394. Baton Rouge: Louisiana State University Press, 1974. $12.95.

The system of special presidential agents is a method by which a president operates in foreign relations without the trained services of State Department officials. Repeatedly resorted to by presidents since Washington's day, it has had a checkered history and, as this book demonstrates, produced in President Woodrow Wilson's relations with Mexico probably the worst fiasco since Cleveland's use of this system in his dealings with the Hawaiian Islands. It created conditions which brought the two nations to a near state of war.

The revolution in Mexico started by Francisco I. Madero eventually degenerated into civil war, and as Wilson found it impossible to recognize any warring faction as the government of Mexico he sent agents to all of them. "This book is a narrative of the activities and the diplomacy of these eleven men and the influence they exerted on Wilson's foreign policy and on the course of the Mexican revolution" (p. x).

Seemingly out of a grab bag Wilson and Secretary of State Bryan pulled a strange assortment of "experts" to advise them on Mexican policy, including a former Episcopal minister, a Protestant, a Mormon, and assorted Catholics. Some were self-important bumblers, others petty intriguers, and others naive amateurs. Sometimes they worked at cross purposes acting beyond their authority and even without credentials. In this study the author presents perceptive vignettes of these men as well as of the revolutionary leaders to whom they were sent as emissaries.

Perhaps a little too detailed in its recital of the intrigues, conferences, and rivalries among the Mexican military chiefs and their relations with Wilson's executive agents, the study nevertheless skillfully keeps the focus upon the latter, giving in general only a skeletal sketch of background events in the revolutionary movement as a whole necessary to an understanding of the roles played at various times by the emissaries of "the puritan in the White House." It supplies important details, largely lacking from more general studies and indispensable to a full understanding of more than two years (June 1913–October 1915) of the Mexican upheaval.

In general this is a record of sordid *personalista* politics by the Mexican revolutionary leaders from Huerta to Carranza, with Obregón and Villa appearing in the most favorable light, and a record of Wilsonian diplomacy in dealing with them in terms of personal predilections and prejudices which it was sought to gloss over by affirmations of the principle of self-determination and professions of high moral purpose. For two years the Wilson administration showed complete misunderstanding of the Mexican mentality and attitudes. It played favorites among the revolutionary leaders transferring its dislikes from Huerta to Zapata to Villa and finally to Carranza, but "in the end," as the author concludes, with Wilson's recognition of the latter, "it was Carranza who won," not because he gained military victories over his Mexican rivals but because he showed himself a stalwart defender of Mexico's national interests.

This is a straightforward, factual, and objective narrative of one of the most shameful sequences in American diplomatic history. From it the irresistible conclusion emerges that hard is the lot and small the rewards of "emissaries to a revolution."

The scholarship of this study is unexceptionable, but it is marred by some spelling errors.

DONALD MARQUAND DOZER
Universidad Autónoma de
    Guadalajara
Guadalajara
Jalisco
Mexico

EILEEN HSÜ-BALZER, RICHARD J. BALZER and FRANCIS L. K. HSÜ. *China: Day by Day*. Pp. xxxvi, 111. New Haven, Conn.: Yale University Press, 1974. $15.00. Paperbound, $7.95.

In the last two years numerous books recounting the experiences of a wide variety of travelers to the People's Republic of China have become quite common. Journalists, scientists, scholars, students, government officials, physicians—as well as "people-to-people" groups—have documented the diverse institutional changes defining socialist China and have evaluated the progress and spirit of the new China. The quality of these travelers' accounts has ranged over a wide spectrum and after reading most of them it would hardly seem likely that another one would be worth reading, or would add to one's sense of new China. And yet this handsome book on China does just that: it presents simply a photographic narrative which felicitously captures the essence of contemporary China. A perceptive introduction to China's cultural values by Francis L. K. Hsü, a noted anthropologist; a vivid running account of life in China's cities and communes by Eileen Hsü-Balzer, a young anthropologist and daughter of Professor Hsü; and over one hundred and fifty apt black-and-white photographs by Richard Balzer, son-in-law of Professor Hsü and husband of Eileen Hsü-Balzer, are effectively combined in this work to present China's current tempo and main theses.

The photographs, which are the heart of the book, make a strong emotional impact by conveying dramatically the mood, sense of purpose, and humanity of the Chinese people. Most of the pictures are of and about the people: at work and play, exercising, relaxing, communicating, swimming, bicycling, shadow-boxing, conversing, marketing, eating, in transit and at rest—going about the day to day activities that are their lives and the reality of China. The black and white photographs have been shot and selected with great sensitivity, catching with great expression the character and temper of individuals and groups in action, and the result is a dynamic picture-essay of new China in flux.

This photographic survey of life in China is made more meaningful by Professor Hsü's insightful introductory discourse on how to understand this vast and ancient country. The introduction focuses on certain basic cultural elements which play a significant role in shaping Chinese social relationships:

continuity, inclusiveness, authority, and asexuality. In this cultural context the Communists' emphasis on cooperation rather than on competition falls on fertile soil and the revolutionary goals of egalitarianism and industrialization-modernization through group-oriented motivation are not in sharp conflict with the four fundamental cultural elements governing social interaction. Professor Hsü contrasts these Chinese cultural characteristics with their American counterparts so that perspective and understanding are gained in dealing with such a different social system. His cultural framework aims at assisting us to "approach the truth by observing the same event from different angles aided by observers of diverse backgrounds."

The remainder of the text material is a running account of the trio's observations by Eileen Hsü-Balzer who succeeds in presenting her story in a careful, knowledgeable and balanced fashion. Fact is separated from what has been reported as fact; personal judgments are closely labeled; and skepticism is voiced in appropriate places and without hostility. The author views China with open sympathy but not with an uncritical eye. Her eye-witness reportage goes beyond what many visitors to China, including this reviewer, have perceived since she enjoyed with her companions the status of *hua ch'iao* (overseas Chinese) which enabled the members of the group to interact more closely and in more varied situations than other types of visitors. Her account thus takes us through the usual array of institutions (factories, schools, health care facilities, nurseries, communes, institutes, universities, hospitals), her reports of which are complete and accurate; as well as into the homes and circles of relatives and other Chinese families whose everyday existence makes the reality of her report more comprehensive and valuable. The result is a compelling, informative journal of contemporary China in revolutionary ferment.

The blend of photographs, introduction, and detailed account of China day by day is a most attractive and readable projection of China today.

CHARLES HOFFMANN
State University of New York
Stony Brook

JOE C. HUANG. *Heroes and Villains in Communist China: The Contemporary Chinese Novel as a Reflection of Life.* Pp. vii, 345. New York: Universe Books, 1974. $15.00.

This is a very difficult book to review, especially in such short space, for though Professor Huang has obviously done a tremendous amount of research and presented us with a fascinating book, this reader doubts that he has fully achieved his stated purpose. As the subtitle suggests, Professor Huang has attempted to explore the operation of the Chinese Communist social system through an examination of approximately 120 novels and novelettes published on the Mainland between 1949 and 1966. He believes that: "Since novels reflect social realities at given times and under given conditions, the structure, order and conditions in society and interpersonal relations may be inferred" (p. vii). He also holds that while a story may not be factual, it can be real, and what makes it real is its artistic quality (p. xi).

Starting from this premise, Professor Huang proceeds to analyze and discuss in some detail the contents of about twenty-one works covering various periods from the formative years of the Communist revolution—as depicted in Ou-yang Shan's *Three Family Lane* —to the beginnings of the Cultural Revolution with its model peacetime hero of the People's Liberation Army, Ou-yang Hai. Of particular interest are the stories dealing with guerrilla warfare and the early years of agricultural collectivization and industrialization.

All these novels concentrate on the revolution at the grass roots level thus making it possible for their authors to discuss numerous problems confronting the revolution without involving major political figures. At the same time the extent of background research involved in the writing of these novels is truly impressive. The attention paid to providing local color and historical detail makes them invaluable sources for the western scholars of modern China whose studies have largely suffered from having so little experience with reality. Furthermore, as Professor Huang points out on several occasions, some of these authors have demonstrated considerable artistic skill in making their characters come to life.

The strength of the book undoubtedly lies in the tremendous amount of material Professor Huang presents from the novels he covers. Through them we see how general policies and ideological formulations emanating from the Party affect the lives of the ordinary people, and how each stage of the revolution presents different kinds of challenges and different sets of contradictions and new struggles among the people. The weakness of the book lies in the fact that it does not hang together very well. Professor Huang starts out to show us how the Chinese Communist society works, how the victory was won, what the goals were, and how they were implemented. To do this he cites numerous passages from various novels, but he makes little attempt to integrate the information contained there into some conceptual framework of changing society aside from some general remarks notably dealing with peasant resistance to collectivization. Thus the social data provided by the novels are more or less left to stand on their own while Professor Huang devotes his discussion to either his evaluation of the work's artistic merits or how the work is treated by Communist critics. This is unfortunate for neither of these is central to the main purpose of the book, and were it the intention of the author to make them so, both subjects deserve much more careful treatment than they received here. In spite of the serious structural failing, however, the book contains enough fascinating material to make the total effort highly commendable.

W. ALLYN RICKETT
University of Pennsylvania
Philadelphia

FRANKLIN W. KNIGHT. *The African Dimension in Latin American Societies.* Pp. v, 148. New York: MacMillan, 1974. $5.95.

Most readers will find that this highly readable summation of the Black experience in the Americas fits somewhere between Roger Bastide's factually loaded *African Civilizations in the New World* and Harry Hoetink's interpretative, analytical *Slavery and Race Relations in the Americas*. Unlike these latter two studies, however, Knight's book is not designed for experts. Rather it will be useful as an introductory study of comparative aspects of Black History.

The author skillfully summarized a number of difficult problems concerning Black History including: European influence on slavery and race consciousness; the development of American attitudes on race; group interaction and group dynamics; and problems with regard to integration. His treatment of the United States, Brazil and Cuba in his chapter on "Group Consciousness" is especially concise and thoughtful.

In order to facilitate his comparative study Professor Knight designed two categories for regions in the Americas: "Settler America" and "Non-Settler America." This differs somewhat from the usual characterization of "Exploitative" and "Farming" colonies. Knight's terms have a distinct advantage when treating the southern United States which was neither entirely exploitative nor farming. There is some strain, however, in classifying Brazil and perhaps Puerto Rico as "Settler" colonies.

Despite Professor Knight's skillful handling of a difficult subject there are several basic problems involved with his comparative approach. First, it is not truly a comparative study in that except for Cuba and Puerto Rico virtually no specific information is included on Spanish America. Cuba and Puerto Rico both evolved as areas of active Spanish economic interest late in the slavery era. The use of these two regions to generalize on Spanish America may well be inappropriate.

Second, the distinction between Spanish policy with regard to Indians and Blacks is never clearly defined. In several instances Knight would have the reader believe that Spanish racial attitudes and legislation for both the Indian and African were directly connected. In fact, the Black, whether as slave or freedman, was never viewed in the same manner as the Indian. Both philosophically and practically the Indian became a special issue for the Spanish. Hence, Knight's inclusion of such things as the Papal announcement of 1537 (*Sublimis Deus*), the New Laws of 1542, and the famous debates between Bartolomé de las Casas and Juan Ginés de Sepúlveda (pp. 29–31, 53–54) need sharper distinction since these issues directly involved the Indian and not the Black.

Finally, Knight stressed the predominantly male nature of Black immigration to the Americas but no statistics on the actual male to female ratio were given. Such information should prove highly significant when applied to various regions of the Americas for comparative purposes.

WILLIAM F. SHARP
Temple University
Philadelphia
Pennsylvania

RODERICK MACFARQUHAR. *The Origins of the Cultural Revolution.* Vol. I. Pp. 439. New York: Columbia University Press, 1974. $14.95.

This is definitely a book for serious students of the Chinese scene, with a superabundance of footnotes (eighty-five pages), an extensive bibliography (ten pages) and a more than adequate index (twenty pages). Originally undertaken as a one-volume study, it has become the first of three, the first being subtitled *Contradictions Among the People, 1956–1957*. It was published for the Royal Institute of International Affairs and Columbia University's East Asian Institute, and the Research Institute on Communist Affairs. It is a really scholarly work with an unusually readable and clear style.

While the general destructive effects of the cultural revolution—"Let a hundred flowers bloom, let a hundred schools contend"—are well known, the author endeavors to indicate its origins and to examine the impact of the main events on the thinking, actions and interactions of the Chinese leaders, particularly Mao Tse-tung, Liu, Shao-ch'i and Chou En-lai, calling attention to their disputes and inconsistencies at various times, over the nature of the ideal of the communist society, the role of the Chinese Communist Party, the validity of the Russian model and the pace of economic development. He describes Mao as a patient man with total self-confidence, having the objective of combining centralism with democracy, discipline with freedom and unity of purpose with personal ease of mind and liveliness. He demonstrates how at different periods Mao first emphasized one element and then the other until in the second half of 1957 he realized the need for more discipline. Liu was said to be bookish, thoughtful and taciturn but persevering, achieving the heights by solid hard work and a gift for organization. Chou's salient characteristics were his unwillingness to elevate policy into principle and his association with policies of moderation; he commanded allegiance on the basis of his personality rather than on vision and really earned the title of supreme negotiator—an ability which enabled him to be a member of the Chinese Politburo for over forty-five years.

Mao himself was the progenitor of the cultural revolution which spawned the Red Guards and threatened to destroy the communist regime until finally Mao ordered the army to restore law and order. We are told that the completion in 1956 of collectivization in China and the 20th Soviet Congress set in motion the processes that led inexorably to the cultural revolution and the purge of the antiparty groups. It is impossible in a few words to recount all the speeches about the liberalization movement, the rectification campaign, the cult of personality and revisionism which the author concludes indicate that the Chairman had changed courses both in domestic and foreign policy.

Certainly this book deserves honorable mention and will be appreciated by scholars for a long time to come. It will be difficult for the coming two volumes to equal or surpass this one.

ALBERT E. KANE
Washington, D.C.

JAY R. MANDLE. *The Plantation Economy: Population and Economic Change in Guyana, 1838–1960*. Pp. ix, 170. Philadelphia, Pa.: Temple University Press, 1973. $10.00.

This slim study condemns the plantation system as a barrier to economic development. The nineteenth-century sugar technology used low-productivity, low-wage labor, kept on the job by slavery, indenture, or other coercive relationships. The plantation thus inhibited labor mobility and a domestic labor market; and, given the small size of the planter class, perpetuated a highly unequal income distribution.

For Mandle, development in Guayana means the emergence of an independent peasantry producing various crops, and high productivity sectors such as industry. But each time the peasantry increased, the planter-dominated colonial policy frustrated the change. After abolition in 1838, Britain limited freedmen's access to public lands, but wages rose anyway, and freedmen purchased private land. Britain then subsidized indentured immigration, mostly East Indian. The immigrants' arrival, and the peasants' inability to support the high costs of drainage and irrigation, reinvigorated the plantations and limited diversification. When sugar prices dropped in the

1890s, unemployed East Indians were permitted easier access to Crown lands, where they grew rice. But village rice production, high cost and low yield, served only to absorb excess plantation labor. World War II obliged Britain to encourage colonial agriculture, but after 1945 the government dismantled the incentive system and refused to help local industry compete with home products.

The Guayana plantation system was shaken but not undone by demographic and political pressures. Following the end of indentured immigration in 1917, government public health measures augmented natural increase. When the larger labor force proved unruly, planters chose to mechanize. Since sugar monopolized prime lands, and other sectors neither absorbed released labor nor facilitated the appearance of local entrepreneurs, the plantation enclave remained dominant. Racial tensions between East Indians and Africans—a legacy of residential segregation under the British—divided the working class and scarred the early years after independence.

Mandle skillfully blends interpretations of demographic and economic data; he is admirably succinct, and usually persuasive. But his insistence upon the plantation's obstacles to development ignores the fact that some plantation areas, notably Brazil's coffee regions, achieved industrialization, and underestimates the possibility that Guayana's main problem may have been colonialism, the lack of capital accumulation and reinvestment by a local elite. Yet he portrays clearly the reciprocal relationship between plantation and colonial policy, and his book will be stimulating reading for economists, demographers, and historians.

PETER L. EISENBERG
Rutgers University
New Brunswick
New Jersey

BRADLEY M. RICHARDSON. *The Political Culture of Japan*. Pp. 282. Berkeley: University of California Press, 1974. $12.50.

One of the later stages in the "modernization" of Japan has been the application of some of the more elaborate forms of quantitative methods research in the social sciences. In this instance, Professor Richardson has selected the political culture approach associated with Professors Almond, Pye, Verba, et al. In addition to surveys of his own, his most important quantitative data were derived from the detailed surveys which have been compiled by the Japanese Fair Election League over an extended period of time.

The findings suggest a Japanese voter in many respects much like his counterpart in other industrialized, democratic states. He believes politics is relevant but he lacks confidence in his ability to understand or to meaningfully affect it. His interest level is low; such as it is, it focuses on pragmatic concerns. He views elections as important, yet he is pessimistic about the results since he tends to be skeptical of his political leaders. He is conscientious about voting but is generally averse to playing an active role in politics. He is more influenced by the candidate than by party label; he wants a candidate of good character who will serve his interests. At middle age he is more involved in politics than in youth or old age.

Sketched in this fashion, however, the portrait is misleadingly simple and fails to capture either the diversity within the voting public or the features which are more particularly Japanese. For example, compared to the Japanese urban voter, the rural voter participates more in politics and tends to be less skeptical. At the same time, Japanese voters, generally, are more interested in local than in national politics, although the level varies among different segments of the public. These findings about urban-rural differences and about the strength of localism quite rightly suggest to the author that revisions may well be in order for certain tenets of modernization theory derived from experience elsewhere. Two other suggestive propositions he advances are that education rather than urban/rural residence may be a critical variable in attitudes about political involvement, and that, based on Japanese experience, social organization (group membership) may be an important variable insufficiently considered heretofore in modernization theory.

The tentatively advanced and carefully reasoned interpretations of data provide the most interesting material in the book which, with its attention to multivariate analysis and its rather heavy style, is not one easy to read. The appeal is more likely to be to those interested in comparative analysis than to area specialists. There is a short appendix on political behavior research in Japan today.

WILLARD H. ELSBREE
Ohio University
Athens

EUROPE

P. A. ALLUM. *Politics and Society in Post-War Naples, 1945–1970.* Pp. ix, 410. New York: Cambridge University Press, 1973. $32.50.

This very expensive book attempts to do three things and in the attempt achieves only partial success. It describes in considerable detail and with much normative complaint the development and operation of two big-city political machines in the Neapolitan electoral constituency, the "Lauro" machine built by the Neapolitan shipowner and Monarchist political leader Achille Lauro, and its successor the "Gava" machine, built by the transplanted Venetian Christian Democratic Senator Silvio Gava and his sons. It also tries to fit this Neapolitan machine-politics model into the larger Italian political system. It attempts to explain why Neapolitan politics developed in the way it did and to forecast how it must (he is an economic determinist) become transformed as a consequence of the industrialization and modernization of the Neapolitan economy and society.

The best part of the book is its description of how these political machines operate (and operated). Having been raised in Chicago in the days of the Kelly-Nash machine and its successors, I could comfortably appreciate, with a sense of easy recognition, the operations of the patronage and clientelistic system. Mr. Allum describes very effectively the role of the "boss" in the development and recruitment of followers and supporters as well as the exploitation of national connections for local political benefits.

My problems with Mr. Allum's effort come from his interpretation of the phenomena he describes. He adopts the dichotomous distinction of the German sociologist Tonnies between "gesellschaft" and "gemeinschaft," between modern society, based on rational calculation of class interests and organized on horizontal class lines, and traditional society based on ascriptive links of personal ties and organized on vertical, hierarchical lines. He finds Neapolitan society to be only just emerging from this traditional, ascriptive society and identifies the inadequate modernization of that society and economy as the cause of the machine-politics which continues to operate. I, unfortunately, do not believe that political machines and patronage politics are only connected to partially-developed societies. I see patronage and clientelistic politics at work in societies at many levels of development. Let us take the process of political recruitment, for example. Mr. Allum shows how successive candidates for parliament from Naples are usually relatives or former aides of political bigshots. In the second congressional district of Connecticut where I now live there are three candidates currently competing for the Democratic Party's nomination for the congressional seat. One is the son of a former candidate for the same seat and is currently an administrative assistant to the Democratic United States Senator from Connecticut; another is the son of a former United States Senator from Connecticut; and the third is the son of the Chairman of the Democratic State Central Committee. Connecticut has the highest per capita annual income of any state in the fifty United States, and the United States has the second or third highest per capita annual income in the world. The conclusion I reach is based on one or the other of two possibilities; there is an awful lot of traditionalism in even the most modern societies or else patronage and cooptation are universal phenomena, transcending time and place.

Mr. Allum quotes Senator Gava's defense that his Neapolitan organization is no different from Andreotti's in Rome, Taviani's in Genoa, Rumor's in Vicenza (and I could add Calleri's in Turin). Almost all these cities he mentions are northern, modern, industrial centers, in a part of the country, in other words, that Allum has identified as based on "gesellschaft" norms. He doesn't reject Gava's defense, yet the challenge to his explanatory framework seems to have escaped him.

He believes that Naples will develop an electorate linked to class conscious, horizontal parties as modernization proceeds and the Neapolitan masses come to identify correctly their proper class locus, their correct class enemy, and the parties which represent their class interests. Machine politics will then disappear. Not being a Marxist I doubt that modernization produces these results, in Naples or elsewhere. In my opinion modernization reduces clear cut class identities and divides populations around other issues. The voting studies of Mattei Dogan have shown that the attitude toward the Catholic Church is a more important divider in Italy than class. Other students have come to at least a tentative conclusion that the influence of class has been declining, in Italy and elsewhere in the Western World. More modern Marxists than Mr. Allum, namely the leaders of the Italian Communist Party, have been engaged for at least two decades in the effort to reach out beyond the traditional proletariat and intellectuals to attract the support of other groups in society. They have succeeded to the point that Professor Giacomo Sani calls the Italian Com-

munist Party a "catch-almost-all" party. Perhaps they see the future more clearly than he does.

NORMAN KOGAN
The University of Connecticut
Storrs

C. C. ELDRIDGE. *England's Mission: The Imperial Idea in the Age of Gladstone and Disraeli, 1868–1880.* Pp. 288. Chapel Hill: University of North Carolina Press, 1974. $10.95.

At the outset of the present century Rudyard Kipling was writing of those "fluttered folk and wild . . . half-devil and half-child," who depended for good government on the willingness of the white man to respond to the obligations of Christianity and civilization by taking up the imperial burden. Kipling was expressing typical late-Victorian sentiments, which remained influential in Britain throughout the next two generations. But his views were not representative of the whole Victorian era, the early part of which has widely been regarded as a time of anti-imperialism, with the mid-Victorian years of 1868–1880 witnessing both the climax of the earlier policy and the change to belligerent expansionism. Some years ago, however, this interpretation was challenged in a seminal article which argued that the Victorians were always imperialists but at first in an informal way, securing effective control of much of the world through commercial and financial activity. "The imperialism of free trade" was the key idea in this new approach. It has in turn been challenged, with some success, but it has left an indelible mark on thinking about the subject. One of its results has been to raise a question about the contribution of the mid-Victorians to the idea and practice of imperialism—the issue which Dr. Eldridge aims to clarify in this carefully-researched and readable book.

His main argument is that the period was much less dramatic than used to be supposed. He says that Gladstone's 1868–1874 ministry was not bent on dismembering the empire, and that although Disraeli, after 1874, often intervened in the tropics, his policy was not one of deliberate expansion. Nor was there a popular imperialist movement in the 1870s. Eldridge does say, however, that Disraeli's concern with India and the route to it led to the vision of a centralized, military empire which helped to pave the way for Britain's involvement in the scramble for territory in Africa, southeast Asia, and the Pacific in the last two decades of the century. But he suggests that this later imperialism was largely a defensive response to changing external circumstances, in particular to the activities of newly-unified and ambitious Germany. In this way Eldridge is able to claim that the period 1868–1880 was indeed a turning point in British imperial history, in that it saw the beginning of the breakdown of that system of cooperation and balance among the European powers which hitherto in the nineteenth century had served them so well. Now their colonial policies and relations were to assume a different shape—as was, in time, much else besides.

ALAN M. JAMES
University of Keele
England

NIGEL GRAY. *The Silent Majority*. Pp. 227. New York: Barnes & Noble, 1973. $10.50.

This book's title and subtitle, *A Study of the Working Class in Post-War British Fiction*, are misleading. It is not about that "majority" of the British population which undoubtedly is working class. It is about a section of the working class which is in some way deprived. Yet deprivation has scarcely been a dominant feature of British working-class life since the Second World War. On the contrary, the contrast with the pre-war period of depression has been so marked that much of the British proletariat, especially its older part, enjoying a hitherto unexperienced material prosperity, has developed a complacent contentment usually associated with the middle classes.

Thus the book, for the most part, is concerned with that minority of the working-class which has not attained this relative affluence, or does not value it and may be in revolt against it. If one excludes the section from Brendan Behan's *Borstal Boy*, the story of an Irishman in the years before 1945 involved in what is scarcely an everyday working-class situation, the various excerpts which Mr. Gray uses to illustrate his theme are taken from novels about children, adolescents, and young men either in conflict with the world, or unable to relate to it.

It is nevertheless true that in one sense the five novels selected for analysis—*Kes*, *Billy Liar*, *Saturday Night and Sunday Morning*, *This Sporting Life* and *Alfie*—are representative of British post-war fiction. They have all been "best sellers" and they have all been adapted for either the large or the small screen. So they have reached vast audiences. Middle-class people, particularly non-British middle-class people, might well, therefore, conclude that they enshrine the British working-class "way of life," though surely that purpose is fulfilled by *Coronation Street*, a long-running television series about life in the backstreets of a North of England industrial town.

Where Mr. Gray's material is authentic is in its background. Rugby League football, pubs, factories and council houses—these carry visual conviction, and this may explain the vividness of their presentation on the media. The values asserted in the selected books, however, are untypical: or so, at least, this reviewer would argue. The British working class is more aggressive than the middle class: nevertheless, one of its most marked features is its gentleness. Again it may be that the British working class is deprived, absolutely if not relatively, but it seldom takes refuge in fantasy or self-pity as do the leading characters in these novels.

These heroes, it could be maintained, are working-class boys who feel unable to accept their own class' compromise with British middle-class values. In

Kes, or *Billy Liar* this leads to withdrawal from the world: in *Saturday Night and Sunday Morning* and *Alfie,* it produces an assertive hedonism. *This Sporting Life* is more subtle: it also has a "mixed-up" heroine, as well as a hero in the same mold as the others. He is unable to relate, though his difficulty is in living above his accustomed standard of living. Thus all the heroes are "different." They are all at odds with, if not all in rebellion against, the ways of an older generation which does not understand their status problems. As so often in contemporary popular sociological writing, generational misunderstandings are explained in terms of lack of communication between classes.

The author who, as he so often reminds us, is a working-class lad, clearly aligns himself with the positions of his uncomprehending and uncomprehended heroes. There is much earnest endeavour to shock the middle classes by using such words as "fuck," "arse" and "pissed." We are introduced to the author's marital problem: he has a middle-class wife who finds him aggressive. Elsewhere there are other biographical details from the 1950s such as his ejection from rock'n'roll films and his membership of a motorbike gang. "When you are down in the working class you are small and ineffectual," he says. (So you are if you are "down" in the middle—or any other— class.) You need a hero.

The book is perceptive in one striking way. It distinguishes an important thread in contemporary British social literature, the plight of the uprooted intellectual or artist whose need to acquire knowledge or express creativity leads to feelings of rebellion against conventional values and "the system." The attempt to translate this into any practical terms is doomed to failure. "I'm talking about revolution," says Mr. Gray in his last sentence. But he is not talking about a working-class revolution. He is talking about the revolt of the clerks.

FRANK BEALEY
University of Aberdeen
Scotland

FELIKS GROSS. *Il Paese: Values and Social Change in an Italian Village.* Pp. 298. New York: New York University Press, 1973. $12.50.

Studies of rural communities and small urban centers brought the social scientists in contact with the real world and the real people. Italian villages and towns became objects of investigation in the postwar period. *Il Paese,* which can be translated as the village, town, or countryside, depending on context, is such a study of a village-town of *Bonagente* (fictitious name), near Frosinone, 65 miles east of Rome, not far from the new Autostrada del Sole, but removed enough from the main lines of circulation to retain the isolated life of the early postwar period.

The study, initially framed in 1957–58 as the study of social organization, was transformed into a study of social change by the surveys of 1969 and 1971. The stagnating social and economic conditions in the fifties, just before the Italian economic boom, provide the scenery of stability but also hopelessness. The traditional mores survived the political upheavals of fascism and the new republic, but could not reestablish the apparent equilibrium of the earlier era. The author surveys the specific conditions of the Bonagente community of two and one-half thousand people. The town with its "cittadini," separated by physical and social walls from the "contadini," peasants of the surrounding area, has a life of its own. The stable relations, responding to the values and goals of the traditional society, were upset by the technological and social innovations of the sixties. It affected the life of everyone, regardless of his social and political status, though it affected everyone differently. The patriarchal structure gave way to a new transformed society, which keeps some social and cultural traditions and at the same time embraces the technical and economic innovations. The apparent and actual conflicts create new relationships, coordinations and conflicts, inconsistencies and disequilibria, which lead to a new adjusted social and economic system. The money economy and market system took over and traditional reliance on established social relationships yielded to new incentives of economic benefits. The improved communications opened employment opportunities in distant Rome, brought in the incipient tourism, electricity and television, broke rigid traditional and provincial barriers and exposed the village to the world. The bewildering experience caught many people unprepared. They were faced with the incongruity of cherishing the old cultural preferences and grabbing the new economic advantages. They were submerged by the overwhelming trust of modernity, not quite prepared to embrace it completely.

The writer appears to be inadequately prepared to face the complexity of this transformation. The description of the static picture of the bucolic remoteness with its intriguing internal stratifications, division of power, money, prestige and property of his first survey is contrasted with the more sketchy description of the new pattern evident in 1969 and 1971, where the dynamic change is more implied than analyzed. Interaction is presented as a relationship between described variables rather than as a dynamic interacting process.

Where does this process of change fit into a large picture of modernization and transformation of the society? How unique or universal is the dynamic process of the Bonagente community? The pseudonym implies that "Il Paese" is not a specific case. We do not learn, however, to what extent the Bonagente community is representative of Italian villages nor for the compact village in general.

The study apparently attempted to satisfy the level of expectations of Italian sponsors, as well as scientific demands of the American professional clientele. By seeking two goals, it produced a compromise: a watered down American field methodology with Italian historical descriptive stress. The assistance of Professor Cerase did not

change this stress. As a consequence, the elementary statistical field survey is too elementary and too biased to have significance. The Italian habit of omitting bibliography and analytical index, and using crude diagrams reduces the scholarly utility of the study. References to authors and studies without footnotes, common in Italian scholarly literature, are of limited value to an American reader.

Nevertheless, the book is an interesting and enjoyable study. I will be looking for Bonagente in the hills of Ciociaria, as I have been for the village of Vaucluse around Rousillon or for the peasants of Orašac in Šumadija. The uniqueness of the Bonagente community becomes a common treatment of villages and their transformation in modern times.

JOSEPH VELIKONJA
University of Washington
Seattle

PAUL C. HELMREICH. *From Paris to Sèvres: The Partition of the Ottoman Empire at the Peace Conference of 1919–1920.* Pp. xi, 376. Columbus: Ohio State University Press, 1974. $15.00.

Of the many problems with which the victorious powers in 1919–1920 contended in their efforts to extract retribution from their erstwhile enemies, to remake the map of Europe, and to introduce a new international order, the fate of the Ottoman Empire was certainly one of the thorniest and most intractable, not to say perhaps the most fateful. The geographic importance of the area was proverbial, the political and administrative weakness of the government appeared incorrigible, and the rivalry for influence and control among the great powers had become traditional. Once the Ottoman government was involved in the great conflict, the Allied powers were agreed at least in this: that the huge conglomeration of territories and peoples under the Sultan's rule should be disrupted and in fact liquidated. From the early days of the war the problems of the

Middle East became enmeshed in numerous and at times contradictory agreements of the utmost secrecy, while conditions in the region were rapidly becoming transformed by Zionist claims and pressures, by the resultant development of Arab nationalism, by the emergence of Venizelos's Greece as a British client and persistent claimant, and by the temporary eclipse of Russia in the years following the Bolshevik Revolution.

The difficulties encountered in the efforts to reconcile conflicting interests in the area have long fascinated historians, and have produced a series of impressive studies, from Harry N. Howard's *The Partition of Turkey, 1913–1923* (1931), through Elie Kédourie's *England and the Middle East: The Destruction of the Ottoman Empire, 1914–1921* (1956) to the comprehensive and impressive volume of Howard M. Sachar: *The Emergence of the Middle East* (1969), to say nothing of a host of specialized studies dealing more particularly with the Arab world and the establishment of the Palestine mandate.

These and other scholars have been able to block out the main lines of the Middle East settlement because of the many documents published by the parties to the dispute, and the abundant material provided by a plethora of biographies and memoirs published in the ensuing years of participants or their apologists. But only in recent years have some of the principal governments undertaken the publication of the relevant documents and have opened their archives to the intensive investigations of scholars.

Mr. Helmreich has been able to exploit this mountainous mass of material in what can only be called a major feat of research. He has done so with commendable thoroughness and with great judiciousness. It would be utterly impossible in the brief scope of a review to comment on even a few of the major issues he has analyzed. Suffice it to say that while he has not altered significantly the main features of the argument, he has provided many

details and has elucidated much that was obscure in the attitudes and policies of individual participants. The reader is led to realize how the great issues of the German treaty and the determination of the British to ensure their preponderance in the Middle East led to constant deferment of decision on the fate of the Ottoman Empire. The reader will also be surprised to find how unimportant a role the issue of oil played in the negotiations, how little importance was attached to the claims of the Arabs, and with what sublime indifference the statesmen viewed the emergence of Turkish nationalism, despite the persistent warnings of their representatives on the spot. Mr. Helmreich's book is particularly valuable for its detailed analysis of the final negotiations disposing of lesser problems and so opening the way to conclusion of the treaty of Sèvres. All in all, this splendid monograph may be said to supersede earlier treatment and to provide an account as definitive as may ever be possible.

Despite the excellence of the book in terms of scholarship, the reviewer cannot refrain from reiterating, in the strongest terms, the objections of scholars to the treatment of the annotations in many serious works. This is, presumably, a matter for the publisher rather than for the author and it has been allowed to go from bad to worse. We have now reached the point where the evidence is not cited at the foot of the page, where it belongs; it is not even collated at the end of the volume, which in itself is an abomination. It has now become the fashion to append the annotations to the end of each chapter, to enumerate them in the text in type so small as to be all but illegible, and to cite materials in the scantest possible form. The inquisitive reader is obliged to keep track of two different texts and, if he desires full information about a book, to consult yet a third place, the bibiliography (which, by the way, is excellent). Furthermore, the references to documentary materials, whether published or unpublished, are often so voluminous and at times so obscure, as to call for a concerted effort at de-cipherment.

When will publishers free them-selves of the delusion that books of this kind can have a popular appeal? When will they overcome their pathological fear of footnotes? Books like the pres-ent one are of great value to scholars and often represent important additions to our knowledge. The footnotes are hardly less important than the text. Consequently the format of the book should be designed for the conveni-ence of those who will use it and not for the convenience of the publisher or of the legendary general reader, so beloved by the publisher. The day may yet come when scholars, driven to desperation, may boycott books that make unconscionable demands on their time and patience.

WILLIAM L. LANGER
Harvard University
Cambridge

FREDERIC C. LANE. *Venice: A Maritime Republic.* Pp. 504. Balti-more, Md.: The Johns Hopkins Uni-versity Press, 1973. $17.50. Paper-bound, $6.95.

WILLIAM H. MCNEILL. *Venice: The Hinge of Europe, 1081–1797.* Pp. ix, 334. Chicago, Ill.: University of Chicago Press, 1974. $10.75.

These two fine books complement each other in a most happy fashion. Both deal with Venetian history from the Middles Ages to the end of Venetian independence. Frederic Lane, the world's foremost authority on Venetian history, gives us a series of splendid essays on the main facets of Venetian political, social, economic, and cultural life in each era of her amazingly stable thousand-year history. William McNeill, famous for his highly success-ful popularizations of global history (*The Rise of the West* [1963]; *Europe's Steppe Frontier* [1964]), tries to explore the complex relations between the changing fortunes of Venice and her function as "the hinge of Europe," a culture transmitter not only from Byzantium to the West, but also from West to East Europe and even to sec-tions of Russia. These two works—one by a specialist, the other by a generalist; one looking at Venice from the inside out, the other from the outside in—together offer almost all one needs to know about the fascinat-ing history of the *Serenissima Repub-blica.*

Neither book, furthermore, assumes much prior historical knowledge. Any-one who remembers something of his freshman Western Civilization course will get along quite well with each of them. Even so, each author has incor-porated the best recent scholarship in his narrative. In the case of Lane, much of what we read is based on his own masterful researches, some of which have recently been incorporated in a Festschrift volume of his articles, *Ven-ice and History* (1966). McNeill's work, as is usually the case with him, leans heavily on the monographs of other scholars; but many of his interpreta-tions are original and merit serious consideration.

No one who has stood on the great piazza of San Marco can help wonder-ing what produced this unique urban gem and kept it so haughtily self-sufficient for so long. Her economically fortunate and easily defendable loca-tion is only part of the explanation. Even more important is the nature of her political system. From one angle, Venice's political history looks like brutal monopoly of government by a jealously limited aristocracy. Looking from another angle, however, one ex-periences a thrill of admiration for the intricate balance so long maintained among overlapping boards of magis-trates that managed to check each other effectively, to give the middle and lower classes decent government, and to win one success after another in war, economic competition, and the clash of culture. The greatest accomplishment of the famous Venetian constitution—a system that was the envy of all political commentators from the thirteenth to the seventeenth century—was its success in avoiding government by faction.

Family life and its economic nexus were just as important to individual Venetians as to Florentines, Genoese, and so on; but in these other city states the repeated and furious internal battles often left them helpless in the face of their enemies. As Lane shows, the manner in which civic responsibilities were shared out among the aristocrats prevented any one family or faction from becoming too powerful. The system was baffling complex and ridiculously ritualized; but it worked.

It was not the quality of Venetian life, therefore, that caused her to shrink to the status of a third rate power. It was, rather, her inability to generate revenues and sustain armed forces that could match those of the rising national monarchies and the Hapsburg and Ottoman empires. After successfully meeting dozens of great challenges over many hundreds of years, Venice finally was presented with one she could not meet—the sheer size of her new rivals.

MARTIN WOLFE
University of Pennsylvania
Philadelphia

PETER H. MERKL. *German Foreign Policies, West and East.* Pp. 232. Santa Barbara, Calif.: ABC-Clio, 1974. $13.00. Paperbound, $4.25.

Professor Merkl's study of West and East German foreign policies might indeed have filled a serious void in the English language literature if he would have pursued a more objective attitude with regard to the contents and effects of Willy Brandt's *Ostpolitik*. Furthermore, it seems that the author is confused about the role the Moscow-controlled Socialist Unity Party of Germany (SED), the East German version of an orthodox communist party, is permitted to play. Thus, it is not the Politbureau of the SED which is responsible for "East Germany's foreign policies," but it is the Politbureau of the CPSU which makes the final decisions. Also, when discussing the part played by the government of the German Democratic Republic (GDR), it

appears that the significance of the formal governmental agencies, such as the Council of Ministers, is highly overrated. The East German communists quite openly stress the role of the SED, thus, when stating the functions of a leader, they always refer to his party office first and only secondly to his "governmental" function. The economic power of the GDR is also overrated as a contributing factor of foreign policy making. The pride of the East German communist leaders—or is it merely their obedience to Moscow's orders—is the increasing integration of the GDR's economy with that of the Soviet Union, respectively COMECON.

On the positive side, it must be pointed out that the author presents a vast amount of material in order to show the emergence of foreign policy orientations in East and West Germany. However, his pre-conceived notion, that is, the great contribution of the *Ostpolitik* to the détente and the obstructionist activities of the CDU, greatly colors the entire presentation. The author is certainly correct in stating that the government of Brandt and Scheel was regarded with greater favor by Moscow than the preceding CDU governments because Brandt was willing to "negotiate" with the East in spite of the fact that Moscow's terms had hardly changed (p. 132). Moscow's short-range *Westpolitik*, namely, the acceptance of the Soviet hegemony over Eastern Europe, the inviolability of *all* borders, the recognition of the GDR, the recognition of "existing realities," all has been accomplished by Brandt's *Ostpolitik*. At the same time the Soviet leaders refused to recognize existing realities in the West, such as the close ties between West Berlin and the FRG. Many of Brandt's policies were allegedly directed to "humanize" the situation of the seventeen million Germans in the GDR and to facilitate their communication with their fellow Germans in the West.

There are some improvements on the access roads to West Berlin, although the communists succeeded in changing "access" which implies a right, to "transit" which is merely granted and therefore can again be withdrawn. On the other hand, the SED leaders counteracted this "concession" by various methods and by "interpreting" the several agreements according to their interests. The amount of money West German visitors must exchange when entering the GDR has been doubled and effectively reduced the number of visitors from the West. All these factual observations are missing in the book under review.

Professor Merkl accurately points out that West German public opinion polls clearly indicated that Brandt's policies had the support of the majority of the people. This also became evident when the Basic Treaty with East-Berlin was signed just prior to the elections in November, 1972. The public as well as the opposition were not fully informed about the contents of the treaty and the vague formulation of various points which presently have given cause for repeated "misunderstandings." If Professor Merkl would examine the present disenchantment prevalent in the FRG about Brandt's Ostpolitik, he would probably change his euphoristic impressions. The second phase of the Ostpolitik now under way will cost the German tax payers immense amounts of money. Moscow, Warsaw, and even East-Berlin demand large credits with low interest rates in order to build up their faltering "socialist" economies.

This book under review is a typical example of the presentation of complex issues against the assumption that détente has already been achieved and that Moscow's version of "peaceful coexistence" is the same as that of the West. Anyone who draws attention to the enormous military buildup of the Soviet Union and the Warsaw Pact is referred to as a cold warrior who just refuses to see the great changes in world politics.

The reader might consider one more fact which came to light after the book manuscript was finished—the arrest of a highly placed East German spy, Guenther Guillaume. He was not only collecting vital information for the East German Ministry of State Security, which his wife admittedly carried to East-Berlin. He, as a close associate of Willy Brandt was an "agent of influence" as well. At this time, it is difficult to assess what influence Guillaume and other individuals had upon the formulation of the Ostpolitik.

The book under review certainly may serve as the basis for a re-evaluation of Brandt's Ostpolitik, but to do this adequately, this reviewer would require equal space.

ERIC WALDMAN
The University of Calgary
Alberta
Canada

GEORG VON RAUCH. The Baltic States: The Years of Independence: Estonia, Latvia, Lithuania, 1917–1940. Pp. 283. Berkeley: University of California Press, 1974. $10.95.

During the final collapse of the Teutonic Order (1558–61), and the disintegration of Sweden's Dominium Maris Baltici (1710–21), the Baltic territories were an important factor in international affairs; so too were the Baltic states during the period of 1917–40.

The fate of the Baltic people has been dealt with only at a very superficial level by the authors of general histories. On the other hand, numerous native Baltic historians have produced comprehensive accounts. Many of these books have been translated but since they deal with historical development on a strictly national basis, the history of a particular people appears as an emanation of the national character of that people, being the product of the nationalistic era. Today, modern historians are concerned with the need to avoid the subjectivism that was such a frequent concomitant of the nationalist ethos, and furnish us with an integrated account of events in the whole of the Baltic era.

This translation of the study of the Baltic geopolitical entity certainly deserves to be included on the shelves of the specialists interested in that area. It

The Thin Blue Line

*International Peacekeeping and
Its Future*

Indar Jit Rikhye, Michael Harbottle,
and Bjørn Egge

As international conflicts continue in
the Middle East and in Southeast Asia,
and new disputes threaten to erupt
around the world, the need for an effective international peacekeeping system
is clear. Drawing from their own experiences as leaders of United Nations
peacekeeping operations and from the
history of international conflict control,
both within and outside the United
Nations, the authors outline how such a
system could be created, structured,
and implemented. $12.50

The Politics of Rights

*Lawyers, Public Policy, and Political
Change*

Stuart A. Scheingold

A book about the role that lawyers and
litigation play in efforts to alter the
course of public policy. The basic question raised is whether legal tactics can
be used in redistributing power and
influence and thus in promoting
political change.

"A stimulating, innovative, and su-
perbly executed project."—Victor G.
Rosenblum $10.00

Congress

The Electoral Connection

David R. Mayhew

Based on the premise that a congressman's principal motivation is reelection,
David Mayhew presents an original
thesis about Congress and congressmen
and comprehensively explores its implications.

"*Congress: The Electoral Connection*
will, in my judgment, become a classic
in legislative studies. I don't think any-
one will study Congress again without
giving sustained thought to Mayhew's
way of looking at it."—Richard F.
Fenno, Jr. $7.95

Impeachment: A Handbook

Charles L. Black, Jr.

"Black's survey is a dispassionate, invaluable beam of light. In terms easily
understood by the layman, this everyman's guide to impeachment outlines
the process leading to the removal of a
President by Congress, places it in historical perspective, discusses the conun-
drums that spring from it and relates it
to many of the specifics of Mr. Nixon's
case. And it does all this with clarity,
thoroughness (yet conciseness), schol-
arliness (without being dull) and above
all, unremitting fairness."—*Newsweek*
Cloth $5.95   Paper $1.95

Decisions in Israel's Foreign Policy

Michael Brecher

A detailed exploration of seven major
cases involving twenty-one strategic
and tactical decisions the Israeli government has had to make since independence: Jerusalem, German Reparations,
the Korean War and China, the Jordan
Waters, the Sinai Campaign, the Six
Day War, and the Rogers Proposals.
$25.00

Yale University Press
New Haven and London

General Maurice Sarrail, 1856-1929

THE FRENCH ARMY AND LEFT-WING POLITICS

by Jan Karl Tanenbaum

By integrating the republican general's military activities with the political aspects of his career, this book makes a valuable contribution to the understanding of the civil-military relationship in the Third French Republic. *312 pages, $12.95*

❧❧❧❧❧❧

The following books are published in association with the Institute of Early American History and Culture, Williamsburg, Virginia:

The Old Dominion in the Seventeenth Century

A DOCUMENTARY HISTORY OF VIRGINIA, 1606-1689

Edited by Warren M. Billings

352 pages, $12.95 (cloth) $4.95 (paper)

The Howe Brothers and the American Revolution

by Ira D. Gruber

412 pages, $14.95

The Gentle Puritan

A LIFE OF EZRA STILES, 1727-1795

by Edmund S. Morgan

506 pages, $15.95

THE UNIVERSITY OF NORTH CAROLINA PRESS
Chapel Hill, North Carolina 27514

"A Very Significant Scholarly Achievement"*

The Papers of John Marshall

VOLUME I

Correspondence and Papers,
November 10, 1775-June 3, 1788
Account Book, September 1783-June 1788

HERBERT A. JOHNSON, *Editor*
CHARLES T. CULLEN, *Associate Editor*

$17.95

This volume, to be published in November, begins the monumental publication of the collected correspondence and papers of John Marshall (1755-1835), fourth chief justice of the United States and principal molder of the American system of constitutional law. Sponsored by the College of William and Mary and the Institute of Early American History and Culture, under the auspices of the National Historical Publications Commission, *The Papers of John Marshall* will be published in approximately ten volumes. Each volume will be published at irregular intervals and priced separately.

*ARTHUR S. LINK, Editor of *The Papers of Woodrow Wilson*

THE UNIVERSITY OF NORTH CAROLINA PRESS
Chapel Hill, North Carolina 27514

is true that it is pretty weak on its historical geopolitical aspects but makes up for this by good surveys of the period between the 1920s and 1930s.

The bibliography (pp. 242–255) refers mostly to the German works and to a very few studies in English. The United States is not included in the index and we would be happier if von Rauch would have included a more extensive coverage of the work of large emigrant communities of former Baltic nations in America, Scandinavia and elsewhere.

JOSEPH S. ROUCEK

Bridgeport
Connecticut

UNITED STATES POLITICS AND HISTORY

DONALD F. ANDERSON. *William Howard Taft: A Conservative's Conception of the Presidency.* Pp. 355. Ithaca, N.Y.: Cornell University Press, 1973. $15.00.

"In retrospect, the conflict between Taft and Roosevelt represented a phase of a long, continuing struggle in American history between those forces pushing for change and reform without regard to constitutional procedures and those demanding conformity to legal procedures even at the cost of immediate justice." That quotation, the first sentence of the last paragraph of the book, states, in capsule, the essence of Professor Anderson's study. The author clearly admires Taft and sympathizes with him in the difficulties which the high-minded and conscientious President faced. Taft's lack of political skill, his real distaste for political maneuvering and his clumsiness in public relations caused public opinion and the press to turn against him and caused estrangement between him and that volatile extrovert who preceded him in the White House.

Roosevelt backed Taft for the Republican nomination for President in 1908, Anderson writes, because Roosevelt believed that Taft would continue his progressive policies. In particular he expected that Taft would follow his foreign policy leads—construction of two battleships per year, vigorous prosecution of the Panama Canal excavation, maintenance of American control over the newly acquired colonial domain and attention to other interests abroad.

Roosevelt was so convinced of his own rectitude and leadership and so impatient with the courts and the Constitution itself and with Congress if they delayed fulfillment of his goals that he felt that he must get around them if necessary to achieve his progressive ends. Taft, who had spent much of his earlier career on the bench in Ohio, was more cautious, perhaps more truthful, and uninterested in projecting himself as an individual on the public screen. The result was the well-known break between the two former close friends and political associates. Anderson writes of Roosevelt's "lies and deceptions."

He offers little if anything that is new or that has not been treated in other biographies of Taft and Roosevelt or general histories of the period. But his study is documented with original manuscript sources or primary sources in published correspondence and documents. It is well done and a valuable study of Taft's personality and of his administration as a way of conducting the high office.

This reviewer was particularly struck by an incident in 1910, which he looked at in relation to President Nixon's expanded public relations structure and quarrel with the news media. As the press turned against Taft, a magazine editor wrote to him that he should try to improve his public relations. No administration before Franklin D. Roosevelt had a "press secretary." Taft answered the editor, "I am not looking for a second term, and I am not going to subject myself to the worry involved in establishing a publicity bureau. . . ."

This book is not a biography nor a history of the Taft administration in the normal understanding of those terms. Only one chapter deals with the subject's life before the 1908 presidential race, and there is nothing about his career after the Presidency or his service on the Supreme Court. The administration's policies are treated topically rather than chronologically. The Pinchot-Ballinger controversy is written into a chapter on the President's theory of administration and his structure of the Cabinet. A chapter deals with Taft's troubled relations with Congress, particularly his difficulties with Speaker Cannon and the "progressives" headed by Senator LaFollette of Wisconsin. That chapter discusses the Payne-Aldrich tariff and the Canadian reciprocity treaty.

Another devotes itself to foreign policy, particularly the President's interest in the Far East and his moves to encourage American private investment in China. And there is a similar study of the break with Roosevelt and the 1912 campaign.

The book concludes with a chapter which reviews and discusses Taft's experience as a study of the general problem of presidential administration.

F. B. MARBUT

Sarasota
Florida

BERNARD BAILYN. *The Ordeal of Thomas Hutchinson.* Pp. vii, 423. Cambridge, Mass.: Harvard University Press, 1974. $12.50.

ROBERT McCLUER CALHOON. *The Loyalists in Revolutionary America, 1760–1781.* Pp. xviii, 580. New York: Harcourt, Brace Jovanovich, 1973. $17.50.

CATHERINE S. CRARY. *The Price of Loyalty: Tory Writings from the Revolutionary Era.* Pp. 481. New York: McGraw-Hill, 1974. $12.50.

Charles Francis Adams once claimed that it was not until 1842 that any American publisher made "an attempt to present to the public of the United States a justificatory memoir of one of the Tories of the Revolution." Two years later Lorenzo Sabine, writing anonymously in *The North American Review,* discussed the then recently published *History of the Operations of a Partisan Corps* by J. G. Simcoe. Sabine stated that he knew of but four published studies, including Simcoe's, that dealt with any aspect of the role of the Loyalists. Three years later Sabine published the first of his two volumes titled *The American Loyalists.*

Such neglect of the defeated partisans in a civil conflict is, of course, neither unusual nor unexpected. Gradually, in the last century and a quarter, Americans have given more consideration to understanding the nature of the political and economic and social attitudes of the Loyalists, and to their role in the War for Independence. In the last two decades there have been many fine studies—biographical, political and military—of the Loyalists. As we move into the Bicentennial, we may expect many more such works.

Bernard Bailyn of Harvard, generally accepted as one of the more insightful of the historians currently delving into the American past, turns his attention to Governor Thomas Hutchinson of Massachusetts, one of the most literate as well as one of the more important of the tens of thousands who chose the side of King rather than that of independence. He sees this present work as "part of a general effort I have been making over the past few years to develop a fuller picture of the origins of the American Revolution than we have had before, and also to exemplify an approach to history that emphasizes balance over argument, context over consequences, and the meaning of the past over the uses of the present" (p. vii).

Professor Bailyn states his purpose as an effort "to convey something of the experience of the losers in the American Revolution. . . . I turn to the losers sympathetically in order to explain the human reality against which the victors struggled and so to help make the story whole and comprehensible" (pp. x–xi). The result is a study carefully researched—a well written biography and an examination of the thinking and the values of one, but a very important one, of the Americans who chose to remain loyal to King. Based largely on the voluminous Hutchinson manuscripts, the author sees his subject as less malicious and less venal than such contemporaries as Hancock and the two Adamses. This is perhaps natural, in view of the materials used, and it is also helpful to the 20th century reader who would overcome previous prejudice in an attempt to understand the Loyalists.

Divided into six parts and 48 chapters, Professor Calhoon has provided a massive analysis and description of the supporters of the Crown. The first part, including a discussion of such men as Cadwallader Colden, Thomas Hutchinson, Joseph Galloway and Jonathan Sewell, deals with the critics of colonial resistance in the 1760s and very early 1770s. Part two, with attention to William Smith, Jr., William Franklin, John Wentworth and Richard Dulany, discusses the "search for accommodation" in the periods 1767–1769 and 1774–1775. Part three, including Samuel Seabury, Peter Oliver, Myles Cooper and Jonathan Boucher, analyzes "the appeal to doctrine" by men who considered any form of resistance as morally wrong.

The last half of the book, sections four, five and six, deals with the years of the Revolution and discusses Tory thinking and activity in the three conventional, geographical sections. The analysis is mature and suggestive, the documentation is helpful and the bibliographical essay is superb. This book adds immeasurably to the availability of interpretations and understandings of those on the losing side.

Professor Bailyn has given us a delightful introduction to the mind and heart of Thomas Hutchinson. Professor Calhoon makes available a most extensive classification and interpretation of Loyalist leaders. Mrs. Crary provides source material from dozens and dozens of largely obscure and little-known Loyalists. Arranging her sources in three parts (October 1773 to July 4,

1776; July 1776 to December 1782; and December 1782 to 1800) and thirteen sections, this interesting and unusual book contains more than 140 different selections. Even that impressive statistic does not adequately describe the contents, as one "selection" contains six different source-statements.

Brief introductions are helpful, and the sources are always indicated. Any reader familiar with the period may find something to criticize in one or another of her introductory statements (this reviewer, for example, is not completely sold on her assertion that James Rivington was, beyond any question, a double agent), but no one should dismiss the fact that Mrs. Crary has made available a wide variety of sources and that in her emphasis on the inconspicuous "little man," she has added a new dimension to our understanding of the Loyalists.

Each of these three volumes has a place in any reader's effort to understand those who chose the losing side in our War for Independence. Together, the three books provide invaluable insight into the Loyalist way of life.

RALPH ADAMS BROWN
State University of New York
Cortland

LEONARD BAKER. *John Marshall: A Life in Law.* Pp. ix, 845. New York: Macmillan, 1974. $17.95.

As this massive biography stresses, America's most noted jurist had four careers—as soldier, attorney-politician, diplomat and Chief Justice. Since these developed essentially in sequence, Leonard Baker's topical approach proceeds rather chronologically. Marshall's Revolutionary soldiering helped make him nationalistic; both legislative experience and his diplomatic mission to France reinforced this thinking and buttressed his conviction that respect for law constitutes the only safeguard against tyranny or anarchy. As Chief Justice he strove—emphasized in a tri-partite section longer than the rest of the book combined—to achieve a truly independent judiciary, make the Union supreme governmentally, and uphold sanctity of contracts as basic to justice and genuine order.

Highly sympathetic and legally knowledgeable, Baker supports Marshall's belief that codes and courts comprise the only alternative to naked force. Refusal to adhere to law threatens the foundation of civilized society. Baker sees this tenet as guiding Marshall's lifework—linked with patriotism and (surprisingly for the justice's reputation, but not inconsistently) cautious judicial restraint. Marshall is depicted as supporting "orderly democracy." No reactionary favoring special interests, he was concerned about individual rights (even for blacks and Indians) and customarily somewhat ahead of his time.

The volume's mammoth fourth section, particularly, demonstrates some difficulty reconciling chronology with Baker's topical organization. Until his death Marshall fought for unfettered courts, and there seems something incongruous about including this (as well as such decisions as *Brown* v. *Maryland*) in a subsection purportedly devoted to contractual obligations.

Perhaps inevitably in such a tome, there are occasional lapses. Burr was scarcely considered Federalist in 1800, the War of 1812 was declared in June (not November), and an unfortunate transposition of digits in the quoted epitaph dates Marshall's marriage to his beloved Polly almost forty years after his demise. Too, if Marshall often irritated critics with dicta beyond his immediate decisions, Baker frequently follows suit with superfluous detail or gratuitous comments promoting his (and usually Marshall's) viewpoints. More stringent editing would have deleted or compressed such items as Burr's conversations with his jailer, and remarks that Americans (contrasted with Britons) "were basically a decent people," among many others in a volume already overly lengthy.

Yet the merit of this work should not be obscured. Excellent background is afforded for Marshall's key cases, and the rulings are admirably presented. While Baker criticizes with apparent reluctance, he reveals Marshall as an appealing figure—humanitarian, gregarious, unostentatious, sometimes troubled, and thoroughly devoted to the Virginia maiden who set her cap for him when she was only fourteen—with an uncanny ability to reach the heart of legal controversies. He makes a good argument for the object of his veneration.

DONALD H. STEWART
State University of New York
Cortland

FRANK M. BRYAN. *Yankee Politics in Rural Vermont*. Pp. xviii, 314. Hanover, N.H.: The University Press of New England, 1974. $12.00.

Illustrated with numerous figures, maps and tables, Professor Bryan's book is more than its title indicates, for although its theme is primarily politics in Vermont, it contains comparative data for many other states as well. The only one-party Republican state, and second only to Alaska in its ruralness, Vermont is of special interest.

The author shows that despite the preponderance of Republican power in the state, Vermont's citizens have not been without some of the advantages of two-party states. Factionalism among Republicans has allowed scope for intraparty competitive views, and Democrats have been strong enough to control ten to twenty percent of the legislature and on occasion to poll a heavy vote for governor. In 1952 it became clear that Democrats had become a serious threat to continued Republican dominance, and six years later they elected the state's only congressman. This was followed in 1962 by the election of Philip Hoff as governor—the first Democrat to hold that post in a century—and by his reelection in 1964 and 1966. Moreover, Democrat Thomas Salmon was elected to the governorship in 1972.

Prior to reapportionment in 1965, the

legislature of Vermont consisted of a House of 246 members, one for each of its towns, and a Senate of thirty members representing the counties. Reapportionment reduced the House to 150 members and by so doing abolished one of the most unrepresentative systems imaginable. Thus before 1965 the average House district had 800 inhabitants, the largest 38,000, and the smallest only thirty-eight.

Analysis by the author of characteristics of Vermont's elected state officials is helpful for an understanding of the state's political leadership, and his use of the cluster-bloc technique to explain voting in the legislature is a striking feature of his study. It must be noted, however, that the book's six chapters are of uneven quality and significance. Thus chapter one on historical background is an undistinguished summary of existing knowledge, whereas chapters two, three and four on the rural elite, rural party politics, and the rural legislature constitute the heart of the book and could pretty well stand alone. Chapter five on defeat in 1936 of the federal Green Mountain Parkway proposal—an interesting example of provincial economic and political psychology—and chapter six on political life in a rural technopolity are less valuable than the three chapters which precede them. Nor is the book without some confusing slips and inconsistencies. Even so, because of its central chapters, it is a welcome addition to state and local political studies.

JENNINGS B. SANDERS
Kensington
Maryland

DENNIS CLARK. *The Irish in Philadelphia: Ten Generations of Urban Experience.* Pp. xvii, 236. Philadelphia, Pa.: Temple University Press, 1973. $10.00.

America as the great melting pot in which immigrants from many lands are all somehow transformed into Americans is a central component in the traditional romantic presentation of our national heritage. In recent decades, the Immigrant-to-American legend has been stripped of its pseudo-miraculous qualities and severely modified in view of the continuing presence of "unmeltable ethnics." Thus, scholars no longer focus only on assimilation; they look at all forms of cultural adjustment. But the basic process remains a key element in American history and historians are still hard at work analyzing it.

Dennis Clark's study of *The Irish in Philadelphia* is a new and valuable contribution to the literature on this subject. Although he opens with a brief survey of the early Irish experience in America, most of the book deals with the nineteenth century, when the immigrants were most numerous. Clark focuses on the various forms of adjustment made by the rural Irishmen in response to American urban conditions. In each case he provides an overview of relevant aspects of the Old Country background and the Philadelphia setting, then discusses the actual experience of his subjects in their new environment.

Clark first presents an excellent analysis of the housing situation: population density, sanitation, and property ownership. He then turns to the Irish work experience in Philadelphia, describing the content of certain commonly-held jobs, the impact of industrialization, the group's occupational profile and mobility patterns. Attention then shifts to the institutions which gave cohesiveness to the Irish community in Philadelphia: the Church, parochial schools, fraternal organizations, the movement for Irish independence, and political activities. In his last three chapters, Clark surveys the changes the Irish experienced from the late nineteenth- through the mid-20th century, then summarizes their adjustment as it occurred in all three centuries of their presence in Philadelphia.

Taken as a whole, Clark's book is a very good traditional history of an urban ethnic group. His writing style is excellent, and while the chapters on the periods before and after the mid-nineteenth century are less thorough than the rest, his theme concerning the balance between participation in and segregation from the outer world is clearly carried forth throughout. The main weakness of the book lies in its failure to adequately utilize the data and methods of the new social history (which draws on the social sciences) along with the traditional materials and methods he uses so well. Thus, for example, Clark relates his findings to previous generalizations on the Irish experience but never to theories of the immigrant adjustment process. In his discussion of housing and work, he fails to examine critical topics such as residential segregation, out-migration, occupational structure and socioeconomic mobility in a rigorous manner. He shows more interest in such topics than many social historians, and has done some statistically-valid sampling to back up his statements; but his concrete data are often scanty or inadequately presented, and he ignores some basic methodological problems such as the accuracy of his sources and the classification of occupations. While on some topics he makes excellent comparisons to the Irish experience in other cities, he neglects to compare his subjects to other groups in Philadelphia; and indeed the data he presents are inadequate for others to make comparisons. Clark also completely ignores a most fundamental social institution: the family. Thus, his study will not completely satisfy historians seeking a rigorous analysis of the basic content of Irish life in Philadelphia. But as traditional histories go, Clark's is much better than most and well worth reading by students of the immigrant experience.

LAURA J. LEFF
University of Pennsylvania
Philadelphia

JAMES S. CHASE. *Emergence of the Presidential Nominating Convention, 1789–1832.* Pp. vii, 332. Urbana: University of Illinois Press, 1974. $8.95.

In their formative years modern political parties in America had much hostility to overcome. Begun in an age which regarded parties as progenitors of "faction" and "sedition," they emerged in the United States at the end of the eighteenth century, and by fits and starts worked out their organizational forms in the half-century which followed. The first parties were organized by the Jeffersonian Republicans and Federalists in the 1790s; seen as emergency expedients which would not be permanent, they dissolved after the War of 1812 when partisan conflict cooled. After a ten-year interval when no national parties were in existence, parties re-appeared in a more acceptable form as the Antimasons, the National Republicans, and the Democrats. Thenceforth American politics would never be without nationally organized political parties.

In *Emergence of the Presidential Nominating Convention, 1789–1832,* James S. Chase, Professor of History at the University of Arkansas, traces the evolution of a most familiar institution of the modern political party. Although the nominating convention was well known to both Republican and Federalist leaders who used it to choose state and local candidates, its adoption as a mechanism for presidential nominations did not take place until 1831–32 when the Antimasons, the National Republicans, and the Democrats held national conventions in Baltimore. Preferring to nominate presidential candidates by more informal methods—the Congressional caucus being the most common—national leaders like Jefferson, Madison, Monroe, and John Quincy Adams were psychologically unprepared to institutionalize party organization, hoping that by "amalgamation" they could put an end to party.

Indeed, the adoption of the presidential nominating convention is itself an index of the final acceptance of party.

With the rise of a new post-Revolution generation of professional party-builders, men were on the lookout for practical methods to rally party rank-and-file, concentrate support behind a chosen candidate, and maximize publicity. As early as 1826 Martin Van Buren and John C. Calhoun were exploring a possible presidential nominating convention as "the best and probably the only practicable mode of concentrating the entire vote of the opposition and of effecting what is of still greater importance, the substantial reorganization of the Old Republican Party" (p. 101). In 1831 the Antimasons, alert for some method to publicize their little-known party, convened the first presidential nominating convention in Baltimore, a meeting primarily designed to spotlight the party's principles and leaders. Immediately thereafter Henry Clay's supporters convened the National Republicans in the same city to rally the faithful around his candidacy. Then it was the turn of the Democratic Republicans who, torn by Jackson's angry feud with Calhoun, held a nominating convention to decide who should be its vice-presidential candidate and to unify the party behind a single ticket.

As for the presidential nominating convention as an expression of emergent democracy, even here party purposes triumphed. By 1832 adoption of the national presidential nominating convention by one party virtually compelled its use by any party claiming itself a vehicle of the people's will. "Lip service to the superiority of democratic government was required of all groups competing for power. The convention, composed of delegates directly commissioned by the entire membership to make a nomination for a particular office, certified that the party met this indispensable condition" (p. 281). Although loudly trumpeted by party managers as the most democratic means of choosing whom the people wanted, the presidential nominating convention was actually the pragmatic instrument of professional politicians whose goal was to gain and hold power through the election process. By viewing the nominating convention as a stage in the development of the modern political party, the book makes an important contribution.

ROGER H. BROWN
The American University
Washington, D.C.

GEORGE DARGO. *Roots of the Republic: A New Perspective on Early American Constitutionalism.* Pp. 187. New York: Praeger, 1974. $8.00.

At the outset of this work historian George Dargo offers a model of constitutional government defined by six criteria: procedural regularity, substantive limitations on government, freedom of expression, government by the consent of the governed, spiritual freedom, and an open political process. Then in chapters dealing with the structure of colonial government, the legal rights of individuals, relations between church and state, the condition of the press, and the character of politics he considers how well American institutions measured up to this model. His finding that a close correspondence existed leads him to the central conclusion that by 1787 Americans had long since achieved a high level of constitutionalism. And they did this, Dargo emphasizes, without a formal written constitution, separation of powers, federalism, and judicial review. While the latter may have become distinctive practices of constitutional government in the United States, they are not in this view essential to the idea of constitutionalism.

Although the book promises a new look at American constitutionalism, it would be more accurate to say that its main contribution is to examine familiar aspects of colonial government and politics in a fresh light, that is, under the heading of constitutionalism. The author reminds us that the foundations of American constitutionalism are deeply embedded in seventeenth and eighteenth century political practices which characteristically worked to limit arbitrary power and make government responsible. Two or three generations ago this point of view was taken for granted: it was the starting point for historical inquiry, not the conclusion. Historiographically the most significant feature of Dargo's book therefore is its conceptualization as an inquiry into the state of constitutional government at a particular time in American history. Ably summarizing recent research on colonial government and politics, the author evinces an interest in the methods of limited, responsible government that reflects the renewed concern for constitutional questions in our own time.

Although Dargo's contention that constitutional government does not require a written constitution or judicial review is well taken, his account obscures the changes in American ideas about constitutionalism produced by the American Revolution. In the struggle against Great Britain, Americans came to regard constitutions as prescriptive—hence the emphasis on documentary fundamental law—rather than descriptive. A constitution was now conceived of as the original of government, the superior yet positive law against which the actions of public officials were to be measured, rather than a caption for, or the equivalent of, existing governmental institutions. Since this development lies outside the period with which he is concerned Dargo is perhaps justified in choosing not to discuss it. Nevertheless his perspective on colonial constitutionalism would have been sharpened by recognition of this fundamental change. Dargo's model of constitutionalism, however, is not so much historical as it is heuristic. Impatient with juridical and legalistic constitutionalism, his account of a mature and realistic political constitutionalism in the colonial era seems intended to evoke a similar approach to government and politics today.

HERMAN BELZ
University of Maryland
College Park

WILLIAM T. GENEROUS, JR. *Swords and Scales: The Development of the Uniform Code of Military Justice.* Pp. vii, 250. Port Washington, N.Y.: Kennikat, 1973. $12.50.

During the past decade considerable attention has been directed towards the military by academicians attempting to understand it themselves and then, aided by their understanding, explain it to others. Recent books and monographs deal extensively with the military, but military justice is hardly mentioned. This book does.

Generous sets the scene by discussing the first major revisions of military justice after World War I and continuing modifications which ultimately result in the Uniform Code of Military Justice (UCMJ) in 1951. Preparation of the *Manual for Courts Martial* (MCM) and political selection of members of the Court of Military Appeals complete the book's basic part.

Then Generous gets closer to the substantive problems of military justice: conflicts between discipline and justice, and between justice and discipline, and command influence. Placing the court's justices on the "input" side, and the reactions of the armed services on the "output" side, he analyzes decisions of the Court of Military Appeals and specific problems such as administrative discharges, non-judicial punishment, federal intervention, and legislation enacting the Military Justice Act of 1968; closing with an epilogue offering "his" suggestions for further reform.

America's defense establishment requires military justice and this book does not alter that. Much of the debate concerning military justice begins and ends with determining "the exact relationship and balance between 'discipline' and 'justice,' " as Professor Keeffe stated after his review of the Navy court martial system in 1946. Reformers "inside" and "outside" the military have broken down the argument that discipline and justice conflict, or vice versa. Today justice has been accepted as a means of creating and enforcing discipline within the armed services.

Problems do exist. However, military justice has matured and provides the soldier with the procedural rights, privileges, and benefits he would enjoy in a federal court; perhaps more so. Utilization of military judges not confounded with command influence (or local politics) and military lawyers practically guarantees a fair trial.

Generous views development of the UCMJ from historical rather than legal perspective and emphasis is clearly placed on "documentary development." His book is neither a legal treatise nor a case rehash and this may lead to criticism by those more familiar with military law than the author. Generous has only begun and is not the ultimate authority. More research is necessary. Abundant primary and secondary materials await those willing to accept the challenge and continue this examination. Someone should.

JOHN D. ELLIOTT
Harford Community College
Bel Air
Maryland

MARJORIE RANDON HERSHEY. *The Making of Campaign Strategy.* Pp. vii, 164. Lexington, Mass.: Lexington Books, 1974. $12.50.

Watergate has taught us the critical importance of campaigns in American democracy. Professor Randon's book is a welcome addition to the small number of studies which systematically probe campaigning.

The data for this study come from interviews with candidates and campaign managers for five statewide offices and all congressional seats in Wisconsin during the 1970 campaign. The study examines campaign participants' tolerance of ambiguity, uncertainty, and role preferences regarding the way campaigns should be conducted, and relates these to campaign decision-making. Professor Randon's book, thus, examines physiological variables of organization rather than variables more common in the literature of organization theory or sociology (for example, conflict, complexity, professionalization). Nor is the study a functional analysis that probes the activity of campaign organizations. After briefly noting the task of campaign organizations in the first chapter, Professor Randon then turns to other concerns.

The central findings of the study are interesting. A campaigner's uncertainty about campaign outcomes affects decision making: the higher the uncertainty the harder one will work and the greater one's desire to avoid changing planned campaign activities. And the lesser one's tolerance of ambiguity, the less one is willing to accept changing planned campaign activities.

This is the first study which examines psychological variables of campaign organization decision-making. The book provides useful insights and makes a positive contribution to the literature on campaign organization. In addition, Professor Randon indicates in great detail the way in which the research was conducted. Those who are interested in learning more about the way in which a carefully executed study is designed will find the appendix of this book to be very useful.

There are, however, several disappointments in the book—disappointments which derive more from the way in which the topic of the book was defined rather than the way the study, as defined by the author, was executed. In the early pages of the study, the author indicates organizational unity and coordination as a major concern, but this topic is not fully explored in the study. In addition, those interested in organizational theory might prefer a study which was tied more directly to the vast literature of this area, which is virtually ignored in this study. Finally, the author provides no explanation as to why she chose the particular variables used in the study. Other relevant psychological variables might have been used. Indicating why the chosen variables were selected would have provided a better theoretical grounding for the study and would have been informative to the reader.

DELMER D. DUNN
University of Georgia
Athens

JUDSON JEROME. *Families of Eden: Communes and the New Anarchism.* Pp. ix, 271. New York: Seabury Press, 1974. $7.95.

Judson Jerome is a former professor of literature at Antioch College who joined a commune called Downhill Farm in the Allegheny Mountains of Pennsylvania to search for "meaning, fulfillment, salvation, for the best use of life. . . ." His book is a combination sociological study, diary and autobiography written to spread the good word about communalism as a "viable alternative to the prevailing system. . . ." It is thoughtfully organized "in terms of economics, communications, political structures, interpersonal and sexual relations, education, religion and changing consciousness. . . ." The "typical" commune Jerome discusses is poor, rural and mainly made up of white, middle-class former hippies, former activists and various workers alienated from their work. The author estimates that 30,000 such communes, including 250 to 300,000 people, are located today throughout the United States.

Jerome describes the "New Anarchism" as living by "natural, organic laws, unstated." It may be defined as "apolitical, ecologically oriented, technologically sophisticated, spiritual and libidinal." Whether the new anarchism will create a new order "depends upon a revolution in consciousness which will restore humankind to its Edenic harmony with the universe."

Jerome's book raises two nagging questions about contemporary communalism. First, what is new about the new anarchism? During the first half of the 19th Century, communes dotted the American landscape from Brook Farm, Massachusetts, to New Harmony, Indiana. Despite the author's attempt to distinguish between 19th and 20th Century communes, much of the new

anarchism reads like old romanticism. Social enclaves based on ideas like "getting back to nature is man's only hope for a peaceful world" or "happiness is never having to submit to any authority" have been tried but do not seem to survive. And even Jerome admits that anarchism is as old as Antigone. Second, what is Edenic about the communes of the 1960s and 1970s? Jerome himself describes communal interpersonal relations as a "pressure-cooker atmosphere," often full of hostility and sometimes tense with paranoia.

Families of Eden realistically describes the pleasures and pains of contemporary communal experiments. But perhaps the book's main virtue lies more in its revelations about a modern man's personal search for an alternative life-style and less in its viability as an image of an ideal America. Crane Brinton's evaluation of romanticism may serve as an appropriate comment on Jerome's faith in communalism and anarchism: "It is a hard faith for us today to live by as we cannot help learning."

DONALD J. ROGERS
New Trier West
Northfield
Illinois

WALTER JOHNSON, CAROL EVANS and C. ERIC SEARS, eds. *The Papers of Adlai E. Stevenson: "Let's Talk Sense to the American People," 1952–1955.* Vol. 4. Pp. vii, 628. Boston, Mass.: Little, Brown, 1974. $17.50.

In early 1952, Adlai E. Stevenson was a national figure for a limited audience of connoisseurs of intelligence, experience, and leadership. His sole political ambition was to be a candidate for reelection as governor of Illinois. He maintained this stance until he was drafted in July as the Democratic nominee for president and thus plunged into the national political arena.

This fourth volume of papers begins on the eve of the 1952 Democratic national convention and ends in mid-November, 1955, when he announced his candidacy for the 1956 nomination. The papers consist mainly of speeches and letters, arranged chronologically. Omitted are the papers for several months in 1953 when he traveled in Europe, the Middle East, and Asia. These will compose the next volume of the planned eight.

Stevenson was a remarkably gifted speaker and writer. Campaign speeches usually make dull reading. Not so with his. He saw the campaign of 1952 "as a great opportunity to educate and elevate a people whose destiny is leadership, not alone of a rich and prosperous, contented country as in the past, but of a world in ferment" (p. 18). "Let's talk sense to the American people," the words of Stevenson, is the appropriate subtitle of the volume.

And these tasks—to educate, elevate, and talk sense—he fulfilled in an extraordinary range of addresses in the 1952 campaign, in working vigorously for his party in the years after his defeat, and on numerous occasions before academic and civic audiences. His onerous speaking schedule required him to rely heavily upon drafts and ideas provided by a dazzling stable of ghosts (Archibald MacLeish, Arthur M. Schlesinger, Jr., Bernard DeVoto, and Barbara Ward, among many). But the Stevenson imprint was always vividly displayed, including qualities of humor, civility, and optimism, generously laced with insights drawn from man's past.

With few exceptions, the speeches in this volume have been published elsewhere. New are the selections from Stevenson's letters and memoranda to family members, close friends, and nationally and internationally known persons in literature, politics, journalism, and the arts. Frequent letters to Harry S. Truman and Lauren Bacall simply hint at the wide range of his friendships. Fascinating to read, the letters reinforce, not contradict, his public image. They magnify his warm personal qualities.

The volume provides a feast for Stevenson aficionados. For the younger who may be disillusioned with politics, it would be great therapy to remind them of the broad tendency of American politics to generate responsible leaders of great integrity. Historians and biographers can mine a few nuggets from the volume but they will find little that is new.

Fortunately for the republic, many people who knew and admired Stevenson and share his philosophy are still active in public life. In selecting correspondence, the editors necessarily had to preserve aspects of their privacy and of others. A definitive biography must await the passage of time.

The book is well-edited. Brief notes are generously provided for transitions and to put the materials in context. The editor and his associates do not mask their biases. For them this is a work of love.

HOLBERT N. CARROLL
University of Pittsburgh
Pennsylvania

PETER LYON. *Eisenhower: Portrait of the Hero.* Pp. xii, 937. Boston, Mass.: Little, Brown, 1974. $15.00.

This is a long and highly detailed and documented work. It has thirty-three chapters, over 3,000 footnotes, and lists over 300 sources—including the official Department of the Army histories. The chapters on the war are too long and, at the same time, omit many events as well as memoirs of other notable participants, such as Montgomery's *The Path to Leadership* (New York, 1961). It is condensed, of course, because it deals with the war exclusively from Eisenhower's point of view.

The story of Eisenhower's personal life is satisfactory: his early life in Abilene, Kansas, near Salina; his deeply religious upbringing by parents who were members of a sect called *River Brethren* (similar to Jehovah's Witnesses); his five brothers; his military education (West Point, 1915); and his later career. He was not permitted to go overseas in World War I because his superiors needed him at home. He had two contacts with General MacArthur: In 1932, at President Hoover's direction, he had to assist MacArthur in routing and dispersing the "Bonus Army." Again, at the General's request, in 1935–1939, he served on MacArthur's staff in the Philippines. He always thought that MacArthur was a brilliant commander—but their relations became strained and Eisenhower returned to America. On December 14, 1940, he was summoned by General Marshall to discuss the Philippines situation. In 1942, he was rapidly promoted from Brigadier General and Chief of Staff, Third Army, to Commander-in-Chief of the American forces in ·Europe (ETOUSA) with specific duties to plan and direct American Activities in Africa.

In 1943, the Allies agreed to President Roosevelt's determination to make Eisenhower Chief Commander of the Allied Forces (SHAEF). Although he had to negotiate with military leaders such as Alanbrooke, Montgomery, a queer assortment of French military leaders, and others he also had to either directly, or indirectly, confer with Churchill and other British statesmen, and of course, with his American superiors.

By concentrating on Eisenhower's role in World War II, Lyon includes far too much of little consequence, and omits significant events such as the British evacuation of Dunkirk, the Commando Raid on Dieppe in August, 1942, the German missile raids on England, the wars of resistance by the Danes, Norwegians, and the Dutch against Germany, and the two wars fought by Finland against the Communists.

There is also practically no mention of such auxiliary forces as the O.S.S. and the O.W.I., not to speak of the 8th and 9th Air Forces. However ably General Eisenhower performed his duties as Commander-in-Chief, the fact of the matter is that allied superiority in men, weapons, instruments and supplies, and the devotion to duty and principles by millions of persons, both military and civilian, in the allied countries, were the authors of the defeat of the axis forces.

Eisenhower's very appearance and behavior, his smile and graciousness, his sense of fairness and his friendliness, all made him popular. A "hero," yes—but let us not forget that sometimes the people choose a lesser man for this acclaim—a Nathan Hale, or a Sergeant York. The fact that later, after the war, and after his temporary service as Commander of SHAPE, Eisenhower won the Republican nomination for the Presidency, and defeated Adlai Stevenson twice, causes some observers to put him in the same class as Grant. Although Grant rated as a failure as President (see Bailey, *Presidential Greatness*, 1967), Eisenhower and Grant are the only two Republican presidents, and the only two West Point generals, to serve two full terms as Chief Executive. Americans have tended to prefer generals as candidates: Eleven generals were elected —Washington, Jackson, W. H. Harrison, Z. Taylor, F. Pierce, U. S. Grant, Hayes, Garfield, Arthur, B. Harrison and Eisenhower—and six generals were nominated, but lost. Strangely, the last three Presidents—Kennedy, Johnson, and Nixon—had served in the Navy. Some of the earlier Presidents, and Presidents in later terms— McKinley, T. R. Roosevelt, and Truman—had seen military service on a level below the rank of general. In other words, a military record is an asset.

Lyon deals exhaustively with the General as a candidate for the Presidency, explaining how Dewey, Lodge and other liberals induced him to agree to accept the nomination and advised him to go easy with Taft and other conservative aspirants. Stevenson, the Democratic candidate, one of the ablest men his party ever produced, had no chance. Mostly the media—in the old forms such as periodicals and the press, and the newer forms such as radio and especially television—were all in the General's camp. Also, like Truman in 1948, he conducted a "whistle stop" campaign. Against this, the Democrats, with their *Fact Book* and *Ikelopedia*, could do little. The author dutifully notes his errors: yielding to McCarthy in Wisconsin; cutting out a favorable reference to his (IKE's) great friend, General Marshall; tolerating Jenner in Indiana; and, many people would add, accepting Nixon as his running-mate after the latter had made his "Checkers" speech.

In conclusion, we must say that this book is much too long and also, incomplete. Even though Lyon tries to cover the war fully and authoritatively, this is a job that cannot be done as part of a book. Most war historians and biographers of generals find that many volumes are needed. Most persons will accept Eisenhower as "A hero"—but not "The hero." Raters of leaders of all kinds, such as Merriam, Bailey and "the experts," as well as Montgomery, used some "yardsticks" or "cardinal virtues." Montgomery, one of Eisenhower's generals, used four Christian virtues: Prudence, justice, temperance, and fortitude. All of these Ike had; but those who think of Ike as a hero and attractive leader put more emphasis on his cheerful disposition, his attractive sturdy figure, and his patience. According to the Bailey experts, Eisenhower was only a fair performer. He wanted peace, but the world became more confused and hostile during his years in the White House. He meant well, but there isn't anything tangible in this long volume that will help us to understand why he is *The Hero*.

ROY V. PEEL
California State University
Northridge

MICHAEL NOVAK. *Choosing Our King: Powerful Symbols in Presidential Politics.* Pp. xviii, 324. New York: Macmillan, 1974. $7.95.

The framers detected the specter of a monarch in the executive they were fashioning at the Constitutional Convention. They went ahead with their work, nonetheless, not because they favored monarchy but because they believed that energetic government was essential to public safety and happiness and that energy was to be found in a single person provided with adequate powers. They hoped they had succeeded in reconciling executive energy to republic government, although some doubted whether such a marriage could be a lasting one. Jefferson and Hamilton were among the doubters, and the one was willing to sacrifice energy to republicanism while the other was willing to run the risk for the sake of good government.

Until very recently, most scholars since the New Deal have seen neither the specter nor the problem of monarchy (under whatever name) in the American Presidency. They have generally approved what energetic Presidents have done and what they might be got to do, and they have accordingly pronounced the Presidential Office to be eminently republican or, as we now say, democratic in all its accrued strength, sometimes the *most* democratic element of our government and not powerful enough. Then we had the Vietnam War under Lyndon Johnson and that and more under Richard Nixon, and now we find scholars joining politicians in discovering the fetus, if not the post-natal monster, of monarchy growing within the Presidency and casting about for ways to abort or subdue it.

Novak appears to take a different tack. The President is king, to be sure, and priest and prophet besides. He symbolizes our power and destiny, sets the terms of our discourse, embodies and expresses our deepest aspirations. But we need him, certainly we need the unity and simplicity he gives to government and the meaning he gives to our lives. Perhaps he has much more power than the framers intended, certainly more than absolute monarchs of the past; but this cannot be helped. We cannot strip the cult of personality from his Office for we cannot do without it.

But wait. There is Nixon in Office, with his "arrogant invasion" of Cambodia, his "flagrant" impounding of funds and vetoing of bills he does not like, his "abuse" of the symbols of

American life; and there is Congress weak, the courts falling under the Presidential appointive power, the media pressured. Something must, after all, be done about the Presidency, not, we are told, because we have treated it as kingship, nor because we have invested it with a sacred quality, not yet because we have placed too much trust in it. Then why? Because one man "is not a sufficient guide to the politics of daily reality." Somehow we may keep the king with all his sacredness and reposed trust, but we must curtail the power that makes a king of him.

What Novak wishes to do is hem in the President with traditional rivals and create new ones. The first purpose would be served by bringing opposition party members into the Cabinet (which, presumably, would become more than a moribund attachment to the Presidency) and by bringing the President before opposition leaders in Congress twice weekly for a public accounting of his actions. To accomplish the second purpose, Novak would have the opposition select a single spokesman, a sort of congressional king, and the American people select two Presidents, the new one to absorb the stately functions of the Office.

These are the proposals, as Novak tells us, of a theologian. He might better be called a theologian-poet, one who defines religion as a structuring of consciousness and the Presidency thus as a religious office. Novak is sensitive to the pluralism—the "civil religions" —of American society and to its influence on the different ways people look upon the Presidency, Presidential aspirants, and each other. His insights into political affairs, which are numerous, are expressed in the language of the poet, or perhaps secular theologian, and they do not fail to charm as they flash before the reader. But to this reader Novak lacks that "high discipline" he finds in contemporary poets and, in his advocacy of a dual Presidency restrained by new institutional devices, he seems not to have reflected upon the reasons for which the Framers rejected similar arrangements in establishing the executive office.

ROBERT SCIGLIANO
Boston College
Chestnut Hill
Massachusetts

GEORGE L. SMITH. *Religion and Trade in New Netherland: Dutch Origins and American Development.* Pp. ix, 266. Ithaca, N.Y.: Cornell University Press, 1973. $12.50.

Professor Smith examines the development of religion in New Netherland in the context of the colony's faltering economy, and what he sees as the "thoroughgoing commercialism" of the Dutch. The first half of the book is an analysis of how the Reformed Church became the only official church in the United Provinces, and yet the Dutch allowed a large measure of de facto religious toleration. The author argues that the Reformed clergy attempted to establish an exclusive Calvinist state, but were thwarted by Dutch leaders who believed that religious toleration was essential for political stability and economic growth. The Reformed Church never commanded majority support, and at a local level, the civil authorities refused to enforce laws against dissenters, who remained prominent in seventeenth century Dutch society. The second half of the book deals with the consequences of this attitude towards religious toleration for the history of New Netherland, where, against the objections of Reformed clergy and some of its own officials, the Dutch West India Company tolerated Jews, Lutherans and Quakers in an attempt to promote commercial prosperity.

The book is based on extensive Dutch and American sources and is clearly presented. There is a good bibliography. Professor Smith seems to over-emphasize narrow economic criteria, but it is useful to have an account of Dutch religious toleration in English. The religious history of New Netherland has not been the subject of a study in English for more than fifty years, and although the author confirms rather than challenges recent studies of the general development of the colony, his book has value in its field. This reviewer was less satisfied with Professor Smith's generalizations about American patterns of church-state relations, and with his sweeping claims for the unique Dutch contribution to American religious pluralism.

LOUIS BILLINGTON
University of Hull
England

DENIS G. SULLIVAN et al. *The Politics of Representation: The Democratic Convention of 1972.* Pp. ix, 152. New York: St. Martin's Press, 1974. $9.95. Paperbound, $3.95.

The topic of this book will appeal to most observers of the 1972 presidential campaigns. The research approach is a fascinating one: Set loose a passel of Dartmouth students and faculty to interview delegates and monitor the proceedings of the 1972 Democratic National Convention. Interviews with 234 delegates were held. Separate studies were made of the delegations from three New England states. CBS News made available its background profiles on the Democratic delegates to the 1968 and 1972 conventions. Data from these sources plus the party platform and its predecessor documents comprise the main evidentiary foundation for the book, which consists of five chapters and appendices that present the sampling procedure and a blank questionnaire.

Chapter One is perhaps the most useful mainly because it states fundamental dilemmas of presidential nominating politics: Who is to participate in the nominating process? Should the allegiances of convention delegates be primarily to the party or to extra-party forces? Which has the higher priority, issue stands or maintenance of the party as an organizational entity? Subsequent chapters explore these questions in these paraphrased topics: reform in representation, innovation in group representation, making the party

platform, and winners and losers: purism and professionalism.

Unfortunately the book is a disappointment. To note its most obvious flaw, there is no conclusion. Perhaps this is because the chapters have different authors but surely someone, if only the copy editor, has the responsibility to assess the book as an entity. Symptomatic of the joint authorship list is the grammatical inconsistency found in the first two footnotes, which respectively begin, "*I* have" and "As *we*" although there is no clue to whom "I" refers. Creative responsibility is further confounded by the questionnaire introduction which refers to the Dartmouth-University of California research group. That is the only mention of a possible University of California role in this enterprise.

There is seeming conceptual confusion when the terms "party member," "convention delegate," "average delegate," and "party activist delegate" are employed (p. 7) but not sufficiently explained and then dropped. There is no mention of the standard typology of the delegate as either a mere agent of the electorate or as their free thinking representative—for example, in Paul T. David, et al., *Politics of National Party Conventions.* Failure to consider these distinctions leads to curious oversights, such as the lack of comment about convention delegates who did not consider themselves Democrats (pp. 76, 118). Why then were they attending a Democratic convention? Similarly, although the abolition of the unit rule is mentioned (p. 7) and the controversy over the California delegation (pp. 19, 47, 53), the inconsistency of a winner-take-all primary with delegates handpicked for their commitment to a candidate and thus functioning as a unit elicits no discussion. On these points and similar ones the analysis deserves elaboration.

There are critical analytic weaknesses. The demographic and experience profiles for 1972 delegates are compared with 1968, the year of McCarthy insurgency. Was it therefore atypical in the number of novice delegates? That question is not posed. Although the sampling commentary indicates the separate periods of interviewing (Sunday-Monday, Tuesday-Wednesday, Thursday) are individually not representative samples, that dimension is a main explanatory variable for Chapter Three, which also uses the chi-square for cells that often have frequencies of less than ten.

Certainly there is much insightful material in the book but as a whole it falls short of the exemplary standards this reviewer is familiar with in the previous works of Sullivan, Pressman, and St. Martin's Press.

T. PHILLIP WOLF
Indiana University Southeast
New Albany

FRANCES LEON SWADESH. *Los Primeros Pobladores: Hispanic Americans of the Ute Frontier.* Pp. xxiii, 262. Notre Dame, Ind.: University of Notre Dame Press, 1974. $9.95.

A condensation of a doctoral dissertation written under the direction of anthropologist Omer Steward, *Los Primeros Pobladores* (the first settlers) is a historical and sociological study of hispanic pioneers who settled in the Chama and San Juan basins in northern New Mexico following the Spanish Reconquest in the 1690s. The scattered settlements were frequently attacked by Indians, particularly Utes and Comanches, and major raids in 1747 caused a temporary abandonment of some areas. Resettlement was ordered in 1750 and included *Genízaros* (detribalized Indians) who received land grants at Abiquiu, one of the most important towns, and Ojo Caliente. In the expansion that followed up the Chama and into the San Luis Valley and San Juan drainage, Hispanic speaking pioneers adapted to the land and developed close relations with their Ute Indian neighbors which provided economic, religious and social benefits for both groups. The society they developed had more social mobility than population centers such as Santa Fe,

and it was a tough and resilient way of life that survives in part to the present.

The first portion of the book is a historical account of expansion into the above mentioned regions while the latter part is a description and analysis of community structure and social relations. The combination of historical, sociological and anthropological approaches and the extensive use of interviews are the book's greatest strengths and weaknesses. Swadesh provides the first scholarly study of Hispanic society on the Ute frontier, but she appears to have accepted oral testimony at face value without testing its reliability. Her interpretation, unsupported by documentation, that the *Genízaros* were detribalized Pueblo Indians rather than nomadic Indians as formerly believed will be challenged by many. More important, her strong sympathy for *Los Primeros Pobladores* has caused her to paint a picture in black and white when describing Hispanic-Anglo relations. Her desire to preserve the culture developed on the frontier would result in a static society and ignores the fact that the very culture she wishes to preserve was, by her own account, the result of adaption and change.

RICHARD N. ELLIS
University of New Mexico
Albuquerque

FRANCIS M. WILHOIT. *The Politics of Massive Resistance.* Pp. 320. New York: George Braziller, 1973. $8.95. Paperbound, $3.95.

THEODORE LEVITT. *The Third Sector: New Tactics for a Responsive Society.* Pp. 182. New York: Amacom, 1973. $11.00.

Clashes in the political arena are of central concern to students of American society, but anyone who ignores the social issues and organizations that lie outside the normal two-party system does so at the risk of misunderstanding much of our national life. In very different ways, these two books address themselves to such major problems that arise without the help of parties, but then come to have importance within the political system.

Francis M. Wilhoit's *The Politics of Massive Resistance* is a solid study of the decade-long movement that arose in the South in response to the Supreme Court's desegregation decision in 1954. Its appearance is welcome. Ever since the urban ghetto revolts of the sixties and the subsequent government investigations, the idea that America contains two societies has become a commonplace. This belated discovery of nothern racism has had one unfortunate side effect—it has tended to blur the fact that the United States, besides being Black and White, also contains a North and a South, regions with divergent histories where racism itself has been manifested in differing modes.

Focusing on the South, Wilhoit—a native of North Carolina—provides both a history and a critical analysis of the origins, politics, leadership and ideology of Massive Resistance. In a graceful style, and with a firm grasp of insights gleaned from history, sociology, psychology, and political science, he dissects the mythology of White Supremacy and States' Rights, portrays leaders like George Wallace, Strom Thurmond, Harry Byrd and Ross Barnett, delves into the workings of the Ku Klux Klan and the White Citizens Councils and recreates those important showdowns in Little Rock, New Orleans and at the Universities of Georgia, Mississippi and Alabama. His depiction of the resistance as, ultimately, a massive failure does not mean Wilhoit is a Pollyanna, for he clearly shows that tokenism rather than full desegregation was, as of the mid-sixties, the new status quo in the South.

Beyond its obvious story, the work gives an insight into that region's social continuities. When the author points out that the price of Massive Resistance was "exile of many of the region's best minds, abridgement of vital press and speech freedoms, curtailment of the right of protest and free association, emasculation of religion and higher education, [and the] further estrange-ment from the mainstream of American life . . . ," he could be describing the South prior to the Civil War.

Theodore Levitt's volume is a study of the Third Sector, those voluntary organizations that lie between the public and private sectors and yet have a great influence on both. Traditionally this sector has included such organizations as labor unions, racial organizations, charity groups like the American Cancer Society and professional ones like the AMA (in 1970 some 3,000 voluntary national organizations existed).

The author's particular interest is in depicting the new Third Sector—groups like the Black Panthers, Common Cause, Nader's Raiders and SDS; and he shows how in recent years they cleverly manipulated the mass media into carrying an "endless flow of news and television reports of mass meetings, marches, non-economic strikes, mill-ins, sit-ins, noise-ins, trash-ins, fires, defacings, bombs and outraged criticisms of almost everything anybody with any power in America did or did not do." Arguing that corporations and government organizations have changed significantly in response to such tactics, Levitt believes that the day for such unrelenting criticism is past, for American society is becoming unbalanced and legitimacy itself is being questioned. Even if true, this argument seems futile. As the work itself shows, the Third Sector arises out of important social needs, and its demands will abate only when its constituents become satisfied (or exhausted), regardless of the logic of arguments advanced by the most reasonable of academics.

ROBERT A. ROSENSTONE
California Institute of Technology
Pasadena

SOCIOLOGY

ARTHUR E. BARBEAU and FLORETTE HENRI. *The Unknown Soldiers: Black American Troops in World War I.* Pp. ix, 279. Philadelphia, Pa.: Temple University Press, 1974. $10.00.

This is the first scholarly study of black American troops in World War I. The importance of the subject, the fair-mindedness of the authors, the weight of their evidence, and the competence of their narrative and analysis make it a significant book. Drawing on military records, war narratives, and personal papers of participants, among a wide range of other sources, Arthur E. Barbeau and Florette Henri show that, despite official pronouncements to the contrary, the United States Army deliberately followed discriminatory policies in its recruitment, training, assignment, and demobilization of black soldiers —policies in which political considerations and racist assumptions outweighed and often militated against military efficiency and effectiveness.

The book deals in detail with black draftees, officer training, service regiments, and fighting units. For nearly 80 percent of the black troops sent overseas in World War I, war service meant menial, often back-breaking work in labor battalions; the "clear and consistent military policy," as Barbeau and Henri establish, was "to make practically all black draftees 'laborers in uniform'" (p. 93). Such a policy was least threatening to social conventions, and it fitted best with the prevailing belief in the cowardice, lack of intelligence, and physical inferiority of black military recruits. But, the authors argue, it was an inefficient, unfair, often counter-productive allocation of manpower.

Barbeau and Henri chronicle the formation, training, and performance of the two black infantry divisions that fought in the front lines in France. Some regiments performed well and were decorated for their heroism in combat—an illustration, the authors maintain, that when blacks were treated as men, they would respond as men. Some performed less successfully—a reflection of limitations in their training, experience, and equipment, and of the expectations of their white commanding officers.

The book has certain weaknesses. The first, second, and concluding chapters in particular demonstrate difficulties in striking a scholarly balance, winnowing important from trivial details, and setting the situation of black troops in a larger interpretive context. Scholars will note that the research, though extensive, is uneven: a number of other manuscript collections, especially, might have been fruitfully explored; there are some surprising omissions of standard secondary works; and the lengthy bibliography might have been more fully exploited in the construction of the narrative.

But despite these limitations, the book spells out in compelling detail the mistreatment suffered by black troops; it demonstrates how the racist presuppositions of white policymakers and officers all too easily became self-fulfilling prophecies; and it points up the irony of a crusade to make the world safe for democracy being waged by a nation unwilling to adhere to some elementary democratic principles at home.

NANCY J. WEISS
Princeton University
New Jersey

SZYMON CHODAK. *Societal Development*. Pp. v, 357. New York: Oxford University Press, 1973. $12.50.

The author of this book is obviously well-educated in the fields of economics, political science, psychology, sociology, and education. Not only is he extremely knowledgeable in these fields and their application to economic development but he also knows all the important relevant literature and which social and economic approaches to the problems have led to false and correct findings. The principal shortcoming of this book is in its conclusions, which do not consider sufficiently the various psychological, sociological, and economic factors which are discussed in detail in the previous chapters.

The author has studied five different development theories and analyzes them comparatively. He first approaches the theory of societal evolutionary development and discusses the theories of certain individuals who were of major historical significance, among them Marx, Comte, Spencer, and Ward; he finds their theories on the whole not sufficiently correct although they developed many propositions of great value, and his assessment of the work of Ward is particularly interesting because it emphasizes its importance whereas until now it has generally not been held in very high esteem.

In the author's second approach he studies the theories of the development of the growing societal systemness. Systemness in the United States, and perhaps in the Western world, was introduced by Talcott Parsons; many of his followers, at least for a time, applied his theories both to a developed and also an underdeveloped state of economics, but today the newness of systemness is not so important nor does it lead to a new interpretation of the political and social histories of countries. Although the Parsons system theories may be correct, they are so general that it is very difficult to find what they actually mean. Predictions made which were based on the systemness of various underdeveloped countries have often been entirely wrong, and Professor Chodak has very ably demonstrated the limitation of systemness of such countries.

The third approach is devoted to theories on causes of development and too many theoretical events have been included in the discussion of Max Weber. In this section, building upon Weber's results, he then discusses the achievement theory of David McClelland. As far as Weber is concerned, the literature, at least in America, is already so rich and contains so many adequate analyses that this book adds little to previously published works. His explanation and discussion of the McClelland theory, on the other hand, is very valuable because he presents the positive proof of achievement and also gives several of the negative aspects of the whole treatment of the theoretical knowledge included in McClelland. This theory, the theory of insecurity

within security, is perhaps the most mature one discussed in the book.

The fourth and fifth sections discuss political and economic development and modernization of underdeveloped areas and include no new findings by Professor Chodak; he analyzes the theories fully, taking into consideration the rather voluminous research that has been done in these fields since 1950. His analysis is of particular value because of the excellent adaptation of the theories to various underdeveloped countries. The presentation is extremely good and contains valuable data and information on Sub-Saharan Africa with which Professor Chodak seems to be extensively acquainted.

In general, I consider this book one of the most outstanding contributions to the literature in the field of sociological study of development. Professor Chodak has raised many complex and challenging questions and reached conclusions which should be of paramount interest generally and to every social scientist especially. I hope the book is widely read.

BERT F. HOSELITZ
The University of Chicago
Illinois

LEWIS A. COSER. *Greedy Institutions: Patterns of Undivided Commitment.* Pp. iv, 166. New York: The Free Press, 1974. $7.95.

It is probably germane to report that when I agreed to review this book I expected it to be a higher level Vance Packard study of advertising and/or consumerism. But, although Coser is clear enough about what he wants to pioneer here in the sociology of politics, to this humanist observer he has just barely turned over a fresh sod. The term "greedy," indeed, is a key to more than one of Coser's intentions. Inasmuch as sociology, by the lack of virtue of its median prose, has long since displaced nineteenth century economics as the dreariest of sciences, the president-elect of the ASA apparently wants to initiate a counterrevolution in the prose of his craft. "Greedy," as we are reminded to the point of wondering whether we are regarded as thick by the writer, is used metaphorically, to indict, really, institutions which demand too much of the private lives of their functionaries. Coser is explicitly polemical about this: there are worse things in the modern (and ancient) world than your Durkheims have ever dreamed of in their philosophies of *anomie*: "While I share with these modish critics their preoccupation with the quality of our lives, I feel obliged nevertheless to point out that attempts to create a 'wholeness' of social involvement might, if unchecked, eventuate in restrictions of individual freedom considerably more damaging to the human spirit than modern fragmentation and segmentation" (pp. 17–18). And greedy is also a spritzy word, a sociologist as it were, aspiring to poetry.

After an introductory overview of the concept of the greedy institution, Coser divides his examples into three parts: serving the ruler (the political functions of eunuchdom, alien Jews and Christian renegades serving alien powers, and the royal mistresses as instruments of rule); serving the public (the servant and the captive housewife); and serving the collective (sects and sectarians, militant collectives— Jesuits, and Leninists, sexual repression in Utopias, and the function of sacerdotal celibacy). The first thing one must be impressed by here is the tremendous range and disparateness of the subjects. When social scientists really do see what is functionally similar in antipodally diverse human milieux, they are of great help to professional humanists as well as general observers trying to place themselves better in a rapidly shifting social landscape. (Leo Lowenthal and Marjorie Fiske's seminal essay, "Art and Popular Culture in Eighteenth Century England," has been such a siting in my own teaching of literature, for example.)

One is less convinced by Coser. For a start, the data—mainly culled from secondary sources which were of uneven validity to begin with—are spotty.

If a humanist tried to fashion a literary hypothesis from as few poems as Coser has mistresses in chapter four, he'd be hooted down. Still we know that sexuality has a heavy status component, and it is *a priori* that the class origins of a mistress would introduce a differential into her relationships with the king and his retainers. But, needless to say, sociology has made a point that *a priorisms* are precisely what it wants to displace with rigorously observed data theoretically organized. Coser's examples tantalize; they don't convince. On the other hand, in his chapter on domestic servants, I had the impression it must have been written out of reading nineteenth century British novels. One can't ask where did he see *that* kind of servant come from, since the genus has disappeared except for us— middle class people who use blacks and students to do our less clean work. That chapter in fact seems more a foil for the one which follows on the housewife who by and large seems to know where she's going anyway, unless she's one of Herbert Gans' blue collars, in which case she seems imperviously content in the serfdoms that seem intolerable to the better educated.

It is not these chapters, however topical they appear to be, that establish the interest of this book or the new discipline Coser would inaugurate. One could retitle the remaining chapters with a frivolous title, *All I Wanted to Say about the Function of SEX in Political Institutions but was Afraid to use that Three Letter Word in Doing So.* Here the humanist observer must note that truth in sociology seems to be polarized between two extremes: ritual apologies for having to force readers to slog through the obvious because Empiricism demands that we not make reality flashy when it is in fact grubby, even obviously so, this sort constituting the bulk of sociological truths; and a tiny lode at the other extreme (one expects that sociologists live from day to day in search of such epiphanies), a truth that contradicts common sense. The big contradiction of this book is that promiscuity and celibacy are the very same under their very different skins, functionally. In short, scratch a Jesuit priest and a randy Leninist and beneath the epidermis one finds the same obsequious soul-seeking total commitment to similarly greedy institutions. Since Coser has brought up the Jesuits I'm tempted to employ a long-discarded aphorism they taught me in metaphysics class: *Quis nimis probat nihil probat*—"Who proves too much proves nothing." Surely, there is some crucial difference in function between a Jesuit order in which men voluntarily gave up dyadic (ugh) sex to embrace secular knowledge for the purposes of the Counterreformation and Leninist revolutionaries who coupled freely through the NEP period to be better able to start and consolidate a secular Revolution with chiliastic overtones. If it is true, that to couple or not to couple (nobody after all gives up sexual drives but rather rechannels them) is the same thing functionally within greedy institutions, then what have we learned about greedy institutions? That sexuality is not important? Manifestly not, since the covert (why does it remain covert?) theme of the book is that a principal task of all power—especially monolithic power—is that it must control sexual energies which have a strong potential for privatizing experience, for engendering disloyalty. It didn't take this book to make that truism evident. That promiscuity or celibacy are both valid human options? I doubt that Coser implies that here although a humane sociology of politics would in my judgment establish precisely that multivalent posture.

Finally, one has the feeling closing this book like that felt finishing early McLuhan, for example, *The Gutenberg Galaxy*. One is grateful for Coser's synoptic searching, introducing one to fascinating bypaths on the human journey, especially in this case the material on eunuchs and royal mistresses. Humanists complain so often about the lack of historical dimension in sociological studies that it would be churlish not to be enthusiastic about this increased access to other times, other places. But as with McLuhan, one is more stimulated than impressed intellectually. And, since Coser clearly wants to remove the incubus of under-readability from the sociological canon, it is sad but necessary to give him no more than a D+ in the prose department. "Socialists attempted to construct a *Gemeinschaft* of like-minded antagonists of the capitalist order who endeavored in their dissent from its guiding assumptions to embody in their lives ideas and ideals that were to prevail in the ideal society of the future" (p. 125). It think I know what he means, but I find its style in linguistic contradiction with the last sentence of his introduction: "I wish it to be clearly understood that I consider it essential that the open society be preserved above all" (p. 18). I only want to make one point perfectly clear: confused prose erodes the open society; so do half-formulated ideas.

PATRICK D. HAZARD

Beaver College
Glenside
Pennsylvania

ALFRED JOHN DIMAIO, JR. *Soviet Urban Housing: Problems and Policies*. Pp. 236. New York: Praeger, 1974. $16.50.

This work compares favorably with several other studies of Soviet matters which I have reviewed in these pages recently. Mr. DiMaio displays a thorough grasp of his subject, an orderly turn of mind, and a degree of sociological sophistication which is quite adequate for his and the reader's purposes.

After an introduction and a brief historical survey, he discusses the following topics: city planning and the planning of housing construction in particular, the organization of the housing construction industry, the allocation of housing, and the rights and obligations of tenants, the administration of housing and the organization of life in the apartment building; and finally, the cooperative housing movement. Each chapter is exhaustively documented and provides the necessary data (at least in terms of legal provisions and administrative measures) for an understanding of its topic. The author has not been able, in the space or with the materials at his disposal, to describe fully the empirical operation of the Soviet housing system. In fact, it is open to question whether such a description would be possible without on-the-spot investigation, which cannot be expected in the near future. DiMaio's material on the operation of this system is necessarily anecdotal in nature; it is mostly taken from the Soviet popular press, and as such is open to charges of biased selection. This, however, is a perennial problem for the Soviet specialist and one which Mr. DiMaio cannot be expected to solve.

The strongest impression which this reviewer derives from the book is that while the introduction emphasizes potential (and to some extent actual) Soviet achievements in housing and the political impact which these can be expected to have, the body of the text stresses the bureaucratic distortions to which the Soviet system is subject in this area as in others. These distortions are in part the result of a deliberate policy decision to use good housing as bait for attracting, holding, and rewarding key personnel; this quite naturally creates special "departmental" vested interests in the control of conveniently located or otherwise desirable housing. DiMaio's handling of this topic, it seems to me, contains a valuable insight.

I am less certain about his attitude toward the housing shortage of the Stalin period, which he regards as a deliberate device to attack the family. I believe that the pressure on the family at that period (and it must be said that if DiMaio's analysis is valid for the Stalin era, then it remains valid in principle today, allowing for differences in degree) can more correctly be interpreted as an unintended consequence, or at most as a price consciously paid for the achievement of internal security.

Specialized arguments and disagreements aside, DiMaio has written a useful and necessary book and has shown himself to be a competent researcher and thinker.

STEPHEN P. DUNN
Berkeley
California

G. WILLIAM DOMHOFF. *The Bohemian Grove and Other Retreats: A Study in Ruling-Class Cohesiveness.* Pp. xvi, 250. New York: Harper & Row, 1974. $7.95.

FREDERIC COPLE JAHER, ed. *The Rich, the Wellborn, and the Powerful. Elites and Upper Classes in History.* Pp. 379. Urbana: University of Illinois Press, 1974. $15.00.

Since *Who Rules America?* (1967), G. William Domhoff has been striving to show us that there *is* a ruling class in the United States and that it is conscious of its own privileged position— in other words, that it is indeed cohesive and that it does exhibit solidarity whenever faced by threats to its own economic interests and especially to the socioeconomic system which rewards it so lavishly. Domhoff's latest book branches out from his basic theme. Rather than exposing the structure of ruling class power, *The Bohemian Grove* gives us an example of how America's elites get to know one another and how they keep in touch.

Fraternization takes place at exclusive schools and clubs, in blue-ribbon panels, in corporate and banking boardrooms, in philanthropic organizations. The Bohemian Grove, one of such spots, is a 2700-acre wooded property near San Francisco. Prestigious, affluent men get together here every summer in a wilderness of redwoods, streams, and meadows, for a fortnight of hiking, swimming, canoeing, music and art, and more: the food is excellent, cigars and liquor the best money can buy, and theatrical productions come from the cream of the season's crop. Of course one could study The Bohemian Grove to learn how "the rich are very different from the rest of us," as F. Scott Fitzgerald might have done, but

Domhoff looks into the social and economic function of this manner of plush enjoyment. Far from being idiosyncratic, exclusivist behavior such as this has a real purpose, Domhoff argues: to strengthen ruling class links and solidarity.

Unlike so many respectable social scientists, who prefer to analyze the poor, ethnics, urban blacks, deviant subgroups, and pressure groups, Domhoff plunges headlong, with obvious relish, into his studies of this nation's economic elite—a never-never land for the probing of which generous foundation grants, for some odd reason, are not readily forthcoming. In *The Bohemian Grove* Domhoff even supplies us with an "appendix of heavies," a list of some 900-odd names of "the most prominent men who were members of two or more of six social clubs and three policy-planning groups between the years 1965 and 1970." The list is cross-classified in terms of men, in-group connections, and major government positions held, and it represents another step forward in the development of badly needed data on the American ruling class. Again, one can only bemoan the reluctance (though it is understandable) of most social scientists to dig into the affairs of the wealthy and powerful. Only historians, sociologists, and economists of the left (old and new), along with a handful of muckrakers, have been doing such work, although there seems to be widening interest in the topic of late (see, for instance, the article by Dye, DeClercq, and Pickering in *Social Science Quarterly*, June 1973).

Exactly how and to what extent the ruling class governs, and how it "controls," is a considerably more complex matter, and it is on this vital point that Domhoff's works have been justly criticized as leading toward, if not encouraging, oversimplified reasoning. Not that Domhoff himself engages in simplistic economic reductionism; not that ruling class power has gone totally unanalyzed (Gabriel Kolko's publications are one key link between the existence of a ruling class and the

actual exercise of its power to attain concrete ends). Yet the mechanism of class power, and the limits to that power, must be carefully examined.

The collection edited by Jaher provides a valuable historical perspective on the rise and fall of ruling classes from Classical Athens and the Roman Republic through the New Deal of Franklin Roosevelt. "Recent pleas to study the so-called inarticulate masses . . . should prompt even the most confrontation-minded historians to realize that they also need systematic analysis of upper classes and elites, if only to 'know the enemy.' " All concerned would agree, and Domhoff, along with the authors gathered into Jaher's volume, has unquestionably turned out several important studies in the existence, composition, and consciousness of the ruling class. Only the study of history and comparative politics, however, can help us find out *how* ruling classes ultimately exercise power and bring some social questions to the agenda at the expense of others, and why the inevitable abuse of their power draws them into fatal contradictions.

RICHARD B. DU BOFF
Bryn Mawr College
Pennsylvania

MARC FRIED. *The World of the Urban Working Class.* Pp. vii, 410. Lawrence, Mass.: Harvard University Press, 1973. $15.00.

The community that was the West End of Boston is no more. The city demolished its tenements and stores and churches, and, in so doing, erased the vibrant network of images, interactions, and attitudes that was the living neighborhood. This monograph is the story of the West End: its creation; its functioning as a way-station wherein immigrant generations assimilated their urban Americanisms before passing on (and up); and its death throes.

The data for this community study derive mainly from pre-relocation and post-relocation interviews with a random sample of about 500 families during the late fifties and early sixties. The topics included residential orientations, community commitments, familial roles, relationship with kin and kith, occupational experiences, attitudes and values, and personality dispositions—with chapters in the book devoted to each. The sampling design resulted in the omission of segments of the population—for example, the unmarried, the aged—about whom information was gathered from a variety of sources including others' surveys, ethnographic observations, Herbert Gans' diary and the like.

Among the conclusions of the study are the following: for many working class residents, neighborhood commitments and satisfactions provide recompense for inadequacies of housing and status; the expansion to neighbors and friends of the warmth and closeness of a familial orientation "uniquely typifies community life in the working class"; unlike people of higher status, marital role behavior among the working class does not become increasingly segregated with age; working class jobs—limited, routinized, and supervised—are less likely to be the sources of satisfaction that they are for middle-class people; rather than reflect ideological commitment, working class attitudes are really pragmatic reflections of pressures for social conformity; the precarious nature of their self-esteem is evident in the sensitivity of many working class people to rebuff, to being slighted or misunderstood.

This is not just another relocation study. It is methodologically intriguing in that the same research project utilized anecdotal descriptions and fragmentary observations, as well as very sophisticated tools of data collection and quantitative analysis. The author takes his readers on a journey through urban history and on an exploration of comparative community in an effort to understand working-class life and outlook. In short, this monograph is an adventure in social science; reading it is a pleasure. And challenging its

conclusions, in light of the evidence presented, is an added delight.

LAWRENCE PODELL
Office of Program and Policy
Research
City University of New York

GEORGE M. VON FURSTENBERG, BENNETT HARRISON and ANN R. HOROWITZ. *Patterns of Racial Discrimination: Housing.* Vol. I. Pp. v, 220. Lexington, Mass.: Lexington Books, 1974. No price.

GEORGE M. VON FURSTENBERG. *Patterns of Racial Discrimination: Employment and Income.* Vol. II. Pp. v, 254. Lexington, Mass.: Lexington Books, 1974. No price.

During the current pause which follows a decade of unprecedented civil rights activism, organized poverty related programming, and public commitment to eliminate racial discrimination, syntheses of what has been accomplished and what has been learned about these matters are highly appropriate. The title of this two-volume set suggests that such a review of racial discrimination in housing and employment might be expected. What is attempted here, however, is far narrower. Two limitations are central: (1) the volumes are concerned only with the contributions of economists; and (2) as an outgrowth of a conference, the books are a rather loose aggregation of rather diverse materials. The bringing together of economists actively in research on racial discrimination has resulted in a state of the art document on discrimination as it has been seen in recent years by academic economists.

Substantively the volumes have been organized according to four topics: (1) interaction of discrimination in housing and employment, (2) racial discrimination in housing, (3) racial discrimination in employment, and (4) measurement of racial inequality in income. Overall, 27 chapters are included representing the efforts of 24 contributors. Some of the authors offer an overview of their research and theory over a period of years including some discussion of conflicting research findings and the views of their critics. Others present findings of recent narrowly focused research on highly specific mathematical models. Included also are scathing critiques of some of the papers presented at the conference. Discussions of policy implication emerge in a number of papers.

For economists with a central interest in research and theory on discrimination, the volumes will be most valuable. In convenient fashion they bring together the major research issues, theoretical formulations, methodological strategies, findings, and policy opinions of economists selected because of their professional achievement in this area. Because there are great differences in problem definition, research approaches, findings, and policy recommendations, the volumes provide a splendid starting point for future academic inquiries which might attempt to reduce some of the discrepancies.

For those with other interests, the volumes will be much less satisfactory. No attempt is made at a balanced, synthesized statement of what is known (and not known) about discrimination. With the exception of income trends which are reported in some detail, there is no systematic description of where the society stands and how discriminatory patterns may have changed. Research on social psychological or sociological forces which underlie discrimination are not treated. Government and other institutional sectors (for example, real estate interests) which can play an important role in supporting or intervening to reduce discrimination are given only passing attention.

Intellectually, some of the material is fascinating. John Kain, for example, presents his argument that the concentration of blacks in inner city ghettos has negative implications for the access of that population to expanding suburban job opportunities. Serious complications, however, are made evident. Although at a slower rate than in suburban areas, central city job opportunities continue to expand. Because they are willing to commute, the dominance of whites in these central city jobs has increased somewhat. When commuting costs are taken in account, many blacks find suburban jobs less attractive than urban work opportunities. For black housewives and teenagers without cars, a suburban residence is likely to be a serious handicap in seeking employment because of the inferiority of suburban mass transit systems.

Blacks are less adequately housed than whites. Much of that difference can be attributed to differences in income. Because of discrimination, some economists argue that ghetto blacks are forced to pay more for housing than do whites for residences of comparable quality. Interestingly because of difficulties in measuring housing quality and in collecting suitable data, an apparently straightforward hypothesis proves difficult to test. Analysis of research data suggests interesting complications. Mahlon Straszheim, for example, finds that blacks pay less for poor housing in black areas than do whites in white areas. High quality housing, however, tends to be more expensive in black than in white areas.

Non-economists are likely also to find themselves seriously troubled with the style of inquiry. Great imbalances in the scholarly endeavor are obvious. Crude, insensitive data are submitted to highly refined quantitative analysis. Elegant mathematical models are presented which cannot be applied because it is not feasible to collect essential data. Policy recommendations are not only sketchy but seem barely related to research findings.

More serious are subtle implications of the way in which problems are defined. An attempt is made to show, for example, that the concentration of blacks in inner city ghettos reduces access to jobs in metropolitan areas. Positive research findings would suggest that black employment opportunities would be enhanced by increased access to suburban housing. But what are we to conclude when research findings are ambiguous? Should efforts to increase access of blacks to suburban housing be held in suspension until clear-cut research findings are available? Victoria Lapham argues that the concentration of blacks and whites in separate portions of the city is a problem only if blacks pay more than whites for housing of comparable quality. Because the research evidence is mixed, she is not ready to conclude that housing segregation is a problem. What to many is a glaring social problem seems to be shunted aside through an arbitrarily narrow definition of housing segregation and an equally arbitrary conservatism in interpreting research findings.

The chapters on employment provide still another example. Economic theories of employment are based on an assumption of a free labor market. Theoretically in a free labor market differences in income are attributable to differences in productivity. The burden of proof, then, is placed on those who would attribute differences in income to other forces such as discrimination. Because productivity can rarely be measured effectively, research results are not available to settle the issue. Should we, therefore, withhold judgment and action on racial discrimination in employment? Information from other sources would suggest that the more reasonable practical judgment is that racial discrimination is a problem which deserves continuing, vigorous attention. Perhaps the burden of proof should more properly be on those who would minimize its importance.

FRANCIS G. CARO
Community Service Society
New York

ANDREW M. GREELEY. *Ecstasy: A Way of Knowing.* Pp. 150. Englewood Cliffs, N.J.: Prentice-Hall, 1974. $6.95.

The intention of this work is to provide a preliminary perspective for the study of ecstatic or mystical experience. Its central thesis is that ecstatic or what is commonly thought of as mystical experience is not something that occurs only to exceptional persons or persons of psychological disturbance or that such experience presupposes divine intervention for its occurrence. It is the author's point that mystical experience is something that can be understood from a social scientific and epistemological point of view. It is his view that the mystical experience is cognitive in character rather than simply an experience of feeling and that such experience is quite common among ordinary people. The author states that research he and William McCready are conducting indicates that one-half of the American population would report experiences of union with "a powerful spiritual force that draws me out of myself" (p. 11).

This is a work written to be understood by the reading public. Perhaps its central attraction for the reader and its central value is that it attempts to make sense of the mystical in an age in which mysticism is seen by the technological mind as aberrant mental behavior or is seen as something so wholly mysterious it forms a basis of attraction for sects of irrationality and cults of the bizarre.

A rather serious defect in the book and one which mars Greeley's attempt at a judicious study of the mystical is his persistent mixing of unargued moral views and on occasion direct moralizing with his analysis—for example, "In our country there is no substitute for precinct work, and a would-be political leader who thinks there is should be given a one-way ticket to the New Mexican desert" (p. 111). Greeley, who is a Catholic priest as well as a sociologist, in his chapter on "Ecstasy through Sex" simply presents his material as if it is clear that sexual activity can function as the occasion for ecstatic experience only within the traditional Christian marriage relationship. This is certainly not the case and one has only to think of the sexual practices of the Tantric sect of Buddhism and other Oriental views and practices to call this into question. Greeley's study which makes no attempt in this regard to think outside his own religious presuppositions is extraordinarily, and disturbingly, limited. Such defects mar much of what is commendable in his aim of a non-reductionistic and reasoned study of mystical experience.

D. P. VERENE
The Pennsylvania State University
University Park

ALFRED KUHN. *The Logic of Social Systems: A Unified, Deductive, System-Based Approach to Social Science.* Pp. ix, 534. San Francisco, Calif.: Jossey-Bass, 1974. $15.00.

Human beings live a unified life. Yet, social sciences, whose purpose is to explain social behavior, have been subdivided into a number of disciplines, each one using its own concepts and methods. In many cases, scientists in various social disciplines are unaware of each other's findings, thus obstructing the understanding of social life as an interrelated whole. Recognizing this problem, a number of social scientists have been developing their research in the direction of an interdisciplinary approach to the study of society. Alfred Kuhn's volume on the logic of social systems goes a step further by proposing a unified social science with common concepts and method of research and a common scientific language. According to the author this approach is imperative, because the reality of social life is complex and its various aspects interact with each other in a variety of ways, including mutual causation and feedback.

All social sciences, therefore, depend upon each others' findings. Such needs would be greatly facilitated if a common social science language were developed. But since each social science has its own specific interests and the need for its own autonomy, there should be within unified social science a division of labor between the generalists and the specialists, but all would use a unified vocabulary. The author suggests a common study of three "basic interactions" in human life: communication (transfer of information); transaction (transfer of values between parties) and organization (effect of interaction between parties).

According to the author, the common basic interests of all social sciences are collecting information about the environment, selecting the response to the environment and executing the selected behavior.

The author does not claim that he has developed the final proposal for a unified social science, but only an attempt to prepare the way to unify social sciences by advancing the "conviction that unification is possible." He believes that it is an experimental obligation for specialists to acquaint themselves with his proposed unified structure and give it a test in their fields. The central point of the volume is that all behavioral and social disciplines "must converge into one comprehensive explanation" of social life expressed in a common scientific language based on a "system analysis" that would cut across all disciplines. He is convinced that "either the specialists will adopt an integrated social science or the integrated social science will become another discipline." This is a thoughtful volume that will contribute to the advance of research both in its interdisciplinary aspects and in its attempts toward unification and will be of interest to the generalists as well as to the specialists in social sciences.

D. A. TOMASIC
Indiana University
Bloomington

ALFRED MCCLUNG LEE. *Toward Humanist Sociology.* Pp. xv, 224. Englewood Cliffs, N.J.: Prentice-Hall, 1973. No price.

The most significant parts of Professor Lee's work are dedicated to demonstrating how sociologists' assumptions, attitudes and methodologies have political and ethical implications. Of specific interest to Lee is the task of exposing how they either passively condone or actively support the various factual and ideological tyrannies of our times. They do this by mistaking *what is* for *what is right* and *what is possible,* by perpetrating abstract and dehumanizing myths about identity, race and ethnicity, by confusing their observations and analysis with such intellectually "sacred" concepts as ideology, alienation, revolution and intellectual, and worst of all (at least in terms of Lee's accent in this work), by subscribing to paradigms of society which affirm elitist and technocratic control of individuals and groups of peoples.

This critique of much of contemporary sociology compliments what can be considered Lee's most encompassing goal in this work: the promotion of a humanist sociology which is committed to the defense of the individual person in modern society. Taking its meaning in a "more radical and earthy, and less doctrinaire sense," Lee advocates an *existential humanism* as the proper perspective for contemporary sociologists. In his words, this humanism should focus "on what is most relevant to man," dismiss questions of "first causes and ultimate consequences, as well as absolutes and infinites as no more than human artifacts," and direct itself to the full understanding and freeing of man. For Lee, this is the spiritual touchstone for a liberating sociology which is politically committed to democracy, ethically inspired by individualism, epistemologically grounded in pragmatism, and spiritually motivated by experimental radicalism.

In claiming that his fundamental preoccupation is the question of autonomy, freedom and individualism, Lee believes himself to belong to a long democratic and humanist tradition which extends from Thomas Jefferson and Walt Whitman to John Dewey, Charles Beard, Williard Waller, and most recently, C. Wright Mills. In showering particular praise on the Sicilian social reformer, Danilo Dolci, as an outstanding example of a practitioner of radical, experimental and nonviolent democracy, Lee leaves no doubt that his brand of sociology must take form in the crucible of research and action.

Chances are that Lee's small but provocative volume will make no friends on either the more radical or conservative sides of the discipline. For those inspired by Marxism, it will be judged to be another example of pick-and-choose bourgeois radicalism. They will find proof of their contention in not only Lee's assertion of the primacy of the individual and his consistent avoidance of concepts like class warfare and revolution, but also in his failure to articulate a historical causality and dialectical methodology to support his brand of sociology. His work will suffer no better fate in the hands of his conservative critics. Lee's accent on individuality, activism and democracy inevitably will be seen by them to be at the expense of tradition, community and culture, and expressive of his failure to enter into a full discussion of relations between authority and order, and power and culture. Lee will have other critics, too. His mixture of democratic experimentalism and critical empirical methodology will satisfy neither the defenders of the academy nor the advocates of a sociology of radical commitment. Lee will be seen, on the one hand, to be too little of the academy to merit the title social scientist and too little of the world of action to be judged a "true revolutionist." He will be said to be unwilling either to defend the academy which shelters him or to enter wholeheartedly into the struggles which undoubtedly attract and energize him.

While in no way a seminal work, *Toward a Humanist Sociology* proves a provocative premier for advanced students and teachers of sociology. And it expresses faithfully the voice of one mature and established sociologist who, since the outset of his career in the 1930s, has willingly admitted the presence of radical change in the modern world, has boldly concerned himself with the ethical responsibilities of his craft, and has attentively listened to much of what is most significant in the debate over the plight of contemporary man, without losing his faith in the ultimate compatability of social science, democracy, and progress.

JOSEPH A. AMATO
Southwest Minnesota State College
Marshall

ALBERT MEHRABIAN and JAMES A. RUSSELL. *An Approach to Environmental Psychology.* Pp. viii, 266. Cambridge, Mass.: The MIT Press, 1974. $12.50.

A classic disagreement between opposing psychological research techniques and philosophies revolves around the controversy over the amount of control one should exercise in measuring the effects of the environment upon human behavior. On one side of course, the argument follows the traditional methods of the physical sciences which require allowance for only one variable acting independently of the controlled environment so that its effects may be measured. This approach also requires reduction of complexities into component elements and then their addition to construct the whole. The book is a classic example of this type of objective analysis and its application to the effects of carefully controlled environmental stimuli upon behavior. As such, it is a most commendable exposition of its type for both its meticulous attention to detail, its use of previous research in a creative manner and as an example of method for both professionals and graduate students. In addition, it is noteworthy because of the conclusions of its research projects, based upon the latest measurement techniques, which provide much information upon relatively little known areas in the environment.

The authors reduce the environment to a single manageable dimension which they label "information rate." This incorporates "complex spatial and temporal arrangements of stimuli within and across settings." It includes stimulation within each sense modality as well. Their hypothesis permits further use of this concept as a basis for measurement of its effects upon behavior as a direct correlate of arousal. Arousal, pleasure and dominance are assumed to be the three major elements of behavioral response. The multiplicity of environmental stimuli are therefore represented in their theory by a variety of information rates, with one,

or all three, of the behavioral responses as a consequence.

This book is largely devoted to a description of the variety of research projects the authors undertook to determine the validity of their hypotheses and a report on their conclusions. It makes for much interesting reading but is not for the casual reader. Those who are most comfortable with the direction of research in the physical sciences should be most satisfied with this report. It has made a substantial contribution to the research literature. Others, who are not in accord with the reductionist technique applied to human behavior in controlled settings, will undoubtably find much here to stimulate classic feuds. However, it is believed that this book will provide material for the research psychologist for some years to come.

I. R. STUART
Herbert H. Lehman College
City University of New York

HERMAN SCHWENDINGER and JULIA R. SCHWENDINGER. *The Sociologists of the Chair.* Pp. 590. New York: Basic Books, 1974. $17.50.

This book by the Schwendingers, which is subtitled *A Radical Analysis of the Formative Years of American Sociology (1883–1922),* is written with a sense of history and a theoretical breadth that is not often found in books written either by or about American sociologists. The Schwendingers are not sociologists, but are professional criminologists, and therefore write about the foundations of sociological theory in the United States and its founding fathers—Ward, Ross, Small, Thomas, Park, Burgess and others—as "outsiders." The perspective they bring to the book, in evaluating the development—and the fate, as they interpret it—of early, and present, American sociology is Marxian. Whether one accepts their evaluation is therefore somewhat directly related to whether one shares this ideological stance.

The book, in fact, is about much more

than the Formative Years. It is about the background to the formative years and their first one hundred and fifty pages are directed to European precursors such as Malthus, Comte and Darwin. In their actual discussion of the Founding Fathers as transitional figures, as they call them (Ward and Small), as well as in their treatment of those who consolidated ideological oppression, as they see it (Thomas, Park, Ward again, Burgess and others), the authors attempt to show that there was a clear link between the emergence and development of sociological theory and the dominant western ideology of liberalism. In the last chapters of the book the authors continue to hammer away at the theme that American sociology never was, nor is it now, "value-free," but is a one-sided enterprise now squarely in the hands of an academic elite.

For those who practice, or pretend to practice value-free science as sociologists, the reading of this book will or should be disturbing. Whether it will be ultimately disturbing will depend upon whether one accepts the authors' historical interpretations and theoretical linkages—and there are many—as well as whether one agrees with their anti-liberalism, Marxist assumptions. In either case, the book is worth reading.

The book contains a rather excellent fifteen page bibliography. Unfortunately the price of the book ($17.50), which is quite within keeping with the liberalism tradition, puts it beyond the hands of most younger, serious students and it is not too conceivable that established (and comfortable) professionals will pay this price to read things that they would find disturbing anyway. For those who do wish to read it, the price to pay will probably mean a trip to the library.

EDWARD L. SUNTRUP
University of Minnesota
Minneapolis

ELIE SHNEOUR. *The Malnourished Mind.* Pp. 216. New York: Doubleday, 1974. $6.95.

The author of this book is to be congratulated on his willingness to "stick his neck out." Even though all the evidence is not yet in, he takes a courageous stand on the need to mobilize national and international resources in the battle against malnutrition. It is his contention that chronic malnutrition during the pregnancy of the mother and the early years of the child's development can seriously impair the development of brain cells with consequent and life-long disability in coping with life. Indeed, chronic malnutrition results in a drastic reduction in the number of brain cells.

The documentation for his thesis is impressive and he argues his case convincingly and with considerable literary style. His indictment of the food industry and the machinery for the distribution of food is damning in the extreme. In sum, the book is more of a tract—an eloquent and powerful statement of the need to mount a frontal attack upon malnutrition because it deprives the body politic of a solely needed pool of talent it can ill-afford to lose.

This reviewer is torn between the horns of a dilemma: to what extent will citizens and their political representatives acknowledge that chronic malnutrition is in fact a serious threat, and, second, is the answer to raise more food, distribute it more wisely and humanely or, alternatively, should a more effective and far-reaching program of birth control be put into operation? An easy, simplistic answer would be: both! But given the limitations of human beings and their massive self-interest, are they likely to respond to Dr. Shneour's challenge?

Not long ago the "green revolution" was widely held to be the answer to world-wide food shortages. It has lost much of its former appeal in the light of recent and sudden scarcities of materials from which to manufacture fertilizers and the overall rise in the number of births on a global basis—many more mouths to feed. Added to these harsh realities is the unpredictability of worldwide harvests—bumper crops one year and scarcities the next. The "have" nations will continue to corner the food supply as best they can; the poor nations will starve— Ethiopia, for example.

This book opens a Pandora's box of basic moral and ethical problems, all of them extremely difficult to answer, and, perhaps, more important, unamenable to rational discussion or to human compassion. People become inured to starvation, particularly that in a distant land and they become jaded and unmoved at the plight of pot-bellied children and emaciated adults searching for a blade of grass in a barren land thousands of miles from their comfortable firesides and heaped dining tables.

Further, the distribution of food to starving populations becomes rife with black-market profiteering and bungled distribution to the point that those who need it the most are denied it.

To this reviewer, Dr. Shneour's proposed remedy is unrealistic and unworkable, tragic as that is. Possibly a more workable alternative is a vastly expanded birth-control program heavily financed by all governments. It is noteworthy in this connection that Argentina intends to *increase* its birthrate!

Dr. Shneour's thesis is forceful, but the problems with which he concerns himself will—in the long run—have to be resolved by decreasing the number of human beings on the planet, rather than appealing to the selflessness and altruism of people who have too much to lose.

FREDERICK E. ELLIS
Yacht "Via Maris"
Dartmouth, Devon
Cornwall
England

CONRAD WEILER. *Philadelphia Neighborhood, Authority, and the Urban Crisis.* Pp. v, 218. New York: Praeger, 1974. $12.50.

This might better have been two works, one an account of recent political events in Philadelphia and the other a "think piece" on the role and future of neighborhood and legitimate political authority in the urban crisis. The author apparently recognized that he had provided little connection between these two topics, despite the promise of the subtitle and the preface. On page 207 he said, "There is a definite theoretical framework throughout the whole book, but ordinarily it has been well covered with ordinary facts and data from the ongoing activities of politics in Philadelphia."

"Well covered," for example, is any clear connection between the events reported in the careers of Joseph S. Clark, Richardson Dilworth, Mark Shedd, Frank Rizzo, and others, and the author's expectation that the "urban crisis" will end in Philadelphia and be shifted to the suburbs by 1980. Certainly 1970 census and more recent data on fiscal problems of cities, crime, educational achievement and school integration, concentration of blacks in central cities, and the minimal movement of either blacks to the suburbs or middle-class whites into the central cities give little support to hopes that somehow things will be getting better in urban America. Philadelphia is by no means an exception. Likewise, a strengthening of neighborhoods as a vehicle for a restored sense of community and the development of a new, respected authority in political life are little more than desirable possibilities in today's rapidly changing world. In short, Weiler's observations on neighborhood, authority, and the future focus of the urban crisis while permissible in themselves, stand curiously apart from the main body of the work, even though all relate to Philadelphia.

For those with an interest in Philadelphia politics since 1950, this book contains many interesting insights beyond what has appeared in the popular press. Philadelphia's political renaissance during these years ranks high in the annals of reform politics in America. The success story of Philadelphia's urban redevelopment programs is well known and is enlarged herein to a lesser degree. But despite these praiseworthy efforts in political and physical reconstruction, the strength of Philadelphia, as the author concludes, "is very easily misconstrued." That city, as with virtually every large city in America, does not have the power to achieve whatever future it may desire for itself.

JAMES R. BELL

California State University
Sacramento

ECONOMICS

WILLIAM G. CAPITMAN. *Panic in the Boardroom: New Social Realities Shake Old Corporate Structures.* Pp. ix, 300. Garden City, N.Y.: Anchor Press/Doubleday, 1973. $7.95.

GEOFFREY VICKERS. *Making Institutions Work.* Pp. 188. New York: Halsted Press, 1974. $13.50.

Both Capitman and Vickers define the major social crisis of developed Western industrial societies as the escalating power and nonresponsiveness of institutions to increasing individual demands for greater economic equality and social justice. Vickers argues abstrusely and academically at the level of John Rawls in A *Theory of Justice*; Capitman writes in a *Business Week*-pop journalistic style. But both authors appear to be profoundly concerned with the crisis they analyze.

Capitman is concerned primarily with the inadequate response of the corporate sector to rising consumer demands. He argues for a fundamental change in corporate thinking and behavior. The profit motive in all business decisions, including those designed to show social responsiveness, will no longer work. At the close of his book, which anecdotally documents the failure of business to understand and to respond to the depth of public criticism, the author concludes: "It is apparent that when a profit standard is attached to all questions of corporate behavior, consistent socially responsible or moral behavior, as it is currently demanded by the public, is virtually

impossible" (p. 135). The dilemma of American business is how "to inject social responsibility into the corporation and still maintain profit margins and the right to determine privately both the amount and distribution of those profits" (p. 144).

But the public has reordered its priorities and concluded that the business system does not deliver. If business fails to take the new public morality seriously, the public rights, on which free enterprise ultimately rests, in Capitman's view, may be withdrawn by that disenchanted public.

Capitman suggests several possible "positive solutions." These are interesting, but sure to raise the hackles of the decision-makers who are now panicking in the boardroom. He suggests that American business managers need reeducation, in a national center, on ideological problems. Consumers need a national court system to deal specifically with disputes between business and the public. This new system could file data nationally and publicize abuses, as well as adjudicate complaints. As economic power becomes more concentrated, the public should be represented directly in corporate decision making. All corporation proceedings would be public, except in cases where secrecy was justified "in the *public* interest."

Finally, individuals could be assigned Social Disability Scores (giving them points for such disadvantages as race, religion, and sex, for example). These scores could be used as chits to cash in toward certain socially determined advantages, such as preference for business loans, educational privileges, real estate loans, and job opportunities.

Capitman raises the interesting general question that, if profits were eliminated from corporate decisions, other possible approaches become viable. For example, if a corporation becomes too big or powerful, why not return it to the public domain? Investors' equity could be assigned a time limit like that of copyright.

Vickers is less radical in his proposals for the necessary institutional response. He argues that both protesting individuals and the institutional objects of their protest operate under constraints, such as limited environmental resources. Protesters are demanding more than any institution— government, business, or labor—can realistically deliver. Therefore, the price of each person's social membership must go up at the same time individual demands are scaled down. The rich will take home much less; but everyone will have to settle for somewhat less (although the most deprived should be lifted into a middle economic class by a negative income tax).

I happen to agree with Capitman's thesis and find his policy proposals attractive, although politically unlikely at this time. His evidence is prodigious. But unfortunately it does not go beyond what is routinely known by any assiduous reader of a good national newspaper and the business press over the past fifteen years. Although this makes the reading tedious for the well-informed, I would hope that the audience for this book would include a number of major corporate directors. Vickers is probably too scholarly to reach any audience beyond other scholars. But the common message of each book is given added cogency by the fact that two such different viewers seem to agree that our very societal survival depends on immediate and drastic institutional change.

KENNETH HENRY
Fairleigh Dickinson University
Teaneck
New Jersey

DONALD R. HODGMAN. *National Monetary Policies and International Monetary Cooperation.* Pp. v, 266. Boston, Mass.: Little, Brown, 1974. $12.95.

RAYMOND F. MIKESELL and J. HERBERT FURTH. *Foreign Dollar Balances and the International Role of the Dollar.* Pp. ix, 124. New York: National Bureau of Economic Research, 1974. $7.50.

Doctrinal history of money contains two extreme positions on origin and role of money. An older view insisted that money was a creation of the state; a newer school limits the role of the state to the supply of money that has to respond reactively to the demand for money created by independent market forces. While these theories were following each other and were intellectually mutually exclusive interpretations, they have become coexisting alternative policies in the current international monetary crisis.

Eurodollar market and independently floating individual currencies have together established a monetary sphere in which market forces rule supreme. An international wholesale market of liquid assets has developed that is not subject to the ordinary controls of money by one central bank. Yet none of the confidently held expectations—namely, that the freely floating currencies would find their truly market determined values; that genuine aggregate demand for money would promptly determine its own supply, would set the required liquidity levels, would gradually eliminate the deficits in the balance of payments, and thus together avoid inflation—has been realized to any significant degree. Our ideological belief in the self-equilibriating power of the market forces has deceived and failed us. Instead of international monetary stability created by automatic adjustments, we have experienced an extreme international currency crisis, expressed by excessive liquidity, absence of any specific limit to money supply, competitive devaluations and appreciations, culminating into recurrent gold and currency speculations, and ending with frantic restrictions of money flows among countries. A peculiar kind of speculative capitalism has been superimposed upon industrial capitalism that invariably suffers from these largely ineffectual efforts at completely free international money markets.

The two books under review address themselves to different aspects of the currency crisis. The book of the National Bureau seeks to determine the size of the market and the relative magnitudes of the various liquid assets. At the end of 1971 the total size amounted to 93 billion dollars of which just over 50 billion were held—mostly involuntarily—by foreign financial institutions. In order to protect their currencies and minimize the imported price inflation, Germany and Switzerland were forced to neutralize most of this unwanted money. Other countries suffered from drastic declines of their monetary reserves, forcing them either into exchange control or dual currency systems. A relatively small portion of the liquid assets functioned as a useful "foreign" exchange market for swaps between central banks and for financing foreign trade, all in one and the same currency. While by no means complete, separating the various kinds of liquid assets and estimating their relative magnitudes constitute an important addition to our knowledge about the market.

Less impressive is the attempted explanation of the operation of this market. The modified portfolio theory used expects these transactions to be self-equilibrating. Individuals hold liquid assets according to the different risks and yields expected and to the savings hoped for by having to pay in only one currency between nations. The financial institutions balance their accounts between claims and obligations for each group or maturity. Most customers are not sensitive to shifts in relative yields (p. 63). This explanation of private and market balances, not tested statistically for lack of data, seems sensible for regular financing of foreign trade and central bank transactions. Obviously, this theory does not come to grips with the speculative motives, the floating different rates, the substantial interest differentials, the sudden capital movements between countries, and the competitive devaluations or imposed appreciations of currencies, followed by renewed governmental controls. A theory of speculative capitalism, initiated by Max Weber, can alone hope to explain these volatile money movements and imported inflations.

The careful analysis of the monetary policies of seven West European countries, done in a masterful fashion by Hodgman, reveals some surprising divergencies in policies among the central banks. Theories—from classical to administrative—guide these policies. In some cases the author finds some of his expectations fulfilled. The more classical the policy, the more independent the central bank from the government. Conversely, the more the central bank is dependent upon the government, the more it is involved in fiscal or corporate finance, the more was monetary policy pushed aside in favor of growth or by credit policy. Yet the third and major effect of the more classical policy (more effective control over money supply means less the price of inflation) could be observed in only one of the countries. For the years of 1960–1970, the average annual rate of inflation was 1.37 percent in West Germany but 4.04 percent in the Netherlands, in spite of the fact that both were committed to two different versions of monetary theory. The rates of inflation by countries using administrative devices lay between these two extremes. Similar variations prevailed in regard to the money supply; the British increase in annual money supply amounted to 5.46 percent but for Italy, 13 percent. How does one explain the differences between intentions and effects of monetary policy?

In the author's view, monetary policy has to be separated from fiscal and credit policy and strictly limited to the management of aggregate demand which clearly indicates how great the money supply ought to be. Such a demand management will assure price stability, even under conditions of economic growth. In our view, such a proposal is only correct under ideal conditions. It calls not only for effective competitive conditions and absence of economic power blocs, but also for political representatives economically free of private interests, and of a presidential policy and budgetary behavior that is strictly limited by the goal of price stability. Complete independence of monetary policy thus calls for a return to a genuine competitive capitalism that seems to be a precondition for the single goal of macro-policy of effective aggregate demand management. Since such a backward-looking reform seems not attainable under prevailing conditions, the new task is to find a series of methods that synchronize the various goals and reconcile the various policies.

ARTHUR SCHWEITZER
Indiana University
Bloomington

F. TOMMASSON JANNUZI. *Agrarian Crisis in India: The Case of Bihar.* Pp. xi, 233. Austin: University of Texas, 1974. $10.00.

Most of this study deals with the broadening gap between public policy in India on agrarian reform and the actual achievement of this policy over some 75–100 years. The author has himself studied the case of Bihar in field work detail over a span of 15–20 years; the book deals mostly with Bihar, and that state probably comprises the most extreme failure among Indian regions in narrowing the policy-performance gap in agrarian reform. Yet the book is appropriately considered an analysis of the situation in India.

It is essentially a story of conflict between wealth and mass poverty in a sociological, cultural and psychological setting where respect for one's fellow man has little universality. The story is persistent: broad social aspirations lose their content in execution. But change is about to come, the author says. The absolute and relative status of the mass of the population has deteriorated to a point where the political framework can not count much longer upon orderly change. Revolution is rapidly becoming the sole alternative.

After accounting for the failures of the past—both in macro terms for the State and in micro village illustrations—Jannuzi analyzes the rapid growth of agrarian tensions over re-

cent decades. His concluding chapter on "The Future of Bihar" sketches the main lines of a program for rural transformation that may still be operable— the last evolutionary, orderly-change, possibility. While this "minimum program" of agrarian reforms and of assistance to small farmers is familiar in current policy directions of both State and Central Governments in India, the unique difference, Jannuzi claims, is the recognition by responsible leaders that now there must in fact be implementation through programs of action. Indeed, Jannuzi argues ". . . that the goals of increased production and better distribution are inseparable in contemporary conditions in rural Bihar . . . [notwithstanding that] to enunciate such a two-fold goal is to contradict established dogma and to reject the conventional wisdom." In other words his minimum program will not only serve to narrow the gap between policy and action, but will also contribute to an improved economic environment for the well-to-do as well as the poor of rural India. Both goals are essential if the program is to work.

It is true that social scientists are increasingly impressed with the possibilities of a two-goal solution in situations like that of Bihar (and indeed of India generally). But such a solution doesn't follow simply from Jannuzi's minimum program. It follows from specific program attributes, pertinent only in some excess capacity and disequilibrium situations. Such conditions must define the specifics of a new program. Jannuzi in no way addresses this problem nor does he seem explicitly to recognize it. His program *may* therefore achieve income transfers, but it need not achieve total income expansion. Deprived of the *double* results, the political achievement of the program may itself be jeopardized.

The book is weakened by this argument. Must we therefore anticipate revolutionary change in Bihar (and India)? Here also the answer rests upon the nature and the strength of the author's "growing tensions" in the

Bihar economy and society. While this reviewer feels confident that Jannuzi needs an altered minimum program to achieve his double *economic* goals, he is more hesitant when he suggests that the societal model appropriate to Bihar (and India) may lead to persistence in poverty rather than to revolutionary change. Despite such differences on two important points, I commend this volume to all who are interested in land reform and land distribution in poor nations. I know no parallel studies that convey so well the nature of the land ownership problem and the obstacles confronting agrarian reform in South Asia.

WILFRED MALENBAUM
University of Pennsylvania
Philadelphia

SUSAN ESTABROOK KENNEDY. *The Banking Crisis of 1933.* Pp. x, 270. Lexington: University Press of Kentucky, 1973. $13.25.

This is a thoroughly researched, narrative account of the banking crisis of 1933. After briefly tracing the evolution of the nation's banking system, the author elucidates the efforts of Hoover and Roosevelt to deal with the problems plaguing that system. In dealing with the Hoover administration, Professor Kennedy focuses on the establishment of the National Credit Corporation, the working of the Reconstruction Finance Corporation, and the changes wrought by the passage of the Glass-Steagall Act. She then describes the rapid deterioration of the national banking situation and the paralysis of federal action stemming from the lack of cooperation between Hoover and Roosevelt. She incisively portrays the inability of Detroit bankers, Michigan politicians, and federal officials to formulate a viable plan for salvaging Michigan's financial structure, and emphasizes the impact of the Pecora hearings on the public's waning confidence in the banking system. The author concludes with three chapters examining the origins of the Emergency Banking Act, describing the procedures for

reopening the banks after the bank holiday, and depicting the legislative compromises leading to the Banking Act of 1933.

Although Professor Kennedy provides some new and interesting material on the Michigan crisis, the Hoover-Roosevelt relationship during the interregnum, and the writing of the Emergency Banking Act, most of her interpretations are along standard liberal lines. She argues that Hoover saw the depression as a crisis in confidence, and therefore failed to initiate fundamental reforms to deal with the banking situation. She also claims that Hoover's efforts to cooperate with the incoming administration during the interregnum were aimed at securing Roosevelt's endorsement of discredited Republican policies. Professor Kennedy criticizes Hoover for not acting on his own responsibility and she maintains that the worsening situation prior to March 4 stemmed from the public's reaction to Hoover's feeble policies and not from public fear of Roosevelt's future actions. In contrast to Hoover, the Democratic President was willing to take bold and pragmatic, yet conservative, steps to deal with the emergency. Although Hoover's advisors conceptualized the Emergency Banking Act and devised the procedures for implementing it, the author contends that Roosevelt's assumption of leadership and willingness to take responsibility ended an era of drift and uncertainty. The restoration of confidence enabled the administration to turn its attention to more permanent reforms which were incorporated in the Banking Acts of 1933 and 1935.

Professor Kennedy's work is rather narrowly conceived. The banking crisis is discussed amost exclusively in terms of the banking system and not in relation to the larger problems afflicting the national and international economy. Similarly, the banking legislation recommended by Hoover and Roosevelt is not examined in the larger context of the monetary, fiscal, and economic policies of the two administrations. Hoover's banking reforms, however, are criticized for not reviving business conditions, but Roosevelt's are not subjected to similar scrutiny. In addition, little emphasis is placed on the congressional impediments to executive action during the last months of the Hoover administration. Thus, while well documented, this descriptive portrayal of the banking crisis leaves some of the larger issues relating to the transition from Hoover to Roosevelt and to the problems of economic recovery unexplored.

MELVYN P. LEFFLER
Vanderbilt University
Nashville
Tennessee

STANLEY D. METZGER. *Lowering Nontariff Barriers.* Pp. vii, 249. Washington, D.C.: The Brookings Institution, 1974. $8.95.

This book is a welcome and important addition to the growing literature on nontariff trade barriers (NTBs). Professor Metzger is not only a distinguished legal scholar in the trade field; he also has a wealth of practical experience in commercial-policy matters because of his former role as Chairman of the Tariff Commission. The result of these assets is a monograph that is outstanding in its legal analysis of U.S. NTBs and rich in insights concerning what is feasible in terms of reducing these barriers.

Six categories of NTBs in the United States are examined: buy-national laws, antidumping and countervailing duties, quantitative restrictions, customs valuation, industrial standards, and governmental aid to industry. All are analyzed very well. In the chapter on buy-national laws, U.S. experience under the provisions of the Buy American Act is carefully examined and evaluated, as is the nature of the various state buy-American policies. A major conclusion is that under existing laws, a relatively effective agreement could be negotiated to lower the restrictive effects of existing U.S. policies in this field.

The author's discussion of U.S. antidumping duties is easily the best that exists. He traces the changing manner in which the 1921 Antidumping Act has been interpreted in practice and effectively points out the drawbacks of permitting the Tariff Commission to make the determination of injury to an industry. His analysis of the ill-fated International Dumping Code is especially outstanding. He is pessimistic concerning the prospects of negotiating significant changes in both antidumping- and countervailing-duty laws but believes much can be accomplished to improve their administration so as to reduce their trade-restricting effects. In his section on quantitative restrictions, Metzger is especially critical of the various mandatory or voluntary quotas on exports that have recently been negotiated. However, he sees little chance that substantive negotiations to reduce quantitative restrictions will be successful. Nevertheless, he does urge that the President undertake more extensive consultations before negotiating further agreements and refrain from making such agreements without at least obtaining a formal finding of serious injury to an industry.

The maze of different U.S. valuation procedures is explained especially well. As Metzger points out, these procedures are a source of much irritation to foreign suppliers and can hardly be justified as being either sensible or fair. Yet U.S. laws covering valuation laws are written in such detail that few changes can be made without explicit authorization of Congress. The failure of the Congress to approve the tentative agreement negotiated in the Kennedy Round on the American selling price method of valuation does not bode well for such authorization. The same is true with respect to subsidies to such U.S. industries as shipbuilding and aviation. On the other hand, progress in harmonizing industrial standards is possible even without a renewal of trade agreements by legislative authority.

Metzger may be too pessimistic about the prospects of securing congressional approval of agreements on nontariff barriers that are inconsistent with domestic legislation. He believes protectionist pressures are too strong for significant use to be made of the procedure contained in the trade bill pased by the House whereby such agreements would go into effect unless disapproved of by a simple majority in either the House or Senate. While there are good grounds based on recent experience for this view, postwar tariff history also indicates that if the groups supporting a liberal trade policy receive strong leadership from the White House, substantial progress can be made in reducing trade distortions.

The study is the first of nine that will deal with the prospects of negotiations on the major trade barriers in the leading industrial countries. If the others are of the same high quality as Metzger's, we can look forward to an extremely valuable series of monographs.

ROBERT E. BALDWIN
University of Wisconsin
Madison

WILLIAM H. RIKER and PETER C. ORDESHOOK. *An Introduction to Positive Political Theory.* Pp. 386. Englewood Cliffs, N.J.: Prentice-Hall, 1973. No price.

ALBERT BRETON. *The Economic Theory of Representative Government.* Pp. 228. Chicago, Ill.: Aldine-Atherton, 1974. $8.50.

The prediction of political events—the task of positive political analysis—requires an understanding of human motives and the political institutions which transform those motives into consequential actions. Predictive analysis must do more than describe. It must offer deductive hypotheses about the central determinants of political outcomes and then test those hypotheses in the natural laboratory of political systems. Two recent books, one by William Riker and Peter Ordeshook (*An Introduction to Positive Political Theory*) and the other by Albert Breton (*The Economic Theory of Representa-*

tive Government), make beginning efforts in this direction. Together they constitute a useful, sometimes stimulating, introduction to the "new" political science.

The Riker and Ordeshook book is offered as a "first attempt to systematize" a deductive theory of political events. The result is a helpful summary of the authors' and their collaborators' own efforts to build a predictive political theory joined unfortunately with heavy-handed, often confusing, chapters on game theory (chapters 5 and 8) and economics (chapters 9 and 10). There are better places for the novice to go for surveys of those literatures and those familiar with the basic results need not waste their time. In contrast, chapter 4 on the paradox of voting is a well-organized, thoughtful review of the literature.

The main value of *An Introduction to Positive Political Theory* is the bringing together of the many recent extensions of the "spatial model" of politics—a model first developed in economics by Hotelling and Smithes to study the location of firms in a market space and later adapted by Anthony Downs (*An Economic Theory of Democracy*) to predict the "location" of political platforms in an "issue space." Given a distribution of *rational* voters' preferences on political issues—measured, for example, in preferred levels of government spending—how will politicians construct their platforms so as to maximize their votes? Will all candidates adopt positions near the preferred position of the majority-creating voter, or will some candidates such as Goldwater or McGovern attempt to win with more extreme stances on the issues? Building on a model of voter participation in chapter 3, chapters 11 and 12 offer one deductive theory, the "spatial model," which attempts to answer these questions. Together, the three chapters provide a valuable overview of this model and its main conclusions. But when all has been said about the "spatial model," the results seem meager at best. Testable predictive hypotheses from the model emerge only in very special cases involving one or more of the following assumptions: symmetric preference distributions (every "pro" voter has a "con" counterpart), full voter participation, two parties, full information, and *always,* accountability through reelection. To be sure, the essence of useful modeling is simplification but not to the point of removing the central facts of the world we are trying to understand. The "spatial models" seem dangerously close to such a sterilization of the political process.

The Economic Theory of Representative Government by Albert Breton is a search in a more fruitful direction. The facts removed by the spatial models are the lens through which Breton visualizes the process of governmental decision-making. In Breton's analysis, politicians are not simple middlemen for an informed public. This fact is the key premise upon which Breton builds his arguments. Representative government with fixed terms of office, uninformed or forgetful voters, and multi-issue platforms all give the politician freedom to act in his own interests (chapter 3). The politician as a public output entrepreneur is the central actor in the Breton model.

Like all of us, the elected official is assumed to behave so as to maximize his satisfaction from employment. He wants to keep his job but he is also interested in pecuniary gains, personal power, and perhaps the well-being of his constituents. He may join with other politicians to form a political party (chapter 7). Operating independently or as a member of a "party-firm" he uses his political office to insure his re-election and to pursue his personal employment goals. His tools of control are the discriminatory distribution of public goods and tax burdens, regulatory favors or penalties, or the alteration of voter preferences (chapter 8). He responds to the pressures of an entrenched bureaucracy (chapter 9) and to those voters who succeed in articulating their preferences through voting for the opposition, pressure groups or, at the local government level, by leaving

town (chapters 5 and 6). The final result of the analysis is a public expenditure equation where expenditures in a given year depend on the relative power of the bureaucracy, the distribution of tax burdens, the level of constituent incomes, the relative costs to constituents of articulating their preferences and constituent perceptions of past government policy (chapter 10).

While Breton's analysis turns us in a promising new direction, it is only a broad-stroked sketch of the mechanisms of political decision-making. Why do politicians join political parties? How are the "spoils" of political victory distributed? Do parties collude to remove competition? How do bureaus compete with politicians and who is likely to win and why? Breton does not answer these questions, but answers are needed if we are to develop empirically testable, entrepreneurial models of political events. Breton's readable book—you can ignore without loss all diagrams and formulas—will hopefully stimulate others to fill in the details and then test the results.

ROBERT P. INMAN
University of Pennsylvania
Philadelphia

HAROLD K. SCHNEIDER. *Economic Man: The Anthropology of Economics.* Pp. 278. New York: The Free Press, 1974. $8.95.

Harold Schneider is an extreme exponent of what is called "formalist" economic anthropology: that the elementary concepts of conventional economics, such as supply, demand, price, maximizing, economizing, and capital, are universally applicable, and that the textbook geometry of indifference curves and Edgeworth boxes is universally illuminating. In short, Schneider believes that aboriginal Africans and Melanesians were maximizing decision-makers, even though they lived in pre-colonial economies without machines, markets, or modern money. Schneider has been asserting these views for many years in opposition to what is called "substantivist" economic anthropology, writings such as those of Karl Polanyi, Paul Bohannan, Marshall Sahlins, and the writer of this review. Now we have an entire book on Schneider's views, a book which will neither please those who are sympathetic to formalist economic anthropology nor surprise the rest of us. The book is a hodgepodge of elementary economics and brief commentaries on dozens of writings in economic anthropology and social exchange theory (Blau, Homans).

It is a mystery to me that such a book gets published. There is no obvious audience addressed: economists will find its economics trivial or wrong; anthropologists will find that it has no economic anthropology in it, merely assertions of what Schneider has been asserting for years and inaccurate summaries of what other people have written. Undergraduates will find it impenetrable and graduate students unreadable. The book is a disaster.

GEORGE DALTON
Northwestern University
Evanston
Illinois

OTHER BOOKS

ALLARDICE, CORBIN and EDMUND R. TRAPNELL. *The Atomic Energy Commission.* Pp. 256. New York: Praeger, 1974. $10.00.

ALLMAND, C.T., ed. *Society at War: The Experience of England and France During the Hundred Years War.* Pp. v, 220. New York: Barnes & Noble, 1974. $11.50. Paperbound, $5.75.

ALLUM, P. A. *Italy: Republic Without Government?* Comparative Modern Governments Series. Pp. ix, 267. New York: W. W. Norton, 1974. $10.00. Paperbound, $2.95.

ALMOND, GABRIEL A. et al., eds. *Comparative Politics Today: A World View.* Pp. viii, 477. Boston, Mass.: Little, Brown, 1974. $11.95.

ANDERSON, CHARLES W., FRED R. VON DER MEHDEN, and CRAWFORD YOUNG. *Issues of Political Development.* Pp. v, 278. Englewood Cliffs, N.J.: Prentice-Hall, 1974. $5.95.

ASTIN, HELEN S., NANCY SUNIEWICK, and SUSAN DWECK, eds. *Women: A Bibliography on their Education and Careers.*

Pp. i, 243. New York: Behavioral Publications, 1974. $10.95.

AUMANN, R. J. and L. S. SHAPLEY. *Non-Atomic Games.* Pp. vii, 333. Princeton, N.J.: Princeton University, 1974. $14.50.

BANFIELD, EDWARD C. *The Unheavenly City Revisited: A Revision of the Unheavenly City.* Pp. vii, 358. Boston, Mass.: Little, Brown, 1974. $4.95. Paperbound.

BARBER, JAMES DAVID, ed. *Choosing the President.* Pp. vii, 208. Englewood Cliffs, N.J.: Prentice-Hall, 1974. $7.95. Paperbound, $2.95.

BARKER, RONALD and ROBERT ESCARPIT, eds. *The Book Hunger.* Pp. 155. New York: Unipub, 1973. $6.00. Paperbound.

BECKWITH, BURNHAM P. *Liberal Socialism: The Pure Welfare Economics of a Liberal Socialist Economy.* Pp. 478. Jericho, N.Y.: Exposition, 1974. $20.00.

BEER, SAMUEL H. *The British Political System.* Reprinted from Patterns of Government, 3rd ed. Pp. viii, 243. New York: Random House, 1974. Paperbound. No price.

BEER, SAMUEL H. *Modern Political Development.* Reprinted from Patterns of Government, 3rd ed. Pp. v, 141. New York: Random House, 1973. Paperbound. No price.

BELIN, DAVID W. *November 22, 1963: You are the Jury.* Pp. ix, 521. New York: Quadrangle, 1973. $12.50.

BELL, J. BOWER. *The Secret Army: The IRA, 1916–1974.* Pp. vi, 434. Lawrence, Mass.: MIT Press, 1974. $4.95. Paperbound.

BERGER, SUZANNE. *The French Political System.* Reprinted from Patterns of Government, 3rd ed. Pp. v, 200. New York: Random House, 1974. Paperbound. No price.

BHAGWATI, JAGDISH N., ed. *Economics and World Order: From the 1970s to the 1990s.* Pp. vii, 365. New York: Free Press, 1974. $3.95. Paperbound.

BICKEL, ALEXANDER M. et al. *Watergate, Politics, and the Legal Process.* Pp. 89. Washington, D.C.: American Enterprise Institute for Public Policy Research, 1974. $2.00. Paperbound.

BIRNS, LAURENCE, ed. *The End of Chilean Democracy: An Idoc Dossier on the Coup and its Aftermath.* Pp. 219. New York: Seabury, 1974. $8.95. Paperbound, $3.95.

BLUHM, WILLIAM T. *Ideologies and Attitudes: Modern Political Culture.* Pp. iii, 385. Englewood Cliffs, N.J.: Prentice-Hall, 1974. $9.95. Paperbound, $6.95.

BLUMBERG, ABRAHAM S., ed. *Current Perspectives on Criminal Behavior: Original Essays on Criminology.* Pp. v, 348.

New York: Alfred A. Knopf, 1974. No price. Paperbound.

BOGGS, JAMES and GRACE LEE BOGGS. *Revolution and Evolution in the Twentieth Century.* Pp. 266. New York: Monthly Review, 1974. $10.00.

BOGUE, ALLAN G., ed. *Emerging Theoretical Models in Social and Political History.* Sage Contemporary Social Science Issues, no. 9. Pp. 152. Beverly Hills, Calif.: Sage, 1973. $3.95. Paperbound.

BRODY, HUGH. *Inishkillane: Change and Decline in the West of Ireland.* Pp. 256. New York: Schocken, 1974. $8.95.

BUTLER, DAVID. *The Canberra Model.* Pp. v, 146. New York: St. Martin's, 1974. $15.95.

CADENHEAD, IVIE E., JR. *Theodore Roosevelt: The Paradox of Progressivism.* The Shapers of History Series. Pp. 384. Woodbury, N.Y.: Barron, 1974. $2.95. Paperbound.

CARTER, WILLIAM D. *Study Abroad and Educational Development.* Pp. 49. New York: Unipub, 1973. $2.65. Paperbound.

CHARVET, JOHN. *The Social Problem in the Philosophy of Rousseau.* Pp. vii, 150. New York: Cambridge University Press, 1974. $8.95.

CLARK, KENNETH B. *Pathos of Power.* Pp. ix, 188. New York: Harper & Row, 1974. $7.95.

CLAUSNER, MARLIN D. *Rural Santo Domingo: Settled, Unsettled, and Resettled.* Pp. vii, 323. Philadelphia, Pa.: Temple, 1973. $11.50.

CLOWARD, RICHARD A. and FRANCES FOX PIVEN. *The Politics of Turmoil.* Pp. v, 365. New York: Pantheon, 1974. $10.00.

COLTON, JOEL. *Leon Blum: Humanist in Politics.* Pp. vii, 512. Cambridge, Mass.: MIT Press, 1974. $4.95. Paperbound.

CONNERY, ROBERT H. and GERALD BENJAMIN, eds. *Governing New York State: The Rockefeller Years.* Pp. vi, 262. New York: Academy of Political Science, 1974. $4.75. Paperbound.

CRATON, MICHAEL. *Sinews of Empire: A Short History of British Slavery.* Pp. vi, 413. New York: Doubleday, 1974. $3.50. Paperbound.

Cultures: Music and Society. Vol. 1. Pp. 282. New York: Unipub, 1973. $7.00. Paperbound.

DALY, DOMINIC. *The Young Douglas Hyde.* Pp. vii, 232. Totowa, N.J.: Rowman and Littlefield, 1974. $13.50.

DATTNER, RICHARD. *Design for Play.* MIT Urban Studies. Pp. 144. Cambridge, Mass.: MIT Press, 1974. $4.95. Paperbound.

DAVENPORT, HORACE W. *The ABC of Acid-Base Chemistry.* 6th ed., revised. Pp. vii, 124. Chicago, Ill.: University of Chicago, 1974. $8.00. Paperbound, $3.45.

DAVIDSON, BASIL. *Africa in History.* Pp. ix, 341. New York: Macmillan, 1974. $6.95. Paperbound, $2.95.

DAVIS, FOREST K. *Journey Among Mountains.* Pp. ii, 226. Adamant, Vt.: Adamant, 1974. $7.50. Paperbound, $5.25.

DENNIS, JACK and M. KENT JENNINGS, eds. *Comparative Political Socialization.* Sage Contemporary Social Science Issues, no. 7. Pp. 135. Beverly Hills, Calif.: Sage, 1970. $3.95. Paperbound.

DIAMOND, STANLEY. *In Search of the Primitive.* Pp. xi, 387. New Brunswick, N.J.: E. P. Dutton, 1974. $14.95. Paperbound, $3.95.

A Digest of Reports of the Carnegie Commission on Higher Education. Pp. 399. New York: McGraw-Hill, 1974. $12.95.

DOGAN, MATTEI and STEIN ROKKAN, eds. *Social Ecology.* Pp. vii, 607. Cambridge, Mass.: MIT Press, 1974. $5.95. Paperbound.

EARLE, PETER, ed. *Essays in European Economic History, 1500–1800.* Pp. 273. New York: Oxford University Press, 1974. $16.00.

EAST, W. G., O. H. K. SPATE, and CHARLES A. FISHER, eds. *The Changing Map of Asia.* Pp. v, 678. New York: Barnes & Noble, 1974. $23.50. Paperbound, $12.00.

EDWARDS, RUTH DUDLEY. *An Atlas of Irish History.* Pp. 261. New York: Barnes & Noble, 1974. $11.50. Paperbound, $5.75.

ELDER, GLEN H., JR. *Linking Social Structure and Personality.* Sage Contemporary Social Science Issues, no. 12. Pp. 160. Beverly Hills, Calif.: Sage, 1973. $3.95. Paperbound.

ETZIONI, AMITAI and EVA ETZIONI HALEVY, eds. *Social Change: Sources, Patterns and Consequences.* 2nd ed. Pp. 576. New York: Basic Books, 1974. $6.95. Paperbound.

EVANS, JOHN LEWIS. *The Communist International: 1919–1943.* Pp. vii, 194. Brooklyn, N.Y.: Pageant-Poseidon, 1974. $7.95.

FAWCETT, J. E. S. and ROSALYN HIGGINS, eds. *International Organization: Law in Movement.* Pp. v, 182. New York: Oxford University Press, 1974. $9.00.

FEINBERG, JOEL. *Doing and Deserving: Essays in the Theory of Responsibility.* Pp. vii, 299. Princeton, N.J.: Princeton University Press, 1974. $2.95. Paperbound.

FIDELL, LINDA S. and JOHN DeLAMATER, eds. *Women in the Professions: What's All the Fuss About?* Sage Contemporary Social Science Issues, no. 8. Pp. 144. Beverly Hills, Calif.: Sage, 1971. $3.95. Paperbound.

FISCHER, FRITZ. *World Power or Decline: The Controversy over Germany's Aims in the First World War.* Pp. 131. New York: W. W. Norton, 1974. $6.95. Paperbound, $1.95.

FOX, RENEE C. *Experiment Perilous.* Pp. 262. Philadelphia: University of Pennsylvania, 1974. $5.95. Paperbound.

FRAZIER, E. FRANKLIN. *The Negro Church in America.* LINCOLN C. ERIC. *The Black Church Since Frazier.* Pp. vi, 216. New York: Schocken, 1974. $10.00. Paperbound, $2.95.

GAGER, NANCY, ed. *Women's Rights Almanac 1974.* Pp. 620. Bethesda, Md.: Elizabeth Cady Stanton, 1974. $4.95. Paperbound.

GEER, BLANCHE, ed. *Learning to Work.* Sage Contemporary Social Science Issues, no. 4. Pp. 112. Beverly Hills, Calif.: Sage, 1972. $3.95. Paperbound.

GIBBS, G. I., ed. *Handbook of Games and Simulation Exercises.* Pp. vii, 226. Beverly Hills, Calif.: Sage, 1974. $12.00.

GOLDMAN, GUIDO. *The German Political System.* Pp. viii, 228. New York: Random House, 1974. No price. Paperbound.

GOLDSTONE, HARMON H. and MARTHA DALRYMPLE. *History Preserved: A Guide to New York City Landmarks and Historic Districts.* Pp. 576. New York: Simon & Schuster, 1974. $12.95.

GREENBERGER, MARTIN et al., eds. *Networks for Research and Education: Sharing of Computer and Information Resources Nationwide.* Pp. vi, 418. Princeton, N.J.: EDUCOM, 1974. $12.50.

GREENBLAT, CATHY, PETER J. STEIN, and NORMAN F. WASHBURNE. *The Marriage Game.* Pp. vii, 135. New York: Random House, 1974. No price. Paperbound.

GROSS, EDWARD and PAUL V. GRAMBSCH. *Changes in University Organization, 1964–1971: A Report Prepared for the Carnegie Commission on Higher Education.* Pp. 257. New York: McGraw-Hill, 1974. $10.00.

HALEVY, DANIEL. *The End of the Notables.* Edited by Alain Silvera. Pp. vii, 225. Middletown, Conn.: Wesleyan University, 1974. $12.50. Paperbound, $3.95.

HANDY, ROLLO and E. C. HARWOOD, eds. *A Current Appraisal of the Behavioral Sciences: Revised Edition.* Pp. viii, 148. Great Barrington, Mass.: Behavioral Research Council, 1974. $12.50.

HARVEY, DODD L. and LINDA C. CICCORITTI. *U.S.-Soviet Cooperation in Space.* Monographs in International Affairs. Pp. v, 408. Washington, D.C.: University of Miami, 1974. No price.

HENIG, RUTH B., ed. *The League of Nations.* Pp. v, 203. New York: Barnes & Noble, 1974. $11.50. Paperbound, $5.75.

HENTHORN, WILLIAM E. *A History of Korea.* Pp. viii, 256. New York: Macmillan, 1974. $3.95. Paperbound.

HOLLANDER, PAUL. *Soviet and American Society: A Comparison.* Pp. xiii, 476. New York: Oxford University Press, 1973. $12.50.

HOROWITZ, MORRIS A. *Manpower and Education in Franco Spain.* Pp. xi, 164. Hamden, Conn.: Shoe String, 1974. $7.50.

HORTON, PAUL B. et al. *Basic Principles of the Social Sciences.* Programmed Learning Aid Series. Pp. v, 189. Homewood, Ill.: Learning Systems, 1974. $3.95. Paperbound.

HUGHES, EMMET JOHN. *The Living Presidency: The Resources and Dilemmas of the American Presidential Office.* Pp. 377. Baltimore, Md.: Penguin, 1973. $2.95. Paperbound.

ISAACS, HAROLD R., ed. *Straw Sandals: Chinese Short Stories, 1918–1933.* Pp. x, 444. Cambridge, Mass.: MIT Press, 1974. $10.00.

JAMES, DOROTHY BUCKTON. *The Contemporary Presidency.* 2nd ed. Pp. vii, 336. Indianapolis, Ind.: Bobbs-Merrill, 1974. $8.95. Paperbound, $4.95.

JOHANNIS, THEODORE B., JR. and C. NEIL BULL, eds. *Sociology of Leisure.* Sage Contemporary Social Science Issues, no. 1. Pp. 128. Beverly Hills, Calif.: Sage, 1971. $3.95. Paperbound.

JONES, ANN. *Uncle Tom's Campus.* Pp. vii, 225. New York: Touchstone, 1973. $2.95. Paperbound.

JORGENSEN, JOSEPH G., ed. *Comparative Studies by Harold E. Driver and Essays in His Honor.* Pp. 248. New Haven, Conn.: HRAF Press, 1974. $20.00.

KARP, WALTER. *Indispensable Enemies: The Politics of Misrule in America.* Pp. x, 324. Baltimore, Md.: Penguin, 1974. $2.95. Paperbound.

KLINE, F. GERALD and PETER CLARKE, eds. *Mass Communications and Youth: Some Current Perspectives.* Sage Contemporary Social Science Issues, no. 5. Pp. 128. Beverly Hills, Calif.: Sage, 1974. $3.95. Paperbound.

KOHLER, FOY D., LEON GOURE, and MOSE L. HARVEY. *The Soviet Union and the October 1973 Middle East War: The Implications for Detente.* Monographs in International Affairs. Pp. iii, 130.

Washington, D.C.: University of Miami, 1974. No price.

KRAINES, OSCAR. *The World and Ideas of Ernst Freund: The Search for General Principles of Legislation and Administrative Law.* Pp. ix, 221. Alabama: University of Alabama, 1974. $8.00. Paperbound, $3.50.

KRAUSSE, ALEXIS. *Russia in Asia: A Record and a Study, 1558–1899.* Pp. viii, 411. New York: Barnes & Noble, 1974. $15.25.

KUTEN, JAY. *Coming Together-Coming Apart.* Pp. ix, 178. New York: Macmillan, 1974. $5.95.

KUTZ, MYER. *Rockefeller Power: America's Chosen Family.* Pp. 288. New York: Simon & Schuster, 1974. $7.95.

LANDSBERGER, HENRY A., ed. *Rural Protest: Peasant Movements and Social Change.* Pp. vi, 430. New York: Barnes & Noble, 1974. $17.50.

LAPALOMBARA, JOSEPH. *Politics Within Nations.* Pp. vii, 624. Englewood Cliffs, N.J.: Prentice-Hall, 1974. $10.50.

LAROCQUE, GAETANE M. *Consumerism: Federal Grants and You.* Pp. vii, 191. Jericho, N.Y.: Exposition, 1974. $8.00.

LASLETT, JOHN H. M. and SEYMOUR MARTIN LIPSET, eds. *Failure of a Dream?* Pp. x, 754. New York: Doubleday, 1974. $5.95. Paperbound.

LAZERSON, MARVIN and W. NORTON GRUBB, eds. *American Education and Vocationalism: A Documentary History, 1870–1970.* Classics in Education, no. 48. Pp. ix, 176. New York: Columbia University, 1974. $5.95. Paperbound, $2.50.

LEEDY, PAUL D. *Practical Research: Planning and Design.* Pp. vii, 246. New York: Macmillan, 1974. $4.95. Paperbound.

LEIF, IRVING. *Community Power and Decision-Making: An International Handbook.* Pp. iii, 170. Metuchen, N.J.: Scarecrow, 1974. $6.00.

LEVINE, EDNA S. *Lisa and Her Soundless World.* Pp. 40. New York: Behavioral Publications, 1974. $4.95.

LEVY, ALAN et al. *The Process of Choice: GEE Group for Environmental Education.* Cambridge, Mass.: MIT Press, 1974. $10.00. Paperbound.

LINDSEY, DAVID. *Andrew Jackson and John C. Calhoun.* The Shapers of History Series. Pp. vii, 438. Woodbury, N.Y.: Barron, 1973. No price.

LYMAN, STANFORD J. *Chinese Americans: Ethnic Groups in Comparative Perspective.* Pp. v, 213. New York: Random House, 1974. No price. Paperbound.

MADDOX, ROBERT JAMES. *The New Left and the Origins of the Cold War.* Pp. ix, 169.

Princeton, N.J.: Princeton University Press, 1974. $2.45. Paperbound.

MAZUR, ALLAN and LEON S. ROBERTSON. *Biology and Social Behavior.* Pp. vii, 199. New York: Free Press, 1974. $2.45. Paperbound.

McCOY, F. N. *Researching and Writing in History: A Practical Handbook for Students.* Pp. 114. Berkeley: University of California Press, 1974. $1.75. Paperbound.

McGOVERN, GEORGE. *An American Journey: The Presidential Campaign Speeches of George McGovern.* Pp. xv, 246. New York: Random House, 1974. $8.95.

McNAMARA, ROBERT S. *One Hundred Countries.* Pp. 150. London, Eng.: Pall Mall, 1973. No price.

MERLI, FRANK J. and THEODORE A. WILSON, eds. *Makers of American Diplomacy: From Benjamin Franklin to Henry Kissinger.* Pp. vii, 728. New York: Charles Scribner's Sons, 1974. $17.50.

MILLER, J. D. B. *Survey of Commonwealth Affairs: Problems of Expansion and Attrition, 1953–1969.* Pp. 550. New York: Oxford University Press, 1974. $35.25.

MILLER, LEO. *John Milton among the Polygamophiles.* Pp. xii, 378. New York: Loewenthal, 1974. $15.00.

MITCHELL, ALLAN and ISTVAN DEAK. *Everyman in Europe: Essays in Social History. The Industrial Centuries.* Vol. II. Pp. vii, 397. Englewood Cliffs, N.J.: Prentice-Hall, 1974. $6.50. Paperbound.

MODELSKI, GEORGE, ed. *Multinational Corporations and World Order.* Sage Contemporary Social Science Issues, no. 2. Pp. 160. Beverly Hills, Calif.: Sage, 1974. $3.95. Paperbound.

MOQUIN, WAYNE, CHARLES VAN DOREN, and FRANCIS A. J. IANNI, eds. *A Documentary History of the Italian Americans.* Pp. 448. New York: Praeger, 1974. $15.00.

MORLEY, JAMES W., ed. *Dilemmas of Growth in Prewar Japan.* Pp. vii, 527. Princeton, N.J.: Princeton University Press, 1974. $3.95. Paperbound.

MORRISON, THEODORE. *Chataugua: A Center for Education, Religion, and the Arts in America.* Pp. vii, 351. Chicago, Ill.: University of Chicago Press, 1974. $10.50.

MORTON, HENRY W. and RUDOLF L. TOKES, eds. *Soviet Politics and Society in the 1970s.* Pp. viii, 401. New York: Free Press, 1974. $12.95.

MOSS, ROBERT. *Chile's Marxist Experiment.* Pp. i, 225. New York: Halsted Press, 1974. $8.95.

MPHAHLELE, EZEKIEL. *The African Image.* Revised ed. Pp. 316. New York: Praeger, 1974. $8.50. Paperbound, $3.95.

MURPHY, WALTER F. and C. HERMAN PRITCHETT. *Courts, Judges, and Politics: An Introduction to the Judicial Process.* 2nd ed. Pp. vii, 719. New York: Random House, 1974. No price.

NICOLAUS, MARTIN, ed. *The Grundrisse by Karl Marx.* Pp. 893. New York: Random House, 1974. $15.00. Paperbound, $3.95.

NORDENSTRENG, KAARLE and TAPIO VARIS. *Television Traffic: A One Way Street.* Pp. 62. New York: Unipub, 1974. $2.00. Paperbound.

PAREKH, BHIKHU, ed. *Bentham's Political Thought.* Pp. 340. New York: Barnes & Noble, 1973. $15.00. Paperbound, $4.95.

PENDLETON, MARY. *Navajo and Hopi Weaving Techniques.* Pp. 158. New York: Macmillan, 1974. $9.95. Paperbound, $4.95.

PENNOCK, J. ROLAND and JOHN W. CHAPMAN, eds. *The Limits of Laws, Nomos XV.* Pp. vii, 276. New York: Lieber Atherton, 1974. $8.95.

PIKE, FREDERICK B. and THOMAS STRITCH, eds. *The New Corporatism: Social-Political Structures in the Iberian World.* Pp. 240. Notre Dame, Ind.: University of Notre Dame, 1974. $8.95. Paperbound, $2.95.

PLATT, ANTHONY and LYNN COUPER, eds. *Policing America.* Pp. v, 216. Englewood Cliffs, N.J.: Prentice-Hall, 1974. $6.95.

RAGGATT, PETER C. M., ed. *Education in the Cities of England.* Sage Contemporary Social Science Issues, no. 11. Pp. 124. Beverly Hills, Calif.: Sage, 1973. $3.95. Paperbound.

REILLY, MARY, ed. *Play as Exploratory Learning: Studies of Curiosity Behavior.* Pp. 317. Beverly Hills, Calif.: Sage, 1974. $15.00.

REYNOLDS, H. T. *Politics and the Common Man: An Introduction to Political Behavior.* Pp. ix, 288. Homewood, Ill.: Dorsey, 1974. $5.95. Paperbound.

ROBERTS, GENE and DAVID R. JONES, eds. *Assignment America.* Pp. viii, 274. New York: Quadrangle, 1974. $8.95.

ROGG, ELEANOR MEYER. *The Assimilation of Cuban Exiles: The Role of Community and Class.* Pp. xii, 241. New York: Aberdeen, 1974. $10.00. Paperbound, $5.95.

RONAIDS, FRANCIS S. *The Attempted Whig Revolution of 1678–1681.* Pp. ii, 202. Totowa, N.J.: Rowman and Littlefield, 1974. $10.00.

ROSE, PETER I. *They and We: Racial and Ethnic Relations in the United States.* 2nd ed. Pp. vii, 256. New York: Random House, 1974. No price. Paperbound.

ROSE, RICHARD, ed. *Lessons from America:*

An Exploration. Pp. 308. New York: Halsted Press, 1974. $14.95.

ROSEN, STEVEN and WALTER JONES. *The Logic of International Relations.* Pp. vii, 390. Cambridge, Mass.: Winthrop, 1974. $6.95. Paperbound.

RUTLAND, ROBERT A. and WILLIAM M. E. RACHAL, eds. *The Papers of James Madison.* Vol. 8. Pp. vii, 560. Chicago, Ill.: University of Chicago, 1973. $20.00.

SCHEINGOLD, LEE D. and NATHANIEL N. WAGNER. *Sound Sex and the Aging Heart: Sex in the Mid and Later Years with Special Reference to Cardiac Problems.* Pp. 168. New York: Human Sciences, 1974. $7.95.

SCHELLENBERG, JAMES A. *An Introduction to Social Psychology.* 2nd ed. Pp. v, 360. New York: Random House, 1974. No price. Paperbound.

SCHORR, ALVIN L. *Children and Decent People.* Pp. xii, 222. New York: Basic Books, 1974. $7.95.

SCHROETER, LEONARD. *The Last Exodus.* Pp. 432. New York: Universe, 1974. $10.95.

SHANAS, ETHEL, ed. *Aging in Contemporary Society.* Sage Contemporary Social Science Issues, no. 6. Pp. 128. Beverly Hills, Calif.: Sage, 1970. $3.95. Paperbound.

SHEPPARD, HAROLD L. and NEAL Q. HERRICK. *Where Have All the Robots Gone?* Pp. iii, 222. New York: Free Press, 1974. $3.95. Paperbound.

SILK, LEONARD et al. *Capitalism: The Moving Target.* Praeger University Series. Pp. ix, 159. New York: Praeger, 1974. $2.95. Paperbound.

SMITH, THOMAS. *De Republica Anglorum: A Discourse on the Commonwealth of England.* Edited by L. Alston. Pp. vii, 210. New York: Barnes & Noble, 1974. $15.00.

SOLO, ROBERT A. *The Political Authority and the Market System.* Pp. iii, 418. Pelham Manor, N.Y.: South-Western, 1974. No price.

SPEER, DAVID C., ed. *Nonverbal Communication.* Sage Contemporary Social Science Issues, no. 10. Pp. 140. Beverly Hills, Calif.: Sage, 1972. $3.95. Paperbound.

SPIEGEL, JOHN P. and PAVEL MACHOTKA. *Messages of the Body.* Pp. vii, 440. New York: Free Press, 1974. $17.95.

STANWORTH, PHILIP and ANTHONY GIDDENS, eds. *Elites and Power in British Society.* Pp. vii, 261. New York: Cambridge University Press, 1974. $15.50. Paperbound, $5.95.

STERLING, RICHARD W. *Macropolitics: International Relations in a Global Society.*

Pp. ix, 648. New York: Alfred A. Knopf, 1974. No price.

STICKLAND, IRINA. *The Voices of Children, 1700–1914.* Pp. 224. New York: Barnes & Noble, 1974. $10.00.

STOCKING, GEORGE, JR., ed. *The Shaping of American Anthropology, 1883–1911: A Franz Boas Reader.* Pp. 354. New York: Basic Books, 1974. $12.95.

STOESSINGER, JOHN G. *The United Nations and the Superpowers: China, Russia, and America.* 3rd ed. Pp. viii, 216. New York: Random House, 1973. No price. Paperbound.

The Study of American History: Reconstruction to the Present. Vol. II. Pp. 699. Guilford, Conn.: Dushkin, 1973. $7.95. Paperbound.

The Study of American History: Exploration to Reconstruction. Vol. I. Pp. 618. Guilford, Conn.: Dushkin, 1973. $7.95. Paperbound.

SUNTHARALINGAM, R. *Politics and Nationalist Awakening in South India, 1852–1891.* Pp. viii, 396. Tuscon, Ar.: 1974. $7.95. Paperbound, $3.95.

SWEEZY, PAUL M. and HARRY MAGDOFF, eds. *Revolution and Counter-Revolution in Chile.* Pp. 169. New York: Monthly Review, 1974. $7.50. Paperbound, $2.75.

SWETZ, FRANK. *Mathematics Education in China: Its Growth and Development.* Pp. 364. Cambridge, Mass.: MIT Press, 1974. $15.00.

TECLAFF, LUDWIK A. and ALBERT E. UTTON, eds. *International Environmental Law.* Pp. vii, 270. New York: Praeger, 1974. $13.50.

THOMSON, R. M., ed. *The Chronicle of the Election of Hugh Abbot of Bury St. Edmunds and Later Bishop of Ely.* Pp. xi, 208. New York: Oxford University Press, 1974. $19.25.

Tilly, Charles. *An Urban World.* Pp. ix, 487. Boston, Mass.: Little, Brown, 1974. $7.95. Paperbound.

TINDER, GLENN. *Political Thinking.* 2nd ed. Pp. vii, 206. Boston, Mass.: Little, Brown, 1974. $3.95. Paperbound.

TUCKER, JERRY. *The Experience of Politics.* Pp. 494. San Francisco, Calif.: Canfield, 1974. $7.95. Paperbound.

TUNSTALL, JEREMY, ed. *Journalists at Work.* Communication and Society Series. Pp. 304. Beverly Hills, Calif.: Sage, 1974. $12.00.

Two Studies on Ethnic Group Relations in Africa: Senegal, the United Republic of Tanzania. Pp. 156. New York: Unipub, 1974. $5.95. Paperbound.

ULAM, ADAM B. *Expansion and Coexistence: Soviet Foreign Policy, 1917–73.* 2nd ed. Pp. 808. New York: Praeger, 1974. $15.95. Paperbound, $6.95.

VON DER MEHDEN, FRED R. *South-East Asia, 1930–1970: The Legacy of Colonialism and Nationalism.* Pp. 144. New York: W. W. Norton, 1974. $7.95. Paperbound, $3.45.

WAKEFORD, GEOFFREY, ed. *Debate: A Digest of Parliamentary Debates and Questions, 1972–73.* Vol. II. Pp. 586. Totowa, N.J.: Rowman and Littlefield, 1974. $35.00.

WALCUTT, CHARLES, JOAN LAMPERT, and GLENN MCCRACKEN. *Teaching Reading: A Phonic/Linguistic Approach to Reading Development.* Pp. v, 471. New York: Macmillan, 1974. $8.95.

WASSALL, GREGORY H. *Tax-Exempt Property: A Case Study of Hartford, Connecticut.* John C. Lincoln Institute Research Monograph No. 3. Pp. iii, 173. Hartford, Conn.: University of Hartford, 1974. No price.

Watergate: Chronology of a Crisis. Vol. II. Pp. iii, 432. Washington, D.C.: Congressional Quarterly, 1974. No price.

WEDDERBURN, DOROTHY, ed. *Poverty Inequality and Class Structure.* Pp. 247. New York: Cambridge University Press, 1974. $15.00.

WELLS, ALAN, ed. *Mass Communications: A World View.* Pp. 276. Palo Alto, Calif.: National Press, 1974. No price.

WENDEL, THOMAS. *Benjamin Franklin and the Politics of Liberty.* The Shapers of History Series. Pp. vii, 454. Woodbury, N.Y.: Barron, 1974. $2.95. Paperbound.

WIRSING, ROBERT G., ed. *International Relations and the Future of Ocean Space.* Studies in International Affairs, no. 10. Pp. v, 146. Columbia, S.C.: University of South Carolina, 1974. $5.95.

THE AAPSS

Inventory Clearance Sale
of the ANNALS

75% REDUCTION

$3.00 paperbound—now $ .75
$4.00 clothbound —now $1.00

This sale applies to issues published prior to September 1963.

Number
of Copies
P   C

The New Europe: Implications for the U. S.   P

Transportation Renaissance   P & C

Conservatism, Liberalism and National Issues   P

American Foreign Policy Challenged   P

Unconventional Warfare   P

Is International Communism Winning?   P

The Rising Demand for International Education   P

Latin America's Nationalistic Revolutions   P

Religion in American Society   P

Agricultural Policy, Politics and the Public Interest   P

Wither American Foreign Policy?   P

International Cooperation for Social Welfare   P

Lagging Justice   P

Perspectives on Government and Science   P & C

Inflation   P

American Civilization and its Leadership Needs   P & C

Resolving the Russian-American Deadlock   P

Partnership for Progress: International Technical Cooperation   P & C

Prevention of Juvenile Delinquency   P

Highway Safety and Traffic Control   P & C

Asia and Future World Leadership   P & C

Number
of Copies
P   C

_____|_____ The Satellites in Eastern Europe   P
_____|_____ A Crowding Hemisphere: Population Change in the Americas   P
_____|_____ Recreation in the Automation Age   P & C
_____|_____ The Future of the Western Alliance   P & C
_____|_____ Current Issues in International Labor Relations   P & C
_____|_____ Disasters and Disaster Relief   P
_____|_____ Japan Since Recovery of Independence. 1952–1956   P
_____|_____ Russia Since Stalin: Old Trends and New Problems   P
_____|_____ The Public School and Other Community Services   P & C
_____|_____ Ethical Standards and Professional Conduct   P
_____|_____ The Future of the United Nations   P
_____|_____ America and a New Asia   P
_____|_____ Bureaucracy and Democratic Government   P
_____|_____ Congress and Foreign Relations   P
_____|_____ NATO and World Peace   P
_____|_____ Judicial Administration and the Common Man   P
_____|_____ The Search for National Security   P
_____|_____ Medical Care for Americans   P
_____|_____ Toward Family Stability   P
_____|_____ Moscow's European Satellites   P
_____|_____ Formulating a Point Four Program   P
_____|_____ Gambling   P
_____|_____ Aiding Underdeveloped Areas Abroad   P
_____|_____ Military Government   P

- **P—Paperbound only; P & C—Paperbound and Clothbound**
- **Quantity and wholesales discounts cannot be applied to this special offer.**
- **Watch for other sales in future issues.**

Please send me the volumes as indicated above.

☐ Enclosed is $_____ Postage and handling: $.50, 1 to 5 books; $1.00, 6 to 10 books; $1.50, 11 or more books.

☐ Please bill me. Postage and handling additional.

Name_____

Address_____

City_____ State_____ Zip_____

THE AMERICAN ACADEMY OF POLITICAL AND SOCIAL SCIENCE

3937 Chestnut Street   Philadelphia, Pa. 19104

INDEX

Accountability, governmental
  see, Auditing, governmental
A-85, A-87, and A-95 circulars
  see, Office of Management and Budget
Agnew, Spiro T., 112
Agreements, intergovernmental service
  municipal and interlocal, 134–136,
    145–146, 161–162, 164–165
  see also, Interstate compacts
Aid to Families with Dependent
  Children, 57
Air Quality Act, 144
Advisory Commission on Intergovernmental
  Relations (ACIR), 10, 13, 31, 44, 57–58,
    80–81, 96, 114, 146, 160–161, 163
Anderson, Robert, 43
Anderson, William, 2
Appalachian Regional Commission (ARC),
  20, 111–112, 114, 115, 117
Appalachian Regional Development Act, 117
Ash Council, 41
Atomic Energy Commission (AEC), 6
Auditing, governmental, 27, 36–39, 62–64

Balance Agriculture with Industry (BAWI)
  program, 109
BEYLE, THAD L., New Directions in Interstate
  Relations, 108–119
Big Seven (public interest groups), 14, 44–45
Bragdon, J. S., 43
British Judicial Committee of the Privy
  Council, 171, 174
British North America Act of 1867 (BNA Act),
  171–172, 174
Budget, U.S. Bureau of the, 43, 161
Budgetary Reform Act, 88
Burger, Warren E.
  and State-Federal Judicial Councils, 75

Campbell, Alan K., 167
Census of Governments, U.S., 79–80
Clark, Jane Perry, 82
Clark, Joseph, 11
Cleveland, Grover, 42
Coalition of Governors, Mayors and County
  Officials, 45

Coastal Zone Conservation Commission, 137
Colorado Basin Compact, 100
Commission on Intergovernmental Relations
  (Kestnbaum Commission), 3–4, 42–43,
    51, 55–56, 60
Committee on Federal-State Relations, 55
Communicable Disease Control Amend-
  ments of 1970, 144–145
Compact for Education, 112
Compacts, interstate
  see, Interstate compacts
CONFLICT IN METROPOLITAN AREAS,
  Henry W. Maier, 148–157
Congress, U.S.
  and Creative and New Federalists, 21
  and governmental auditing, 37
  and judicial system, 69, 71, 73
  and metropolitan planning, 142–145
  and preemptive legislation, 101–102
  legislative reorganization of 1946, 8
  see also, Grants-in-aid, federal, and
    Revenue sharing, federal
Conservative party
  and intergovernmental relations in Britain,
    184, 186, 192–193
Constitution, U.S.
  and Dillon's Rule, 126
  and intergovernmental relations, 102–104,
    121–132 passim
  and interstate compacts, 100
  and judicial system, 69, 73
Constitutional Convention of 1787, 69
Corry, J. A., 172–173
Corwin, E. S., 2–3
Council of State Governments, 44, 46,
  105–107, 160, 168
Council on Municipal Performance, 150
Councils of governments (COGs), 13, 31, 139,
  143–145, 156, 163–164
COUNTIES: THE EMERGING FORCE, Bernard
  F. Hillenbrand, 91–98
Courts, U.S.
  and dual court system, 68–76
  see also, Supreme Court, U.S.
Covell v. Heyman, 74
Creative Federalism, 10–11, 18–22, 53

275

Kindly mention THE ANNALS *when writing to advertisers*